Integrated Series in Information Systems

Volume 24

Series Editors

Ramesh Sharda
Oklahoma State University, Stillwater, OK, USA

Stefan Voß
University of Hamburg, Hamburg, Germany

For further volumes:
http://www.springer.com/series/6157

Ned Kock
Editor

Evolutionary Psychology and Information Systems Research

A New Approach to Studying the Effects
of Modern Technologies on Human Behavior

 Springer

Editor
Ned Kock
Department of MIS and Decision Science
Texas A&M International University
University Boulevard 5201
78041 Laredo Texas
USA
nedkock@tamiu.edu

ISSN 1571-0270
ISBN 978-1-4419-6138-9   e-ISBN 978-1-4419-6139-6
DOI 10.1007/978-1-4419-6139-6
Springer New York Dordrecht Heidelberg London

Library of Congress Control Number: 2010928642

Printed on acid-free paper

Springer is part of Springer Science+Business Media (www.springer.com)

Preface

This book is a compilation of chapters written by leading researchers from all over the world. Those researchers' common characteristic is that they have investigated issues at the intersection of the fields of information systems (IS) and evolutionary psychology (EP). The main goal of this book is to serve as a reference for IS research building on EP concepts and theories (in short, IS-EP research). The book is organized in three main parts: Part I focuses on EP concepts and theories that can be used as a basis for IS-EP research; Part II provides several exemplars of IS-EP research in practice; and Part III summarizes emerging issues and debate that can inform IS-EP research, including debate regarding philosophical foundations and credibility of related findings.

IS-EP research is generally concerned with the use of concepts and theories from EP in the study of IS, particularly regarding the impact of modern information and communication technologies on the behavior of individuals, groups, and organizations. From a practitioners' perspective, the most immediate consumers of IS-EP research are those who develop and use IS, of which a large contingent are in businesses that employ IS to support marketing, order-taking, production, and delivery of goods and services. In this context, IS-EP findings may be particularly useful due to the present need to design web-based interfaces that will be used by individuals from different cultures, and often different countries, and whose common denominator is their human nature.

EP has the potential to become one of the pillars on which IS research can take place. The explanatory power of EP comes from the fact that its underlying ideas relate to the basic design of our brain (and, more generally, our body, including endocrine glands that strongly influence our brain processes and our behavior), and thus can form the basis on which fundamental explanations of behavior in the context of IS design and use can be developed. EP also arguably holds the key to many counterintuitive explanations of behavior toward modern technologies, because many of the evolved instincts that influence our behavior are below the level of our conscious awareness. Often those instincts lead to behavioral responses whose motivations and patterns are not self-evident to the individuals involved – e.g., the fact that we tend to develop vivid memories of facts surrounding a surprising event, whether that event occurs in a real or technology-created (virtual) environment.

The range of topics covered by the authors of the chapters that make up this book arguably represents the state of the art of IS-EP research today. Moreover, several of the chapters in this book raise issues that are likely to feature prominently in the future debate on and application of IS-EP research, not only in the fields of IS and EP, but in several other fields, such as marketing and economics. Among the key reasons for these positive aspects of this book is that its contributing authors are certainly among the most influential thinkers and practitioners of IS-EP research in the world today, not only in IS but also in a few other related disciplines. Those authors are also pioneers, sometimes "swimming against the current" in their fields or subfields of research, and their chapters will hopefully pave the way for the future of IS-EP research.

I am indebted to the authors for their hard work and for contributing well-researched and truly thought-provoking chapters to this book. I would also like to thank the team at Springer for their support of this book project. In particular, I would like to thank Gary Folven, who has recently retired from his editorial duties at Springer, but who strongly encouraged me to pursue this book project, which I first discussed with him in 1999, and Neil Levine, for taking the editorial lead on this book project at Springer. Thanks are also due to series editors Ramesh Sharda and Stefan Voss for their support, comments, and suggestions early on in this project.

I would also like to thank my colleagues at Texas A&M International University for supporting my research and scholarship. Special thanks go to my doctoral students, especially Jesus Carmona, Ruth Chatelain-Jardón, and Vanessa Garza, for collaborating with me in various IS-EP research projects; my colleagues at the Division of International Business and Technology studies, particularly Rick Hicks, Pedro Hurtado, Jackie Mayfield, Milton Mayfield, Max Mukherji, Kamal Parhizgar, and Rolando Sanchez, for contributing to a work environment that is conducive to research and scholarship; and university staff and administrators, especially President Ray Keck and Provost Pablo Arenaz, for their strong commitment to high-quality research and scholarship.

Last, but certainly not least, I would like to thank my wife Leticia and children Eliseu (Al), Arthur, Monica, and Nathan for their love and support. This book is dedicated to them.

Laredo, Texas   Ned Kock

Contents

Contributors

Chon Abraham Operations and Information Systems Management Department, College of William and Mary, 101 Ukrops Way, Williamsburg, VA 23187, USA, chon.abraham@mason.wm.edu

Robert Aunger Disease Control and Vector Biology Unit, Department of Infectious & Tropical Diseases, London School of Hygiene & Tropical Medicine, Keppel Street, London WC1E 7HT, UK, robert.aunger@lshtm.ac.uk

Ina Blau Department of Psychology and Education, Open University of Israel, 1 University Road, Ra'anana, Israel, ina.blau@gmail.com

Jesus Carmona Division of International Business and Technology Studies, Texas A&M International University, 5201 University Boulevard, Laredo, TX 78041, USA, jcarmona@tamiu.edu

Avner Caspi Department of Psychology and Education, Open University of Israel, 1 University Road, Ra'anana, Israel, avnerca@openu.ac.il

Ruth Chatelain-Jardón Division of International Business and Technology Studies, Texas A&M International University, 5201 University Boulevard, Laredo, TX 78041, USA, chatelain@students.tamiu.edu

Barbara Fasolo Department of Management, London School of Economics and Political Science, London WC2A 2AE, UK, b.fasolo@lse.ac.uk

Christopher J. Ferguson Department of Behavioral Sciences, Applied Sciences and Criminal Justice, Texas A&M International University, 5201 University Boulevard, Laredo, TX 78041, USA, cferguson@tamiu.edu

Penelope Sue Greenberg School of Business Administration, Widener University, One University Place, Chester, PA 19013, USA, psgreenberg@mail.widener.edu

Ralph H. Greenberg The Fox School of Business, Temple University, 1801 Liacouras Walk, Philadelphia, PA 19122, USA, ralph.greenberg@temple.edu

Ana Ortiz de Guinea Service de l'enseignement des technologies de l'information, HEC Montréal, 3000, chemin de la Côte-Sainte-Catherine, Montréal, QC, Canada H3T 2A7, ana.ortiz-de-guinea@hec.ca

Donald A. Hantula Department of Psychology, Temple University, Weiss Hall (265-67), Philadelphia, PA 19122, USA, hantula@temple.edu

Stefan Hrastinski Department of Media Technology, KTH Royal Institute of Technology and Uppsala University, Lindstedtsv. 3, SE-100 44 stockholm, Sweden, stefanhr@kth.se

Iris Junglas Decision and Information Sciences Department, 334 Melcher Hall, University of Houston, Houston, TX 77204-6021, USA, ijunglas@uh.edu

Ned Kock Division of International Business and Technology Studies, Texas A&M International University, 5201 University Boulevard, Laredo, TX 78041, USA, nedkock@tamiu.edu

Alison P. Lenton Department of Psychology, University of Edinburgh, 7 George Square, Edinburgh EH8 9JZ, Scotland, a.lenton@ed.ac.uk

Henry F. Lyle Department of Anthropology, Box 353100, University of Washington, Seattle, WA 98195-3100, USA, lyle3@u.washington.edu

Sakthi Mahenthiran College of Business, Butler University, 4600 Sunset Ave., Indianapolis, IN 46208, USA, smahenth@butler.edu

Ahmed Y. Mahfouz Department of Management Information Systems, Prairie View A&M University, 1501 Harvey Rd #526, College Station, TX 77840, USA, aymahfouz@pvamu.edu

M. Lynne Markus Department of Information and Process Management, Smith Technology Center 325, 175 Forest Street, Watham, MA 02452-4705, USA, mlmarkus@bentley.edu

Zack Mendenhall John Molson School of Business, Concordia University, 1455 de Maisonneuve Blvd. West, Montreal, QC, Canada H3G 1M8, z_mend@jmsb.concordia.ca

Marcelo Vinhal Nepomuceno John Molson School of Business, Concordia University, 1455 de Maisonneuve Blvd. West, GM 1002-03, Montreal, QC, Canada H3G 1M8, m_nepomu@jmsb.concordia.ca

Andreas G. Philaretou Department of Social & Behavioral Sciences, European University Cyprus (formerly Cyprus College), 6 Diogenes Street, Engomi, PO Box 22006, 1516 Nicosia, Cyprus, aphilare@hotmail.com

Jaana Porra Management Information Systems, Department of Decision and Information Sciences, University of Houston, C.T. Bauer College of Business, 280G Melcher Hall, Houston, TX 77204-6282, USA, jaana@uh.edu

Gad Saad Department of Marketing, John Molson School of Business, Concordia University, 1455 de Maisonneuve Blvd. West, Montreal, QC, Canada H3G 1M8, gadsaad@jmsb.concordia.ca

Bernd Carsten Stahl Department of Informatics, Centre for Computing and Social Responsibility, De Montfort University, The Gateway, Leicester LE1 9BH, UK, bstahl@dmu.ac.uk

Roger J. Sullivan Department of Anthropology, California State University, Sacramento, 6000 J Street, Sacramento, CA 95819, USA, sullivar@csus.edu

Antonis Theocharous Department of Hotel and Tourism Management, Cyprus University of Technology, Saripolou 2-8, 3036 Lemesos, Cyprus, antonis.theocharous@cut.ac.cy

Peter M. Todd Indiana University, Psychology Building, Room 369, Informatics East, Room 302, Bloomington, IN 47406-7512, USA, pmtodd@indiana.edu

About the Editor

Ned Kock is professor of information systems and director of the collaborative for International Technology Studies at Texas A&M International University. He holds degrees in electronics engineering (B.E.E.), computer science (M.S.), and management information systems (Ph.D.). He has previously served as Founding Chair of the Division of International Business and Technology Studies and Chair of the Department of MIS and Decision Sciences at Texas A&M International University, and as a research center director at Lehigh University and Temple University. He is an active member of the Human Behavior and Evolution Society and the Association for Information Systems and has recently guest-edited the Special Issue on Darwinian Perspectives on Electronic Communication published in the *IEEE Transactions on Professional Communication*. Ned has authored and edited several books, including the bestselling Sage Publications book titled *Systems Analysis and Design Fundamentals: A Business Process Redesign Approach*. He has published his research in a number of high-impact journals including *Communications of the ACM, Decision Support Systems, European Journal of Information Systems, European Journal of Operational Research, IEEE Transactions (various), Information & Management, Information Systems Journal, Journal of the Association for Information Systems, MIS Quarterly*, and *Organization Science*. He is the Founding Editor-in-Chief of the *International Journal of e-Collaboration*, Associate Editor for Information systems of the journal *IEEE Transactions on Professional Communication*, and Associate Editor of the *Journal of Systems and Information Technology*. His main research interests are biological and cultural influences on human–technology interaction, electronic communication and collaboration, action research, ethical and legal issues in technology research and management, and business process improvement.

About the Authors

Chon Abraham is an assistant professor at the Operations and Information Systems Department in the Mason School of Business at the College of William & Mary. Before she received a Ph.D. from the University of Georgia, she worked as a systems analyst and has a military background. Chon has published in *Communications of the ACM, Decision Support Systems, Database, Encyclopedia of Healthcare Information Systems, Computers Informatics Nursing,* and written monographs for IBM Center for Healthcare Management and the Healthcare Information Management Systems Society (HIMSS). She received a 2008–2009 Fulbright Research award to conduct healthcare information technology research. Her research interests include healthcare information systems, wireless/ubiquitous computing, and organizational decision making for information systems and technology.

Robert Aunger has a master's degree in urban planning from the University of Southern California and a Ph.D. in biological anthropology from UCLA. He has taught at the Northwestern University, the University of Chicago, and King's College, Cambridge, in psychology, biology, and anthropology. He worked for 15 years on the theoretical, methodological, and empirical problems of studying cultural evolution, which resulted in a series of academic articles, as well as a trade science book, *The Electric Meme: A New Theory of How We Think* (The Free Press, 2002), and an edited volume, *Darwinizing Culture: The Status of Memetics as a Science* (Oxford University Press, 2001). These books begin the task of using evolutionary theory to understand cultural trends, including developments in technology. A third book, called *Reflexive Ethnographic Science*, concerns anthropological research methods. Currently, he works in the areas of psychological behavior change theory, identifying the natural kinds of human behavior at the London School of Hygiene & Tropical Medicine. He has also worked on the problems of rigorously identifying periods in macro-scale history from the Big Bang to contemporary times and the types of technologies that have evolved in human history.

Ina Blau is a faculty member in the Dept. of Education and Psychology at the Open University of Israel, and in the Dept. of Education at the Western Galilee College. She is also a member of Chais Research Center for the Integration of Technology in

Education. Her doctorate, from the University of Haifa, is in the field of E-Learning and CyberPsychology. Her research interests include social aspects of Internet use and e-communication, online participation patterns, and integration of innovative technologies in teaching and learning.

Jesus Carmona is a doctoral student in the MIS concentration of the Ph.D. Program in International Business Administration, Texas A&M International University. He is also an adjunct professor in that University's Division of International Business and Technology Studies. He holds a B.A. degree in agronomy from the Instituto Tecnologico de Estudios Superiores de Monterrey (ITESM) and an M.S. degree in information systems from Texas A&M International University. His research interests include e-collaboration, software engineering, and human–computer interface design.

Avner Caspi is a faculty member at the Open University of Israel, Department of Education & Psychology. He holds a B.A. in behavioral sciences (Tel-Aviv Yaffo Academic College) and Ph.D. in cognitive psychology (Tel Aviv University). His major research and publication interests focus on social aspects of communication technologies, mainly in the area of learning and instruction.

Ruth Chatelain-Jardón is a doctoral student of the Ph.D. Program in International Business Administration with concentration in MIS at Texas A&M International University, where additionally, she is an adjunct professor of the Division of International Business and Technology Studies. She holds degrees in international trade (B.B.A. and M.B.A.), international logistics (M.S.), and management information systems (M.S.). Her research interests include knowledge transfer, human–computer interface, e-collaboration, and business process improvement.

Dr. Barbara Fasolo is lecturer in decision sciences at the Department of Management of the London School of Economics and Political Sciences. Economist and psychologist by training (B.Sc. economics, Universita' Bocconi, Italy; M.Sc. decision sciences, London School of Economics; Ph.D. psychology, University of Colorado, USA), her area of expertise is "behavioral decision science," the empirical study of how people make judgments and choices. Her research explores how people choose in situations characterized by conflict, information overload, and risk and ways to improve their decision making – with applications to consumer, medical, and financial decision making, marketing, policy making, regulatory decisions, and decision analysis.

Christopher J. Ferguson is associate professor of clinical and forensic psychology at Texas A&M International University. He has published numerous articles on the subject of video game and other media violence and their potential influence on violent behavior, visuospatial cognition, and other outcomes. He is currently directing a longitudinal study of youth violence outcomes in a primarily

Hispanic population of youth. Other research has focused on evolutionary influences on aggression and sexual behavior. His work has been published in a number of high-impact journals including *Journal of Pediatrics*, *American Psychologist*, *Review of General Psychology*, *Professional Psychology: Research and Practice*, *Criminal Justice and Behavior*, *Aggression and Violent Behavior*. He has published an edited book, *Violent Crime: Clinical and Social Implications*, through Sage Publications. He is licensed as a psychologist in Texas.

Penelope Sue Greenberg is associate dean and director of graduate programs for the School of Business Administration at Widener University. She earned her doctorate at the Ohio State University. She has done international consulting and teaching in the areas of performance management, internal control, and knowledge management. She is active in several professional organizations including serving on the board of directors for the Philadelphia Chapter of the Association of Business Process Management Professionals. Her teaching interests include knowledge management and business process management. She has frequently presented research papers at academic conferences and has published in numerous international journals including *Business Process Management Journal*, *Journal of Computer Information Systems*, *Journal of Management Accounting Research*, *Journal of Accounting Literature*, *Behavioral Research in Accounting*, and *Business Horizons*. Her current research interests include trust in virtual teams and in business process outsourcing, and intra- and inter-organizational collaborative planning, performance measurement, and control.

Ralph H. Greenberg is associate professor of accounting in the Fox School of Business and Management at Temple University. He earned his doctorate at the Ohio State University. He has done international teaching in the Peoples' Republic of China, the National Republic of China (Taiwan), Japan, and Indonesia. He is active in the American Accounting Association. His teaching interests include management accounting and accounting information systems. He has frequently presented research papers at academic conferences and has published in many international journals including *Business Process Management Journal*, *Journal of Computer Information Systems*, *Journal of Management Accounting Research*, *Journal of Accounting Literature*, *Behavioral Research in Accounting*, and *Business Horizons*. His current research interests include trust in virtual teams and in business process outsourcing, and intra- and inter-organizational collaborative planning, performance measurement, and control.

Ana Ortiz de Guinea is an assistant professor in the Department of Information Technologies of HEC Montréal. She holds a Ph.D. from Queen's University, an M.Sc. from the University of Lethbridge, and a graduate degree in computer science and engineering from the Universidad de Deusto. Her work has been published in *MIS Quarterly*, the *Journal of Global Information Management*, and in the proceedings of numerous conferences.

Donald A. Hantula is an organizational psychologist, associate professor of psychology, and director of the Decision Making Laboratory at Temple University. He is the past executive editor of the *Journal of Social Psychology*, current associate editor of the Journal of Organizational Behavior Management and has edited special issues of other journals on topics such as experiments in e-commerce, evolutionary perspectives on consumption, Darwinian perspectives on electronic communication, and *Consumer Behavior Analysis*. He served on the National Science Foundation's Decision Risk and Management Sciences review panel and remains an ad hoc reviewer for government and private research funding agencies. Don has published in many high impact journals including the *Journal of the American Medical Association, Journal of Applied Psychology, Journal of Economic Psychology, Organizational Behavior and Human Decision Processes*, and *Behavior Research Methods*. His research in evolutionary behavioral economics combines behavior analytic and Darwinian theory to focus on questions in financial and consumer decision making, escalation of commitment, performance improvement, and human/technology interactions.

Stefan Hrastinski is assistant professor of Media Technology at KTH Royal Institute of Technology and Research Fellow of Information Systems at Uppsala University, Sweden. He is a member of the Swedish IT-User Centre and alumni member of the Swedish Research School of Management and IT. Stefan received his Ph.D. in informatics from Lund University and Jönköping International Business School with a thesis titled "Participating in Synchronous Online Education." It focused on computer-mediated communication and participation in online education and included both evolutionary and social psychological perspectives. Stefan has authored or co-authored more than 50 peer-reviewed articles published in, for example, the journals *Computers & Education* and *Information & Management*, and in the proceedings of the *International and European Conferences on Information Systems*, the *International and European Conferences on e-Learning*, and the *Internet Research Conference*. He regularly serves as guest editor, committee member and associate editor. Stefan's research is focused on learning, collaboration and innovation in online settings.

Iris Junglas is an assistant professor in the Decision and Information Sciences Department at the University of Houston's C.T. Bauer College of Business. Before receiving her Ph.D. from the University of Georgia, she has worked as a consultant for PricewaterhouseCoopers. She has published in *European Journal of Information Systems, Communications of the ACM, Decision Support Systems, MISQ Executive, Database, Communications of the AIS, International Journal of Mobile Communications*, among others. She is an associate editor for the *European Journal of Information Systems*. Her research interests include m-business, technology innovators, and construct development.

Alison P. Lenton is a lecturer in social psychology in the School of Philosophy, Psychology, and Language Sciences at the University of Edinburgh. From 2002 to 2004, she was a lecturer in social psychology in the Faculty of Social and Political Sciences at Cambridge University. Lenton received a Ph.D. in social psychology from the University of Colorado at Boulder in 2002, an M.A. in psychology from California State University, Long Beach, in 1997, and a B.A. in women's studies from the University of California at Santa Barbara, in 1994. Lenton's research interests and publications span the field of social psychology and include studies of automatic stereotyping, social biases in healthcare and legal decisions, the processes underlying judgments of sexual intent, and – most recently – context effects in mate choice.

Henry F. Lyle is a Ph.D. candidate in biocultural anthropology at the University of Washington, Seattle. His research draws from evolutionary theory to investigate collective action, unconditional generosity, and risk-taking behavior. He has conducted research on these topics in a variety of contexts, including blood donations in industrialized societies and collective action management in Andean Peru.

Sakthi Mahenthiran is the Carl Doty Professor Accounting at Butler University in Indianapolis. He received his M.B.A. and Ph.D. from Temple University in Philadelphia. In 2002–2003, he served as a Fulbright Scholar at University Institute of Technology Mara in Malaysia, and continues to serve as a visiting professor. He teaches and does research in the areas of management accounting, information systems, and corporate governance. To his credit, he has 17 publications in reputed journals such as *Journal of Management Accounting Research* and *Journal of Contemporary Accounting and Economics*.

Ahmed Y. Mahfouz, Ph.D., is an assistant professor of management information systems (MIS) at Prairie View A&M University, Prairie View, Texas, USA. He has a Ph.D. in information and operations management (MIS track) from Texas A&M University. He has an M.B.A. and a B.S. in management science from Virginia Tech. His research interests include electronic commerce, online consumer behavior, flow theory, IS strategy, research methodology, and interdisciplinary IS research and education. Dr. Mahfouz' research appears in several journals, such as *Computers in Human Behavior* and the *Journal of Internet Commerce*, as well as in four books, including *Handbook for Research on Contemporary Theoretical Models in Information Systems*; *Inquiring Organizations: Moving from Knowledge Management to Wisdom*; and *Internet Management Issues: A Global Perspective*. In addition, he taught for 3 years at Texas A&M University. He is a member of the Association for Information Systems (AIS).

M. Lynne Markus is the John W. Poduska, Sr. professor of information and process management at Bentley University and senior editor in charge of the Theory and

Review Department of *MIS Quarterly*. She was named a fellow of the Association for Information Systems in 2004 and received the AIS Leo award in 2008.

Zack Mendenhall is an M.Sc. student at Concordia University in the John Molson School of Business. He holds a B.S. (2008) in psychology with a minor in human evolutionary ecology from the University of New Mexico. He has been involved in research projects including rhythmic ability and symmetry, pathogenic risk and testosterone, digit ratio and product preferences, and conspicuous consumption within a virtual world. His research interests include evolutionary psychology, psychometrics, consumer behavior, and virtual worlds.

Marcelo Vinhal Nepomuceno is a Ph.D. student at the John Molson School of Business. He holds a B.Sc. (2004) and M.Sc. (2007) in psychology from the University of Brasilia. In Brazil, he has worked in the advertisement and banking industries, in both public and private sectors. He has published papers in *Estudos de Psicologia* (Natal), *Revista Psicologia Organizações e Trabalho*, and *Revista de Administração Mackenzie*. He also has forthcoming papers in the *Journal of Consumer Marketing* and *Educar em Revista*, as well as several recent submissions to other international journals. His research interests include social psychology, consumer behavior, and evolutionary psychology.

Andreas G. Philaretou, Ph.D., PMCMFT, CFLE, author and lecturer, is currently an associate professor in the Department of Social & Behavioral Sciences at European University Cyprus (formerly Cyprus College) and a special scientist in the Department of Psychology at the University of Cyprus. His research and teaching interests revolve mainly around topics of social psychological significance, specifically, gender and sexuality, sexualized work environments, psychosexual well-being, as well as leisure and entertainment. Dr. Philaretou's research appears in various journals, such as the *Journal of Men's Studies*, the *International Journal of Men's Health, Sexuality and Culture, Sexual Addiction and Compulsivity: The Journal of Treatment and Prevention, Computers in Human Behavior, The International Journal of Travel & Tourism Educators*. In addition, he is currently a member of the American Sociological Association (ASA), the Society for the Scientific Study of Sexuality (SSSS), and the American Men's Studies Association (AMSA).

Dr. Jaana Porra is an associate professor at the University of Houston, C.T. Bauer College of Business, Department of Decision and Information Sciences. Her research interests include group level evolution theory, group level speciation, systems theory and its application to human colonies, virtual communities, and online groups. She has published in journals such as *Journal of the Association for Information Systems, Information Systems Research, MIS Quarterly, Communications of the ACM, Decision Support Systems*, and *Database*. She currently serves on the *Journal of the Association for Information Systems* and *Journal of Information Systems and E-Business Management* editorial boards.

Gad Saad is a professor of marketing at Concordia University (Montreal, Canada) and the holder of the Concordia University Research Chair in Evolutionary Behavioral Sciences and Darwinian Consumption. He has held visiting associate professorships at Cornell University, Dartmouth College, and the University of California – Irvine. He was listed as one of the "hot" professors of Concordia University in both the 2001 and 2002 Maclean's reports on Canadian universities. He received his Faculty's Distinguished Teaching Award in June 2000. His book titled *The Evolutionary Bases of Consumption* (Lawrence Erlbaum, 2007) is the first academic book to demonstrate the links between evolutionary theory and consumption. He has published 55+ scientific papers many of which lie at the intersection of evolutionary psychology and a broad range of disciplines including consumer behavior, marketing, advertising, medicine, and economics. He is currently working on an edited book, to be published by Springer (2011), tentatively titled *Evolutionary Psychology in the Business Sciences*, as well as a trade book tentatively titled *The Consuming Instinct: What Juicy Burgers, Ferraris, Pornography, and Gift Giving Reveal About Human Nature* (Prometheus Books, 2011). Dr. Saad is a highly popular blogger for *Psychology Today*. Since November 2008, his posts have amassed 429,500+ total views. He received a B.Sc. in mathematics and computer science (1988) and an M.B.A. (1990) both from McGill University, and his M.S. (1993) and Ph.D. (1994) from Cornell University.

Bernd Carsten Stahl is professor of critical research in technology in the Centre for Computing and Social Responsibility at De Montfort University, Leicester, UK. His interests cover philosophical issues arising from the intersections of business, technology, and information. This includes the ethics of computing and critical approaches to information systems. He is the editor-in-chief of the *International Journal of Technology and Human Interaction*.

Roger J. Sullivan is an associate professor of anthropology at California State University Sacramento, and assistant adjunct professor of psychiatry at the University of California, Davis, Medical School. Sullivan is a biological anthropologist whose research focuses primarily on evolutionary medicine with a special emphasis on psychiatric conditions such as schizophrenia, cognitive deficits, and substance use. He conducts fieldwork of strategic social interactions and mental health in Oceania. Sullivan's inter-disciplinary research has appeared in biology, medicine, and anthropology journals including *Current Anthropology*, *American Journal of Psychiatry*, *Proceedings of the Royal Society B*, and *Neuroscience*.

Antonis Theocharous, Ph.D., is lecturer in the Department of Hotel and Tourism Management in the Faculty of Economics and Management, Cyprus University of Technology. He received his Ph.D. in business administration from the University of Sunderland. At Cyprus College, he was assistant professor in the school of business, coordinator of the under/postgraduate programs in tourism and hospitality management, and director of the research center, for which he secured international recognition and over 2 million CYP in research funds. He is the national representative of the Program Committee for Social Sciences and Humanities of the EU's 7th Framework Program. Dr. Theocharous has also served as national coordinator for two ESFRI projects: the European Social Survey (ESS) and the Digital Research Infrastructure for the Arts and Humanities (DARIAH). His research focuses on links between political instability and tourism development as well as risky behaviors and social networks in tourism and leisure. He has published in leading academic journal articles on topics such as political instability and tourism development, cross-cultural examination of the impact of political instability on tourism development at the regional level, various models of tourism destination choice, mass media depictions of various facets of political instability, sexual harassment at the workplace, and risky behaviors in tourism and leisure.

Peter M. Todd received an M.Phil. in computer speech and language processing from Cambridge University and a Ph.D. in psychology from Stanford University for his thesis on neural network models of the evolution of learning. In 1995 he moved to Germany to help found the Center for Adaptive Behavior and Cognition (ABC), which has been at the Max Planck Institute for Human Development in Berlin, since 1997. The center's work culminated in the book *Simple Heuristics That Make Us Smart* (Gigerenzer, Todd, and the ABC Research Group; Oxford, 1999); the sequel, focusing on environment structures and their impact, is forthcoming. In addition, Todd has co-edited three books on neural network and artificial life models in music and has written papers on topics ranging from social decision processes in rats to modeling patterns of age at first marriage. Since 2005 he has been professor of cognitive science, informatics, and psychology at Indiana University, Bloomington. His research interests cover the interactions between decision-making mechanisms and decision environments, including how the two co-evolve over time, in domains including mate choice, food choice, and spatial and mental search.

Part I
Theoretical and Conceptual Issues

Chapter 1
Evolutionary Psychology and Information Systems Theorizing

Ned Kock

Abstract Evolutionary Psychology is a relatively new field of research focusing on evolved mental traits and their impact on human behavior. It provides the basis on which innovative theoretical models can be developed in the context of information systems research, which is usually concerned with human behavior toward information and communication technologies. Yet it is important to recognize that not all information systems phenomena can be fully explained based on human evolution, a problem that can be addressed by the careful and selective integration of evolutionary and non-evolutionary information systems theories. This chapter discusses opportunities and difficulties associated with evolutionary information systems theorizing, provides an example of an evolutionary information systems theory (media naturalness theory), and shows how that theory can be profitably integrated with a non-evolutionary information systems theory.

Keywords Information systems · Evolutionary psychology · Theory development · Media richness theory · Media naturalness theory · Channel expansion theory

1 Introduction

While information systems as a distinct area of research has the potential to be a reference for other disciplines, it is reasonable to argue that information systems theorizing can benefit from fresh new insights from other fields of inquiry, which may in turn enhance even more information systems' reference potential (Baskerville and Myers 2002). After all, to be influential in other disciplines, information

N. Kock (✉)
Division of International Business and Technology Studies, Texas A&M International University, 5201 University Boulevard, Laredo, TX 78041, USA
e-mail: nedkock@tamiu.edu

N. Kock (ed.), *Evolutionary Psychology and Information Systems Research*,
Integrated Series in Information Systems 24, DOI 10.1007/978-1-4419-6139-6_1,
© Springer Science+Business Media, LLC 2010

systems research should address problems that are perceived as relevant by those disciplines' scholars and in ways that are consistent with those scholars' research traditions.

The likelihood of obtaining fresh new insights is especially high in connection with fields that bring in notions yet unexplored in information systems theorizing. A field of inquiry that appears to hold much promise in this respect is evolutionary psychology (Barkow et al. 1992; Buss 1999). This field of inquiry builds on concepts and ideas related to human evolution, primarily human evolution during the period that goes from the emergence of the first hominids, the Australopithecines (Boaz and Almquist 2001), up to the present day. (The term "hominid" is used here as synonymous with "hominin." In this sense, recent evidence supports the existence of even more ancient hominids, the Ardipithecines).

Evolutionary psychologists generally believe that many of our modern brain functions evolved during the period that goes from the emergence of the first hominids around 3.5 million years ago until the emergence of modern humans about 100,000 years ago (Buss 1999; Cartwright 2000).

Evolutionary psychology has the potential to become one of the pillars on which information systems theorizing can take place. The explanatory power of evolutionary psychology comes from the fact that its underlying ideas relate to the basic design of our brain and thus can form the basis on which fundamental explanations of behavior can be developed (Barkow et al. 1992; Cosmides et al. 2003; Kock 2004; Tooby and Cosmides 1990). Evolutionary psychology also arguably holds the key to many counterintuitive predictions of behavior toward technology, because many of the evolved instincts that influence our behavior are below the level of conscious awareness (Barkow et al. 1992; Buss 1999; Cartwright 2000). Often those instincts lead to behavioral responses that are not self-evident to the individuals involved. One example of this is the recent evolutionary psychology-inspired study by Kock et al. (2008), which shows that including a Web page showing a large picture of a snake in attack position in between Web pages with text-based knowledge content leads to a significant improvement (of as much as 38%) in the absorption of the content on the Web pages adjacent to the snake page.

Past research has rarely employed evolutionary psychological explanations and predictions regarding human behavior for the understanding of information systems phenomena. There have been few studies building on human evolution ideas, and to some extent on evolutionary psychological ideas, in the areas of mobile technology use (Junglas et al. 2009), electronic consumer behavior (Hantula et al. 2008; Rajala and Hantula 2000; Smith and Hantula 2003), computer-mediated communication (Kock 2004, 2005; Kock et al. 2008), virtual team leadership (DeRosa et al. 2004), electronic user interface design (Hubona and Shirah 2006), online mate selection (Saad 2008), and information search and use behavior (Spink and Cole 2006). These few studies reflect the potential of evolutionary psychology to explain behavior toward technology. Nevertheless, with even fewer exceptions (Hantula et al. 2008; Hubona and Shirah 2006; Junglas et al. 2009; Kock 2004, 2005), these studies have been published in outlets or addressed topics that are generally considered outside the field of information systems.

An attempt is made here to break new epistemological ground (Audi 2003) through the proposal, not of a new epistemology, of a theory development and integration framework for information systems theorizing based on evolutionary psychology that can be used within the scope of most epistemological traditions used in the field of information systems (Klein and Myers 1999; Orlikowski and Baroudi 1991). The theory development and integration framework builds on an extensive interdisciplinary review.

The framework is illustrated based on an analysis of the development of a new evolutionary theory, namely media naturalness theory (Kock 2004, 2005). This new theory was developed to fill a theoretical gap in connection with a non-evolutionary theory known as media richness theory (Daft and Lengel 1986; Daft et al. 1987). While evolutionary theories can bridge gaps left by non-evolutionary theories, it is also argued here that evolutionary theories of information systems generally need to be integrated with other non-evolutionary theories in order to provide a more precise and testable picture of the information systems phenomena that they try to explain. This has not been fully accomplished by media naturalness theory and is presented as leading to some limitations in explanatory and predictive power. A proposal is advanced on how media naturalness theory can be integrated with one non-evolutionary theory that seems to be a good complement to it, namely channel expansion theory (Carlson 1995; Carlson and Zmud 1999).

Notwithstanding the focus on communication media studies adopted in the illustrative examples provided, it is argued here that the framework can be used in a wide variety of theory development efforts not only in communication media research but also in the field of information systems. Traditional and emerging information systems topics that could also benefit from evolutionary psychological theorizing include (but are not limited to) the following: information systems development (e.g., visual programming and other cognitively natural approaches), technology-mediated learning (e.g., technology-mediated storytelling and other natural cognitive aids), human–computer interface design (e.g., chunking approaches to address cognitive limitations that have an evolutionary basis), and use of virtual worlds to simulate and predict large-scale group behavior in catastrophic situations (where evolved flight-or-fight instincts are likely to strongly influence behavioral responses).

2 Darwin's Theory of Evolution and Evolutionary Psychology

Evolutionary psychology builds on the modern synthesis (Mayr and Provine 1998) of Charles Darwin's (1859, 1871) theory of evolution of species by selection, which comprises evolution by natural (or environmental) selection in general (Darwin 1859), as well as in response to the more specific evolutionary force of sexual selection (Darwin 1871). Evolutionary psychology applies notions from the modern synthesis to the understanding of the evolution of the human brain and the complex set of brain modules that regulate human behavior.

Renewed interest in evolutionary explanations of human behavior, particularly since the mid-1990s (Zimmer 2001), may suggest that Darwin's theory has been somehow rediscovered by modern researchers. This is incorrect. Researchers interested in evolutionary theories that can be used for information systems theorizing should be aware that there has been steady progress over the years in the expansion and refinement of the original theory of evolution. Much of that progress has been made by researchers who resorted to mathematical formalizations of evolutionary phenomena building on fundamentals of genetics (Hartl and Clark 2007) and who published their conclusions primarily in academic journals. By and large those conclusions have been hidden from the popular and out-of-field academic literature for many years and have been partially disseminated through the efforts of best-selling authors such as Dawkins (1990), Miller (2000), and Pinker (2002).

Also interesting but less relevant for the discussion presented here is the fact that the main ideas of the theory of evolution were in fact published in 1858 as part of an essay by Alfred Russel Wallace, which prompted Darwin to rush his momentous book into publication in 1859; Darwin gave Wallace proper credit, and the theory is sometimes referred to as the Darwin–Wallace theory of evolution (Kutschera 2003). The theory of evolution was plagued by controversy up until the early 1900s (Fox and Wolf 2006; Quammen 2006). It was the rediscovery of Gregor Mendel's pioneering work on the fundamentals of genetics (of which Darwin and Wallace were unaware) by Hugo de Vries and others in the early 1900s that provided the impetus for a better understanding of how variation occurs in plant and animal traits (Mayr and Provine 1998; Quammen 2006). That variation is the main fuel used by natural selection to shape the wide variety of adaptive traits observed in organic life (Maynard Smith 1998; Rice 2004). Even though Hugo de Vries and other early geneticists were very critical of the theory of evolution, their rediscovery of and subsequent work on genetics eventually provided a solid basis on which the theory of evolution stood even more convincingly than when it was originally proposed (Boaz and Almquist 2001; Fox and Wolf 2006).

The progress in the expansion and refinement of the original theory of evolution continues up to this day, particularly due to new discoveries in various fields such as molecular genetics (Hartl and Clark 2007). The original formulation of the theory of evolution has been supported by a vast amount of empirical data, successfully withstanding the test of time (Mayr and Provine 1998; Zimmer 2001). Nevertheless many key theoretical contributions have been made over the years to explain evolutionary phenomena that were not fully addressed by Darwin, Wallace, or any of their contemporaries. A large proportion of these contributions have been made in the period going from 1910 to 1980, after which evolutionary theorizing has generally branched out into more specialized fields. One of these specialized fields is the field of evolutionary psychology (Barkow et al. 1992).

Evolutionary psychology essentially assumes that the human brain is like a computer with a number of interacting programs, or mental modules, and that those modules have been developed over successive generations in response to evolutionary pressures (Barkow et al. 1992). Most of those mental modules are believed to have been developed to solve problems faced by our ancestors in the Stone

Age. As pointed out by Buss (1999, p. 20), modern humans "... carry around a stone-aged brain in a modern environment."

Several researchers have made key contributions to the field of evolutionary psychology since the 1980s. Robert Trivers not only has made key contributions to evolution theory but is also among the pioneers in the field of evolutionary psychology (for a collection of influential papers, see Trivers 2002). Jerome Barkow, Leda Cosmides, and John Tooby are widely recognized for having taken the first steps in the path of establishing evolutionary psychology as a field of investigation with a clear identity (Barkow et al. 1992; Cosmides and Tooby 1981; Cosmides et al. 2003; Tooby and Cosmides 1990). Another pioneer of the field is psychologist David Buss (1995, 1999), who has conducted groundbreaking cross-cultural studies on the evolutionary psychological mechanisms underlying human sexuality, aggression, and mental disorders. Two other notable psychologists who pioneered the field are Martin Daly and Margo Wilson, having provided key evolutionary psychological explanations of violent and criminal behavior (Daly and Wilson 1999; Wilson et al. 2002). Among linguists and language development researchers who have contributed to the establishment of the field of evolutionary psychology are Jeffrey Laitman (Laitman 1984; Laitman and Reidenberg 1997), Philip Lieberman (Lieberman 1998, 2000), Derek Bickerton (Bickerton 1990), William Calvin (Calvin and Bickerton 2000), and Steven Pinker (Pinker 1994, 2002, 2003). Notable anthropologists who also have greatly contributed to the establishment of the field are Napoleon Chagnon (Chagnon 1977, 1988) and Robin Dunbar (Dunbar 1993, 1998).

3 The Evolution of Psychological Traits by Natural Selection

The diagram in Fig. 1.1 depicts how a psychological trait P would have evolved in our evolutionary past by natural selection (Cartwright 2000; McElreath and Boyd 2007; Price 1970). The trait P was associated with a genotype G, which was a set of interrelated genes (Boaz and Almquist 2001; Hartl and Clark 2007; Maynard Smith 1998) that influenced the formation of P. An example of psychological trait

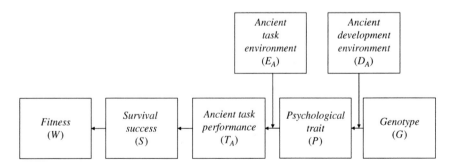

Fig. 1.1 Evolution of psychological traits by natural selection

P would be "attention to colors". Individuals possessing this trait would have an instinctive response to objects displaying colors other than black and white, paying more attention to them. Individuals not possessing this trait would pay no particular attention to those objects.

Like most gene–trait relationships, the relationship between G and P was moderated by the ancient development environment D_A. The term "environment" is used here broadly, generally meaning all factors that were not genetic in nature, such as social, nutritional, climatic, and other related factors (Boaz and Almquist 2001; McElreath and Boyd 2007; Pinker 2002; Wilson 2000). The environment D_A was the environment surrounding our hominid ancestors in their formative years, that is, while they developed from fertilized egg stage to reproductive maturity. For example, if a mother's milk was very low in certain nutrients, proper development of color vision could have been impaired. Even in the presence of the same genotype G, that impairment could make attention to colors impossible due to color blindness.

The psychological trait P influenced ancient task performance T_A, or the performance of an individual in an ancient task such as hunting or foraging (Boaz and Almquist 2001; Hubona and Shirah 2006). For example, let us assume that T_A was associated with the task of foraging for nutritious fruits. In this case, individuals who paid attention to colors would generally have higher T_A than individuals who did not, because colors are indicative of the presence of important nutrients in fruits (Boaz and Almquist 2001; Cartwright 2000). The relationship between P and T_A was moderated by the ancient task environment E_A.

Individuals who were more successful at the task of foraging for nutritious fruits would also be more resistant to disease, and thus would survive in higher quantities (Gillespie 2004; Maynard Smith 1998). They would have a higher survival success (S). Since one must be alive to procreate and care for offspring, those individuals would also have higher fitness (W). In population genetics (Graur and Wen-Hsiung 2000; Hartl and Clark 2007; Kimura 1994; Maynard Smith 1998; McElreath and Boyd 2007), the term fitness (usually indicated as W, as we do here) generally refers to the success with which an individual's genes are passed on to successive generations. It is usually measured through the number of surviving offspring or grand-offspring of an individual (Gillespie 2004; Maynard Smith 1998; McElreath and Boyd 2007; Rice 2004).

The process above, repeated generation after generation, would lead the genotype G and the related psychological trait P to spread from one single individual to the vast majority of our ancestors. This process is what is generally referred to as evolution by natural selection (Boaz and Almquist 2001; Maynard Smith 1998; Rice 2004). As a result, G and P would be widely observed in modern humans, leading to the emergence of what is often referred to as a human universal (Brown 1991). The term "human universal" does not refer to a trait that is present in every single living individual but to a trait that is widespread among humans, regardless of cultural differences.

In summary, the evolution of any psychological trait P through natural selection is the direct result of the emergence, usually by chance, of a genotype G, which in turn positively affects fitness W through a chain of effects (Maynard Smith 1998;

McElreath and Boyd 2007). The chain of effects is as follows: genotype G influences psychological trait P, psychological trait P influences ancient task performance T_A, ancient task performance T_A influences survival success S, and survival success S influences fitness W. It can be shown that the product of the correlations between each of these pairs of constructs must be greater than zero for this evolution to take place (see Kock 2009, Appendix F; the seminal article by Price 1970). That is, each of the causal links does not have to be seen as a deterministic causation; it is the *correlation* implied by those links, and thus ultimately the *correlation* between genotype G and fitness W, that provides the basis on which evolution takes place.

4 How Evolved Psychological Traits Affect Modern Human Behavior

The same genotype (G) and related psychological trait (P) that evolved in our evolutionary past can have an impact in the context of modern behavior toward technology, often affecting modern task performance in tasks where technology is used. However, that would not normally be related to the survival success or the fitness of modern humans, because modern humans are no longer subject to the same selection pressures that our ancestors faced in our evolutionary past (Boaz and Almquist 2001; Buss 1999; McElreath and Boyd 2007).

For example, the psychological trait "attention to colors" could affect the performance of individuals in information search tasks using computer interfaces that employ various colors, compared with interfaces that used no colors other than black and white. Yet, this psychological trait would have no impact on the survival success or the fitness of modern humans.

Fig. 1.2 Evolution of psychological traits by natural selection

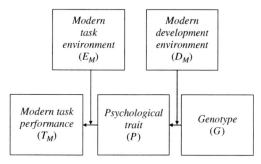

Figure 1.2 depicts the process above. The genotype G influences the development of a psychological trait P, which in our example is attention to colors. This relationship is moderated by the modern development environment D_M, which is the environment surrounding modern humans in their formative years as they develop from fertilized eggs to reproductively mature individuals.

The psychological trait P influences modern task performance T_M, which refers to the performance of an individual in a modern task such as searching for information using a computer interface. Individuals who possess the evolved psychological trait P (attention to colors) would have better T_M with a color-enabled computer interface than with a computer interface that displays only black and white objects.

Similarly to E_A's moderating effect on the relationship between P and T_A, the relationship between P and T_M is also moderated by a construct, namely the modern task environment E_M. This is the environment surrounding modern humans, as they perform modern tasks. For example, a task environment E_M with poor lighting could negatively influence the relationship between P and T_M when compared with a well-lit environment, where P is attention to colors and T_M is the performance on a computer-based information searching task.

5 Evolutionary Information Systems Theorizing

What characterizes information systems theorizing based on evolutionary psychology is the search for an evolved psychological trait P, whose development is influenced by a genotype G, and for a technology-related impact on the performance of a modern task T_M. In these scenarios, the technology usually adds elements that help shape a modern task environment E_M in which the task is accomplished.

The main focus of evolutionary psychology theorizing is the relationship between genotype G and evolved psychological trait P (Barkow et al. 1992; Buss 1999), as indicated in Fig. 1.3. On the other hand, the main focus of information systems theorizing based on evolutionary psychology is the relationship between an evolved psychological trait P and the performance of a modern task T_M, in a modern environment E_M. The modern environment E_M is shaped by technology created by modern

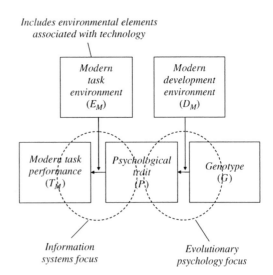

Fig. 1.3 The foci of information systems and evolutionary psychology research

humans, as well as by associated social structures aimed at technology appropriation (Bélanger and Watson-Manheim 2006; DeSanctis and Poole 1994).

If there is no evolved psychological trait P involved in the theorizing effort, and thus no assumption about the existence of a related genotype G, then the effort cannot be characterized as information systems theorizing based on evolutionary psychology. Two examples that illustrate this approach to theorizing are the development of media naturalness theory (Kock 2004, 2005) and the use by Hantula et al. (2008) of ancestral foraging theory to predict the behavior of online buyers.

The development of media naturalness theory (Kock 2004, 2005) is an example of how evolutionary theorizing can be used to fill gaps left by a non-evolutionary theory. Media naturalness theory was developed to fill gaps arguably left by media richness theory (Daft and Lengel 1986; Daft et al. 1987). Those gaps were related to empirical findings suggesting media richness theory's success in explaining users' perceptions about electronic communication media richness (Daft et al. 1987; Kock 2005), but not those users' actual choices of media (Markus 1994b) or task performance when using media of low richness (Kock et al. 2006).

The research conducted by Hantula et al. (2008) is an example of how evolutionary theorizing can be used to develop innovative and precise predictions of information systems phenomena. Hantula et al.'s (2008) research is based on ancestral foraging theory and includes predictions about how modern humans make decisions in an online environment. Based on ancestral foraging theory, those researchers predicted that online buyers would react rather negatively to online in-stock verification delays. Their prediction was mathematically precise: the higher the delays, the lower the proportion of purchases and shopping times observed, following a hyperbolic decay function. Their empirical results provided strong support for their theoretical predictions, which are part of an evolving theoretical framework known as the behavioral ecology of consumption (Rajala and Hantula 2000; Smith and Hantula 2003).

6 Natural Selection Versus Sexual Selection

The discussion presented here does not cover all forms of evolutionary information systems theorizing; its main focus is on what is often referred to as "natural" selection or selection of traits that enhance the survival success of individuals in a population. Different evolutionary psychology outlets and institutions place emphasis on different forms of evolutionary theorizing. Particularly noteworthy is sexual selection theorizing, which builds on what is sometimes referred to as Darwin's (1871) *other* theory or the theory of sexual selection (Miller 2000).

Modern Darwinian evolutionary thinking builds on two main biological processes: natural selection (Darwin 1859) and sexual selection (Darwin 1871). In a nutshell, the first refers to evolution in connection with survival success, whereas the second refers to evolution in connection with mating success. In sexual selection, the selective pressures come not from the physical environment surrounding an individual but from members of the opposite sex who find certain traits attractive. The classic example of sexual selection is that of the male peacock's train, which is actually a survival handicap (Petrie et al. 1991; Zahavi and Zahavi 1997).

Sexual selection has been used to explain the evolution of our appreciation of artistic expression, which in our evolutionary past would have little survival value (Miller 2000, 2001). This type of theorizing is fairly rare, and possibly nonexistent, in information systems. Sexual selection could be used to explain why the external design of computers is perceived by certain buyers as being fairly important, even though computers are primarily purchased for their functionality. Sexual selection is also associated with the emergence of sex differences, which have (the sex differences) often been the target of information systems theorizing, sometimes based on evolutionary arguments. For instance, Hubona and Shirah (2006) built on hunter–gatherer theory to argue that modern-day differences between men and women in spatial and cognitive abilities result from different roles played by our male and female hominid ancestors. They studied males and females performing visual spatial tasks using two- and three-dimensional virtual worlds, finding that females underperformed males in matching and positioning tasks, and outperformed males in resizing tasks. Analogous differences have been found in other studies (see, e.g., Stenstrom et al. 2008). There are several difficulties associated with theorizing about sexual differences.

7 Theorizing About Sex Differences: A Difficult Task

It is undeniable that human males and females differ in their genetic makeup. The genetic differences between men and women are very likely the largest within the human species. In humans, genetic material is organized in 23 pairs of chromosomes. One of these pairs, often referred to as the sex chromosomes, differs in men and women. Men have what is often referred to as an XY pair, where the X chromosome is inherited from the mother and the Y from the father; women have an XX pair (Boaz and Almquist 2001; Hartl and Clark 2007).

Information systems researchers interested in evolutionary theorizing may be tempted to hypothesize sexual differences based on the known genetic differences between men and women. Those researchers are likely to encounter several difficulties. One of them is that many traits that have been evolved because of selective pressures on one sex are also present, at least to a certain extent, in the other sex. For example, men have nipples. This phenomenon is often referred to as gene correlation (Gillespie 2004; Maynard Smith 1998). It creates a particularly serious problem for information systems researchers trying to hypothesize sex differences in behavior toward technology based on assumptions about different selective pressures on men and women in our evolutionary past. Even when different selective pressures are clearly identified, it is often difficult to argue convincingly that evolved brain mechanisms associated with behavioral responses have been passed on only to men or women, and not both.

Another difficulty awaiting information systems researchers trying to explain sex differences based on evolutionary thinking is that sex differences are often associated with sexually selected traits. Many of these traits confer no survival advantage to the individuals that possess them; some actually handicap those individuals (Zahavi and Zahavi 1997). Sexually selected traits are generally used in mate choice, meaning that they evolved because they were considered attractive by members of the other sex. The classic example of sexually selected trait is the big and bright train of the male in the peacock species, which is actually a handicap from a survival perspective (Petrie et al. 1991; Zahavi and Zahavi 1997). Examples of traits in the human species that are hypothesized to be at least in part sexually selected are testosterone markers in men such as angular facial features and fertility markers in women such as a 0.7 waist-to-hip ratio (Buss 1995, 1999; Miller 2000). Many other examples exist (see, particularly, Buss 1995) that can be used as a basis for the formulation of hypotheses on human behavior toward technology and differences in that behavior displayed by men and women.

Sexually selected traits used in mate choice pose another problem for information systems researchers because they often present a much greater level of variability than do traits evolved in response to other environmental pressures. This higher variability of mate choice traits is a general phenomenon that extends well beyond the human species (Boaz and Almquist 2001; Miller 2000; Zahavi and Zahavi 1997). Therefore, hypothesized sex-linked instincts affecting behavior toward technology may present a great deal of variation among any sample of individuals. A high level of variability leads to problems in empirical tests employing quantitative data collection and analysis techniques, and may lead to misleading conclusions even in qualitative studies. For example, it poses restrictions on the types of tests that can be employed and requires quantitative tests with large statistical power. Moreover, since in most cultures, attitudes toward men and women are different and have a differential effect on how men and women behave, a great deal of variability in connection with a hypothesized effect may make it very difficult to isolate genetic from cultural influences.

Yet another difficulty may be faced by information systems researchers trying to explain sex differences based on evolved behavioral patterns. It comes from the fact that the variability of many traits differs in men and women (Buss 1995; Miller 2000), with variability often being higher in men than women. For example, general intelligence scores present a higher variation in men than in women, even though on average men and women score equally well in general intelligence tests (Deary et al. 2007). From a statistical standpoint, this is reflected in a flatter (i.e., higher variance) normal distribution of the trait for men than for women. This finding has led to what is sometimes referred as the "more idiots, more geniuses" effect, i.e., there are more idiots and geniuses among men than among women (Deary et al. 2007; Miller 2000).

Differences in within-sex variability may create difficulties in empirical tests and lead to misleading interpretations of differences in behavior toward technology. For example, a random sample of men and women may contain a higher percentage of men than women unable to effectively use a computer system with a very complex interface and also a higher percentage of men than women showing extremely high proficiency at using the computer system, even though a comparison of mean proficiencies may suggest no significant differences between men and women.

The above discussion is not meant to imply that information systems researchers should avoid theorizing about sex differences in behavior toward technology based on evolved psychological traits. What should be clear is that such line of research will be generally more difficult to undertake than theorizing about human universals that apply to both sexes. Empirical tests of hypotheses related to sex differences will probably require large cross-cultural samples to be convincing.

8 Why There Is a Need to Integrate Evolutionary and Non-evolutionary Theories

In many cases, evolutionary information systems theories will have to be integrated with non-evolutionary theories to fully explain certain information systems phenomena. There are four main reasons for this: (a) not all information systems phenomena have an evolutionary basis; (b) differences between ancient and modern tasks may prevent task-specific theorizing; (c) differences between ancient and modern task environments may prevent technology-specific theorizing; and (d) differences between ancient and modern development environments may prevent generation-specific theorizing.

Not all information systems phenomena have an evolutionary basis. While evolutionary psychology holds great promise as a basis for information systems theorizing, there are probably many facets of information systems phenomena that have no clear evolutionary basis. Evolutionary theorizing may lead to explanations and predictions of some facets of an information systems phenomenon, but not others, which calls for the integration of evolutionary information systems theories with non-evolutionary theories.

For example, one may be tempted to develop a fully evolutionary explanation of why flat keyboards are so widely used by individuals from different cultures. Yet, there has been no selective pressure in our evolutionary past in favor of flatness of typing surfaces. The task of typing is a very recent human invention, too recent to have shaped the morphology of our hands or the design of our brain, in any significant way (Kock 2004). It would be possible to find a distant analogue of the task of typing in our evolutionary past, such as stone tool making (Boaz and Almquist 2001), but that would probably go only some way toward explaining the general flatness of modern typing surfaces. Moreover, past research suggested that the flat keyboard design is not the most optimal design from an ergonomics standpoint (Gilad and Harel 2000). The main conclusion one can reasonably reach based on that past research is that the flat design is quite widespread due to primarily being an efficient design from manufacturing perspective.

Differences between ancient and modern tasks may prevent task-specific evolutionary theorizing. Building parallels between ancient task performance (T_A) and modern task performance (T_M) may be difficult due to differences in the tasks themselves. This makes it difficult to develop fully evolutionary theories to make predictions about some specific modern tasks. High-level, or generic, tasks, such as the task of communicating knowledge, may be largely the same irrespective of whether performed today or by our hominid ancestors (Miller 2000; Pinker 2003; Spink and Cole 2006; Wilson 2000). Low-level, or more specific, tasks may be significantly different.

The task of communicating knowledge about foraging for a specific type of food was carried out in our evolutionary past (Boaz and Almquist 2001; Cartwright 2000) and is also carried out today in non-urban societies. On the other hand, the task of communicating knowledge about the design of a new car engine is carried out only by modern humans. Therefore, it is difficult to build a fully evolutionary theory of, say, electronic communication of knowledge about the design of new car engines. One could, however, build a fully evolutionary theory of electronic communication of knowledge (Kock 2004) and then integrate it with a non-evolutionary theory to explain various aspects of electronic communication of knowledge about the design of new car engines.

Differences between ancient and modern task environments may prevent technology-specific evolutionary theorizing. Modern task environments (E_M) frequently differ, sometimes significantly, from ancient task environments (E_A), and those differences are often due to the use of technology. While this may not prevent evolutionary theorizing in connection with high-level, or generic, technologies, it may make it difficult to conduct evolutionary theorizing in connection with low-level, or specific, technologies. Evolutionary psychological theories rely on predictions associated with Stone Age problems and with how those problems have led to the development of brain mechanisms to deal with them in order to maximize reproductive success (Barkow et al. 1992; Buss 1995). A look back at our evolutionary past leads to the conclusion that our brain is probably designed for face-to-face communication, the mode of communication used by our ancestors during over 99% of our evolutionary history, where learning was an integral part of hominid survival and mating strategies (Boaz and Almquist 2001; Lieberman 1998; Wilson 2000). As a corollary, one can also conclude that our brain is probably maladapted for the use of communication media that suppress too many of the elements found in face-to-face communication in learning tasks.

Yet, when we look at the virtual environments created by online learning technologies, it is undeniable that electronic media are widely used by modern humans for online learning in universities and other educational institutions (Summers et al. 2005). This would not be the case if the vast majority of the students who have taken courses online had failed them due to their brain being designed for face-to-face communication. The widespread use of electronic media for online learning allows students who live in rural areas, and also those who are unable to attend classes due to working full time, to obtain the education that they need to improve their lives. The existence of factors such as living in rural areas and working full time, which strongly influence the use of electronic communication technologies for online learning, is probably not best explained by evolutionary forces, if it can be explained at all in that way. This illustrates the need to integrate evolutionary and non-evolutionary theories to explain phenomena associated with the use of a specific type of technologies, namely the technologies that shape online learning environments.

Differences between ancient and modern development environments may prevent generation-specific evolutionary theorizing. Differences between modern (D_M) and ancient development environments (D_A) may lead to differences in the way a genotype G influences the formation of a psychological trait P. This is likely to be especially true with different generations of individuals (e.g., baby boomers, generation X, generation Y). In fact, each new generation of modern humans may develop psychological traits somewhat differently, even though those traits may be coded for by the same genotype G. As a result, it may be very difficult to explain generation-specific information systems phenomena entirely based on evolutionary theorizing.

Except for some rare traits, such as blood type, the vast majority of human traits are the result of a complex interplay between genotypes and developmental influences (Boaz and Almquist 2001; Wilson 2000). Often events experienced during the early developmental stages of one's life affect behavior later in life fairly strongly (Chagnon 1977; Dunbar 1998; Wilson 2000). In those cases, the effects of genetic influences can and should still be studied, as they may shed light on intriguing patterns of behavior, but researchers must be mindful that developmental influences can also have a strong effect on behavior. The study by Kock et al. (2008) of surprise-enhanced cognition can be used to illustrate this.

Kock et al. (2008) provided an evolutionary explanation for the phenomenon associated with unpleasant unexpected events causing enhanced cognition within their temporal vicinity, namely a few minutes before and after they occur. This is a well-documented phenomenon, sometimes referred to as flashbulb memorization (Brown and Kulik 1977; Nairne et al. 2007; Schutzwohl and Reisenzein 1999). Kock et al. (2008) argued that the reason for such enhanced cognition is that it was adaptive in our evolutionary past, because unpleasant unexpected events (e.g., a snake attack) were often associated with survival threats in our evolutionary past and those threats often occurred within predictable contexts (e.g., a snake's habitat) with clear markers such as specific terrain and rock formations.

For example, most animals seem to live in well-defined habitats, which were likely invaded by our human ancestors, as they generally are today in non-urban societies, a few minutes before and after the attacks (Hung 2004; Manipady et al. 2006). Therefore, having vivid memories associating an animal attack with habitat markers would have helped an ancestor avoid future animal attacks after the first was experienced; this assumes that animal attacks were not always fatal. This surprise-enhanced cognition notion was used to explain an unusual experimental finding in Kock et al.'s (2008) study. The inclusion of a Web page showing a large picture of a snake in attack position, in between Web pages with text-based knowledge content, led to a significant improvement in test scores on the content of the Web pages adjacent to the snake page.

However, studies of responses to surprise events of a social nature suggest that we tend to be much more surprised by events that affect the social group to which we are taught to belong, as we grow up, than those that affect other groups; e.g., news of an invasion of our native country as opposed to a country about which we have never heard (Berntsen and Thomsen 2005). Analogously, for the effect observed in Kock et al.'s (2008) study, that effect might not have been the same for individuals who were used to handling snakes from an early age, as those individuals might have been desensitized to the use of that type of stimulus as a source of unpleasant surprise. This illustrates the need to integrate evolutionary theories with non-evolutionary theories that incorporate influences associated with modern developmental environments (D_M) that shaped psychological traits of certain individuals, especially during childhood.

Integration of evolutionary and non-evolutionary theories may be only a first step in the development of progressively more comprehensive information systems theories. Once the integration of theories A (evolutionary) and B (non-evolutionary) is complete, it is possible that a new evolutionary theory C may be developed, where C encompasses A and B. However, there are a few good reasons to believe that evolutionary information systems theories will often have to be complemented by non-evolutionary theories. The continuously changing nature of information systems phenomena, often fueled by the development of ever new technologies, places constant pressure for the identification of theoretical frameworks to explain those new phenomena. New theories take time to develop, and existing non-evolutionary information systems theories far outnumber evolutionary ones, making the use of non-evolutionary theories almost inevitable in many theory-based information systems research investigations.

9 Four Important Preconditions for Theoretical Integration

The discussion above provides arguments in favor of the integration of evolutionary and non-evolutionary theories of information systems phenomena. Fundamental epistemological contributions, such as those made by Popper (1992) and others (see, e.g., Audi 2003; Stinchcombe 1968), suggest that for this integration to take place successfully, some preconditions should be satisfied. It is argued here that four important preconditions are the following: (a) the theories should refer to the same general type of task; (b) the theories should refer to the same general type of technology; (c) the theories should comprise similar theoretical constructs; and (d) the theories should complement each other. For simplicity, the discussion presented here focuses on information systems theorizing that gravitates around the development of causal models (Bagozzi 1980; Davis 1985) depicting the relationships between independent, intervening, moderating, and dependent constructs (Kline 1998; Rosenthal and Rosnow 1991). Causal modeling can generally be used in information systems research employing various research approaches, data collection and analysis methods, and epistemologies (Davis 1985; Klein and Myers 1999; Orlikowski and Baroudi 1991).

The theories should refer to the same general type of task. Since the discussion is presented here in an information systems context, an object-oriented analogy (Chuang and Yadav 2000; Sircar et al. 2001) may help clarify this precondition for theoretical integration. This precondition is equivalent to saying that evolutionary and non-evolutionary theories should refer to the same task *class*, even though either theory may refer to a *subclass* of the task. Task performance attributes, such as task outcome quality and task performance efficiency, are frequently included in causal models as dependent constructs (Davis 1985; Rosenthal and Rosnow 1991) Therefore, without this precondition being satisfied, it could be difficult to identify task-related constructs that could serve as dependent constructs in a causal model depicting the complete theoretical framework including both evolutionary and non-evolutionary theories.

Our previous discussion provides a good example; one could build a fully evolutionary theory of electronic communication of knowledge (Kock 2004) and then integrate it with a non-evolutionary theory to explain various aspects of electronic communication of knowledge about the design of new car engines. In this example, both theories refer to the same task class, which could be seen as the task of electronic communication of knowledge. One of the theories refers to a subclass of this task, namely electronic communication of knowledge about the design of new car engines.

The theories should refer to the same general type of technology. Again using an object-oriented analogy (Chuang and Yadav 2000; Sircar et al. 2001), this precondition is equivalent to saying that evolutionary and non-evolutionary theories should refer to the same technology *class*, even though either theory may refer to a *subclass* of the technology. In information systems investigations, technology-related attributes, such as the naturalness of an asynchronous electronic collaboration technology, are often included in causal models as independent constructs (DeLuca et al. 2006; Simon 2006). Therefore, without this precondition being satisfied, it could be difficult to identify technology-related constructs that could serve as independent constructs in a causal model depicting the complete theoretical framework.

Using the same example as above, a fully evolutionary theory of electronic communication of knowledge may be integrated with a non-evolutionary theory to explain various aspects of electronic communication of knowledge about the design of new car engines. Here both theories refer to the same technology class, namely the class of electronic communication technologies. While no technology subclasses are mentioned in this example, either theory might have referred to a subclass of electronic communication technologies, such as instant messaging technologies, which would not prevent theoretical integration.

The theories should comprise at least one similar theoretical construct. This precondition is closely related to the preconditions above. It is challenging to integrate two theories that refer to constructs that are very different, and a good indication of construct discrepancy is the inability to measure the two theories' constructs in the same way or in using the same instrument (Davis 1985; Popper 1992; Rosenthal and

Rosnow 1991). This refers to constructs that are measured objectively (e.g., an individual's age) or subjectively (e.g., perceived amount of knowledge communicated). The latter are usually referred to as latent constructs (Schumacker and Lomax 1996; Rencher 1998).

Let us refer again to the example of a fully evolutionary theory of electronic communication of knowledge, being integrated with a non-evolutionary theory to explain various aspects of electronic communication of knowledge about the design of new car engines. In this example, one of the constructs that provide a bridge between the two theories is communication of knowledge, which could be measured in the same way for both theories through a latent construct. The latent construct in question could reflect the answers to a few question statements related to the perceived amount of knowledge communicated, during a specific time interval, about the design of new car engines.

The theories should complement each other. In this precondition, what is meant by complementing each other is essentially that the theories should add elements that enlarge a single causal model depicting the integrated theoretical framework. These elements can be new constructs or new relationships between constructs, in addition to the constructs and relationships of one or the other theory. The constructs here can be independent, intervening, moderating, or dependent constructs; the relationships can be direct, indirect, or moderating effects (Bagozzi 1980; Davis 1985; Kline 1998; Rosenthal and Rosnow 1991). Theories that are not complementary in this sense cannot be integrated, as they would lead to two or more separate causal models.

It should be noted that evolutionary and non-evolutionary theories that predict competing effects can still be seen as complementary, as long as the competing effects can be depicted in the same causal model. Let us assume that a fully evolutionary theory of electronic communication of knowledge predicts that electronic communication media in general decrease the performance in knowledge-intensive tasks of short duration. Let us also assume that a non-evolutionary theory developed to explain various aspects of electronic communication of knowledge about the design of new car engines predicts that electronic communication media in general *increase* the performance in knowledge-intensive tasks of long duration, such as the task of new car engine design. These two theories would still be complementary, because they can be combined in one single causal model, where the relationship between medium and task performance is moderated by task duration.

10 Theoretical Integration in Practice: Media Naturalness and Channel Expansion

This section provides a discussion and critical review of an evolutionary theorizing effort and the integration of the resulting evolutionary theory with a non-evolutionary theory. The discussion starts with a review of media richness theory (Daft and Lengel 1986; Daft et al. 1987) and the identification of a theoretical gap associated with empirical findings that contradicted it. It then proceeds with the development of media naturalness theory (Kock 2004, 2005), in response to the theoretical gap left by media richness theory. The discussion then moves to recent attempts to overstretch the explanatory and predictive scope of evolutionary theorizing to overcome some limitations of media naturalness theory and the proposal of a solution to overcome those limitations. That solution is the integration of media naturalness theory with a non-evolutionary theory, channel expansion theory (Carlson 1995; Carlson and Zmud 1999).

10.1 Media Richness Theory

Media richness theory (Daft and Lengel 1986; Daft et al. 1987) is an ingenious theory of organizational communication that makes predictions about behavior and outcomes in connection with various communication media. Within the scope of media richness theory's predictions were also electronic media, even though the theory was originally developed well before the emergence of the Internet and the widespread use of electronic communication technology that is seen today. Media richness theory is one of the most widely cited theories in the field of information systems (Dennis et al. 1999; Kahai and Cooper 2003; Kock 2005). In this theory, different media are classified according to their degree of richness, which varies depending on the degree to which media incorporate certain characteristics.

Four main characteristics define the richness of a medium, according to media richness theory. Two of them are given special prominence by Daft and Lengel (1986); they are the medium's ability to convey multiple communicative cues (e.g., facial expressions and voice intonations) and enable immediate feedback on the message being conveyed (a characteristic of synchronous communication). The other two are given less prominence by Daft and Lengel (1986, p. 560), who appear to imply that they either follow from or are related to the first two; they are the medium's support for language variety and personalization of messages. These four characteristics are evocative of unencumbered face-to-face interaction, although media richness theory does not explicitly use the face-to-face medium as a basis for richness comparisons. That is, media richness theory does not define rich media based on their degree of similarity to the face-to-face medium.

The notion of equivocal task is central to media richness theory. A task is equivocal when there are multiple interpretations of the problem that is being solved through the task (Daft and Lengel 1986; Daft et al. 1987). In equivocal tasks, complex knowledge, as opposed to simple pieces of information, must be exchanged in order for the task to be successfully accomplished (Speier et al. 2003). For example, the task of designing a new car engine with the goal of saving an ailing automaker plagued by decreasing revenues will most likely be an equivocal task. Conversely, the task of buying a commercially available metal pipe that will go into that new engine will probably not be an equivocal task.

In the context of equivocal tasks, media richness theory makes two main predictions (Daft and Lengel 1986; Daft et al. 1987). The first is essentially that effective communication media users will choose the richest possible media available to them. For example, an effective team developing a new car engine will probably, according to media richness theory, choose to communicate face-to-face instead of via e-mail if only these two media are available to them. The second prediction by media richness theory is that, when the choice of media is constrained (e.g., only e-mail is available), the use of a lean communication medium will lead to a corresponding degradation in task outcome quality. For example, if two teams are tasked with developing a new car engine and one communicates only face-to-face while the other communicates only via e-mail, then the theory's prediction is that the face-to-face team will develop a better car engine than will the one developed by the e-mail team.

The above predictions may seem fairly intuitive and, at first glance, quite correct. However, there is a substantial amount of empirical evidence showing that individuals often choose lean media to carry out equivocal team tasks and that the use of lean media often leads to the same or even better outcomes than if rich media were used (Bélanger and Watson-Manheim 2006; Burke and Aytes 2001; Crowston et al. 2007; Dennis and Kinney 1998; El-Shinnawy and Markus 1998; Hasty et al. 2006; Kock et al. 2006; Markus 1994a, b; Ngwenyama and Lee 1997; Ocker et al. 1995). In other words, media richness theory has essentially been falsified multiple times.

In spite of the above, there is strong evidence that lean media do pose obstacles to communication in equivocal team tasks (Burke and Chidambaram 1999; DeLuca et al. 2006; DeRosa et al. 2004; Graetz et al. 1998; Kahai and Cooper 2003; McKinney and Whiteside 2006; Simon 2006). This evidence is to a certain extent contradictory with the evidence that falsified media richness theory and suggests the existence of a theoretical gap. Moreover, the finding that lean media pose obstacles to communication seems to be associated with a variety of different studies and has even been reported in multi-country studies (Kock and DeLuca 2007; Tan et al. 1998; Wainfan and Davis 2004).

10.2 Media Naturalness Theory

Media naturalness theory (Kock 2004, 2005) is an evolutionary theory that was developed to address theoretical problems with media richness theory, which were brought to light by many focused empirical tests. One of those problems is that there is solid evidence that electronic media that suppress face-to-face communication elements do seem to pose communication obstacles in equivocal team tasks (DeLuca et al. 2006; Graetz et al. 1998; Kahai and Cooper 2003; Simon 2006). This finding may be seen as supporting media richness theory. However, media richness theorists provided an explanation for it, namely low medium richness, which is not well grounded on fundamental psychological mechanisms. The proponents of media richness theory seem to have assumed as a postulate that what they refer to as rich media present certain characteristics that make those media particularly well suited to support communication in the context of equivocal tasks.

A simple thought experiment highlights this fundamental problem that plagues media richness theory. Let us assume that the human species had evolved in an ancestral environment without light. If that were the case, modern humans would all be blind, and therefore a communication medium's ability to convey facial expressions and body language would be irrelevant for effective communication. Conversely, a medium's ability to convey smell might be fairly important for effective communication. This illustrates the fact that one cannot define a medium's ability to support effective communication without taking into consideration characteristics of the communicators. Of these, biological characteristics often have an evolutionary basis. (Since those biological characteristics are hypothesized to present a high degree of similarity across different people, one can call them media naturalness characteristics, even though they are not tied to the media, but rather to the biological design of humans. In this sense, one could argue that "media naturalness theory" is a misnomer, even though it is how the theory is normally referred to – see, e.g., Simon 2006).

The problem highlighted by the thought experiment has been vital to the development of media naturalness theory (Kock 2004, 2005). The lack of a solid scientific basis for media richness theory's predictions was akin to that created by the explanation that objects fall to the ground because they are attracted to it, which was consistent with the geocentric view of the universe proposed in the first century by the great mathematician and astronomer Ptolemy. This explanation would in fact be consistent with many observations of objects falling to the ground, perhaps in most modern everyday situations. However, this explanation would fail to account for some exceptions, relatively rare in modern everyday life, such as the behavior of objects in a free-falling airplane. It would also fail to explain more general cases that are not part of most people's daily routines, such as the observation of planetary orbits. In other words, even though it would be wrong, the explanation would appear intuitive and correct to most people.

More modern explanations of the phenomenon of objects falling to the ground, now known as gravitational attraction, were later provided by Isaac Newton and Albert Einstein. Those explanations were consistent with the behavior of objects in free-falling airplanes and with astronomical observations. The search for a more fundamental explanation to the phenomenon associated with the communication obstacles posed by non-face-to-face media led to the development of media naturalness theory, similarly but certainly in a vastly smaller scale than the theoretical developments by Newton and Einstein.

A relatively simple argument is at the core of media naturalness theory. The argument is that since our Stone Age hominid ancestors have communicated primarily face-to-face, evolutionary pressures likely have led to the development of a brain that is consequently designed for that form of communication (Kock 2004, 2005). Other forms of communication are too recent and unlikely to have posed evolutionary pressures that could have shaped our brain in their direction (Boaz and Almquist 2001; Wilson 2000). Using communication media that suppress key elements found in face-to-face communication, as many electronic communication media do, thus ends up posing obstacles to communication. This is particularly the case in the context of equivocal tasks, because such tasks seem to require more intense communication over extended periods of time than do non-equivocal tasks (Kock 2004).

It appears that the face-to-face medium has been the primary communication medium used during over 99% of the hominid evolutionary history that led to the emergence of the human species (Boaz and Almquist 2001; Cartwright 2000). During that time, our ancestors have developed several adaptations that seem obviously aimed at face-to-face communication employing speech and facial expressions. Among those adaptations are a larynx located relatively low in the neck and a customized vocal tract, which combined with corresponding brain modules allow us to generate the large variety of sounds needed to speak most modern languages (Laitman 1984; Laitman and Reidenberg 1997; Lieberman 1998). Another interesting adaptation is a very complex web of facial muscles, which allow humans to generate a large variety of communicative expressions and whose main function seems to be primarily related to facial communication (Bates and Cleese 2001; McNeill 1998).

The naturalness of a communication medium is defined, in media naturalness theory, as the degree of similarity of the medium with the face-to-face medium (Kock 2004, 2005). The face-to-face medium is presented as the medium enabling the highest possible level of communication naturalness, which is characterized by the following five key elements: (1) a high degree of co-location, which would allow the individuals engaged in a communication interaction to see and hear each other; (2) a high degree of synchronicity, which would allow the individuals to quickly exchange communicative stimuli; (3) the ability to convey and observe facial expressions; (4) the ability to convey and observe body language; and (5) the ability to convey and listen to speech. The ability to convey tactile stimuli or smell is not part of the definition of naturalness of a communication medium; some unique research results suggest that media naturalness theory could benefit from taking them into consideration—see, e.g., Sallnas et al. (2000).

Similar to media richness theory, the main independent construct in media naturalness theory is the degree of naturalness of a communication medium. Unlike media richness theory though, the main dependent constructs of media naturalness theory do not refer to media choice or task outcome quality. They instead refer to the following attributes regarding the use of a medium to perform a collaborative task: (a) cognitive effort, reflected in perceptions regarding mental effort expended; (b) communication ambiguity, or the likelihood of misinterpretation of communication cues; and (c) physiological arousal, reflected in perceptions related to physical stimulation or excitement. Kock (2004, 2005) provides a detailed discussion of these constructs and suggestions on how they can be measured. Media naturalness theory's main prediction is that, other things being equal, a decrease in the degree of naturalness of a communication medium leads to the following effects in connection with a collaborative task: (a) an increase in cognitive effort, (b) an increase in communication ambiguity, and (c) a decrease in physiological arousal.

10.3 Naturalness Versus Richness: What Is the Difference?

Some may feel inclined based on the above discussion to argue that media naturalness theory is too similar to media richness theory, even though it has a different
theoretical basis and different dependent constructs. There are two key predictions,
however, that illustrate the fundamental differences between the two theories. The
first is in connection with the place of face-to-face communication in the naturalness
or richness scale (Kock 2004, 2005). The second is in connection with what Kock
(2004) refers to as the speech imperative proposition.

The place of face-to-face communication. Media naturalness theory predicts that
any electronic communication medium that allows for the exchange of significantly
less *or more* communicative stimuli per unit of time will pose cognitive obstacles
to communication than does the face-to-face medium (Kock 2004, 2005). In other
words, media naturalness theory places the face-to-face medium at the center of a
one-dimensional scale of naturalness, where deviations to the left or the right, so
to speak, are associated with decreases in naturalness. Media richness theory, on
the other hand, leaves the door open for the assumption that certain media can be
higher in richness than is the face-to-face medium. It does so because its focus is on
the physical properties of the communication medium (Daft and Lengel 1986), and
not on the biological constraints on the communicators using the medium, which is
the focus of media naturalness theory. For example, a virtual reality medium that
enables individuals to interact with more than one individual at the same time, without the interlocutors knowing, could be classified as richer than the face-to-face
medium (Kock 2004), based on media richness theory (Daft and Lengel 1986).

Electronic media that enable the exchange of significantly *more* communicative
stimuli per unit of time are classified by media naturalness theory as having a lower
degree of naturalness than does the face-to-face medium (Kock 2005). As such,
those media are predicted to be associated with higher cognitive effort, in this case
primarily due to a phenomenon known as information overload (Kock 2004), which
is characterized by individuals having more communicative stimuli to process than
they are able to. This phenomenon may also happen with the use of electronic media
that are significantly simpler than virtual reality media. The electronic communication media created by group decision support systems, which are systems that allow
groups of users to exchange large amounts of textual information without the need
to share airtime as in face-to-face meetings, have been shown to induce a certain
amount of information overload (see, e.g., Dennis 1996).

The speech imperative proposition. Complex speech was enabled by the evolution of a larynx located relatively low in the neck (Lieberman 1998), which
considerably increased the variety of sounds that our species could generate; this is
actually one of the most important landmarks in the evolution of the human species.
However, that adaptive design also significantly increased our ancestors' chances
of choking on ingested food and liquids, and suffering from aerodigestive tract diseases such as gastroesophageal reflux (Laitman and Reidenberg 1997). This leads
to an interesting conclusion, which is that complex speech must have been particularly important for effective communication in our evolutionary past, otherwise the

related evolutionary costs would prevent it from evolving through natural selection. This argument is similar to that made by Zahavi and Zahavi (1997) in connection with evolutionary handicaps. If a trait evolves to improve the effectiveness in connection with a task, in spite of imposing a survival handicap, then the trait should be a particularly strong determinant of the performance in the task to offset the costs it imposes.

Media naturalness theory builds on this evolutionary handicap conclusion to predict that the degree to which an electronic communication medium supports an individual's ability to convey and listen to speech is particularly significant in defining its naturalness (Kock 2004). Media naturalness theory predicts, through its speech imperative proposition, that speech enablement influences naturalness significantly more than does a medium's degree of support for the use of facial expressions and body language. This prediction is consistent with past research showing that removing speech from an electronic communication medium significantly increases the perceived mental effort associated with using the medium to perform knowledge-intensive tasks (see, e.g., Graetz et al. 1998). This prediction could not have been derived from media richness theory.

10.4 Taking the Evolutionary Argument a Bit Too Far?

While media naturalness theory provides what one could call deep-level explanations for some key findings in the electronic communication literature, its predictions do not address task outcomes. This is a problem because predictions about task outcomes are often very relevant in information systems research, as they provide the basis on which practical implications for information systems users can be developed (Baskerville and Myers 2002; DeSanctis and Poole 1994; Easley et al. 2003; Fjermestad 2004; Straub and Karahanna 1998; Zigurs and Buckland 1998).

Let us take the case of online delivery of university courses for example. Media naturalness theory allows for the prediction that students taking a course through an online delivery medium will have different, and possibly more negative, perceptions about their experience than do students taking the same course face-to-face. Any online course delivery medium, even a very sophisticated one, will present a lower degree of naturalness than will the face-to-face medium. Therefore, students in the online medium are predicted by media naturalness theory to experience higher levels of cognitive effort and communication ambiguity, and lower levels of physiological arousal.

What media naturalness theory cannot predict is whether the students taking the course online will learn less than, more than, or the same as the students taking the course face-to-face. This is an important type of prediction in the context of online learning (Summers et al. 2005), which like face-to-face learning is a highly equivocal task that involves intense communication and knowledge exchange over an extended period of time. At first glance one could argue that more cognitive effort and communication ambiguity, combined with less excitement, is very likely to lead to impaired learning performance. Yet, media naturalness does not allow for that type of conclusion because there may be other influences that compete with naturalness and that contribute to improved learning performance (Kock 2005).

Even with the obstacles posed by electronic communication media in general, it is undeniable that the use of those media for course delivery is widespread and growing (Newlin et al. 2005; Summers et al. 2005). It would be surprising if that proliferation was taking place in spite of evidence that online delivery had a negative impact on student learning. In fact, much of the evidence from studies in which performance is measured through course grades obtained by students suggests that online delivery has no negative impact on learning outcomes (Newlin et al. 2005). The impact is not positive either; it seems to be generally neutral, which is still seen as an encouraging finding since online delivery allows students with time or geographic constraints and physical disabilities to attend university courses virtually. This has led to a rather optimistic view of online delivery of university courses that became known as the "no-significant-difference" perspective (Summers et al. 2005).

Since online learning is a task with peculiarities that make it rather different from ancestral learning tasks, the above findings would call for the integration of media naturalness theory with an appropriate non-evolutionary theory as a first step to better explaining them. In spite of that, media naturalness theory has not yet been integrated with any non-evolutionary theory that could have complemented it. Instead, it has been expanded to incorporate another phenomenon, namely that of compensatory adaptation (Kock et al. 2006, 2007), which is also presented as having an evolutionary basis.

Compensatory adaptation is presented as a general brain mechanism, or a mental meta-module, that is associated with the rewiring of the brain's neo-cortex whenever obstacles are posed to an individual carrying out a task. The evolutionary relevance of compensatory adaptation is presented on the basis that our hominid ancestors have faced a number of task-related obstacles for which specialized adaptation would have been impractical. Therefore, a general mechanism such as compensatory adaptation should have been favored by natural selection (Cartwright 2000; Kock et al. 2007), particularly in the Pleistocene, the period in which *Homo sapiens* is believed to have emerged (Boaz and Almquist 2001).

While appealing and perhaps generally correct, the compensatory adaptation argument goes too far in a strictly evolutionary theorizing path in this case. Attempts to overstretch the limits of evolutionary theorizing may face some key challenges, such as that the tasks carried out by and task environments surrounding our hominid ancestors were often much different from the ones in connection with modern humans. Presumably natural selection shaped human morphology, physiology, and behavior to deal with tasks routinely carried out by our human ancestors. Those tasks involve mating, foraging, hunting, and socializing. Learning about computer topics (Kock et al. 2007) and developing new products (Kock et al. 2006) are too dissimilar from tasks performed routinely by our ancestors. Invoking general adaptive mechanisms, such as compensatory adaptation, to overcome this task dissimilarity problem is likely to only weaken the predictive and explanatory power of any related theoretical model. The reason is that such invocation and related hypotheses are difficult if not impossible to falsify.

The above argument can be illustrated through a critical review of the study reported by Kock et al. (2007), which was conducted in the context of an online learning task. The study builds on the analysis of mid-semester and final grades obtained by two groups of students taking the same course with the same instructor, with the difference that one group took the course online and the other face-to-face. One of the main findings of the study was that while grades at the middle of the semester were lower in the online than in the face-to-face condition, the difference disappeared at the end of the semester. Compensatory adaptation was invoked to explain that finding, even though the notion of compensatory adaptation is so general that it could also have been invoked to explain: (a) compensatory adaptive reactions leading to any increase in grades online between the middle and the end of the semester, even if the increase had not led the online grades to catch up with the face-to-face grades at the end of the semester and (b) a strong compensatory adaptive reaction that led the students in the online condition to obtain grades that were significantly better at the end of the semester than those in the face-to-face condition.

10.5 *Integration with Channel Expansion Theory*

A critical analysis of the compensatory adaptation notion suggests that it can be invoked to explain various changes in grades, including the change in grades observed in Kock et al.'s (2007) study. In other words, compensatory adaptation theory is not very amenable to falsification in this type of context, which may impair its usefulness as a piece of a larger theoretical model addressing related information systems phenomena (Popper 1992).

One theory that is compatible with the change in grades observed in Kock et al.'s (2007) study is channel expansion theory (Carlson 1995; Carlson and Zmud 1999), a non-evolutionary theory. A key prediction of channel expansion theory is that continued use of a lean (or unnatural, in media naturalness theory's terminology) communication medium over time, with the same individuals and to perform the same task, will lead to an expansion of what is called the channel capacity of the medium. In their explanation of the channel expansion phenomenon, Carlson and Zmud (1999, p. 157) note that: "As individuals develop experience communicating with others using a specific channel, such as e-mail, they may develop a knowledge base for more adroitly applying this communication channel ... For example, e-mail users may become aware of how to craft messages to convey differing levels of formality or of how to use channel-specific metalanguage to communicate subtleties. Similarly, these individuals are also likely to interpret messages received on this channel more richly because they can interpret an increasing variety of cues."

In order words, users of an unnatural medium are predicted to possibly become better at communicating through the medium over time to perform a specific task. This could explain the "no-significant-difference" effect in connection with the use of online course delivery media, since students normally have a full semester to adapt to an online delivery medium and the instructor's style of use of the medium for communication. Therefore, channel expansion theory can be seen as a good complement to media naturalness theory.

Channel expansion theory (Carlson 1995; Carlson and Zmud 1999) also allows for a much more specific prediction, which is that average grades in the online and face-to-face conditions would converge as the semester progresses. This is exactly what happened in Kock et al.'s (2007) study. In fact, the grades at the end of the semester were on average lower than grades in the middle of the semester, for both the online and face-to-face conditions; the key change observed was that the differences in grades between conditions were significant in the middle of the semester and insignificant at the end of the semester (Kock et al. 2007) In this case, a non-evolutionary theoretical proposition (i.e., channel expansion) provides a better complement to an evolutionary proposition (i.e., media naturalness) than yet another evolutionary proposition (i.e., compensatory adaptation). The non-evolutionary theoretical proposition provides a better theoretical "glue," so to speak, with which one can integrate (a) predictions from a theoretical model developed based on ancient human behavior with (b) predictions about human behavior in connection with modern tasks.

The integration of the media naturalness and channel expansion theories is facilitated by channel expansion theory referring to media richness, or channel richness, in a way that makes it interchangeable with media naturalness. If channel expansion theory referred to richness in a way that implied that super-rich virtual reality media would be even more natural than the face-to-face medium, then it would be difficult to integrate the media naturalness and channel expansion theories in the context of use of such super-rich virtual reality media. An example of a super-rich virtual reality medium would be a medium that enabled individuals to interact with more than one individual at the same time, without the interlocutors knowing, thus potentially enabling the exchange of significantly more communicative stimuli than would the face-to-face medium. According to media naturalness theory, such a super-rich virtual reality medium would be less natural than face-to-face communication. In this case, the integration would probably not be impossible, but one theory or the other would have to be amended prior to their integration.

11 Discussion

As can be inferred from the above discussion, the theories of media naturalness and channel expansion can be integrated to provide a more reasonable predictive and explanatory framework within which Kock et al.'s (2007) empirical findings can be understood. This section provides a conceptual link between the above discussion and the earlier discussion on information systems theorizing based on evolutionary psychology, the need to integrate evolutionary and non-evolutionary theories, and the four preconditions for integrating evolutionary and non-evolutionary theories.

Figure 1.4 shows the elements involved in the evolution of face-to-face communication modules, and thus face-to-face media naturalness, in our ancestral

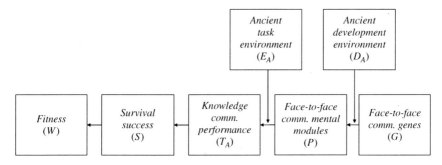

Fig. 1.4 Evolution of face-to-face communication mental modules through natural selection

past. The genotype G is indicated as "Face-to-face comm. genes," which is the configuration of genes that coded for a brain design optimized for face-to-face communication. The genotype G coded for the general psychological trait P, indicated as "Face-to-face comm. mental modules," which were the mental modules designed for face-to-face communication. The trait P positively influenced the ancient task performance T_A, indicated as "Knowledge comm. performance," which was the performance in the high-level task of communicating knowledge. The ancient task performance T_A positively influenced survival success S, which in turn positively influenced fitness W. Over many generations, the genotype G spread to be point of being largely observed among modern humans. So did the psychological trait P. The relationship between G and P was moderated by the ancient development environment D_A, and the relationship between P and T_A was moderated by the ancient task environment E_A.

Why was knowledge communication performance (T_A) positively associated with survival success (S) in our evolutionary past? The reason is that it enabled ancient humans to occupy what Pinker (2003) called the cognitive niche, which was yet unoccupied by other species. Knowledge communication enabled our ancestors to make predictions about events that were likely to affect their survival without having to experience those events. This placed our human ancestors at a tremendous advantage compared with most other animal species, even those species with relatively large brains such as apes, because those other species had to generally live through or directly observe survival threats to learn how to avoid them (Pinker 1994; Wilson 2000). The ability to communicate knowledge, which is highly and uniquely developed in humans, allowed our ancestors to avoid survival threats, and also engage in survival-enhancing behaviors, simply by learning about them from other individuals. This likely co-evolved with many socialization drivers that are believed to have also been the result of selection and that have led our ancestors to congregate in increasingly larger and more complex social groups (Boaz and Almquist 2001; Cartwright 2000). One of the most fundamental of those socialization drivers is the universal human instinct called reciprocal altruism (McElreath and Boyd 2007; Trivers 2002), without which our ancestors would be disinclined to share knowledge with one another.

Fig. 1.5 Evolved
face-to-face communication
mental modules and online
learning

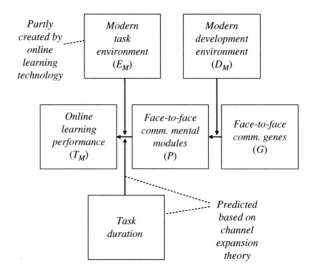

Figure 1.5 shows how the evolution of face-to-face communication modules plays a role in the modern task of online learning investigated in Kock et al.'s (2007) study. The genotype G is indicated as "Face-to-face comm. genes"; G codes for the general psychological trait P, indicated as "Face-to-face comm. mental modules." The relationship between G and P is moderated by the modern development environment D_M. The trait P negatively influences T_M, indicated as "Online learning performance," since the trait P is optimized for face-to-face communication.

The relationship between P and T_M is moderated by the modern task environment E_M, which is partly created by the online learning technology. The more the technology suppresses face-to-face communication elements, the stronger the negative relationship between P and T_M. The moderating effect predicted based on channel expansion theory is indicated at the bottom as "task duration." Channel expansion theory allows for the prediction that the longer the task, the weaker the negative effect of P on T_M.

Media naturalness and channel expansion theories fit relatively well in terms of the four preconditions for integration discussed earlier. The two theories refer to the same general type of task, the task of electronic communication of knowledge; both theories allow for predictions regarding this general task. The two theories refer to the same general type of technology, electronic communication technology; both theories allow for predictions regarding this general technology. The two theories comprise at least one similar theoretical construct, namely media naturalness; channel expansion actually refers to media richness, but in a way that makes it interchangeable with media naturalness. Finally, the two theories complement each other. Media naturalness predicts that face-to-face communication modules (P) have the potential to negatively affect online learning performance (T_M). Channel expansion theory provides a moderating effect complement by supporting the prediction that this relationship between P and T_M is weakened as task duration increases.

The above discussion illustrates the integration of the media naturalness and channel expansion theories in the context of online learning. In different contexts, such as virtual new product development (Kock et al. 2006) and virtual team leadership (DeRosa et al. 2004), other non-evolutionary theories may be needed to complement media naturalness theory.

It is possible that the media naturalness and channel expansion theories will be subsumed within a broader evolutionary theory as a result of future theoretical efforts. This will happen as long as the phenomenon Carlson and Zmud (1999) called channel expansion can be fully explained from an evolutionary perspective. Once that is achieved, if it is achieved at all, the resulting naturalness–expansion theory can be used as a basis for integration with other non-evolutionary theories as needed, in a progressive process of theory development and integration (Popper 1992) that is not unlike that underlying the evolution of social theories (Stinchcombe 1968).

12 Conclusion

Hopefully the framework for information systems theorizing based on evolutionary psychology and theoretical integration put forth here will serve as a guide for information systems researchers, especially those interested in understanding how evolved brain modules and mechanisms may influence human behavior toward technology. The use of the framework was partially illustrated here through one main example in connection with theorizing about human behavior toward communication media. While much of the discussion focuses on electronic communication studies, one main contention made here is that the framework can be used in a wide variety of theory development efforts in the field of information systems.

The framework proposed here is likely to be particularly useful in efforts aimed at developing theories that explain and predict universal behavior of humans toward technology. The emphasis of the framework is on behavior that is likely to be observed in all human beings regardless of possible differences between subgroups, even small genetic differences (e.g., men and women). Media naturalness theory is a good example of this type of theory development effort. These theories would apply to both men and women whose genetic differences are likely to influence certain types of behavior but not others. For instance, men and women have been shown to differ significantly in their mate search and selection patterns (Buss 1995; Miller 2000), which would naturally lead to different theoretical predictions regarding certain types of technology-related behavioral patterns such as those in online dating contexts.

The discussion of the integration of evolutionary and non-evolutionary information systems theories put forth here also opens up a new line of theoretical inquiry for information systems researchers. This new line of inquiry relates to the integration of different information systems theories into theoretical models that are amenable to rigorous empirical testing. Examples are provided in the context of communication media issues, which are issues that have been gaining increasing attention over the years, and are among the most intensely investigated among information systems researchers (Dennis et al. 1999; Te'eni 2001; Watson-Manheim and Bélanger 2007). With a few notable exceptions (see, e.g., Trevino et al. 2000; Webster and Trevino 1995; Watson-Manheim and Bélanger 2007), rarely different communication media theories have been integrated before into testable models.

It may seem at first glance that the discussion presented here is only of academic value, but industry practitioners can benefit greatly (although indirectly) from theory development efforts conducted through the framework and related information technology developments. The emergence of the Internet and the global economy are two key reasons for that, because they create a central challenge for most organizations. The challenge is that of having to sell goods and services, using electronic interfaces, to buyers from a wide variety of backgrounds and cultures. The main common denominator among those buyers is their human nature. In spite of increasing efforts toward personalization of interfaces, many of which are undeniably successful, designing interfaces for electronic commerce that build on human universals is likely to be a fundamental part of the solution to the challenge of selling goods and services to geographically disperse and culturally diverse buyers.

In addition to providing a guide for researchers interested in developing new information systems theories based on evolutionary psychology, another obvious goal here is to stimulate this type of theorizing among researchers who have not considered it yet. However, a note of caution, already discussed as part of the framework, needs to be emphasized. Information systems phenomena are unlikely to be always fully explained based only on evolutionary psychology notions. Thinking otherwise would probably do more harm than good for the field of information systems, as it has been the case elsewhere.

History has taught us (on a much broader scale) that a blind belief in deterministic evolutionary explanations and predictions of human behavior can lead to many problems. After all, that blind belief was at the source of once influential schools of thought such as race-based eugenics and social Darwinism, which in turn formed the basis for the development of ideas that led to racism, wars, and genocide. Evolutionary explanations of behavior, including behavior toward technology, must be developed cautiously and fully tested before they are accepted and used in practice. Moreover, their results should be used only to the extent that they are compatible with the highest standards of ethics, morality, and concern for the well being of all human beings.

Acknowledgements This chapter is a revised version of an article by the author published in 2009 in the journal *MIS Quarterly*. The author would like to thank the senior editor, the associate editor, and reviewers of that article for their excellent comments and suggestions. Special thanks are due to the senior editor, M. Lynne Markus. The author thanks Nap Chagnon, Leda Cosmides, Martin Daly, Don Hantula, Allen Lee, John Nosek, Achim Schutzwohl, John Tooby, Rick Watson, and Margo Wilson for ideas and enlightening discussions on the various topics discussed in this chapter. Thanks are also due to the following individuals for comments and suggestions on earlier versions of this chapter: Chon Abraham, Robert Boyd, Geoffrey Miller, and Steven Pinker.

References

Audi R (2003) Epistemology: a contemporary introduction. Routledge, New York

Bagozzi RP (1980) Causal models in marketing. John Wiley & Sons, New York

Barkow JH, Cosmides L, Tooby J (eds) (1992) The adapted mind: evolutionary psychology and the generation of culture. Oxford University Press, New York

Baskerville RL, Myers MD (2002) Information systems as a reference discipline. MIS Q 26(1): 1–14

Bates B, Cleese J (2001) The human face. DK Publishing, New York

Bélanger F, Watson-Manheim MB (2006) Virtual teams and multiple media: structuring media use to attain strategic goals. Group Decis Negot 15(4):299–321

Berntsen D, Thomsen DK (2005) Personal memories for remote historical events: accuracy and clarity of flashbulb memories related to World War II. J Exp Psychol Gen 134(2):242–257

Bickerton D (1990) Language and species. University of Chicago Press, Chicago

Boaz NT, Almquist AJ (2001) Biological anthropology: a synthetic approach to human evolution. Prentice Hall, Upper Saddle River

Brown DE (1991) Human universals. McGraw-Hill, New York

Brown R, Kulik J (1977) Flashbulb memories. Cognition 5(1):73–99

Burke K, Aytes K (2001) Do media really affect perceptions and procedural structuring among partially-distributed groups? J Syst Inf Technol 5(1):10–23

Burke K, Chidambaram L (1999) How much bandwidth is enough? A longitudinal examination of media characteristics and group outcomes. MIS Q 23(4):557–580

Buss DM (1995) The evolution of desire: strategies of human mating. Basic Books, New York

Buss DM (1999) Evolutionary psychology: the new science of the mind. Allyn & Bacon, Needham Heights

Calvin WH, Bickerton D (2000) Lingua ex machina: reconciling Darwin and Chomsky with the human brain. The MIT Press, Cambridge

Carlson JR (1995) Channel expansion theory: a dynamic view of media and information richness perception. Doctoral dissertation, Florida State University, Tallahassee

Carlson JR, Zmud RW (1999) Channel expansion theory and the experiential nature of media richness perceptions. Acad Manage J 42(2):153–170

Cartwright J (2000) Evolution and human behavior: Darwinian perspectives on human nature. The MIT Press, Cambridge

Chagnon NA (1977) Yanomamo: the fierce people. Holt, Rinehart and Winston, New York

Chagnon NA (1988) Life histories, blood revenge, and warfare in a tribal population. Science 239(4843):985–992

Chuang T, Yadav SB (2000) A decision-driven approach to object-oriented analysis. Database Adv Inf Syst 31(2):13–34

Cosmides L, Tooby J (1981) Cytoplasmic inheritance and intragenomic conflict. J Theor Biol 89(1):83–129

Cosmides L, Tooby J, Kurzban R (2003) Perceptions of race. Trends Cogn Sci 7(4):173–179

Crowston K, Howison J, Masango C, Eseryel UY (2007) The role of face-to-face meetings in technology-supported self-organizing distributed teams. IEEE Trans Prof Commun 50(3): 185–203

Daft RL, Lengel RH (1986) Organizational information requirements, media richness and structural design. Manage Sci 32(5):554–571

Daft RL, Lengel RH, Trevino LK (1987) Message equivocality, media selection, and manager performance: implications for information systems. MIS Q 11(3):355–366

Daly M, Wilson M (1999) The truth about Cinderella: a Darwinian view of parental love. Yale University Press, New Haven

Darwin CR (1859) On the origin of species by means of natural selection. Harvard University Press, Cambridge, MA (Facsimile of the first edition, reprinted in 1966)

Darwin CR (1871) The descent of man, and selection in relation to sex. John Murray, London

Davis JA (1985) The logic of causal order. Sage, London

Dawkins R (1990) The selfish gene. Oxford University Press, Oxford

Deary IJ, Irwing P, Der G, Bates TC (2007) Brother–sister differences in the g factor in intelligence: analysis of full, opposite-sex siblings from the NLSY1979. Intelligence 35(5):451–456

DeLuca D, Gasson S, Kock N (2006) Adaptations that virtual teams make so that complex tasks can be performed using simple e-collaboration technologies. Int J e-Collab 2(3):64–90

Dennis AR (1996) Information exchange and use in group decision making: you can lead a group to information, but you can't make it think. MIS Q 20(4):433–455

Dennis AR, Kinney ST (1998) Testing media richness theory in the new media: the effects of cues, feedback, and task equivocality. Inf Syst Res 9(3):256–274

Dennis AR, Kinney ST, Hung YC (1999) Gender differences and the effects of media richness. Small Group Res 30(4):405–437

DeRosa DM, Hantula DA, Kock N, D'Arcy JP (2004) Communication, trust, and leadership in virtual teams: a media naturalness perspective. Hum Resour Manage J 34(2):219–232

DeSanctis G, Poole MS (1994) Capturing the complexity in advanced technology use: adaptive structuration theory. Organ Sci 5(2):121–147

Dunbar RIM (1993) Coevolution of neocortical size, group size and language in humans. Behav Brain Sci 16(4):681–735

Dunbar RIM (1998) Grooming, gossip, and the evolution of language. Harvard University Press, Cambridge

Easley RF, Devaraj S, Crant JM (2003) Relating collaborative technology use to teamwork quality and performance: an empirical analysis. J Manage Inf Syst 19(4):247–269

El-Shinnawy M, Markus L (1998) Acceptance of communication media in organizations: richness or features? IEEE Trans Prof Commun 41(4):242–253

Fjermestad J (2004) An analysis of communication mode in group support systems research. Decis Support Syst 37(2):239–263

Fox CW, Wolf JB (eds) (2006) Evolutionary genetics: concepts and case studies. Oxford University Press, New York

Gilad I, Harel S (2000) Muscular effort in four keyboard designs. Int J Ind Ergon 26(1):1–7

Gillespie JH (2004) Population genetics. The Johns Hopkins University Press, Baltimore

Graetz KA, Boyle ES, Kimble CE, Thompson P, Garloch JL (1998) Information sharing in face-to-face, teleconferencing, and electronic chat groups. Small Group Res 29(6): 714–743

Graur D, Wen-Hsiung L (2000) Fundamentals of molecular evolution. Sinauer Associates, Sunderland

Hantula DA, Brockman DD, Smith CL (2008) Online shopping as foraging: the effects of increasing delays on purchasing and patch residence. IEEE Trans Prof Commun 51(2):147–154

Hartl DL, Clark AG (2007) Principles of population genetics. Sinauer Associates, Sunderland

Hasty BK, Massey AP, Brown SA (2006) Role-based experiences, media perceptions, and knowledge transfer in virtual dyads. Group Decis Negot 15(4):367–387

Hubona GS, Shirah GW (2006) The Paleolithic Stone Age effect? Gender differences performing specific computer-generated spatial tasks. Int J Technol Hum Interact 2(2):24–46

Hung D-Z (2004) Taiwan's venomous snakebite: epidemiological, evolution and geographic differences. Trans R Soc Trop Med Hyg 98(2):96–101

Junglas I, Abraham C, Ives B (2009) Mobile technology at the frontlines of patient care: understanding fit and human drives in utilization decisions and performance. Decis Support Syst 46(3):634–647

Kahai SS, Cooper RB (2003) Exploring the core concepts of media richness theory: the impact of cue multiplicity and feedback immediacy on decision quality. J Manage Inf Syst 20(1): 263–281

Kimura M (1994) Population genetics, molecular evolution, and the neutral theory. The University of Chicago Press, Chicago

Klein HK, Myers MD (1999) A set of principles for conducting and evaluating interpretive field studies in information systems. MIS Q 23(1):67–93

Kline RB (1998) Principles and practice of structural equation modeling. The Guilford Press, New York

Kock N (2004) The psychobiological model: towards a new theory of computer-mediated communication based on Darwinian evolution. Organ Sci 15(3):327–348

Kock N (2005) Media richness or media naturalness? The evolution of our biological communication apparatus and its influence on our behavior toward e-communication tools. IEEE Trans Prof Commun 48(2):117–130

Kock N (2009) Information systems theorizing based on evolutionary psychology: an interdisciplinary review and theory integration framework. MIS Q 33(2):395–418

Kock N, DeLuca D (2007) Improving business processes electronically: an action research study in New Zealand and the US. J Global Inf Technol Manage 10(3):6–27

Kock N, Lynn GS, Dow KE, Akgün AE (2006) Team adaptation to electronic communication media: evidence of compensatory adaptation in new product development teams. Eur J Inf Syst 15(3):331–341

Kock N, Verville J, Garza V (2007) Media naturalness and online learning: findings supporting both the significant- and no-significant-difference perspectives. Decis Sci J Innov Educ 5(2):333–356

Kock N, Chatelain-Jardón R, Carmona J (2008) An experimental study of simulated Web-based threats and their impact on knowledge communication effectiveness. IEEE Trans Prof Commun 51(2):183–197

Kutschera U (2003) A comparative analysis of the Darwin–Wallace papers and the development of the concept of natural selection. Theory Biosci 122(4):343–359

Laitman JT (1984) The anatomy of human speech. Nat History 20(7):20–27

Laitman JT, Reidenberg JS (1997) The human aerodigestive tract and gastroesophageal reflux: an evolutionary perspective. Am J Med 103(5):2S–8S

Lieberman P (1998) Eve spoke: human language and human evolution. W.W. Norton & Company, New York

Lieberman P (2000) Human language and our reptilian brain: the subcortical bases of speech, syntax, and thought. Harvard University Press, Cambridge

Manipady S, Menezes RG, Bastia BK (2006) Death by attack from a wild boar. J Clin Forensic Med 13(2):89–91

Markus ML (1994a) Finding a happy medium: explaining the negative effects of electronic communication on social life at work. ACM Trans Inf Syst 12(2):119–149

Markus ML (1994b) Electronic mail as the medium of managerial choice. Organ Sci 5(4): 502–527

Maynard Smith J (1998) Evolutionary genetics. Oxford University Press, New York

Mayr E, Provine WB (eds) (1998) The evolutionary synthesis: perspectives on the unification of biology. Harvard University Press, Cambridge

McElreath R, Boyd R (2007) Mathematical models of social evolution: a guide for the perplexed. The University of Chicago Press, Chicago

McKinney VR, Whiteside MM (2006) Maintaining distributed relationships. Commun ACM 49(3):82–87

McNeill D (1998) The face: a natural history. Little, Brown and Company, Boston

Miller GF (2000) The mating mind: how sexual choice shaped the evolution of human nature. Doubleday, New York

Miller GF (2001) Aesthetic fitness: how sexual selection shaped artistic virtuosity as a fitness indicator and aesthetic preferences as mate choice criteria. Bull Psychol Arts 2(1):20–25

Nairne JS, Thompson SR, Pandeirada JNS (2007) Adaptive memory: survival processing enhances retention. J Exp Psychol Learn Mem Cogn 33(2):263–273

Newlin MH, Lavooy MJ, Wang AY (2005) An experimental comparison of conventional and web-based instructional formats. North Am J Psychol 7(2):327–335

Ngwenyama OK, Lee AS (1997) Communication richness in electronic mail: critical social theory and the contextuality of meaning. MIS Q 21(2):145–167

Ocker R, Hiltz SR, Turoff M, Fjermestad J (1995) The effects of distributed group support and process structuring on software requirements development teams: results on creativity and quality. J Manage Inf Syst 12(3):127–153

Orlikowski WJ, Baroudi JJ (1991) Studying information technology in organizations: research approaches and assumptions. Inf Syst Res 2(1):1–28

Petrie M, Halliday T, Sanders C (1991) Peahens prefer peacocks with elaborate trains. Anim Behav 41(2):323–331

Pinker S (1994) The language instinct. William Morrow and Co, New York

Pinker S (2002) The blank slate: the modern denial of human nature. Penguin Putnam, New York

Pinker S (2003) Language as an adaptation to the cognitive niche. In Christiansen M, Kirby S (eds) Language evolution: states of the art. Oxford University Press, New York, pp 16–37

Popper KR (1992) Logic of scientific discovery. Routledge, New York

Price GR (1970) Selection and covariance. Nature 227(1):520–521

Quammen D (2006) The reluctant Mr. Darwin: an intimate portrait of Charles Darwin and the making of his theory of evolution. W.W. Norton & Company, New York

Rajala AK, Hantula DA (2000) Towards a behavioral ecology of consumption: delay-reduction effects on foraging in a simulated Internet mall. Manage Decis Econ 21(1):145–158

Rencher AC (1998) Multivariate statistical inference and applications. John Wiley & Sons, New York, NY

Rice SH (2004) Evolutionary theory: mathematical and conceptual foundations. Sinauer Associates, Sunderland

Rosenthal R, Rosnow RL (1991) Essentials of behavioral research: methods and data analysis. McGraw-Hill, Boston

Saad G (2008) Advertised waist-to-hip ratios of online female escorts: an evolutionary perspective. Int J e-Collab 4(3):40–50

Sallnas EL, Rassmus-Grohn K, Sjostrom C (2000) Supporting presence in collaborative environments by haptic force feedback. ACM Trans Comput Hum Interact 7(4):461–476

Schumacker RE, Lomax RG (1996) A beginner's guide to structural equation modeling. Lawrence Erlbaum, Mahwah

Schutzwohl A, Reisenzein R (1999) Children's and adults' reactions to a schemadiscrepant event: a developmental analysis of surprise. Int J Behav Dev 23(1):37–63

Simon AF (2006) Computer-mediated communication: task performance and satisfaction. J Soc Psychol 146(3):349–379

Sircar S, Nerur SP, Mahapatra R (2001) Revolution or evolution? a comparison of object-oriented and structured systems development methods. MIS Q 25(4):457–471

Smith CL, Hantula DA (2003) Pricing effects on foraging in a simulated Internet shopping mall. J Econ Psychol 24(5):653–674

Speier C, Vessey I, Valacich JS (2003) The effects of interruptions, task complexity, and information presentation on computer-supported decision-making performance. Decis Sci 34(4):771–799

Spink A, Cole C (2006) Human information behavior: integrating diverse approaches and information use. J Am Soc Inf Sci Technol 57(1):25–35

Stenstrom E, Stenstrom P, Saad G, Cheikhrouhou S (2008) Online hunting and gathering: an evolutionary perspective on sex differences in website preferences and navigation. IEEE Trans Prof Commun 51(2):155–168

Stinchcombe AL (1968) Constructing social theories. Harcourt Brace, New York

Straub D, Karahanna E (1998) Knowledge worker communications and recipient availability: toward a task closure explanation of media choice. Organ Sci 9(2):160–175

Summers J, Waigandt A, Whittaker T (2005) A comparison of student achievement and satisfaction in an online versus a traditional face-to-face statistics class. Innov Higher Educ 29(3):233–250

Tan BCY, Wei K, Watson RT, Clapper DL, McLean ER (1998) Computer-mediated communication and majority influence: assessing the impact in an individualistic and a collectivistic culture. Manage Sci 44(9):1263–1278

Te'eni D (2001) A cognitive-affective model of organizational communication for designing IT. MIS Q 25(2):251–312

Tooby J, Cosmides L (1990) On the universality of human nature and the uniqueness of the individual: the role of genetics and adaptation. J Personal 58(1):17–68

Trevino LK, Webster J, Stein EW (2000) Making connections: complementary influences on communication media choices, attitudes, and use. Organ Sci 11(2):163–182

Trivers R (2002) Natural selection and social theory. Oxford University Press, Oxford

Wainfan L, Davis PK (2004) Challenges in virtual collaboration: videoconferencing, audioconferencing and computer-mediated communications. RAND Corporation, Santa Monica

Watson-Manheim MB, Bélanger F (2007) Communication media repertoires: dealing with the multiplicity of media choices. MIS Q 31(2):267–293

Webster J, Trevino LK (1995) Rational and social theories as complementary explanations of communication media choices: two policy-capturing studies. Acad Manage J 38(6):1544–1573

Wilson EO (2000) Sociobiology: the new synthesis. Harvard University Press, Cambridge

Wilson M, Daly M, Pound N (2002) An evolutionary psychological perspective on the modulation of competitive confrontation and risk-taking. Horm Brain Behav 1(1):381–408

Zahavi A, Zahavi A (1997) The handicap principle: a missing piece of Darwin's puzzle. Oxford University Press, Oxford

Zigurs I, Buckland BK (1998) A theory of task-technology fit and group support systems effectiveness. MIS Q 22(3):313–334

Zimmer C (2001) Evolution: the triumph of an idea. HarperCollins Publishers, New York

Chapter 2
Group-Level Evolution and Information Systems: What Can We Learn From Animal Colonies in Nature?

Jaana Porra

Abstract In this chapter, we describe 10 central properties and a speciation process for a certain type of real and virtual human collective that is comparable with animal colonies in nature. This theory, called *colonial systems* and its application to information systems-supported groups called *information colonies,* is based on those characteristics of mobile animal colonies that may contribute to the survivability of these formations under varied environmental circumstances. We propose that like animal colonies, human equivalents participate in group selection processes and thus have lineages. Like animal colonies, human colonies create offspring, which inherits their evolutionary history and evolutionary mechanism. We call this group-level evolutionary mechanism *punctuated prototyping*. In this chapter, we discuss human colonies from the following perspectives: *phylogeny* (evolutionary history); *ontogeny* (members' lifetime histories); *change; boundaries, complexity, structure, growth, goals, power,* and *control*. We propose that the theory of human colonies provides a novel perspective on human collectives in real and virtual settings.

Keywords Group evolution theory · Group speciation · Systems theory · Human colonies · Punctuated equilibrium · Punctuated prototyping · Information systems · Information colonies · Virtual communities · Phylogeny · Evolutionary history · Ontogeny · Lifetime history · Change · Boundaries · Complexity · Structure · Growth · Goals · Power · Control · Virtual communities · Online communities · Group identity · Humanness

J. Porra (✉)
Management Information Systems, Department of Decision and Information Sciences, University of Houston, C.T. Bauer College of Business, 280G Melcher Hall, Houston, TX 77204-6282, USA
e-mail: jaana@uh.edu

N. Kock (ed.), *Evolutionary Psychology and Information Systems Research*,
Integrated Series in Information Systems 24, DOI 10.1007/978-1-4419-6139-6_2,
© Springer Science+Business Media, LLC 2010

1 Introduction

Studying human groups is more important than ever. Developments like the Internet and mobile computing have stimulated the group-level ecosystem. Human collectives are able to share information effortlessly across geographic boundaries. Yet, little theory about the structural characteristics of groups or how these evolve exists (Backstrom et al. 2006). Since the publication of the theory of colonial systems (Porra 1999), little academic discourse has taken place around the topic. Yet, we believe that in order to understand modern society better, it is essential to learn more about how human groups evolve through generations.

One of the reasons for the lack of discourse in the area is that until recently, group-level evolution theory has not been in the spotlight of any field. For decades, group-level evolution theories were unpopular even amongst biologists, evolutionists, and paleontologists (Wilson and Wilson 2007). Just a few decades ago, the winning viewpoint amongst scientists was that groups do not have enough closure in order to participate in speciation or selection processes.

Over the past decade, however, the scientific viewpoint has shifted in favor of group-level evolution. Over the past decade, research on group selection has experienced a renaissance (Sober and Wilson 2000; Borrello 2005; Van Veelen and Hopfensitz 2007; Marek 2008; Wilson and Wilson 2008; Van Veelen 2009). New theory (cf., Gardner and Grafen 2009), new empirical research (Shavit 2005; Scheuring 2009), and novel perspectives on old theory (Shavit 2004; Wilson and Wilson 2007) have contributed to a renewed interest in the phenomenon. This dramatic change of heart in evolutionary theory has contributed to our conviction that a group-level evolution perspective could also benefit social sciences, organizational theory, and information systems research.

In particular, we believe that evolutionary theory can provide a fresh perspective on how humans use computers. This viewpoint is based on the assumption that "humans are social animals" (cf., O'Gorman et al. 2008). Thus collectives formed by people (and their information systems) may evolve in ways comparable with other social species. This leads to a simple conclusion that like the evolution of other species, human evolution is a complex, multi-level phenomenon (cf., O'Gorman et al. 2008; Lehmann et al. 2007). Therefore we should study human evolution with matching complexity and levels of inquiry.

Today, the conviction that human groups are ontologically real is gaining in popularity (Campbell 1994). Human groups develop boundaries relying on mutual monitoring, in-group solidarity creation mechanisms, homogeneity of belief, and discipline. Research on social processes shows that human group formation begins in 2 hours in arbitrarily assembled groups (Campbell 1982). Thus a human collective begins to separate itself from the environment soon after it is born.

The ability to form boundaries through phenomena such as "group selfishness" means that a group can turn into an independently evolving unit (Campbell 1994). From an organizational theory and information systems research viewpoint, this means that a human group can insulate itself from the environment and evolve independently from an organization or a society at large. We have argued that these kinds of groups are their own kind of "being in the world" (Porra 1996, 1999). We have shown that like animal colonies, human colonies have origins, evolutionary paths, and histories (Porra 1996, 1999; Porra et al. 2005, 2009; Porra and Parks 2006).

In our prior research, we have described 10 essential systemic properties of *human colonies* (Porra 1996, 1999). We have illustrated the impact of information systems on human colonies and called these *information colonies* (Porra 1996, 1999). Finally, we have described how human colonies create offspring and thus how their evolution results in inheritance and lineages. We have called the human colonies' speciation mechanism *punctuated prototyping*. In this chapter, we will summarize our prior work and present some examples in the light of recent empirical research results (Porra et al. 2005, 2009; Porra and Parks 2006).

Colonies are but one example of how to build theory about human groups on evolutionary theory, sociobiology, and paleontology (Wilson 2008). If it is true, as we believe, that societies are replete with human colonies, which evolve using sophisticated information systems, there is a vast blank spot on the academic radar. In the following, we will give an example of how one might begin to tackle this new area of research from both a theoretical and an empirical standpoint.

2 Group-Level Evolution

The primary problem for pursuing human group evolutionary research continues to be that few theories exist in this area (cf., Backstrom et al. 2006; Porra 1999). Most research on organizational evolution is based on the idea that entire populations of organizations, organizations or organizational units transform (Singh et al. 1986; Carroll and Hannan 1989; Baum 1990; Ginzberg and Buchholtz 1990; Miner et al. 1990; Baum and Oliver 1991; Delacroix and Swaminathan 1991; Kelly and Amburgey 1991; Haveman 1992; Amburgey et al. 1993; Baum and Singh 1994a; Pouder and St. John 1996; Romanelli and Tushman 1994; Haveman et al. 2001). In intra-organizational evolutionary research, the focus is mostly on tasks such as strategy making (Burgelman 1991) or social–psychological processes of organizing (Weick 1979; Gersick 1991).

At the group level of analysis, research has traditionally focused on individuals, tasks, and routines and not on the human collective as the evolving unit (Baum and Singh 1994a). Since information systems research largely builds on organizational theory, evolutionary research on information systems topics tends to focus on similar units of analysis (cf., Lassila and Brancheau 1999; Street and Meister 2004; Lyytinen and Newman 2008). Outside organizational theory, information systems researchers have considered a computer-based information system as an evolving unit (cf., Arnott 2004).

Moreover, with few exceptions (cf., Baum 1989; McKelvey 1982; Ulrich and McKelvey 1990), organizational evolutionary research has focused on the ecological perspective and not on the systematics of evolution (Baum and Singh 1994b; van de Ven and Poole 1995). The popular assumption is that evolution occurs

mainly through natural selection. Theories in this class called "ecological evolutionary theories" are focused on the ecology of organizations and the cumulative
effect of variation and selection over time (Baum and Singh 1994a). From this perspective, organizations (and groups) are believed to mainly provide the raw material
for environmental forces.

Our theory of human colonies, information colonies, and punctuated prototyping
is an example of a less popular class of evolutionary theories entitled "genealogical
evolutionary theories" (Baum and Singh 1994b). The focus of these theories is on
organizational speciation: the structures and processes of organizational inheritance
and transmission over generations (Baum 1989). Theories in this class are about
organizational reproduction and lineages. They seek to shed light on how organizations (and groups) change within and across generations in order to respond
to environmental shifts (cf., Hull 1980, 1988). Compared to the mainstream ecology class of theories, little is known about this *other side* of the evolution (Baum
1989). Outside our work on human colonies (Porra 1996, 1999; Porra et al. 2005;
Porra and Parks 2006), little research exists that would consider human groups as
independently evolving multi-generational phenomena.

In Fig. 2.1, we illustrate how our theory of human colonies (Porra 1996, 1999)
fits in with a classification of organizational evolution theories.[1] The number of levels and categories in the figure shows how vast the research area of the evolution

Genealogical hierarchy		**Ecological hierarchy**
		Ecosystem
		↑↓
Polyphyletic group	→ ←	Community
		↑↓
Organizations as a species	→ ←	Population
		↑↓
Organization	→ ←	Organization
		↑↓
Human colony	→ ←	Work group
		↑↓
Routines	→ ←	Job

Fig. 2.1 Two hierarchies of organizational evolution (Baum and Singh 1994a)

[1] We have adapted Baum and Singh (1994a) by illustrating where the *colonial systems* theory
belongs in the hierarchy.

of human collaboration can be. There are many other categorizations of organizational evolution theory (cf., Aldrich 1979; Baum 1988; Burgelman 1991; Burgelman and Singh 1987; Campbell 1974a, b, 1990; Carroll 1984; Csányi 1989; Hannan and Freeman 1977, 1989; Hawley 1950, 1986; Lumsden and Singh 1990; McKelvey 1982; Miner 1991, Singh and Lumsden 1990). We chose this one, because it illustrates where the colonial systems theory belongs in a hierarchy of organizational evolution theories.

In Fig. 2.1, the units of analyses relevant to organizational evolution are nested within one another. Wholes are composed of parts at lower levels of organization and are themselves parts of more extensive wholes. Communities are composed of populations of organizations, which in turn are formed by individual organizations. Individual organizations consist of work groups, and so on. The nesting of entities into larger entities at a higher level of organization creates a system of levels. An important aspect of this hierarchy is that it is not reductionist. Every level is a discrete class of organizational entities, each with their own theories of evolution.

To summarize, our colonial system theory is a group-level genealogical theory. It is mainly focused on the speciation processes of human colonies and the inherited characteristics of these kinds of human groups. The colonial systems theory is also a theory about group lineages and evolutionary histories. Our thesis is that human colonies evolve independently from organizations and society at large and may be the carrier of the evolutionary history of the humanity and thus what we call *humanness* (Porra 1996, 1999).

Humanness means that each human colony has unique social qualities (Porra 1996, 1999). Every new generation colony develops its own identity founded on its parent's history and adapted to the current environment. We believe that *humanness* is the essential substance of a colony (Porra 1996, 1999). Colony's humanness can be described by labels such as "IS professionals," "geeks," "study groups," or "catastrophe rescue teams," but these will not adequately capture the fact that each colony's humanness is as old as the lineage.[2]

3 Colonies

Human colonies may not seem like elephant, dolphin, or insect colonies, but we believe that they share several common systemic characteristics with colonies of other species. Yet in many ways, human colonies appear like ordinary human groups. They may have been initiated for a specific goal or project. They may emerge spontaneously around an ideal or a purpose. They may apply information systems or live without. They may meet face-to-face or online. But unlike many other kinds of human groups, human colonies will not dissolve after the task is accomplished or the project is over.

---

[2] For a comprehensive discussion of "humanness," see Porra (1996, 1999).

A common characteristic of all colonies is their longevity. They persist through calm times and survive environmental shifts. They change suddenly and radically. They abandon and recreate structures without losing their essence. They are an outcome of generations of evolution. Colonies are amongst the most sustainable life forms known today. Some are over 3 billion years old. We believe that it is important to learn about the systemic characteristics of animal colonies in order to understand persistent human groups (Porra 1996, 1999).

In a strict biological sense, a *colony* is a society of organisms that are highly integrated either by physical union of the bodies or by division into specialized individuals and groups or by both (Wilson 1980). In the biological vernacular and even in some technical texts, the word "colony" can refer to almost any group of organisms. In this paper, we are most interested in mobile colonies. These colonies have individuals with independent structures; so they can choose to stay or leave the colony at will. Specifically, we are interested in those systemic qualities of colonies that are common across species. On the surface, finding commonalities in animal group behavior seems challenging. Such is the diversity of the behaviors colonies portray (Wilson 1980).

> In some colonies, individuals have highly specialized tasks (insect colonies) that may last for a lifetime (wasp colonies) or relatively short periods of time (ant colonies). Males (dolphins) or females (asp colonies) may start colonies. Colonies may portray hierarchical relationships (wasp colonies), or they may be leaderless individuals acting in concert (schools of fish). Individuals join some colonies for life (termite colonies), others are joined on a temporary basis (schools of fish). For some colonies nomadism has been determined as a necessary condition (schools of fish), while in others individuals carry on diverse activities such as grooming and playing (whiptail wallaby). Some colonies portray altruistic cooperative behaviors (dolphins). Some colonies have only few individuals, while others are known to have thousands (dolphins). Some colonies travel far (dolphins) and others stay near the parent colony. Many colonies occur in plains and savannas among nonterritorial herds dividing casually while traveling (vicuria). Others build permanent immobile homes (termites). Some colonies form around matriarchs while males lead solitary lives throughout their lives (elephants). Chimpanzee colonies are known for their high degree of cooperation, while orangutans don't form colonies at all. Some colonies exchange their members with other colonies they encounter (chimpanzees); others do so only reluctantly (elephants) (Porra 1999, p. 51).

Prior research shows, however, that all colonies form through three complementary processes: (1) weakening of the individuality of the members; (2) intensification of the individuality of the colony through shared appearances and behaviors; and (3) the development of *colonies within colonies* (Beklemishev 1969). Across species, colonies develop a collective identity and an ability to create offspring.

We believe that qualities that best describe a colony (i.e., dolphiness, fishness, or humanness) occur at the level of the collective (Porra 1996, 1999). In our prior work, we have argued that dolphiness, fishness, or *humanness* of a colony is a result of being a particular kind of a system (Porra 1996, 1999). We have defined *colonial systems* as "systems that facilitate the formation of collections of interdependent members and evolution of characteristics that maintain collective stasis and can create or respond to change through collective awareness." (Porra 1999, p. 51).

We have proposed that like animal colonies in nature, human colonies form spontaneously and have an ability to evolve like a species (Porra 1996, 1999). From this perspective, societies and organizations are an environment in which human colonies have histories, identities, and destinies of their own. This group-level perspective portrays an environment where colonies evolve through and within organizations as independent entities with their own systemic qualities and evolutionary mechanisms. Thus viewing groups as colonies creates a new perspective on collective human behavior.

We have defined a human colony as a "voluntary collection of individuals with the shared characteristics of (1) a common evolutionary social history (phylogeny); (2) a common method for realizing both stability and radical change (species level evolution); and (3) a common local context (being in the world)" (Porra 1999, p. 39). Thus colony's members are volunteers who share a unique perspective on colony's past and local conditions. They cooperate in order to maintain collective's stability during calm times. They work together to carry out radical change during environmental shifts using a method we have called *punctuated prototyping* (Porra 1996, 1999). Today many human colonies use information systems to support their humanness. We have called these kinds of colonies *information colonies* (Porra 1996, 1999).

4 Punctuated Equilibrium

For human colonies, the most consequential type of change is evolution (Porra 1996, 1999). Most essentially, a human colony changes from one generation to another as a collective. Each colony has its unique origins and contains its own evolutionary history or *phylogeny*. Each colony has an evolutionary mechanism for producing offspring or next generation colonies. Based on animal colonies, we have theorized how human colonies evolve. In Porra (1996, 1999), we have proposed that human colonies' evolutionary pattern corresponds with the *punctuated equilibrium* model (Eldredge and Gould 1972).

Eldredge and Gould's (1972) punctuated equilibrium model is a suggestion that new species emerge from small isolated populations. When a group becomes isolated from the species at large geographically or otherwise (cf., Wilson 1992), the sub-population may rapidly evolve into a new species. Eldredge and Gould propose that evolution is not necessarily gradual and continuous unfolding of minute changes in entire populations as many mainstream Darwinists believe, but that observed gaps in the fossil record are real. Because the new generation species is better adapted to the local environment than the ancestor, it may take the terrain over in a sudden shift. The new species punctuates. This kind of speciation from small, isolated populations is called *allopatric speciation* (Mayr 1982).

Since its introduction, the punctuated equilibrium model has been a target of both criticism and misunderstanding (Schwartz 1999). The fact remains that the origins of most major groups of organisms remain unknown. There is not enough evidence in the fossil record to prove or disprove gradualism or punctuated equilibrium. "New species seem to appear as abruptly as old ones disappear into the oblivion of extinction" (Schwartz 1999).

We have adopted the viewpoint that Darwinian gradualism and the punctuated equilibrium model are not mutually exclusive (Porra 1996, 1999; Schwartz 1999). According to this perspective, the punctuated equilibrium model is a form of gradualism in the sense of ecological continuity (Eldredge and Gould 1972). Change still occurs incrementally from one generation to the next (Gould 1991). While change may seem dramatic, it is gradual when measured on a geological scale.[3]

In the applications of the punctuated equilibrium model to social phenomena, researchers apply radically shorter time frames. Stable times and punctuations are commonly measured in months, years, or decades (cf., Romanelli and Tushman 1994; Haveman at al. 2001; Sabherval et al. 2001; Silva and Hirschheim 2007). As Eldredge's and Gould's model has been adapted to the human realm, evolution's velocity has been increased tens of thousands of times (cf., Gould 1991).

That social evolution proceeds significantly faster than natural evolution may not be a theoretical mistake (Wilson 2008). A prerequisite for rapid social evolution is human potential for varied behavior (Porra 1999). Wilson (2008) has argued that such variability is vast in socially advanced species. Add communications capabilities and we may find social evolution proceeding at unforeseen rates. While large organizations and societies may struggle to respond to sudden environmental shifts due to their size and relatively open boundaries (cf., Palla et al. 2007), small groups with effective intrinsic or extrinsic isolation mechanisms may be more successful (Wilkins 2007). In our prior research, we have found human colonies that lived stable times for years or decades (Porra et al. 2005). On the other hand, we have identified two generations of a rescue colony occurring within just a few days (Porra et al. 2009).

It is important to note that a body of research that applies punctuated equilibrium at the group level of analysis exists. Typically these studies include change patterns similar to Eldredge and Gould's (1972) model. Groups are considered to evolve through punctuations and stable times (cf., Gersick 1991). Typically, however, this change pattern refers to phases in group development relating to completing a task (cf., Gersick 1988, 1989; Okhuysen and Waller 2002; Chang and Duck 2003).

5 Ten Characteristics of Human Colonies

The colony perspective highlights that like animal colonies, human colonies have lineages, generations, and a speciation mechanism. Human colonies know innately how to create offspring and pass their heritage down the lineage. Thus human colonies are long-lasting systems with characteristics that ensure the continuity

---

[3] How we reconcile between gradual and radical change in the colonial systems theory is presented in detail in our previous work (Porra 1996, 1999).

of the "species." In Porra (1996, 1999), we have identified 10 common characteristics that all colonies appear to share. These include *phylogeny* (evolutionary
history), *ontogeny* (lifetime history), *change, boundaries, complexity, structure,
growth, goals, power, and control.*

5.1 Phylogeny (Evolutionary History)

Building on Eldredge and Gould's model (1972), we have proposed (Porra 1996,
1999) that human colonies have generations. In order to produce offspring, human
colonies evolve through four stages: (1) splitting of lineages; (2) rapid development of these lineages; (3) speciation from the resulting subpopulations; and (4)
speciation from small parts of the geographical distribution.

In the first phase, a group of humans develops unique characteristics. These can
emerge from a variety of social qualities such as professional expertise, social or
organizational status, common interest or ideology. In the second phase, the group
rapidly develops these characteristics. It fosters a distinct culture, language, dress
code, customs, etc. It mentors future leaders and cultivates entrepreneurial attitudes.
In the third phase, the colony initiates sub-colonies in preparation for the fourth and
final phase: a potential release of the offspring to the environment. In the colonial
systems theory, we have called this four-step method *punctuated prototyping* (Porra
1996, 1999).

During stable times, sub-colonies operate as part of the parent colony (Porra
1996, 1999). They blend into the structures and activities of their surroundings. For
example, a department (cf., Porra et al. 2005), a team, a virtual community (cf.,
Porra and Parks 2006) or specially trained employees (cf., Porra et al. 2009) can
be sub-colonies in the making. Sub-colonies share an ability to continue their life
independently after being dispersed into the environment.

Several studies illustrate how punctuated prototyping works in practice. For
example, at Texaco, a colony that resided in the IT function moved to Chevron
after the firm's acquisition (Porra et al. 2005). At St. Joseph's academy, high school
students formed colonies around voluntary and required school activities (Porra
and Parks 2006). During Katrina, a rescue worker initiated two generations of rescue colonies as she pursued the parent organization's original mission (Porra et al.
2009).

5.2 Ontogeny (Lifetime History)

Because evolution is the most consequential type of change in human colonies,
their members' ontogenies (lifetime histories) have a limited impact (Porra 1996,
1999). From the perspective of the colony, individual-level change affects the colony
only to some degree. During the 47 years of the evolution of Texaco's IT function,
many members joined and left the colony. While this change is significant from

the individual perspective of the affected members, the colony's identity was not severely impacted (Porra et al. 2005).

Just like any other collective phenomenon, however, colonies can be studied at the individual level of inquiry. For example, colonies can be identified by study-ing members' perceptions (Porra and Parks 2006). If members perceive that their group has characteristics of a human colony, it may be one. Colonies tend to last beyond their existing membership, but the current members are the embodiment of its history and future potential.

5.3 Change

A third type of change related to colonies is internal change during stable times. When times are calm, colonies can change locations, grow, or diminish their mem-bership. They can change their ideals, goals, or practices. They may alter their information systems. While changes like these may seem dramatic and sudden to the colony's members at the time, they usually represent minor fluctuation from the perspective of the lineage (Porra 1996, 1999). Throughout its lifetime, Texaco's IT colony's membership changed through retirement and normal turnover and its infor-mation systems evolved with new technologies (Porra et al. 2005). Over the 47 years of its existence, these changes did not significantly affect the colony.

Minor fluctuation during stable times can sometimes, however, lead into a punc-tuation (Porra 1996, 1999). For example, a key individual leaving the colony may soon be followed by a large outflow of members. Changes in information systems may also lead to similar results if they alter colony's access to its stored knowl-edge and communications capabilities too suddenly or dramatically. During Katrina, many rescue groups dissolved, because they lost access to their information systems (Porra et al. 2009).

Finally, during stable times, colonies have an ability to hibernate. We have described inactive colonies as *latent* (Porra 1996, 1999). A latent colony disappears by temporarily dispersing its members and information systems into its environment while waiting for better times. As the circumstances improve, the colony reappears seemingly from nowhere. We can speculate, for example, that some of the rescue groups scattered during Katrina to take shelter from the storm to continue their mission as the weather improved and as they recovered access to their information systems.

5.4 Boundaries

Colonies can emerge wherever people meet. They can form based on geographical proximity (i.e., living in the same neighborhood, participating in local community activities, working for the same organization), long-lasting common interests (i.e., around hobbies), family relations, or friendship. Colonies are not synonyms for organizations, their units, project, or work groups, but these can be colonies if they develop colonial boundaries (cf., Porra et al. 2005, 2009; Porra and Parks 2006).

Human colonies develop adequately closed boundaries to be able to evolve as a collective (Porra 1996, 1999). While the boundaries of formal organizations and work groups are founded on short-term contracts, colonies' boundaries are based on an innate human need to spend time in the company of familiar people. Thus colony's boundaries form when a group of people commits to within-group co-operation and altruism for the long haul.

Shared long-term focus on colony's well being creates the conditions for colony's unique *humanness* to develop and evolve (Porra 1996, 1999). Members learn from one another by listening, observing, and doing together as the colony lives its every-day existence. As the members evolve together, they contribute to colony's unique identity, which in turn strengthens colony's boundaries.

Indirectly, the evolution of a colony's humanness can be observed by the reactions of the environment. At Texaco, the IT colony was first recognized by the rest of the firm as "go getters" and "highly skilled experts," who would "get the job done". Over the decades as the environment changed, business units reconsidered their perceptions of the quality of IT's humanness. When the IT colony eventually moved to Chevron, it was still considered to embody past expertise, but it was not seen to be a leader or a high achiever. That Texaco at large perceived its IT colony differently over time indicates that the colony evolved independently from the firm at large (Porra et al. 2005). At Texaco, IT colony's humanness remained relatively unchanged for decades, while the firm changed around it. As a result, the IT colony was appreciated less over time.

From a theoretical standpoint, human colonies' boundaries are based on *reach* (Porra 1996, 1999). *Reach* means that potentially everything in the reach of the senses of its members becomes included into colony's humanness. Reach has both spatial and temporal dimensions. *Spatial reach* closes in the collective at a given point of time. Thus membership is achieved by physically (or virtually) being present in the colony. While the idea of spatial boundaries is conceptually easy to grasp, its practical implications may be counterintuitive. Like other types of human groups, human colonies make decisions about their membership, but colony's spatial boundaries are also a function of attendance (Porra 1996, 1999). Thus a receptionist who is present influences colony's humanness more that day than an absent leader.

Human colonies can take advantage of their spatial reach. They often tolerate or even encourage lurkers and visitors because these bring outside influences and keep the colony's humanness from stagnating. The lack of outside influences on Texaco IT colony's humanness may have led to the relative stagnation of its identity, which eventually alienated the rest of the firm (Porra et al. 2005).

Another dimension of colonies' boundaries is called *temporal reach* (Porra 1996, 1999). Each member's influence on the colony is a function of time (Porra 1996, 1999). The longer the actual time spent in the colony, the deeper the influence on its humanness. At Texaco, members with the longest tenure with the IT colony shaped its identity most (Porra et al. 2005).

Temporal reach highlights the historical and future dimensions of colonies' boundaries (Porra 1996, 1999). While it is not known how old human colonies are, it is possible that their temporal boundaries go back in time to the origins of the collective life form more than 3 billion years ago. Thus colony's temporal boundaries close in all individuals who have spent time with the colony or its ancestor colonies.

Temporal boundaries also reach into the future until the colony's extinction with the death of its last member (Porra 1996, 1999). The choices each colony makes over the course of generations shape its humanness and thus its potential to survive environmental shifts. Texaco's IT colony was considered a laggard at Texaco, but it survived the shift to Chevron and continued its evolution in the new surroundings (Porra et al. 2005).

5.5 Complexity

The implication of colonial boundaries is that each human colony is a vast repository of information it has received through all senses of all of its members through generations since its inception (Porra 1996, 1999). Storing human experiences in their actual historical contexts of people, places, and things is a mind-boggling task. If human minds were like computer-based information systems, containing this much information would result in unforeseen complexity, which would end the system (Pagels 1989).

Unlike human-made information systems, however, human collectives are able to regulate their complexity as they evolve. Complexity regulation in human colonies occurs at least at the level of an organism, individual mind, and the collective (Porra 1996, 1999). In this chapter, we are most interested in complexity regulation at the level of the colony as it relates to speciation.

At the level of the collective, human colonies use punctuations for complexity regulation (Porra 1996, 1999). During a punctuation, they can dramatically reduce their structure by shedding people and abandoning information systems in order to adapt to new circumstances. Due to the experiences with punctuations, older colonies are more prepared to deal with uncertainty and risk related to the speciation process. Colony's past acts as a repository for finding simpler and more efficient ways under pressure.

During Katrina, a rescue unit punctuated two times (Porra et al. 2009). Both times the colony left behind everything but its leader. She relocated and recreated the human and information systems structures initiating two consequent successful generations of the rescue colony. Amongst the rescue stories, this example is unusual on two counts. The rescue effort was a success. The colony completed a large part of its original task (Porra et al. 2009). Another unusual aspect of this story is that speciation took place within days. We contribute the success of the Katrina rescue effort to the experience and training of the rescue worker and the long history of her rescue organization in dealing with catastrophic circumstances.

While the time frame is short, the direction of the punctuation in the Katrina example is typical. Mostly colonies punctuated to a smaller structure, because it is easier for smaller colonies to make radical changes in their structures. Human colonies can, however, also punctuate into a more complex form (Porra 1996, 1999). We can speculate that during a hurricane, a rapid, dramatic, and temporary increase in the size of a rescue colony may be necessary in order to respond to the victims' needs in a timely, effective manner.

While adding people and information systems may be necessary in order to successfully respond to immediate environmental pressures, increased complexity consumes energy (Porra 1996, 1999). Thus more structure does not necessarily translate into better preservation of the colony's humanness. For this reason, human colonies tend to preserve their complex form only until a shift to a simpler structure is possible (Porra 1996, 1999). In short, simplicity has turned out to be a useful quality in a species (Wilson 1992).

5.6 Structure

Traditionally, human colony's structure has essentially consisted of people. Colony's members are the carrier of its evolutionary history and thus its identity and humanness (Porra 1996, 1999). In order for the colony to survive, at least one member must move on to the next generation.

During Katrina, a rescue colony replaced all of its information systems in the speciation process (Porra et al. 2009). After finding that she was the only member still on the mission, the leader found a new location and recruited new members from local volunteers. Opportunistically, she then stopped a communications truck and recreated the necessary information systems relying on the expertise of the truck owner.

Colonies' information systems can also preserve their evolutionary history, identity, and humanness (Porra 1996, 1999). It is conceivable that a human colony may survive even when all of its members are replaced. We can speculate that some online communities are *information colonies* (Porra 1996, 1999). They preserve much of their evolutionary history and their humanness in their information systems even after members leave.

5.7 Growth

Human colonies are founded on physically being in one another's company (Porra 1996, 1999). Humanness forms when members have opportunities to spend time in one another's reach. The Katrina example illustrates that a colony can consist of one person (Porra et al. 2009). We have also speculated that colony's humanness can be passed on to a new generation in an information system. In nature colonies, colonies' membership varies from a few to thousands (Wilson 1980). How large human colonies can grow is an open question. It is likely, however, that human colonies too remain relatively small because as they grow large, they become less efficient (Porra 1996, 1999).

Today the Internet allows sharing colony-like experiences over distances. These experiences may not, however, have the same quality of reach as face-to-face colonies (Porra 1996, 1999). Colony's humanness is based on spatial and temporal reach through all senses. Computer-based reach is yet to provide similar experiences. Yet it seems plausible that humans form *information colonies* online. Our study shows that when virtual community members also meet in person, they tend to perceive that their virtual communities have characteristics of human colonies (Porra and Parks 2006). Whether humanness forms in purely on-line colonies and how large these can grow remains to be seen.

On of off-line, however, human colony's growth follows the punctuated equilibrium model (Eldredge and Gould 1972). From a distance, colonial growth patterns look like "Gould's onions" (Porra 1996, 1999). Onions sprout new onions from their sides. Some of the sprouts die, while others lead to new onions. The onion is a parent colony and sprouts are new generation colonies it sends to the environment. These become populous or die.

In order to study the growth patterns of Texaco's IT colony, we could start from the initiation of the IT function half a century ago. From its ancestor colonies at Texaco's business units (onions), we would see individuals (sprouts) join the new IT unit and form a colony (the stem of the onion). Over the years the IT colony would become populous (the lower half of the onion) and then diminish in size as the firm went through several cycles of downsizing (the top half of the onion). At the end of Texaco in 2001, we would see a sprout leaving Texaco IT colony (the top of the onion) to join IT at Chevron.

5.8 Goals

Colonies have ideals (Porra 1996, 1999). These collective-level goals are long lasting, often beyond current membership. Members shape and act out colony's ideals for as long as they remain with the colony. For example, the Katrina rescue colony continued its mission through two punctuations after losing all contact with the parent organization (Porra et al. 2009). This colony held humanitarian ideals and these ideals were inherited by each new generation.

The Katrina rescue story also shows that colony's ideals are not driven by short-term goal setting because such behavior is risky (Porra 1996, 1999). The ultimate purpose of colonies is survival, which requires that they preserve their evolutionary history and thus their *humanness*. The Katrina rescue colony had many acceptable reasons to interrupt its mission, but it held high its humanitarian ideals and pursued to overcome catastrophic circumstances (Porra et al. 2009).

When colonies change their ideals, they proceed cautiously. New ideals can emerge from the environment, colony's evolutionary history, or its understanding of its future potential and capacity to survive radical change (Porra 1996, 1999). This means that even over generations, colonies' ideals tend to remain unchanged. Thus Texaco's IT colony retained its professional ideals and the Katrina rescue colony its humanitarian ideals under varying circumstances (Porra et al. 2005, 2009).

5.9 Power

Human colonies may appear leaderless (Porra 1996, 1999). Unlike formal organizations, they do not necessarily have clear power structures or methods for goal setting or control. Human colonies lack hierarchies and individual centered authority (Porra 1996, 1999). When necessary, however, like during a rescue mission, a colony can adopt any type of organizational structure and authority scheme it finds beneficial for its purpose. Thus colonies change their power structures at will.

Another central aspect of power is that colonies operate independently from outside authorities. No outside entity can impose its authority over a colony without its consent. This kind of power is called *endogenous authority* (Porra 1996, 1999). A colony has full authority over itself and no power over others. This perspective on power is useful in situations like the Katrina rescue mission (Porra et al. 2009). The rescue colony improvised its power structures based on who was there and made independent decisions about the rescue process as it went along.

In human colonies, power means influence (Porra 1996, 1999). Members influence the colony by being present. The longer the time spent with the colony, the greater the influence on the colony. In the Texaco's IT colony, several senior members were considered leaders and mentors of the colony, but they did not hold the highest organizational positions (Porra et al. 2005).

5.10 Control

We have described human colonies as systems (Porra 1996, 1999). From this perspective, control is a central characteristic. As systems, human colonies have feedback and feedforward mechanisms. These terms, familiar from cybernetics, describe a system that is able to adapt to its environment and use goal-setting primitives (Coulter 1968, 1975, Locker and Coulter 1976, Parks and Steinberg 1978).

Traditionally, cybernetics is concerned with mechanistic and organic microlevel control mechanisms (Porra 1996, 1999). Thus "feedback" and "feedforward" are associated with a machine or an organism. Since human colonies are collectives, their control mechanisms may be different from mechanistic and organic feedback and feedforward systems, but it is likely that something analogous is being used at the collective level of the colony. What kinds of feedback and feedforward mechanisms colonies use remains an open question.

We have described colonial-level feedback and feedforward mechanisms as a product of the evolution of the colony (Porra 1996, 1999). It is likely that these are delayed, complex, and varied like the human collectives that portray the mechanisms. Moreover, the impact of the feedback and feedforward processes is always at the discretion of the colony. Thus colonies choose their actions based on the feedback they receive from the environment. Texaco's IT colony had several choices based on environmental feedback (Porra et al. 2005). It could move to Chevron, start a new firm, or dissolve. Also the Katrina rescue colony had choices (Porra et al. 2009). It could continue its rescue mission under extreme circumstances or quit and go home.

6 Empirical Research

While studying human collectives from an evolutionary standpoint is in its infancy, the colonial systems theory has been used in several empirical studies.[4] For example, colonial systems theory has been used to interpret the 47-year history and the eventual failure of the Texaco's IT function (Porra et al. 2005). We found that there was an IT colony at the firm, which had an identity, history, and evolutionary path distinct from the organization at large.

Another empirical study at an all-female high school shows that the colonial properties form a construct that predicts member perceptions of their community being sustainable (Porra and Parks 2006). A third study is a story of a successful Katrina rescue effort that can be interpreted as a sequence of two colonial speciation episodes (Porra et al. 2009).

These three empirical research projects have taught three important lessons about human evolution at the group level: (1) human groups can have distinct evolutionary paths from the organization at large; (2) group members perceive their groups to be sustainable (or not sustainable) early on in the group formation process and commit to contributing to the longevity of the groups they perceive long lasting; and (3) groups able to leave behind their parent organization, abandon, and recreate their human and IS structures can survive when the organization at large struggles.

7 Concluding Remarks

In this chapter, we have discussed an alternative perspective on human groups. This perspective is founded on animal colonies in nature (Porra 1996, 1999). Based on our earlier work, we have discussed their 10 characteristics. We have used examples

---

[4] In this chapter, we have used examples from these studies to illustrate some points about human colonies.

from three empirical studies to illustrate them (Porra et al. 2005, 2009; Porra and Parks 2006).

The human colony approach provides a novel perspective on studying human collectives. The central ideas that (1) humans form colonies and that (2) these have lineages and (3) inherit characteristics from their ancestors can shed new light on studying groups in all social and organizational contexts.

A principle idea behind the theory of human colonies is that these kinds of collectives may be capable of speciation through radical change. The colony perspective shifts the focus away from individual members, specifics of the information systems, and short-term tasks. It highlights some essential characteristics of the collective that may be important for the long-term survival of their humanness. It underscores that from this perspective, all individuals and their information systems are replaceable and the collective's identity irreplaceable. If a human colony loses its evolutionary history, the lineage becomes extinct.

The human colony perspective opens up new research areas. One such area is the study of group lineages. How do new generations of human colonies emerge from old ones? What does the offspring inherit from the ancestors? What are the evolutionary conditions under which groups survive? What characteristics do long-lasting groups and lineages have? What are the long-term dynamics between groups and their environment?

Finally, the study of human colonies is not limited to groups in traditional organizational settings. While groups such as expert groups, virtual teams, project groups, and rescue teams have been studied from this perspective (Porra et al. 2005, 2009; Porra and Parks 2006), this theory can be useful in understanding the evolution of virtual communities and online groups. It can also be helpful in understanding underground movements such as criminal and terrorist activities, where group-level activity is of central importance (cf., Mumford 1999).

We have patterned our theory of human colonies after mobile animal colonies. While there appear to be many similarities in the behavior of these living systems, the colony idea is merely a useful metaphor, not a scientific fact. How human social behavior is coded or passed on to future generations in genes remains an open question. We have described 10 systemic characteristics mobile living collectives appear to have in common based on paleontology, evolutionary biology, systems theory, psychology, and the social sciences.

What the significance of human colonies may be remains to be seen. According to the punctuated equilibrium theory by Eldredge and Gould (1972), speciation occurs from small parts of geographical distribution. They claim that most significant change in a species occurs from small collectives, not as a uniform transformation in all humanity. While Eldredge and Gould's (1972) theory is about genes, we hold that metaphorically, something very similar may be taking place in the social evolution of human colonies.

Acknowledgment   This chapter is based on an article by the author, published in 1999 in volume 10, issue 1 of the *Information Systems Research* journal.

References

Aldrich HE (1979) Organizations and environments. Prentice-Hall, Englewood Cliffs

Amburgey TL, Kelly D, Barnett WP (1993) Resetting the clock: the dynamics of organizational failure. Admin Sci Q 38:51–73

Arnott D (2004) Decision support systems evolutions: framework, case study and research agenda. Eur J Inf Syst 13:247–259

Backstrom L, Huttenlocher D, Kleinberg J, Xiangyang L (2006) Group formation in large social networks: membership, growth and evolution. In: Proceedings of the 12th ACM SIGKDD international conference on knowledge discovery and data mining, Philadelphia, pp 44–54

Baum JAC (1988) Ecological aggregates and heritable units: towards an evolutionary perspective on organizations. A paper presented at the Academy of Management national meetings, Anaheim, CA. In: Baum JAC, Singh JV (eds) (1994a) Evolutionary dynamics of organizations. Oxford University Press, New York

Baum JAC (1989) A population perspective on organizations: a study of diversity and transformation in child care service organizations. Ph.D. Thesis, Faculty of Management, University of Toronto

Baum JAC (1990) Inertial and adaptive patterns of organizational change. Academy of Management best papers proceedings, Academy of Management, San Francisco, pp 165–169

Baum JAC, Oliver C (1991) Institutional linkages and organizational mortality. Admin Sci Q 36:187–218

Baum JAC, Singh JV (eds) (1994a) Evolutionary dynamics of organizations. Oxford University Press, New York

Baum JAC, Singh JV (eds) (1994b) Organizational hierarchies and evolutionary process: some reflections on a theory of organizational evolution. In: Evolutionary dynamics of organizations. Oxford University Press, New York, pp 3–22

Beklemishev WN (1969) Principles of comparative anatomy of invertebrates, In: Kabata Z (ed) Promorphology, vol 1. Chicago University Press, Chicago, IL xxx + 490

Borrello ME (2005) The rise, fall and resurrection of group selection. Endeavour 29(1):43–47, March

Burgelman RA (1991) Intraorganizational ecology of strategy-making and organizational adaptation: theory and field research. Organ Sci 2:239–262

Burgelman RA, Singh JV (1987) Strategy and organization: an evolutionary approach. Paper presented in the Academy of Management meetings, New Orleans. In: Baum JAC, Singh JV (eds) (1994a) Evolutionary dynamics of organizations. Oxford University Press, New York

Campbell DT (1974a) Downward causation in hierarchically organized biological systems. In: Ayala F, Dobzhansky T (eds) Studies in the philosophy of biology. University of California Press, Berkeley, pp 179–186

Campbell DT (1974b) Evolutionary epistemology. In Schilpp PA (ed) The philosophy of Karl Popper. Open court Publishing, LaSalle, pp 413–463

Campbell DT (1979) Comments on the sociobiology of ethics and moralizing. Behav Sci 24:37–45

Campbell DT (1982) Legal and primary-group social controls. J Sociol Biol Struct 5: 431–438

Campbell DT (1990) Levels of organization, downward causation, and the selection-theory approach to evolutionary epistemology. In: Greenberg G, Tobach E (eds) Theories of the evolution of knowing, the T.C. Schneila conference series, Vol 4. Lawrence Erlbaum Associates, Hillsdale, pp 1–17

Campbell DT (1994) How individual and face-to-face-group selection undermine firm selection in organizational evolution. In: Baum JAC and Singh JV (eds) Evolutionary dynamics of organizations. Oxford University Press, New York, pp 23–38

Carroll G (1984) Organizational ecology. Annu Rev Sociol 10:71–93

Carroll G, Hannan MT (1989) Density delay in the evolution of organizational populations: a model and five empirical tests. Admin Sci Q 34:411–430

Chang A, Duck J (2003) Punctuated equilibrium and linear progression: toward new understanding of group development. Acad Manage J 48(1):106–117

Coulter NA (1968) Towards a theory of teleogenic control systems. Gen Syst 13:85–89

Coulter NA (1975) The self determinism of teleogenic systems. Cybernetics 5(3):9–12

Csányi V (1989) Evolutionary systems and society: a general theory. Duke University Press, Durham

Delacroix J, Swaminathan A (1991) Cosmetic, speculative, and adaptive organizational change in the wine industry: a longitudinal study. Admin Sci Q 28:274–291

Eldredge N, Gould S (1972) Punctuated equilibria: an alternative to phyletic gradualism. In Schopf TJM (ed) Models in paleobiology. Freeman, Cooper & Company, San Francisco, pp 82–115

Gardner A, Grafen A (2009) Capturing the superorganism: a formal theory of group adaptation. Eur Soc Evol Biol 22:659–671

Gersick CJG (1988) Time and transition in work teams: toward a new model of group development. Acad Manage J 31(1):9–41

Gersick CJG (1989) Marking time: predictable transitions in task groups. Acad Manage J 32(2):274–309, June

Gersick CJG (1991) Evolutionary change theories: a multilevel exploration of the punctuated equilibrium paradigm. Acad Manage Rev 16(1):10–36

Ginzberg A, Buchholtz A (1990) Converting to for-profit status: corporate responsiveness to radical change. Acad Manage J 33:447–477

Gould J (1991) Opus 200. Nat Hist 100:12–18, August

Hannan MT, Freeman JH (1977) The population ecology of organizations. Am J Sociol 32: 929–964

Hannan MT, Freeman JH (1989) Organization ecology. Harvard University Press, Cambridge

Haveman HA (1992) Between a rock and a hard place: organizational change and performance under conditions of fundamental environmental transformation. Admin Sci Q 37:48–75

Haveman HA, Russo MV, Meyer AD (2001) Organizational environments in flux: the impact of regulatory punctuations on organizational domains, CEO succession, and performance. Organ Sci 12(3):253–273, May–June

Hawley AH (1950) Human ecology: a theory of community structure. Ronald, New York

Hawley AH (1986) Human ecology: a theoretical essay. University of Chicago Press, Chicago

Hull DL (1980) Individuality and selection. Annu Rev Ecol Syst 11:311–332

Hull DL (1988) Science as a process: an evolutionary account of the social and conceptual development of science. Chicago University Press, Chicago

Kelly D, Amburgey TL (1991) Organizational inertial and momentum: a dynamic model of strategic change. Acad Manage J 34:591–612

Lassila KS, Brancheau JC (1999) Adoption and utilization of commercial software packages: exploring utilization equilibria, transitions, triggers, and tracks. J Manage Inf Syst 16(2):63–90

Lehmann L, Keller L, West S, Roze D (2007) Group selection and kin selection: two concepts but one process. Proc Natl Acad Sci U S A 104(16):6736–6739

Locker AN, Coulter A (1976) Recent progress towards a theory of teleogenesis. Kybernetes 5: 67–72

Lumsden CJ, Singh JV (1990) The dynamics of organizational speciation. In: Singh JV (ed) Organizational evolution: new directions. Sage, Newbury Park, pp 145–163

Lyytinen K, Newman M (2008) Explaining information systems change: a punctuated socio-technical change model. Eur J Inf Syst 17:589–613

Marek K (2008) Darwin 200: the needs of the many. Nature 256(7220):296–299

Mayr E (1982) The growth of biological thought. Harvard University Press, Boston

McKelvey B (1982) Organizational systematics. Taxonomy, classification, evolution. University of California Press, Berkeley

Miner AS (1991) Organizational evolution and the social ecology of jobs. Am Sociol Rev 56: 772–785

Miner AS, Amburgey TL, Stearns TM (1990) Interorganizational linkages and population dynamics: buffering and transformational shields. Admin Sci Q 35:689–713

Mumford E (1999) Dangerous decisions. Kluwer Academic/Plenum Publishers, London

O'Gorman R, Sheldon KM, Wilson DS (2008) For the good of the group? Exploring group-level evolutionary adaptations using multilevel selection theory. Group Dyn 12(1):17–26

Okhuysen GA, Waller MJ (2002) Focusing on midpoint transitions: an analysis of boundary conditions. Acad Manage J 45(5):1056–1065

Pagels HR (1989) The dreams of reason—the computer and the rise of the sciences of complexity, Bantam edn. Bantam Books, New York

Palla G, Barabási A-L, Vicsek T (2007) Quantifying social group evolution. Nature 446(5):664–667, April

Parks MS, Steinberg E (1978) Dichotic property and teleogenesis. Kybernetes 7:259–264

Porra J (1996) Colonial systems, information colonies and punctuated prototyping, Jyvaskyla studies of computer science, economics and statistics, vol 33. University of Jyvaskyla Press, Jyvaskyla

Porra J (1999) Colonial systems. Inf Syst Res 10(1):38–69, March

Porra J, Parks MS (2006) Sustaining virtual communities: suggestions from the colonial model. Inf Syst e-Bus Manage 4:309–341

Porra J, Hirschheim R, Parks MS (2005) The history of Texaco's Corporate IT FunctionA general systems theoretical interpretation. Manage Inf Syst Q 29(4 I):721–746, December

Porra J, Parks MS, Day J, Junglas I (2009) Organizational survival from colonial speciation during Katrina – What temporary organizations and ad hoc information systems can do to aid rescue, Working paper

Pouder R, St. John CH (1996) Hot spots and blind spots: geographical clusters of firms and innovation. Acad Manage Rev 21(4):1192–1225, October

Romanelli E, Tushman ML (1994) Organizational transformation as punctuated equilibrium: an empirical test. Acad Manage J 37(5):1141–1166

Sabherval R, Hirschheim R, Goles T (2001) The dynamics of alignment: insights from a punctuated equilibrium model. Organ Sci 12(2):179–197, March–April

Scheuring I (2009) Evolution of generous cooperative norms by cultural group selection. J Theor Biol 257(3):397–407, April

Schwartz JH (1999) Sudden origins—fossils, genes, and the emergence of species. John Wiley and Sons, New York

Shavit A (2004) Shifting values partly explain the debate over group selection. Stud Hist Philos Biol Sci 35(4):697–720, December

Shavit A (2005) The notion of 'group' and tests of group selection. Philos Sci 72:1052–1063

Silva L, Hirschheim R (2007) Fighting against windmills: strategic information systems and organizational deep structures. Manage Inf Syst Q 31(2):327–354

Singh JV, Lumsden CJ (1990) Theory and research in organizational ecology. Annu Rev Sociol 16:161–195

Singh JV, House RJ, Tucker DJ (1986) Organizational change and organizational mortality. Admin Sci Q 31:587–611

Sober E, Wilson DS (2000) "Was Hayek right about group selection after all?" Review essay of unto others: the evolution and psychology of unselfish behavior. Rev Austrian Econ 13(1):81–95, February

Street CT, Meister DB (2004) Small business growth and internal transparency: the role of information systems. Manage Inf Syst Q 28(3):473–506

Ulrich D, McKelvey B (1990) General organizational classification: an empirical test using the United States and Japanese electronic industries. Organ Sci 1:99–118

van de Ven AH, Poole MS (1995) Explaining development and change in organizations. Acad Manage Rev 20(3):510–540, July

Van Veelen M (2009) Group selection, kin selection, altruism and cooperation: when inclusive fitness is right and when it can be wrong. J Theor Biol 259(3):589–600, August

Van Veelen M, Hopfensitz M (2007) In love and war: altruism, norm formation, and two different types of group selection. J Theor Biol 249(4):667–680, December

Weick KE (1979) The social psychology of organizing, 2nd edn. Random House, New York

Wilkins J (2007) The dimensions, modes and definitions of species and speciation. Biol Philos 22:247–266

Wilson EO (1980) Sociobiology—the abridged edition. The Belknap Press of Harvard University Press, Cambridge

Wilson EO (1992) The effects of complex social life on evolution and biodiversity, vol 63. OIKOS, Copenhagen, pp 13–18

Wilson EO (2008) One giant leap: how insects achieved altruism and colonial life. Bioscience, 58(1):17–25, January

Wilson DS, Wilson EO (2007) Rethinking the theoretical foundation of sociobiology. Q Rev Biol 82(4):327–348, December

Wilson DS, Wilson EO (2008) Evolution "for the good of the group". Am Sci 96(5):378–389, September/October

Chapter 3
Applying Evolutionary Psychology to the Study of Post-adoption Information Technology Use: Reinforcement, Extension, or Revolution?

Ana Ortiz de Guinea and M. Lynne Markus

Abstract How and why people use information technology (IT) after initial adoption is a growing area of research in the information systems (IS) field. For the most part, IS scholars have approached this area of study with conceptual tools well honed in the study of initial IT adoption and acceptance – specially, with theories of reasoned action that emphasize the conscious formation of beliefs, attitudes, and intentions to engage in IT use behavior. At the same time, continuing IT use researchers have recognized the importance of non-reflective action – specifically, habitual behavior – in the explanation of post-adoption IT use. In this chapter, we inquire about the relevance and implications of evolutionary psychology, a theoretical paradigm recently introduced to the IS community, for the study of continuing IT use. We compare the core concepts and basic assumptions of both areas of study and we explore three ways in which IS scholars could use evolutionary insights: (1) to reinforce and justify current research approaches, (2) to extend current theory and methods in important new ways, such as by linking objective technical characteristics to cognitive belief formation, or (3) to revolutionize current approaches, for instance, by respecifying the role of emotion in behavior and by redefining the concept of habit.

Keywords Evolution · Evolutionary psychology · Continuing IT use · IT continuance · Post-adoption IT usage · Automatic behavior · Habit · Emotion · Cognition · Intention · Reasoned action · Planned behavior

A. Ortiz de Guinea (✉)
Service de l'Enseignement des Technologies de l'Information, HEC Montréal, 3000, Chemin de la Côte-Sainte-Catherine, Montréal, QC, Canada H3T 2A7
e-mail: ana.ortiz-de-guinea@hec.ca

M.L. Markus
Department of Information and Process Management, Smith Technology Center 325, 175 Forest Street, Watham, MA 02452-4705, USA
e-mail: mlmarkus@bentley.edu

N. Kock (ed.), *Evolutionary Psychology and Information Systems Research*,
Integrated Series in Information Systems 24, DOI 10.1007/978-1-4419-6139-6_3,
© Springer Science+Business Media, LLC 2010

1 Introduction

For the past 20 years, explaining individuals' information technology (IT) use has been a central theme in information systems (IS) research. From early work on technology adoption and acceptance (Davis 1989; Davis et al. 1989), researchers moved to technology continuance use decisions (Bhattacherjee 2001; Bhattacherjee and Premkumar 2004; Kim and Malhotra 2005a, b; Limayem et al. 2007). This move directed scholars' efforts to the explanation of post-adoption IT use (Jasperson et al. 2005), understood as the patterns of IT use behavior after an individual has started using a particular IT and learned at least the rudiments of how to use it.

Research on post-adoption IT use has built, for the most part, on theories of reasoned action that portray IT use as a rational decision-making process. In this view, IT use is driven by conscious intentions that result from a conscious cognitive process involving beliefs, expectations, and reflections on past experience. Over time, in stable contexts, continuing IT use is believed to become habitual, so that the automatic execution of well-learned behavior sequences can be triggered by environmental cues. This model reflects the intellectual traditions of social and cognitive psychologies.

In this chapter we inquire about the relevance and implications of evolutionary psychology for the study of continuing IT use. Evolutionary psychology has only recently been introduced to the IS community, through the efforts of scholars such as Kock (2004, 2009), who has shown how an evolutionary perspective can augment IS theorizing about the use of communication media. The fact that other IS scholars have independently begun exploring related theoretical ideas from branches of environmental psychology (Johnston et al. 2005; Markus and Silver 2008; Waller et al. 2006) suggests that evolutionary psychology has great potential to inform IS research.

The question is *how* IS scholars will employ the insights of evolutionary psychology for the study of continuing IT use. Analysis of the core concepts and basic assumptions of both areas of study shows both strong similarities and a few important differences. IS scholars could choose to exploit only the similarities or some subset of the differences. In this chapter we consider three potential applications of evolutionary theorizing to IS research on continuing IT use. First, IS scholars could co-opt evolutionary psychology as providing greater legitimacy for existing approaches to the study of post-adoption IT use. Second, evolutionary psychology could be used to extend current IS theory and methods related to post-adoption IT use in various ways, principally, to make connections between specific IT features and the formation of particular attitudes and beliefs about information technology. Third, application of evolutionary insights could revolutionize the study of continuing IT use, through a redefinition of habitual behavior and a reformulation of the role of emotion in IT use behavior.

In the next section, we briefly summarize the core concepts and assumptions in current research on post-adoption IT use and we compare them to those in evolutionary psychology. Along the way, we surface the intellectual controversies that could affect how evolutionary ideas are applied in an IS context. In the following section, we delve deeper into the three ways we see evolutionary psychology being employed for the study of ongoing IT use: as reinforcement, for extension, and for revolution. The chapter concludes with a brief discussion of what such conflicting applications of evolutionary theory mean for the IS research community.

2 How Evolutionary Psychology Relates to the Study of Post-adoption IT Use

One of the most welcome recent developments in the IS field has been the growing interest in post-adoption IT use, following decades in which the major preoccupation of many IS scholars was explaining and predicting whether or not an individual would decide to use an information technology. In principle, the concept of post-adoption IT use can be defined very broadly, to include the "mindless" repetition of well-learned behavior, the learning of new capabilities of a currently (under) used technology, the application of a familiar IT to new tasks, or even the generalization of known capabilities to new tools *and* new tasks. If the concept is thus defined broadly, a wide variety of theoretical perspectives would appear to be relevant to explaining post-adoption IT use, including especially evolutionary psychology, with its links to biological mechanisms and to the study of animal tool use.

In practice, however, post-adoption IT use has been more narrowly defined, either as "the IT continuance decision" – a conscious choice to continue to use a currently used IT (where "use" itself is considered an unproblematic concept that does not require definition or qualification) – or as "the myriad feature adoption decisions, feature use behaviors, and feature extension behaviors made by an individual user after an IT application has been installed, made accessible to the user, and applied by the user in accomplishing his / her work activities" (Jasperson et al. 2005, p. 531). In addition, post-adoption IT use has been studied using a narrow range of theoretical perspectives at the intersection of social and cognitive psychologies that focus mainly on mental events without reference to biological processes or to non-living objects.

In this section, we try to establish the relevance of evolutionary psychology as a theoretical perspective on post-adoption IT use by locating both areas of inquiry in a broader intellectual space and comparing and contrasting their basic concepts and assumptions.

2.1 Current IS Research on Post-adoption IT Use

With a few important additions, the study of post-adoption IT use maintains considerable theoretical continuity with an earlier stream of research on initial IT adoption and acceptance. (See Ortiz de Guinea and Markus (2009), for a fuller discussion of the issues in this section.) Research on IT adoption and acceptance has predominantly employed one or another variety of the social psychological theory of

reasoned action (Fishbein and Ajzen 1975). Examples include the technology acceptance model (TAM) (Davis 1989; Davis et al. 1989), the unified theory of acceptance
and use of technology (UTAUT) (Venkatesh et al. 2003), and their numerous extensions (Bhattacherjee and Sanford 2006; Karahanna et al. 2006; Venkatesh and Davis
2000). These theories concern the *conscious* mental events that lead up to an intention to use (or continue to use) an information technology (Bhattacherjee 2001;
Bhattacherjee and Premkumar 2004; Karahanna et al. 1999; Taylor and Todd 1995;
Venkatesh et al. 2008).

Among the important constructs in these theories is that of "attitudes," such as
satisfaction with an IT, which is often in the IS literature referred to as "emotions" or
"feelings." Attitudes are conceptualized as determined by cognitive beliefs about, or
evaluations of direct experiences with, IT (Bajaj and Nidumolu 1998; Bhattacherjee
2001; Kim et al. 2007), and they are also viewed as inputs to conscious intentions to
use IT. Thus, attitudes or emotions are to a great extent conflated with cognitions –
in the sense that attitudes stem from cognitive beliefs – in a conscious, rational
calculus about whether to use (or to continue to use) an IT.

Where the present study of post-adoption IT usage departs from the theory of
reasoned action and its variants is in the inclusion of non-conscious elements, such
as habit. When they turned their attention to the continuing use of IT, IS scholars recognized that not all behavior is the result of a currently conscious decision.
Rather, some post-adoption IT use behavior is viewed as the non-reflective repetition of well-learned sequences of actions that were once intentional but subsequently
became subject to activation by environmental cues and automatic repetition without conscious intentions. In some studies, habit is said to affect IT use (Kim and
Malhotra 2005a; Limayem and Hirt 2003), or intentions to use IT (Gefen 2003),
directly. In other studies, habit is argued to moderate the impact of intentions on IT
use (Cheung and Limayen 2005; Kim et al. 2005; Limayem et al. 2003, 2007).

These concepts and basic assumptions locate the study of post-adoption IT use
entirely within the realm of psychology at the intersection of social and cognitive psychologies (see Fig. 3.1 and Table 3.1). Post-adoption IT use research is

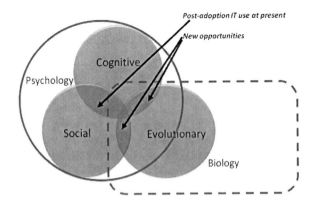

Fig. 3.1 How the disciplines intersect

Table 3.1 Overlapping disciplines relevant to the study of post-adoption IT use

Discipline	Description	Comments
Biology	The study of living beings	Includes numerous subfields, including evolutionary biology, neuroscience (the study of the nervous system), neurobiology, and ecology
Evolutionary biology	The study of development of living beings over time; specifically concerned with changes in genetic makeup as a result of natural or sexual selection	Includes a focus on animal tool use, which is highly relevant to the study of human use of information technology
Neuro-biology	The study of the neurosystem as it relates to information processing and behavior	Forms an intersection between biology and neuroscience. Overlaps with numerous other subfields of neuroscience, including several that impinge on cognitive psychology and neuropsychology
Ecology	The study of living beings and the non-living parts of their environments	Relevant, because environments include tools, but not explicitly examined in this chapter
Psychology	The study of mind and behavior	Includes numerous subfields, like cognitive, social, neuro-, evolutionary, and ecological psychologies
Cognitive psychology	The study of mental processes, specifically, mental representations and the rules involved in information processing	Includes the study of both conscious and non-conscious mental processes. Does not directly address the connections between material objects and their mental representations
Social psychology	The study of how people's thoughts, feelings, and behaviors are influenced by other people	Includes the study of both conscious and non-conscious mental processes. Influenced the development of the theory of reasoned action, which has been widely used in the study of IT use
Neuro-psychology	The study of the brain and its relationship to psychological processes and behavior	Forms an intersection between biology (specifically, neurobiology), philosophy (specifically, the philosophy of mind), and psychology (where it has much in common with cognitive psychology in its focus on both conscious and non-conscious information processing)

Table 3.1 (continued)

Discipline	Description	Comments
Evolutionary Psychology	The study of psychological processes and behavior as evolutionary adaptations, that is, the results of natural or sexual selection	Forms an intersection between biology (specifically, evolutionary biology) and psychology (specifically, cognitive psychology). Differs from cognitive psychology in that evolutionary psychology is concerned with the adaptive problems that psychological mechanisms evolved to solve (whereas cognitive psychology is "functionally agnostic") and thus conceptualizes the mind as consisting of many specialized mechanisms (whereas cognitive psychologists assume that the mind is a general-purpose information processing device)
Ecological psychology	The study of psychological processes and behavior in environmental contexts that include non-living elements	Consists of several different schools of thought. Relevant, because it emphasizes the role of non-living aspects of the environment such as tools, but not explicitly addressed in this chapter
Theory of reasoned action (social psychology and cognitive psychology)	A social–psychological perspective on the relationship between subjective norm, attitudes (and cognitive beliefs), intentions, and behaviors	Deals exclusively with conscious mental processes, specifically, intentional decisions to act on the basis of various inputs such as attitudes and subjective norms. Extensively used in the study of information technology use, where emotions are for the most part conceptualized as attitudes
Theory of planned behavior (social and cognitive psychology)	An extension of the theory of reasoned action that adds behavioral control as another determinant of behavioral intentions	Adds perceived behavioral control to the study of information technology use and acceptance
Post-adoption IT usage (information systems)	A subset of the study of information technology use concerned with how people use information technology after initial adoption	Relies heavily on the theory of reasoned action, but also includes a focus on non-reflective, habitual behavior, which would generally be considered outside the scope of the theory of reasoned action and within the scope of social psychology more broadly or of other branches of psychology that deal with non-conscious mental processes

concerned primarily with mental events that explain and predict behavior, specifically, with mental representations of internal states or external objects. In this theoretical perspective, the biological bases of those internal states or the material conditions of those environmental objects do not play a role. For the most part, this theoretical perspective is premised on the "concept that cognition is central to human nature and that the best way to begin the complex task of understanding and helping other people is by focusing on conscious thought" (Lee 1998, p. 97). The assumption is that people plan and then act; behavior is attributed to an assumed rational system of beliefs and desires (Foxall 2004). At the same time, non-conscious states such as non-reflective habit figure importantly in the study of post-adoption IT use. All things considered, then, the study of post-adoption IT use assumes a human information processor for whom emotions are conflated with cognition and are inputs to consciously or unconsciously driven behavior – a position very much in keeping with the discipline of cognitive psychology.

2.2 Evolutionary Psychology and Its Relevance for the Study of Post-adoption IT Use

Evolutionary psychology brings biological evolution into the psychological realm. Evolution refers to "change over time in organic (living) structure" (Buss 2008, p. 3). Evolutionary biology explains not only why these changes take place over time but also how new species come into being (Buss 2008). Darwin's theory of natural selection posits that organisms change "over time due to the differential reproductive success of inherited variation" (Buss 2008, p. 33). Other major contributions to the theory of evolution include Huxley's (1942) "modern synthesis" of genetics and natural selection, and the etiology movement (also spelled ethology and aetiology) (Tinbergen 1951), which sought to understand the causes or origins, development, evolution, and function of animal behavior.

One thing that makes evolutionary biology so intriguing for the study of information technology use is its inclusion of the use of tools by various species of animals. Sea otters and owls, for instance, are capable of tool use (Dunsworth 2007). The sporadic use of tools is common among a wide range of animals, but everyday tool use is only found in some primates, such as orangutans and gorillas (Dunsworth 2007). A further distinction concerns the ability to modify found objects for use as tools – a capability exclusive to chimpanzees and humans (Dunsworth 2007). It is believed that humans evolved the ability to construct and use tools to solve environmental problems (Lieberman 2000).

Evolutionary psychology is a multidisciplinary field that combines ideas from many different disciplines, such as cognitive science and evolutionary biology (Dunsworth 2007). The field originated as a reaction to what some scholars called the "standard social science model (SSSM)," a perspective in which humans are viewed as blank slates, who have to learn "our social practices and customs, our ways of life and manners of relating to one another" (Levy 2004, p. 460) from scratch. In other words, "though we might have innate learning strategies, little else is built in" (Levy 2004, p. 460). According to evolutionary psychologists, the existence of human universals across different cultures (i.e., males' tendency to control resources) cannot be explained by the SSSM. As a result, evolutionary psychologists state that innate psychological adaptations are able to better account for human universals. This tenet of the founders of evolutionary psychology is subject to considerable debate (see Barkow et al. 1992; Hampton 2004; Levy 2004), and some evolutionary psychologists have proposed alternative hypotheses. The role of innate psychological adaptations is highly relevant to the applicability of evolutionary psychology to the study of continuing IT use, which we will discuss later.

Less controversially, evolutionary psychology applies the principles of evolution to the study of human behaviors. It holds that human behavior can be explained by psychological adaptations that evolved over time to enable humans to successfully deal with the challenges they faced in ancestral environments (Buss 2008). For example, evolutionary psychology posits that the human brain and body coevolved to facilitate tool making. Certain human bodily characteristics, such as the anatomy of the wrist and hand, that evolved to make tools (Dunsworth 2007), were accompanied by the evolution of human brain functions need to control these physical and anatomic characteristics (Buss 2008; Cosmides and Tooby 1992; Plotkin 1998; Tooby and Cosmides 1992). The evolutionary psychology approach of explaining interactions between evolved adaptions and environmental inputs (Plotkin 1998) has even been used to explain the social behaviors of humans (Dennnett 1991; Pinker 1997).

2.2.1 Evolutionary Psychology Compared and Contrasted with Cognitive Psychology

As mentioned above, the study of continuing IT use has many points of similarity with the field of cognitive psychology. Although evolutionary psychology arose in response to some scholars' dissatisfaction with the "standard social science model" and not with cognitive science per se, comparing and contrasting evolutionary psychology with cognitive science will facilitate our subsequent analysis of how evolutionary psychology can be applied to the study of continuing IT use.

Cognitive psychology views the human mind as an information processing device and attempts to understand the internal mental processes involved in solving problems. Likewise, "when evolutionary psychologists refer to the mind, they mean the set of information processing devices, embodied in neural tissue, that is responsible for all conscious and nonconscious mental activity, that generates all behavior, and that regulates the body" (Tooby and Cosmides 2005, p. 16). Thus, evolutionary psychology is similar to cognitive psychology in that both disciplines emphasize the information processing activities that lie behind human behavior. Both disciplines employ the concepts of computation and reasoning rules to describe the role of human mind in the production of human behavior.

Despite these clear similarities between evolutionary psychology and cognitive science, there are also major points of difference. Evolutionary psychologists believe that we cannot explain the way humans process information, make decisions, retrieve and store information, without understanding the functions that these cognitive mechanisms were designed to accomplish (Buss 2008; Cosmides and Tooby 1992; Tooby and Cosmides 2005). By contrast, cognitive psychology is characterized by "functional agnosticism" (Buss 2008, p. 386). That is, cognitive psychology studies information processing mechanisms "without understanding the adaptive problems they were designed to solve" (Buss 2008, p. 386).

This key philosophical difference results in divergent theoretical developments. Because cognitive psychology ignores the functional problems that lead to the evolution of cognitive mechanisms, cognitive psychologists assume that "the human mind includes only general-purpose rules of reasoning and that these rules are few in number and content-free" (Cosmides and Tooby 1992, p. 179). In other words, to the cognitive psychologist the mind is a general-purpose computer, designed to solve whatever problems come its way.

By contrast, the founders of evolutionary psychology believed that the "mind is likely to consist of a large number of specialized mechanisms, each tailored to solving a different adaptive problem," such as food selection or mating (Buss 2008, p. 386). As a result, they further argued that inconvenient consequences might result if humans were to apply the reasoning rules that evolved for a certain adaptive problem to a different class of problems (Tooby and Cosmides 1992). Since the environmental problems in each domain of human activity are unique, they cannot be solved by the general-purpose system depicted by cognitive psychology, and thus, "different special purpose reasoning procedures" are needed (Tooby and Cosmides 1992, p. 179). (Some subsequent evolutionary psychologists disagreed).

In short, whereas cognitive psychology portrays the human mind as an integrated, general-purpose computational device, evolutionary psychology generally depicts it as a modular computational system in which the modules evolved to deal with specific adaptive problems successfully. As we discuss below, controversy surrounds this modularity assumption in evolutionary psychology as well as its beliefs about the role of emotion in human behavior.

2.2.2 Controversies Relevant to the Study of Post-adoption IT Use

Evolutionary psychology, like other scientific fields, is not without controversy. Numerous debates exist within the field itself (see Segestråle 2000; Smith et al. 2001). In addition, critics from the biology and neuroscience fields find fault with the lack of supporting evidence for evolutionary psychological theories and question its scientific status (see Buller 2009; Panksepp and Panksepp 2000).

Two areas of controversy are particularly relevant to the study of post-adoption IT use. The first has to do with the implications of evolutionary psychology's view of the mind as a set of domain-specific adaptive systems for human learning, particularly, for the human ability to generalize learning from one domain to another (see Atkinson and Wheeler 2004; Krill et al. 2007). As Kock (2009) pointed out, the learning question is highly salient for the study of IT use, since the cognitive mechanisms posited by evolutionary psychology evolved long before humans began using IT.

As discussed earlier, the view of the founders of evolutionary psychology was that the mind is domain-specific. Evidence in support of the domain-specificity hypothesis comes from neuro-imaging studies among other sources (Platek et al. 2005; Takahashi et al. 2000). This evidence suggests that animals are pre-conditioned to learn associative responses connected to specific adaptation problems faster than they learn responses to stimuli that are not connected to such problems (DaSilva et al. 1977). Other scholars argue that a general-purpose cognitive mechanism is necessary for solving novel problems (Chiappe and MacDonald 2005). Empirical evidence supporting this view comes from studies of humans as well as animals such as ravens and rats. These studies show that animals are able to solve novel problems innovatively without having to resort to trial and error (Henrich 2000) and that they can combine steps learned in solving separate tasks to accomplish novel tasks (Anderson 2000).

An integrative theory combines elements of both domain-specificity and general-purpose adaptive mechanisms (Geary 1995). This theory distinguishes between primary biological activities, such as food-getting and mating, that involve domain-specific adaptations, and secondary biological activities, in which domain-general capabilities can be applied to solve novel problems. This integrative theory seems more in line with the study of post-adoption IT use than the domain-specific assumptions of the founders of evolutionary psychology.

A second controversy relevant to the study of post-adoption IT use concerns the role of emotion in human behavior. The majority of evolutionary psychologists tend to conflate cognitive and emotional processes (e.g., Parrot and Schulkin 1993; Tooby and Cosmides 2000). In a typical treatment emotions and cognitions are depicted as operating together in the production of human behavior. More extreme descriptions portray emotions in highly cognitive terms (e.g., Tooby and Cosmides 2000) that imply that cognitive processing controls highly emotional experiences. Although these particular views of the role of human emotions square quite well with the views of cognitive psychologists, they have come under fire by neurobi-ologists and psychobiologists (Panksepp and Panksepp 2000). Much evolutionary evidence supports the conclusion that the human emotional system is much older and more primitive than are the higher cognitive functions (Panksepp and Panksepp 2000). The emotional system can, and often does, override the cognitive system, especially during strong emotional experiences (Damasio et al. 2000; Fischer et al. 2000).

The relevance of the controversy over emotions to the study of post-adoption IT use is clear. The views of founding evolutionary psychologists are highly compatible with those of cognitive psychologists and to current perspectives on post-adoption IT use. The views of evolutionary theorists who emphasize the temporal sequence of development of the human nervous system suggest that current perspectives on post-adoption IT use may require revolutionary change.

2.3 Summary and Implications

In this section, we have argued that the concepts and basic assumptions of current research on post-adoption IT use fall at the intersection of social and cognitive psychology. Evolutionary psychology provides a particularly interesting framework for the study of post-adoption IT use because of its grounding in evolutionary biology, which accords the making and use of tools a prominent role in human evolution. The similarities between evolutionary psychology and cognitive psychology will also likely make evolutionary psychology appealing to IS scholars. At the same time, two key controversies suggest that the application of evolutionary psychology to the study of post-adoption IT use is by no means clear-cut.

As discussed in the next section, we see three possibilities. The first is that evolutionary psychology may be co-opted by IS researchers as "biological" justification for the current perspective on post-adoption IT use. The second is that evolutionary psychology may be employed by IS researchers to extend the current perspective in the form of an explanation for the attitudes and beliefs that are proposed to drive continuing IT use behavior. The third is that evolutionary psychology may stimulate some novel IS theoretical developments and empirical research by challenging current assumptions about the role of emotions and the nature of habits.

3 How Evolutionary Psychology Could Influence the Study of Post-adoption IT Use

There should be little doubt that evolutionary psychology is *relevant* to the study of post-adoption IT use. The question remains how the IS field can or will actually *employ* this theoretical framework in theorizing about continuing IT use. Will evolutionary psychology be used as reinforcement of current perspectives, for purposes of theoretical or methodological extension, or for revolutionary new directions in post-adoption IT use theory and research?

3.1 Reinforcement: An Evolutionary or Biological Justification for the Current Perspective

A likely, but limited, outcome would be for IS scholars to co-opt evolutionary psychology into the current perspective on post-adoption IT use, employing evolutionary ideas merely as justification for prevailing views. That mainstream evolutionary psychology is similar to current IS views in several important respects makes this outcome plausible.

To recap our earlier discussion, IS research on post-adoption IT use focuses on mental events using the metaphor of the human mind as an information processing device. Emotions are viewed as inputs to conscious information processing or as part of the basic cognitive process. Non-reflective behavior in the form of habitual repetition can also occur when previously intended behaviors have been well learned.

Mainstream evolutionary psychologists hold very similar views. First, their view of humans as information processors tends to conflate emotions and cognitions (Parrot and Schulkin 1993; Tooby and Cosmides 2000), as Panksepp and Panksepp (2000) point out. "[E]motions … are viewed as inherently cognitive … because their purpose could not be accomplished without cognitive appraisal" (Parrot and Schulkin 1993, p. 48). Emotions are thought of as "programs" (Tooby and Cosmides 2000, p. 115) or as sets of rules for dealing with various circumstances. Some evolutionary psychologists even seem to imply that the emotional system evolved more recently in the evolutionary timescale than the cognitive system as noted by Panksepp and Panksepp (2000). (This idea is contradicted by the evidence of evolutionary biologists).

Tooby and Cosmides's (2000) conceptualization of the role of fear in behavior illustrates the conflation of emotions and cognitive capabilities. The fear system is portrayed as a superordinate module that coordinates lower level modules of cognition and self-regulation. During fearful situations, the fear system is said to select cognitive capabilities in ways that increase the likelihood of an adaptive behavioral response.

A similar conflation of emotion and cognition can be seen in IS research on post-adoption IT use. Concepts such as satisfaction or attitudes are viewed as emotions that influence intentions to continue using systems. Such emotions are assumed (1) to have resulted from the formation of cognitive beliefs based on prior experiences using a technology and (2) to be updated over time as users evaluate whether subsequent use experiences confirm prior expectations (Bhattacherjee and Premkumar 2004; Karahanna et al. 1999). Thus, in this view, the emotional mechanism is intimately bound up in the operation of a conscious cognitive system of intention formation.

A second major assumption of evolutionary psychologists may also be used to reinforce the current IS perspective on post-adoption IT use. The prevailing view of the mind, held by mainstream evolutionary psychologists, as composed of numerous adaption mechanisms that evolved over eons to address the special-purpose survival challenges of our human ancestors, does not easily accommodate the idea that humans may be able to generalize learned behaviors to novel situations. The implication seems to be that behavior sequences acquired through practice are capable of literal repetition, but that they would require conscious effort to change. This, in a nutshell, is the current IS portrayal of the concept of habit.

The upshot of the similarities is that evolutionary psychology could be co-opted into the study of continuing IS use without much consequence, if IS scholars were so inclined. Doing so could be seen as providing additional legitimacy to an existing line of research – as establishing an evolutionary (or even a biological) justification for current conceptualizations and research methods. Although plausible, that outcome would, we believe, be a narrow application of the theory. Therefore, we next consider how evolutionary psychology could be used to extend, and even to revolutionize, the existing stream of IS research.

3.2 Extension: A Springboard for Explanatory and Methodological Innovation

IS scholars could also adopt evolutionary psychology as a framework for research on post-adoption IT use in a way that, while not significantly altering the current theoretical paradigm, also adds considerable value by stretching the post-adoption theory beyond its current bounds. We see two primary ways this could happen. First, evolutionary psychology could be used to provide an explanation for the cognitive beliefs that are a fundamental concept in post-adoption theory. Second, evolutionary biology could provide a rationale for conceptualizing the influence of information technology per se (not just mental representations of IT, as in current post-adoption theorizing) on the formation of cognitive beliefs.

As discussed earlier, theorizing about post-adoption IT use rests upon the idea that IT users form cognitive beliefs, such as ease of use or perceived usefulness of a system, which in turn affect their intentions to continue using the system. Recently, scholars have argued for the need to identify the building blocks and antecedents of such cognitive beliefs (Benbasat and Barki 2007). Let us see by example how evolutionary psychology could fulfill such demands.

Poisonous animals and plants often show aposematic coloration – bright colors that are believed to have evolved to warn away potential predators (Lev-Yadun 2001; Terrick, Mumme, and Burghardt 1995). We might propose that ancestral humans who were better able to distinguish and pay attention to bright colors would have been more able to identify and avoid poisonous plants or animals, thus increasing their chances of survival. The "attention to bright colors" trait could, then, have spread to the majority of humans through the process of natural selection. (See Kock 2009, for a fuller discussion on the psychological trait "attention to color").

Nowadays, the trait "attention to bright colors" is not as critical for survival as it was during the Pleistocene era, but it may still have consequences for our inter- actions with the modern world. For example, since bright colors continue to elicit human attention, use of bright colors in the interface of a computer application could be expected to create arousal and draw attention away from the task at hand. Using such applications could tire people's eyes and minds, making it harder for them to concentrate, eventually forming a perceptual bias that leads to the construction of the belief that the brightly colored application (and others like it) is "hard to use."

Evolutionary explanations like this one can accomplish two benefits for research on post-adoption IT use. First, they can explain the origins of specific cognitive beliefs by reference to actual (not just perceived) characteristics of technology and to the biological characteristics of humans. Second, they suggest a methodology by which IS scholars can predict and test for likely human responses to various technological characteristics. Thus, evolutionary psychology could make a real contribution to the study of continuing IT use by extending prevailing theory and promoting methodological innovation. However, it is also possible for evolutionary thinking to lead to a profound reformulation of the current IS perspective on continuing IT use. We consider this possibility next.

3.3 Revolution: A Radical Departure from Current IS Theory

A third way in which IS scholars could adopt evolutionary psychology for the study of continuing IT use would be to undertake radical changes in current theorizing. We see two major opportunities for revolutionary change in IS theorizing enabled by *non-mainstream* aspects of the evolutionary paradigm. First, evolutionary logic could be used to reconceptualize the role of emotions in continuing IT use. Second, evolutionary arguments could be used to rethink the concept of habit.

3.3.1 Direct Effects of Emotion on Behavior

Although mainstream evolutionary psychologists view human emotions quite similarly to the way that many IS scholars do, evolutionary scholars who are more biologically oriented disagree. They cite empirical evidence for their belief that the emotional system is much older and more primitive than the cognitive system in the evolutionary timescale and thus in some ways more powerful and determinant of human behavior. If one accepts this view that emotion can sometimes override conscious cognitions and intentions, the implications for human behavior in general and for IT use in particular are obvious: Emotions can have a direct effect on behavior and can occasionally derail intended actions formed through careful cognitive evaluations of experience and even deeply held beliefs.

Such a view is clearly articulated in Mohr's (1996) "affect-object paradigm" (a theoretical synthesis of research from a wide range of disciplines, including brain physiology). In this paradigm, intention plays a small and indirect role in driving human behavior. Indeed, the starting point for Mohr's analysis was the observation of how frequently people behave differently from their conscious intentions. Mohr (1996, p. 71) posited a region of the brain "populated with neural representations of . . . objects [including material objects, concepts, thoughts, feelings, etc.] that are constantly in flux and are contenders for influence over behavior." People may be unaware of such objects, which become connected by rich webs of association. "Affect tags" are linked with every object as a result of learning or genetic programming, and the affect tags associated with an object can be updated through experience. Behavior is driven by the affect–object pair that has greatest valence or intensity for the individual at the very moment of behavior. Thus, the affect–object mechanism frequently overrides conscious intentions, even those formed moments before behavior (Mohr 1996) – a proposition that differs substantially from the role given to emotions in IS research.

Much research grounded in evolution supports Mohr's arguments about the role of emotion in behavior. As explained earlier, some scholars assert that the basic emotional circuits in our brain came into being much earlier in the evolutionary timescale than those that perform higher cognitive capabilities (Damasio et al. 2000; Panksepp 1998). Other scholars go further to claim that humans are more like other mammals at the affective level than we may like to believe: humans process emotional experiences using brain functions that are similar in all mammals (Panksepp and Panksepp 2000). It is in the higher cortico-cognitive layers that the human brain differs significantly from that of other animals (MacLean 1990). Not only are the psychological systems involved in the processing of emotions older in evolutionary terms and distinct from those involved in the processing of cognitions (although the two systems are related), but the emotional systems are also much more rapid in terms of processing time than cognitive ones are (Tomkins 1981; Zajonc 1980). This means that some affective "phenomena occur outside of and prior to consciously controlled thought" (Spielman et al. 1988, p. 297).

As proposed by Mohr (1996), emotional responses can drive behavior directly, without the intervention of higher cognitive processing. This is not to say that higher cognitive processing can never drive behavior. At the same time, research shows that the evolutionarily primitive emotional circuits are essential in shaping appropriate behavior. For example, neuroleptic drugs (antipsychotic drugs known to regulate affect and mediate between sensory inputs and action) can block emotions that result from certain behaviors (e.g., eating) and thus erase the usual motor responses associated with particular objects (e.g., food) (German 1982; Mueller 1984; Panksepp 1982a). Animals and humans whose amygdala have been removed and people with limbic system damage do not react to stimuli that would otherwise be meaningful to them (Aggleton and Mishkin 1986; Mishkin and Appenzeller 1987). Moreover, such individuals are unable to make simple decisions (Eslinger and Damasio 1985) and engage in effective behavior (Bechara et al. 2000).

A primary function of emotion, then, is the enhancement of important stimuli, which serves to prioritize human responses (Anderson and Phelps 2001). The presence of a strong emotion or affect represents a call for a response to which that emotion is relevant, thus derailing whatever goal was then being pursued (Carver and Scheier 1981). Even further, when people experience strong emotions, their brain's higher cortical regions (where higher cognitive capabilities are believed to lie) have a tendency to slow down (i.e., show lower activity) (Damasio et al. 2000; Fischer et al. 2000). In other words, in the presence of strong emotions, human behavior is driven primarily by emotions, not by higher cognitive processing. During such episodes, attention is driven toward the provoking stimuli; although the process is not necessarily conscious, actors' sensory organs are directed to take in the stimulus (Elfenbein 2007). This and other evidence, such as the mere exposure effect (Zajonc 1968, 1980), show that human behavior has a built-in bias to respond to emotions.

What does this imply about post-adoption IT use? Simply put, relatively stable cognitive beliefs and attitudes derived from prior expectations and experiences (e.g., Bajaj and Nidumolu 1998; Bhattacherjee 2001; Bhattacherjee and Premkumar 2004;

Karahanna et al. 1999) are *not* the only, or even the major, drivers of ongoing IT use behavior. Immediate experiences during IT use can provoke strong or even intense emotional reactions – such as the frustration associated with a system crash or the pleasure aroused while playing a computer game – and these emotions may override even the most carefully reasoned intentions and may direct subsequent behaviors (Ortiz de Guinea and Markus 2009).

Such emotional experiences may indeed result in updated expectations, cognitive beliefs, and attitudes, as mainstream IS post-adoption researchers argue. But we conclude that these mechanisms may not be as central in the explanation of IT use as most IS scholars believe. The evidence that emotion is a more basic driver of human behavior than conscious decision making and that emotional processing occurs largely outside of people's conscious awareness suggests that emotions might be key to explaining continuing IT use behaviors and that IT use behaviors may be more automatic and less consciously cognitive than current IS theorizing allows.

3.3.2 Unconscious Generalizations

Another way in which evolutionary theorizing could revolutionize IS research on post-adoption IT use is by provoking a rethinking of non-reflective behavior, generally referred to as habit. Habit is often understood as the unthinking performance of a well-learned and originally intentional behavioral sequence, without variation, in a stable context, triggered by environmental cues (Cheung and Limayen 2005; Kim and Malhotra 2005a; Kim et al. 2005; Limayem et al. 2003, 2007; Limayem and Hirt 2003). However, evolutionary theorizing and research suggest that the IS portrayal of non-reflective behavior could be limited and constraining in several ways.

As discussed earlier, the mainstream evolutionary psychology view of mind as consisting of a large number of specialized adaptations to specific survival problems has been criticized for its inability to deal effectively with learning, particularly the generalization of learned responses to new problems. Some evolutionary biologists and neuroscientists think of the mammalian brain as a more general-purpose system capable of producing a whole range of different survival-oriented behaviors (Panksepp 1982b, 1998; Robinson and Berridge 1993). Yet, it is not necessary to abandon the insights of evolutionary psychology entirely and to accept the "functionally agnostic," cognitive science, view that the brain is entirely a general-purpose computing machine. Indeed, a dual process theory was proposed by Geary (1995), with both highly specialized adaptive mechanisms for primary biological needs and general-purpose mechanisms that can be devoted to novel problems.

The important point of the evolutionary perspective is that the ability to learn and generalize is hardwired into the nervous system of mammals and necessarily requires neither conscious awareness nor intention for operation: the ability to generalize has even been observed in non-human animals (Anderson 2000; Henrich 2000). And, just as habit is said to be activated by environmental cues, some researchers believe that the brain is "capable of constructing goal-directed behavior patterns based on the confluence" of contextual contingencies (Panksepp and Panksepp 2000, p. 119). Furthermore, some believe that, among mammals, humans have the most "plastic" brain (Dennnett 1991; Gardner 1985). This evolved plasticity is believed to determine the capacity of humans to learn (Lieberman 2000; Pinker 1997). Put differently, not all learning occurs by means of conscious effort; the evolutionary heritage of humans is such that we may be able to apply learned goals and behaviors to new environments – such as new information technologies and new tasks – without necessarily employing the higher level mechanisms of conscious cognitive processing and intention formation.

How does this analysis apply to post-adoption IT usage? We agree with mainstream IS researchers on continuing IT use that much of the psychological literature on habit tends to emphasize the activation of well-learned behaviors in stable contexts. However, habit thus defined is a subset of automatic human behavior, and we believe that the study of continuing IT use could be broadened to address the whole spectrum of automaticity (Ortiz de Guinea and Markus 2009). Automatic behavior is defined as behavior that occurs (1) without intention, (2) without conscious awareness, and (3) without interfering with other mental activity (Posner 1978). Leading authorities on automaticity have explained automatic behavior as a result of the development of an association between the mental representations of goals and the features of certain situations in which the goal (not the behavior) was "repeatedly and consistently chosen and pursued in the past" (Bargh et al. 2001, p. 1015). Furthermore, the goal itself is not necessarily conscious: in experiments, subjects were easily primed with goals without their awareness or intention; later, in similar situations, the goal-related behavior was automatically activated. Bargh and Gollwitzer (1994) interpreted this result as "direct control over behavior by the environment" (p. 76). A key point here is that what is triggered by the environment is a set of goals and the means that have previously been developed to achieve those goals and not a behavioral sequence per se.

The goals activated in automatic behavior do not need to have been consciously intended by the individual. As Wood et al. (2002) put it, "people engaged in habitual actions do not consciously access habit intentions, either because they do not need to do so in order to repeat well-learned intentional responses or because the behavior was not intended to begin with and perhaps became well learned as a byproduct of some other action sequence" (p. 1283). Priming studies further support this point by showing that participants are able to form impressions of persons or things in the environment and to alter their behavior without becoming aware of such influence (Bargh and Fergusson 2000).

This research also suggests that, once goals have been activated by the environment, the automatically triggered behavior may differ from previously learned action sequences. That is, automatic behaviors do not need to follow exactly previously learned patterns, but can "operate autonomously in complex interaction with the environmental events – once they are in operation, conscious choices and guidance to completion are no longer necessary" (Bargh and Fergusson 2000, p. 933).

As a result, automatic sequences of actions do not need to be identical to behaviors that a person practiced in the past, but can represent "generalizations" – in which a behavior learned in one situation is transferred to new situations. As a result, it is possible for people, while operating automatically and not under the control of conscious intentions, to learn how to pursue old goals in new contexts. The standard psychological example is a child generalizing from buttoning a shirt to butting dresses, sweaters, and coats. The IT analogy might be generalizing from inputting, deleting, or saving in one application to performing those tasks in another application. It is even possible that users might be able, not only to learn how to apply known IT features in entirely new sequences and contexts but also to "learn" how to use entirely new IT features, through unconscious generalizations.

In short, insights from the evolutionary paradigm suggest a radical rethinking of the concept of habit as currently understood in IS research on post-adoption IT use. Whether or not the human brain is a general-purpose computing device, the capacity to learn is to some extent hardwired into the human system. At least after the acquisition of a certain level of skill at using an information technology, people may be able to invent new IT use behaviors to deal with novel circumstances without even having to think about it. Hypotheses such as this suggest important new research questions and methodologies that have the potential to revolutionize IS research on continuing IT use.

4 Discussion and Conclusion

We have shown how an evolutionary view can reinforce, extend, or revolutionize current theoretical and methodological traditions in IS research on post-adoption IT use. Use of evolutionary psychology could simply reinforce existing theories about the role of cognitive beliefs, attitudes, and conscious intentions in post-adoption IT use. Another possibility is that evolutionary psychology could suggest ways to significantly extend current approaches to the study of post-adoption IT use, for instance, by showing how objective IT characteristics can explain the origins of users' cognitive beliefs about IT. Third, IS scholars could mine evolutionary theorizing and research for insights that could revolutionize the study of post-adoption IT use. Two particularly promising directions involve reconceptualizing the role of emotion as having the potential to drive IT use behavior directly and reformulating ideas about habit to include other kinds of automatic behavior such as non-conscious behavioral generalizations across technologies and/or tasks.

Is it a problem for our field that evolutionary ideas could be applied to a single area of study in such different ways? Controversies such as the ones in evolutionary psychology are not uncommon in multidisciplinary fields, where large and diverse bodies of research must be scrutinized and, if possible, synthesized. Indeed, scientific eras characterized by disagreement can be extremely productive of innovative ideas and findings (Kuhn 1996).

In that spirit, we do not take a strong position here on which is the right course for our field to pursue with respect to the application of evolutionary psychology to the study of continuing IT use. We do believe it would be a conservative application if the IS field merely used evolutionary psychology to justify and reinforce the existing perspective and methods without any change. But we are agnostic about whether extension or revolution would produce better outcomes. Most likely, the field would benefit most by pursuing both approaches in tandem.

That said, we believe there are two keys to the productive application of evolutionary insights to the study of post-adoption IT use. The first should not require stating: IS scholars should exploit, not ignore or gloss, differences of definition, assumption, fact, or conclusion, and we should describe our ideas and propositions explicitly and in detail and differentiate them carefully from those of our peers. Only then will we collectively be able to assess the extent to which our results are cumulative or conflicting. This scientific discipline is core to our ability to progress as a field.

A second key is to examine the arguments and evidence with an open mind. For example, our previous discussion provides some support for the argument that continuing IT use may be best explained by cognitive (not necessarily conscious) processing of a special-purpose type. But it also supports the argument that continuing IT use may be driven as much by emotions as by cognitions (or more so), in a way that is inconsistent with the tenets of cognitive psychology. Support for the former proposition comes from founding evolutionary psychologists. Support for the latter comes from neuroscience and evolutionary neurobiology – fields that emphasize the study of the human brain (e.g., the organization of the neocortex). The IS field as a whole cannot afford to select one of the arguments and ignore the other. Nor should IS scholars simply try to combine them in integrated models without carefully analyzing their potential contradictions. Each of these arguments must be evaluated on its own terms as well as in relation to the other.

In short, we believe that evolutionary ideas have enormous potential to extend or even transform IS research on continuing IT use. We hope that our discussion of the contributions and controversies of evolutionary theorizing will motivate our colleagues to apply evolutionary ideas critically and creatively to the study of people's use of information technology after initial adoption.

Acknowledgments We gratefully acknowledge the developmental contributions of Carol Saunders to our earlier work and the constructive feedback of Ned Kock and the anonymous reviewers on this chapter.

References

Aggleton JP, Mishkin M (1986) The amygdala: sensory gateway to emotions. In: Plutchik R, Kellerman H (eds) Emotion: theory, research, and experience, vol 3. Academic Press, Orlando, pp 281–299
Anderson B (2000) The g factor in non-human animals. In: Bock GR, Goode JA, Webb K (eds) The nature of intelligence. Wiley, New York, pp 79–95
Anderson AK, Phelps EA (2001) Lesions of the human amygdala impair enhanced perceptions of emotionally salient events. Nature 411(6835):305–311

Atkinson AP, Wheeler M (2004) The grain of domains: the evolutionary-psychological case against domain-general cognition. Mind Lang 19(2):147–176

Bajaj A, Nidumolu SR (1998) A feedback model to understand information system usage. Inf Manage 33(4):213–224

Bargh JA, Fergusson MJ (2000) Beyond behaviorism: on the automaticity of higher mental processes. Psychol Bull 126(6):925–945

Bargh JA, Gollwitzer PM (1994) Environmental control of goal-directed action: automatic and strategic contingencies between situations and behavior. Nebr Symp Motiv 41:71–124

Bargh JA, Gollwitzer PM, Lee-Chai A, Barndollar K, Trötschel R (2001) The automated will: nonconscious activation and pursuit of behavioral goals. J Pers Soc Psychol 81(6):1014–1027

Barkow JH, Cosmides L, Tooby J (1992) The adapted mind: evolutionary psychology and the generation of culture. Oxford University Press, New York

Bechara A, Damasio H, Damasio AR (2000) Emotion, decision making and the orbitofrontal cortex. Cereb Cortex 10(3):295–307

Benbasat I, Barki H (2007) Quo vadis, TAM? J Association Inf Syst 8(4):211–218

Bhattacherjee A (2001) Understanding information systems continuance: an expectation-confirmation model. MIS Q 25(3):351–370

Bhattacherjee A, Premkumar G (2004) Understanding changes in belief and attitude toward information technology usage: a theoretical model and longitudinal test. MIS Q 28(2): 229–254

Bhattacherjee A, Sanford C (2006) Influence processes for information technology acceptance: an elaboration likelihood model. MIS Q 30(4):805–825

Buller DJ (2009) Evolution of the mind: 4 fallacies of psychology. Scientific American, January

Buss DM (2008) Evolutionary psychology: the new science of the mind, 3rd ed. Pearson Education Inc, Boston

Carver CS, Scheier MF (1981) Attention and self-regulation: a control-theory approach to human behavior. Springer-Verlag, New York

Cheung CMK, Limayen M (2005) The role of habit in information systems continuance: examining the evolving relationship between intention and usage. Proceedings of the twenty-sixth international conference on information systems, Las Vegas

Chiappe D, MacDonald K (2005) The evolution of domain-general mechanisms in intelligence and learning. J Gen Psychol 132(1):5–40

Cosmides L, Tooby J (1992) Cognitive adaptations for social exchange. In: Barkow JH, Cosmides L, Tooby J (eds) The adapted mind: evolutionary psychology and the generation of culture. Oxford University Press, New York, pp 163–228

Damasio AR, Grabowski TJ, Bechara A, Damasio H, Ponto LB, Parvizi J et al (2000) Subcortical and cortical brain activity during the feeling of self-generated emotions. Nat Neurosci 3(10):1049–1056

DaSilva P, Rachman SJ, Seligman MEP (1977) Prepared phobias and obsessions: therapeutic outcomes. Behav Res Ther 15(1):65–77

Davis FD (1989) Perceived usefulness, perceived ease of use, and user acceptance of information technology. MIS Q 13(3):319–340

Davis FD, Bagozzi RP, Warshaw PR (1989) User acceptance of computer technology: a comparison of two theoretical models. Manage Sci 35(8):982–1003

Dennnett DC (1991) Consciousness explained. Little, Brown and Company, Boston

Dunsworth HM (2007) Human origins 101. Greenwood Press, Westport

Elfenbein HA (2007) 7 Emotion in organizations. Acad Manag Ann 11(1):315–386

Eslinger PJ, Damasio AR (1985) Severe disturbance of higher cognition after bilateral frontal lobe ablation: Patient EVR. Neurology 35(12):1731–1741

Fischer H, Anderson JLR, Furmark T, Fredrikson M (2000) Fear conditioning and brain activity: a positron emission tomography study. Behav Neurosci 114(4):671–680

Fishbein M, Ajzen I (1975) Belief, attitude, intention, and behavior: an introduction to theory and research. Addison-Wesley, Reading

Foxall GR (2004) Context and cognition: interpreting complex behavior. Context Press, Reno

Gardner H (1985) The mind's new science. Basic Books, New York

Geary DC (1995) Reflections on evolution and culture in children's cognition: implications for mathematical development and instruction. Am Psychol 50(1):24–37

Gefen D (2003) TAM or just plain habit: a look at experienced online shoppers. J End User Comput 15(3):1–13

German DC (1982) Dopamine neurons, reward, and behavior. Behav Brain Sci 5(1):59–60

Hampton SJ (2004) The instinct debate and the standard social science model. Psychol Evol Gend 6(1):15–44

Henrich B (2000) Testing insight in ravens. In: Heyes C, Huber L (eds) The evolution of cognition. MIT Press, Cambridge, pp 289–305

Huxley JS (1942) Evolution: the modern synthesis. Allen & Unwin, London

Jasperson JS, Carter PE, Zmud RW (2005) A comprehensive conceptualization of post-adoptive behaviors associated with information technology enabled work systems. MIS Q 29(3): 525–557

Johnston RB, Waller V, Simon SK (2005) Situated information systems: supporting routine activity in organisations. Int J Bus Inf Syst 1(1/2):53–82

Karahanna E, Straub DW, Chervany NL (1999) Information technology adoption across time: a cross-sectional comparison of pre-adoption and post-adoption beliefs. MIS Q 23(2):183–213

Karahanna E, Agarwal R, Angst CM (2006) Reconceptualizing compatibility beliefs in technology acceptance research. MIS Q 30(4):781–804

Kim SS, Malhotra NK (2005a) A longitudinal model of continued IS use: an integrative view of four mechanisms underlying postadoption phenomena. Manage Sci 51(5):741–755

Kim SS, Malhotra NK (2005b) Predicting system usage from intention and past use: scale issues in the predictors. Decis Sci 36(1):187–196

Kim SS, Malhotra NK, Narasimham S (2005) Two competing perspectives on automatic use: a theoretical and empirical comparison. Inf Syst Res 16(4):418–432

Kim HW, Chan HC, Chan YP (2007) A balanced thinking-feelings model of information systems continuance. Int J Hum-Comput Stud 65(6):511–525

Kock N (2004) The psychobiological model: towards a new theory of computer-mediated communication based on Darwinian evolution. Organ Sci 15(3):327–348

Kock N (2009) Information systems theorizing based on evolutionary psychology: an interdisciplinary review and theory integration framework. MIS Q 33(2):395–418

Krill AL, Platek SM, Goetz AT, Shackelford TK (2007) Where evolutionary psychology meets cognitive neuroscience: a précis to evolutionary cognitive neuroscience. Evol Psychol 5(1):232–256

Kuhn TS (1996) The structure of scientific revolutions, 3rd ed. University of Chicago Press, Chicago

Lee C (1998) Alternatives to cognition: a new look at explaining human social behavior. Lawrence Erlbaum Associates Inc, Mahwah

Lev-Yadun S (2001) Aposematic (warning) coloration associated with thorns in higher plants. J Theor Biol 210(3):385–388

Levy N (2004) Evolutionary psychology, human universals, and the standard social science model. Biol Philosophy 19(3):459–472

Lieberman P (2000) Human language and our reptilian brain: the subcortical bases of speech, syntax, and thought. Harvard University Press, Cambridge

Limayem M, Hirt SG (2003) Force of habit and information systems usage: theory and initial validation. J Assoc Inf Syst 4(1):65–97

Limayem M, Cheung CMK, Chan GWW (2003) Explaining information systems adoption and post-adoption: toward an integrative model. Proceedings of the twenty-fourth international conference on information systems. Seattle, December

Limayem M, Hirt SG, Cheung CMK (2007) How habit limits the predictive power of intention: the case of IS continuance. MIS Q 31(4):705–737

MacLean PD (1990) The triune brain in evolution: role in paleocerebral functions. Plenum Press, New York

Markus ML, Silver MS (2008) A foundation for the study of IT effects: a new look at the DeSanctis and Poole's concepts of structural features and spirit. J Assoc Inf Syst 9(10/11):609–632

Mishkin M, Appenzeller T (1987) The anatomy of memory. Sci Am 256(6):80–89

Mohr LB (1996) The causes of human behavior: implications for theory and method in the social sciences. University of Michigan Press, Michigan

Mueller JS (1984) Neuroanatomic correlates of emotion. In: Temoshok L, Van Dyke C, Zegans LS (eds), Emotions in health and illness: theoretical and research foundations. Grune and Straton, New York

Ortiz de Guinea A, Markus ML (2009) Why break the habit of a lifetime? Rethinking the roles of intention, habit, and emotion in continuing information technology use. MIS Q 33(3):433–444

Panksepp J (1982a) The pleasure in brain substrates of foraging. Behav Brain Sci 5:71–72

Panksepp J (1982b) Toward a general psychobiological theory of emotions. Behav Brain Sci 5(3):407–467

Panksepp J (1998) Affective neuroscience: the foundations of human and animal emotion. Oxford University Press, New York

Panksepp J, Panksepp JB (2000) The seven sins of evolutionary psychology. Evol Cogn 6(2):108–131

Parrot WG, Schulkin J (1993) Neuropsychology and the cognitive nature of the emotions. Cogn Emot 7(1):43–59

Pinker S (1997) How the mind works. Norton & Company, New York

Platek SM, Keenan JP, Mohamed FB (2005) Sex differences in neural correlates of child facial resemblance: an event-related fMRI study. NeuroImage 25(4):1336–1344

Plotkin H (1998) Evolution in mind: an introduction to evolutionary psychology. Harvard University Press, Cambridge

Posner MI (1978) Chronometric explorations of mind. Erlbaum, Englewood Heights

Robinson TE, Berridge K (1993) The neural basis of drug craving: an incentive-sensitization theory of addiction. Brain Res Rev 18(3):247–291

Segestråle U (2000) Defenders of the truth: the sociobiology debate. Oxford University Press, Oxford

Smith EA, Mulder MB, Hill K (2001) Controversies in the evolutionary social sciences: a guide for the perplexed. Trends Ecol Evol 16(3):128–135

Spielman LA, Pratto F, Bargh JA (1988) Automatic affect. Am Behav Sci 31(3):296–310

Takahashi H, Matsuura M, Yahata N, Koeda M, Suhara T, Okubo Y (2000) Men and women show distinct brain activation during imagery of sexual and emotional infidelity. NeuroImage 32(3):1299–1307

Taylor S, Todd PA (1995) Understanding information technology usage: a test of competing models. Inf Syst Res 6(4):144–176

Terrick TD, Mumme RL, Burghardt GM (1995) Aposematic coloration enhances chemosensory recognition of noxious prey in the garter snake Thamnophis radix. Animal Behav 49(4):857–866

Tinbergen N (1951) The study of instinct. Oxford University Press, New York

Tomkins SS (1981) The quest for primary motives: biography and autobiography of an idea. J Pers Soc Psychol 41(2):306–329

Tooby J, Cosmides L (1992) The psychological foundation of culture. In: Barkow JH, Cosmides L, Tooby J (eds) The adapted mind: evolutionary psychology and the generation of culture. Oxford University Press, New York, pp 19–136

Tooby J, Cosmides L (2000) The evolutionary psychology of the emotions and their relationship to internal regulatory variables. In: Lewis M, Haviland-Jones J, Barrett FL (eds) Handbook of emotions. 3rd ed. Guilford Press, New York, pp 114–137

Tooby J, Cosmides L (2005) Conceptual foundations of evolutionary psychology. In: Buss DM (ed) The handbook of evolutionary psychology. Wiley, New York pp 5–67

Venkatesh V, Davis FD (2000) A theoretical extension of the technology acceptance model: four longitudinal field studies. Manage Sci 45(2):186–204

Venkatesh V, Brown SA, Maruping LM, Bala H (2008) Predicting different conceptualizations of system use: the competing roles of behavioral intention, facilitating conditions, and behavioral expectation. MIS Q 33(3):483–502

Venkatesh V, Morris MG, Davis FD (2003) User acceptance of information technology: toward a unified view. MIS Q 27(3):425–478

Waller V, Johnston RB, Milton S (2006) An action-centred approach to conceptualising information support for routine work. Proceedings of the 6th information systems foundations workshop. Australian National University, Canberra

Wood W, Quinn JM, Kashy DA (2002) Habits in everyday life: thought, emotion, and action. J Pers Soc Psychol 83(6):1281–1297

Zajonc RB (1968) Attitudinal effects of mere exposure. J Pers Soc Psychol 9(2):1–27

Zajonc RB (1980) Feeling and thinking: preferences need no inferences. Am Psychol 25(2): 151–175

Chapter 4
The Behavioral Ecology of Human Foraging in an Online Environment: Of Omnivores, Informavores, and Hunter–Gatherers

Donald A. Hantula

Abstract The basic decision rules by which we live were shaped by natural selection. Among the most fundamental problems to be solved for humans, or any other creature, is the problem of finding, securing, and using resources; or in more general terms, foraging. Foraging is the naturally selected way in which we manage patchy and stochastic environments. In the behavioral ecology literature, foraging theory is a well-developed set of theoretical propositions and empirical models that address common questions about decision rules for predators. To introduce foraging theory and its relevance for behavior in technologically rich environments, basic concepts such as marginal value theorem, matching, and delay discounting are introduced. Just as we foraged on the savannas, we now forage online. Two independent streams of research on online foraging "the behavioral ecology of consumption" and "information foraging" have delineated foraging functions in an online environment over the past decade. This chapter reviews the respective work in each research stream and summarizes the current state of knowledge in modern human foraging.

Keywords Behavioral ecology · Foraging theory · Matching · Delay discounting · Behavioral ecology of consumption · Information foraging

1 Introduction

We are problem solvers, decision makers, hunter–gatherers. The basic decision rules by which we live were shaped by natural selection. Among the most fundamental problems to be solved for humans, or any other sentient creature, is the problem of finding, securing, and using resources, or in more general terms, foraging. In the

D.A. Hantula (✉)
Department of Psychology, Temple University, Weiss Hall (265-67), Philadelphia, PA 19122, USA
e-mail: hantula@temple.edu

N. Kock (ed.), *Evolutionary Psychology and Information Systems Research*,
Integrated Series in Information Systems 24, DOI 10.1007/978-1-4419-6139-6_4,

behavioral ecology literature, "foraging" is a rubric encapsulating a variety of theoretical propositions and empirical models that address common questions about decision rules for predators (Stephens and Krebs 1986). However foraging is not limited solely to decisions about prey items per se but rather is a general-purpose set of rules and strategies for adapting to environmental risk and uncertainty, yielding both prey items and information (Stephens et al. 2007). Foraging is not constrained to our ancestral environments; it is the naturally selected way in which we manage any patchy and stochastic environment, even today. Just as we once foraged on the savannas, we now forage online. Two independent streams of research on online foraging the behavioral ecology of consumption (Hantula et al. 2001) and information foraging (Pirolli and Card 1999) have delineated foraging functions in technologically rich environments over the past decade. This chapter reviews the respective work in each research stream, summarizes the current state of knowledge and provides suggestions for future research in online foraging.

Behavioral ecology is the organizing framework for this review. Behavioral ecology adopts a deterministic, selectionist stance, as does evolutionary psychology, but the behavioral ecology approach differs from the evolutionary psychology approach in fundamentally important ways (Smith 2000; White et al. 2007). Behavioral ecology focuses on links between ecological factors and adaptive behavior, or the question of what environmental factors select for or against a behavior. It is concerned with modeling as a research strategy and decision rules as an outcome of investigations. Evolutionary psychology, in contrast, often focuses on presumed mechanisms that underlie psychological phenomena, positing evolved "mental modules" as its chief explanatory device (however, some evolutionary psychologists question the "massive modularity" position; e.g., Miller 2000). It is concerned with survey and one-shot experiments as a research strategy and specialized cognitive mechanisms for very specific adaptive outcomes.

2 Foraging Is a Biobasic Behavior

The famous "4Fs" (feeding, fighting, fleeing, and fornicating) are the basic components of fitness in an evolutionary sense, with the first three directed toward survival so that the organism has a chance to engage in the fourth. Perhaps "feeding" should be changed to "foraging" in this quadruplet; foraging includes but encompasses more than feeding. All organisms seek out goods in their environments such as food, nesting materials, and rudimentary tools. Some organisms even seek out gift items, as gift giving occurs across a wide spectrum of species (Jonason et al. 2009). Hills (2006) summarizes current neuroscience evidence showing that dopaminergic activity is involved in both area-restricted foraging as well as goal-directed thought in human beings. Foraging yields more than material resources or food. Foraging also yields rich information about the forager's environment, including distance between patches, prey density, and presence of other foragers or predators (the term "patch" refers to any bounded spatial or temporal co-location of prey items). Hence, foraging is the common mechanism for finding goods and information about important goods in stochastic and uncertain environments.

3 Foraging Research

Research in foraging cuts across disciplines such as anthropology, biology, computer science, library science, marketing, and psychology. Some of these investigations are qualitative studies in the anthropological tradition, focusing on food foraging with indigenous peoples in field (e.g., Smith 2000) and in library science (Sandstrom 1994) describing how library researchers search for scientific literature. Quantitative work in foraging spans species from wasps to humans and disciplines such as behavioral ecology (e.g., Stephens et al. 2007), operant psychology (e.g., Fantino 1985; Fantino and Abarca 1985), cognitive psychology (e.g., Rode, Cosmides et al. 1999), information systems (e.g., Pirolli 2007), and consumer psychology (e.g., Foxall and James 2003).

4 Foraging Theory

Foraging theory is a descriptive and inductive framework. Its fundamental assumption is that foraging is not a random action, but rather is a strategic behavior. Researchers have built elegant mathematical models of forager decision making that have occasioned much laboratory and field research. The resulting data strengthened the field to the point that the cutting edge of foraging theory is comparison of quantitative models. Foraging is explicitly viewed as a behavior distributed across time; therefore, temporal components are important in its models. All foraging models presuppose that the forager has a finite amount of energy that must support basic metabolic activities, foraging, and other behaviors throughout the day. Further, the forager is attempting to maximize energy intake per unit time or energy expenditure, within certain constraints. The major variables in foraging models are probability (e.g., of prey encounter, capture), delay (in patch travel, to consume prey), and cost (e.g., to procure or consume). Foraging models are classified as prey or patch models. Prey models concern the decision to capture or not capture a prey item; patch models concern the decision to stay in a patch or leave it.

Foraging theory delineates three major phases of foraging, namely searching, handling, and consumption (Stephens and Krebs 1986). In foraging theory, searching describes the time and energy devoted to finding patches and prey items and handling denotes time and energy devoted to a prey item after it has already been acquired or captured and before any energy can be derived from it. For organisms that exploit patches, this might involve cracking the shell of a seed or a nut; for predators, this might involve transporting a prey item to a safe location and cleaning it before consumption. It is important to note that handling does not guarantee consumption; the prey item may be abandoned or lost during handling. A nut or other food item may be dropped or discarded during shelling; a prey animal may escape a carnivore after a capture response is emitted.

Foraging theorists recognize two major assumptions about any foraging species that must be considered. The first is a currency assumption. It is assumed that all foragers "spend" energy and time as a currency in foraging. Foragers may also spend energy and time for other "commodities" such as basic somatic functions, grooming, avoiding predation, nesting, and mating. Foragers also "earn" currency in the form of energy. The particular form of currency varies according to the forager's species; for example, meat would not be a form of currency for a herbivore. The second assumption is a constraint assumption. All foragers have limitations that constrain their ability to forage, and a successful forager is one that works within their constraints. Constraints are generally conceptualized as interactions between the forager and its environment; the forager's phylogenetic endowments dictate their capabilities, while the environment limits the availability of prey and information. This interactionist idea is important in understanding foraging; for example, although there may be an abundance of prey in a patch, if the prey is out of the forager's reach, or too fast for the forager, the prey is functionally non-existent.

It should be clear from the foregoing discussion that modern foraging theory takes the concept of foraging a few steps further, casting foraging not as much as an issue of feeding per se but one of a more general adaptation to uncertainty. Given the stochastic nature of the foraging environment, uncertainty pervades. The successful forager is the forager that can not only consume calories but also can glean information from the environment and make choices. Indeed, "foraging" may probably be best understood as the naturally selected way in which any sentient organism navigates the rocky shoals of a constantly risky, patchy, and equivocal environment. This conceptual focus is also a good example of the difference between the behavioral ecology approach taken in this chapter and the more common evolutionary psychology approach. Rather than positing several "modules" for feeding, information, risk, and decision making as is done in evolutionary psychology, a behavioral ecology approach works inductively from environmental constraints to identify a more general constellation of adaptive behavior. Given that risk and uncertainty are ubiquitous in the natural environment, it is more efficient or economical from an evolutionary perspective to have a flexible and adaptable means for managing uncertainty than to have many modules for the different components of foraging.

5 Foragers Are Financiers

A particularly straightforward way to understand foraging theory is to view foragers as finned, feathered, and furry financiers. The maximization assumptions and temporal perspective in foraging theory portray foraging as an economic system, or a system of exchange between the forager and the environment. At the beginning of each day (for a diurnal forager), the forager invests time and energy in foraging activities and must turn a profit – that is take in more energy than is expended. If the forager turns a sufficient profit, it may then have the time and energy to engage in other behaviors such as grooming, socializing, and perhaps even mating. If the forager does not turn a profit, it may be able to survive until the next day, but if it is running too large an energy deficit, it may perish by nightfall. Although energy is fungible (to a point), time is not. For a forager, time is a continually decreasing resource that cannot be replenished. If it is assumed that a forager is attempting to maximize energy intake per unit time, the temporal dimensions of a decision will be more important than any potential energy intake. This becomes especially important as nightfall approaches and foraging time draws to a close. The forager who has the good fortune of an energy surplus will become increasingly risk averse, preferring low variance prey items over those with a higher variance. Conversely, the forager running an energy deficit will become increasingly risk-seeking, choosing higher variance prey items over low variance prey items and displaying "go for broke" choices (Stephens and Charnov 1982).

6 Marginal Value Theorem

The marginal value theorem (Charnov 1976) occupies a central place in foraging theory. According to the marginal value theorem, all prey occur in a patch. When a forager is in a patch, it balances the yield of that patch against the yield of other available patches if the forager were to leave the patch and move to another patch. The first important insight from the marginal value theorem is that foragers do not find a patch, exploit it, and remain in the patch until all prey are depleted. Rather foragers will "leave some money on the table" and depart a patch when the rate of return in the patch falls below the average rate of return available from other patches in the environment. The second important insight is that the travel time between patches is a critical variable in determining how long a forager will remain in a depleting patch. The longer the travel time is, the longer the forager will endure a scarce and spotty patch. As shown in Fig. 4.1, the value of any patch or prey item is not an intrinsic property of that patch or prey item but is a relativistic assessment in the dynamic context of the patch, the prey item, the depletion rate, and the travel time.

7 Matching

The marginal value theorem has proven very useful in understanding many different aspects of foraging (Stephens et al. 2007). However, it begs an important question: how does the forager "know" or come to know the average rate of return provided by patches in the environment? The answer comes from a venerable stream of operant psychology research on the matching law (Herrnstein 1961, 1970). Simply stated, the matching law holds that in any choice situation, behavior will be distributed

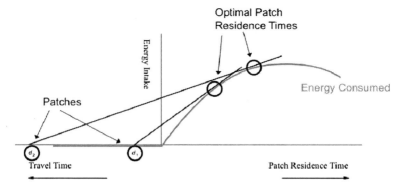

Fig. 4.1 The marginal value theorem (redrawn from Charnov 1976). The abscissa represents time. The left side of the figure shows travel times to two different patches (d_1 and d_2), while the right side of the figure shows patch residence time. The ordinate represents energy intake, depicted by the curve on the right side

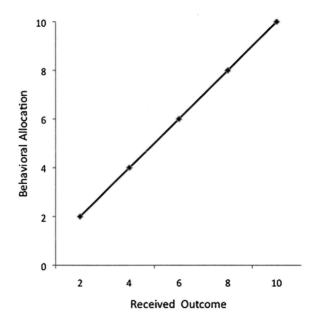

Fig. 4.2 Illustration of the functional relation between behavioral allocation and received outcome in matching. Note that the abscissa and the ordinate are arbitrary units

between alternatives in a rough (or sometimes fairly close) "match" to their relative rates of return. Foragers will allocate their behavior among options in proportion to the outcomes obtained as shown in Fig. 4.2. Matching is ubiquitous; nearly all sentient species match (Davison and McCarthy 1988; Herrnstein et al. 1997), and evidence now suggests that matching is not a learned behavior, but rather is innate (Gallistel et al. 2007). Matching shares an important feature with the marginal value theorem: the prediction that a forager will not deplete a patch entirely before leaving (or maximize) but rather will depart a patch before depletion or engage in patch sampling. Matching and the resulting patch sampling guarantees that the forager will contact other patches in the environment over time, thus is the mechanism by which the organism comes to "know" the average rate of return in the environment. Although matching may appear to be sub-optimal at first glance, a more nuanced look at matching in terms of overall fitness tells a different story. Sakai and Fukai (2008) have shown that matching is a long-term optimal strategy. Further, in a stochastic and scarce environment, patches may disappear without warning, and prey items in patches may deplete quickly due to exogenous factors such as competing foragers or environmental changes. The forager who stayed exclusively in a "rich" patch (or a maximizer) would be at an incredible survival disadvantage if that patch were to vanish. However, the forager that matches will most likely have a ready alternative.

8 Delay Discounting

Matching is the naturally selected, innate, long-term optimal choice strategy for foragers. A next step is to ask whether there is a particular decision rule that would produce matching. Such a decision rule would have to be as ever-present as matching and would most likely appear to be sub-optimal at first glance. Delay (or temporal) discounting is the mechanism by which matching occurs. For any forager, the value of a prey item is a decreasing function of delay to that prey item, or in common parlance, a dollar today is worth more than a dollar tomorrow. The fact that value is a function of delay is not controversial; however, the shape of the discount function is. Classical economic and rational choice theories hold that such a discount function would be exponential as shown in the following equation:

$$V = Ae^{-rD} \tag{4.1}$$

where V represents the time-discounted value of the outcome, A is the non-time-discounted value of the outcome, e is the base of the natural logarithm, and D is the delay between a choice response and the outcome. However, much research has now clearly established that the discount function is in fact hyperbolic (Ainslie and Haslam 1992; Green and Myerson 2004; Rachlin 2006; Smith and Hantula 2008) as shown in the following equation:

$$V = A/(1 + kD) \tag{4.2}$$

where V is the value of the delayed outcome, A is the non-time-discounted amount of the outcome, D is the intertemporal delay between choice and outcome, and k is an index of sensitivity to delay.

Hyperbolic discounting differs from exponential discounting in many important ways. First and most important is the shape of the discount curve. A hyperbolic discount curve is more steeply bowed than an exponential curve with a rapid decrement in value as a function of time at the beginning of the curve and a gradual decrease afterward. Second, while exponential curves are parallel across time, hyperbolic curves will cross, predicting preference reversals. Third, like matching, hyperbolic discount curves are found across species; exponential discount curves are not normally found. The hyperbolic curve's steep discount function yields a very strong preference for the immediate and a diminished preference for the delayed. Essentially, the forager chooses the most valuable outcome on a moment-by-moment basis in a process called momentary maximizing. This seeming over-sensitivity to, and preference for, immediate outcomes leads to matching (Shimp 1966).

8.1 Human Foraging in an Online Environment: Behavioral Ecology of Consumption

Online shopping is a natural modern-day analogue to foraging in the savannah or the arboreal environment. In an online shopping environment, consumer items are prey, stores are patches, travel time between patches is a function of connection speed, system speed, and other delays involving leaving an online store and entering another one. This functional similarity between foraging and online shopping is the basis for a research program called the behavioral ecology of consumption (Hantula, et al. 2001) that applies foraging theory to modern human shopping choices. The behavioral ecology of consumption assumes that the multiple phases of foraging activities, including searching, choosing between alternatives, and handling, as described by Lea (1979) are mirrored in human consumption decisions. It also assumes that consumption behaviors emerge because of their adaptive characteristics, consistent with evolutionary theory.

The first studies in the research program used a microworld-simulated (DiFonzo et al. 1998) online music mall to study delay discounting and its effects on store visits, purchasing, and satisfaction. Participants shopped for CDs among five virtual stores. CD prices varied but were equivalent across stores as was selection and "travel time" between stores. The primary independent variable was delay to feedback indicating whether or not a desired CD was in stock. In-stock probability was constant at 0.80.

In a two-phase experiment by Rajala and Hantula (2000), eight participants shopped in the virtual mall in which the delay to in-/out-of-stock feedback in a store was either 0.5, 2, 4, 8, or 16 s. In the first phase of the experiment, there was minimal travel time between stores (leaving one store and entering another), but in the second phase, participants had to engage in additional mouse clicks to leave a store and enter another, increasing travel time (known as a change over delay or COD in operant psychology parlance). Purchase data were fit to the hypothesized hyperbolic function. Overall, the increase in travel time increased the fit from $r^2 = 0.30$ to 0.41. Closer analysis of individual data revealed that of the eight participants, four discounted nearly exactly as predicted ($r^2 = 0.91$), while the other four evidenced a nearly flat function across delay times, indicating little to no sensitivity to the delay manipulation.

Adult humans in post-industrial societies have poor time perception (Smythe and Goldstone 1957), especially when compared to non-human animals. Clocks, watches, and other external timing devices have obviated the need to learn the nuances of time passage. Consequently, DiClemente and Hantula (2003) hypothesized that placing a clock on the screen would increase time sensitivity and accordingly make participants' choices closer to the hyperbolic model. In a systematic replication and extension of Phase 2 of Rajala and Hantula (2000), a control group repeated the conditions in Rajala and Hantula, while a second had an ascending "time-on-line" clock placed on the screen and a third had a descending clock on the screen. The control group's purchase data replicated the previous study, while the ascending and descending clock groups showed strong ($r^2 > 0.90$) fits to a hyperbolic function, with the ascending clock group showing the best fit. Customer satisfaction data collected at the end of the experiment showed that in all conditions, satisfaction was significantly negatively correlated with delay value.

Replications are rare in behavioral sciences in general, but it is a central feature of scientific research and it is especially important in the present case where establishing stable quantitative relationships between variables is at issue. DiClemente and Hantula (2003) used the same delay values as Rajala and Hantula (2000) and while these two studies are part of a systematic research program and used different participants, it is possible that the delay values used in and of themselves may have contributed to artifactual results. That is, the results may have been idiosyncratic to the delay values used. The experimental artifact has been long recognized as a critical issue in research methodology in behavioral research with humans (Strohmetz 2006). Replication, especially systematic replication using varying participants and parameters, is the most basic control for artifacts.

Accordingly, Hantula et al. (2008) conducted a systematic replication of the ascending clock condition of DiClemente and Hantula (2003) but doubled the delay values to 2, 4, 8, 16, 32 s and used a participant population of experienced online shoppers. This study also delved deeper into foraging theory by analyzing the amount of time spent in each store as patch residence. The purchase data again showed a strong fit to the hyperbolic function ($r^2 = 0.96$), as did the patch residence (time spent in each store) data ($r^2 = 0.85$). These data demonstrate that delay discounting online is not an artifactual function of participants or delay parameters.

Figure 4.3 shows the purchase data interpolated from the ascending clock condition of DiClemente and Hantula (2003) and Hantula et al. (2008). Delay values on the abscissa are normalized logarithmic values. The obtained hyperbolic curves are clearly evident, but the two points of origin differ by almost 50%. The store with the shortest delay accounted for nearly three-quarters of the purchases in DiClemente and Hantula's data, whereas the store with the shortest delay accounted for slightly more than half of the purchases in Hantula et al.'s data. The shortest delay value in DiClemente and Hantula was 0.5 s, while the shortest delay value in Hantula et al.

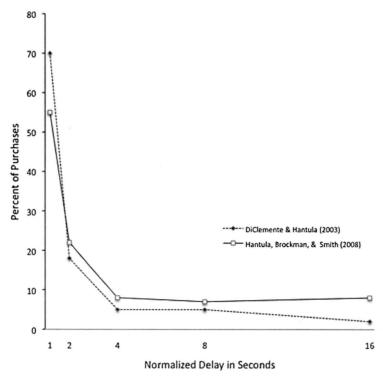

Fig. 4.3 Interpolated purchase data with normalized delay values on the ordinate from DiClemente and Hantula (2003) and Hantula et al. (2008)

was 2 s. All delays and values are evaluated relative to one another in matching, as is evident in these data. Consistent with Mazur's (1984; 1986) equivalence rule for valuing delayed outcomes, it appears that the extremely short delay value of 0.5 s exerts heightened control over behavior in these studies. These results are also consistent with those from other e-commerce (Rose et al. 2005) and human–computer interaction studies (Szameitat et al. 2009) showing that in general, people who are accustomed to working with broadband systems find delays of only a few seconds very aversive.

Energy is the classic currency in foraging theory. However, humans in post-industrial societies are not as concerned with energy intake and outflow as they are with money intake and outflow. For humans, monetary budgets are accumulated through time allocated to labor in exchange for wages. In foraging, animal energy budgets are accumulated through foraging activities, and total accumulated energy is analogous to cash accrual. In both cases, the accumulation of resources represents somatic effort on the part of the individual organism. Foraging theory contends that an alternative offering the most favorable E/T (energy per unit time) ratio should be selected, underscoring the importance of temporal values in assessing the economic efficiency of foraging models. Each temporal phase commands some portion of the total foraging time associated with acquiring that prey item, but may also be seen as contributing to delay to reinforcement and lessening the E/T ratio. Though no literal food foraging occurs in post-industrial human society (despite its persistence in non-industrialized human groups), commodity acquisition may still be modeled in successive temporal phases after the manner of animal models (DiClemente and Hantula 2003; Rajala and Hantula 2000; Hantula et al. 2008).

A major temporal component of human commodity acquisition is comprised of working for tokens, or monetary accrual. Before any consequences are experienced, tokens must be accumulated and exchanged. Thus, the cost of a commodity may be regarded as a component of the total foraging time associated with a particular prey item (commodity) (Fantino 1985; Fantino and Abarca 1985) because its purchase represents an exchange for temporally extended responding on some type of monetary pay schedule. In literal terms, the time spent working for money is a phase of foraging, analogous to the handling phase described by (Lea 1979). Framed in this way, the effects of price on preference should conform to the same hyperbolic discount function as delay. Smith and Hantula (2003) varied CD prices in each store systematically such that the mean CD price increased by \$2 between stores. The mean price for the lowest priced store was \$9.99; the mean price for the most expensive store was \$17.99. CD prices in each store were drawn pseudo-randomly within a \$4 range around the mean values using the Goltz and Northey (1998) algorithm. In-stock probability was constant among stores at 0.80 as was delay to in-stock feedback at 0.5 seconds. Purchase data fit the hyperbolic decay function well ($r^2 = 0.89$). In a very real sense, time is money.

Consistent with foraging theory and matching, the patch residence time data showed that patch sampling occurred in all of the behavioral ecology of consumption online shopping studies. Adapting the foraging environment to account for organismic constraints (poor time perception) in DiClemente and Hantula (2003) and extending the temporal discounting model to include money, a more appropriate currency, in Smith and Hantula (2003) illustrates how these basic assumptions of foraging theory derived from research on non-human animals in natural environments map on to the behavior of adult humans in complex, technologically rich environments. We are, as Kock (2001) notes, the ape who used e-mail – as well as e-commerce.

9 Human Foraging in an Online Environment: Information Foraging

Sandstrom (1994) described the functional similarity between foragers and humans searching for information in a reference library. Similarly, Pirolli (2005, 2006, 2007) noted the functional similarity between foragers and humans seeking information on the Internet. Pirolli and Card's (1999) information foraging theory holds that information is a resource like any other and that humans searching for information in an online environment do so in a way that follows from foraging. Specifically, humans attempt to optimize the utility of the information gained relative to the cost of obtaining it; just as foraging theory assumes overall maximization of E/T, information theory assumes maximization of I/T (information per unit time).

In keeping with the methodology in much human foraging research in the anthropology literature, Pirolli and Card (1999) conducted qualitative studies of a technology analyst gathering information for writing a business intelligence newsletter and MBA students seeking information to prepare a strategic management analysis of a food and beverage company. Employing the concept of "information diet," Pirolli and Card found that in both cases, researchers did not use or consume every piece of information encountered; much like an arboreal forager does not capture and consume every prey item encountered. Instead the researchers discarded much of the information, even relevant information, after a quick scan, opting for short reports that contained much information for its size and rejecting larger but potentially more information-rich reports, maximizing I/T.

An important component of information foraging theory is the SNIF-ACT model (Fu and Pirolli 2007). According to the SNIF-ACT model, people use "information scents" to determine which links to follow and use the mean information scent value to determine whether to stay on a particular Web site (information patch) or to travel to another Web site, similar to foragers in the physical environment. Note that in this context, "scent" does not refer to actual olfactory stimulation, but rather to traces of information or abbreviated representation of content (such as a link on a webpage) that may lead to more information of interest. Using data from logs of two tasks employed in usability studies (searching for information in Yahoo Help and searching information in ParcWeb, an intranet), Fu and Pirolli found that their SNIF-ACT 2.0 model fit the data well ($r^2 = 0.69$ and 0.91 for the two different tasks).

We are informavores from the perspective of information foraging theory. As informavores, our online behavior is also subject to constraints. Fu and Pirolli (2007) identified the physical placement of a link on a webpage as an important constraint. Humans appear to be more attracted to links placed nearer to the top of a page than nearer to the bottom, regardless of information utility. Information is the currency in an online environment for informavores. In contrast to physical foraging, somatic effort and energy expenditure are negligible; instead time is the important expenditure. Informavores seek to maximize I/T; so the information richness of a particular site or an article is constantly balanced against the time it takes to read and process that information.

10 Conclusions

The idea that a researcher working in a modern technologically advanced building and a pigeon looking for food outside the office window would have much in common besides being carbon-based life forms is incredulous to many. Further, the supposition that this researcher and this pigeon may be using the same fundamental processes to solve the same basic problems at the same time would seem dubious at best. However, this is what behavioral ecology and foraging theory tell us – the business of balancing risk and return while securing the things we need differs only in structure, not function between species.

A behavioral ecology perspective asks us to question assumptions about the nature of human decision making and provides insights into new answers, telling us to look outside in the environment, not inside the organism to determine how and why decisions are made; it is an ecological account, not a mediational account of behavior. The features of the environment that may select for or against particular decision or decision strategies are what are important.

Further, a behavioral ecology account supplies logical explanations for seemingly "irrational" behavior. Take, for example, matching. Matching is an innate long-term survival decision strategy that in the short term may appear sub-optimal. One implication of matching for online (or any) marketers is that consumers will not engage in brand loyalty nor will they always buy the least expensive product. Rather than assuming that consumers are fickle al la Stigler and Becker (1977), it may be more profitable to understand that consumers are adaptive and to analyze their behavior from that perspective. Consumers will stray from "choice" brands and stores; patch sampling is not a function of capriciousness but one of natural selection.

Time is critical in a behavioral ecology account of decision making. Whether in the more general E/T case or the more specific I/T case, the temporal dimension of foraging is more than simply a denominator; it is a primary determinant of choice. Taking time seriously also questions the "irrationality" of some choices. The hyperbolic discounting function that gives rise to matching (over-valuing the immediate over the future) is often referred to in unduly pejorative terms such as "impetuosity" or "impulsiveness" (Smith and Hantula 2008). However, individuals who discount steeply are more successful in competitive group foraging situations (Critchfield and Atteberry 2003), and such steep discounting may also be associated with entrepreneurial success (Hantula 2006). Delay determines value. Information foragers will reject potentially rich but lengthy reports in favor of shorter but less rich reports Pirolli and Card 1999). Online delays decrease customer satisfaction (Rose et al. 2005). Further, in an online instructional environment, delays degrade learning (Davis and Hantula 2001). For a forager, delay is not simply vexing – delay is deadly.

11 Different Species, Same Choices

Kock's (2001, 2004) evolutionary-based psychobiological model of computer-based communications and extensions to virtual teamwork (DeRosa et al. 2004) have enriched IT research. Behavioral ecology and foraging theory applied to technology complements the communication work, tying more of our online behavior to basic naturally selected processes. It is now clear that new theories are not needed to understand new technology, but rather newer understanding of the wisdom of older theories is what is necessary. Darwin never used a word processor, but his text remains relevant to those of us who do.

References

Ainslie G, Haslam N (1992) Hyperbolic discounting. In: Loewenstein G, Elster J (eds) Choice over time. Russell Sage Foundation, New York, pp 57–92

Charnov EL (1976) Optimal foraging, the marginal value theorem. Theor Popul Biol 9(2):129–136

Critchfield T, Atteberry T (2003) Temporal discounting predicts individual competitive success in a human analogue of group foraging. Behav Process 64(3):315–331

Davis E, Hantula D (2001) The effects of download delay on performance and end-user satisfaction in an Internet tutorial. Comput Hum Behav 17(3):249–268

Davison M, McCarthy D (1988) The matching law: a research review. Lawrence Erlbaum Associates, Inc., Hillsdale

DeRosa DM, Hantula DA, Kock NF, D'Arcy J (2004) Trust and leadership in virtual teamwork: a media naturalness perspective. Hum Resour Manage 43(2/3):219–232

DiClemente D, Hantula D (2003) Optimal foraging online; increasing sensitivity to delay. Psychol Mark 20(9):785–809

DiFonzo N, Hantula DA, Bordia P (1998) Microworlds for experimental research: having your (control and collection) cake and realism too. Behav Res Methods Instrum Comput 30(2):278–286

Fantino E (1985) Behavior analysis and behavioral ecology: a synergistic coupling. Behav Anal 8(2): 151–157

Fantino E, Abarca N (1985) Choice, optimal foraging, and the delay-reduction hypothesis. Behav Brain Sci 8(2):315–330

Foxall G, James V (2003) The behavioral ecology of brand choice: how and what do consumers maximize? Psychol Mark 20(9):811–836

Fu W, Pirolli P (2007) SNIF-ACT: a cognitive model of user navigation on the World Wide Web. Hum Comput Interact 22(4):355–412

Gallistel C, King A, Gottlieb D, Balci F, Papachristos E, Szalecki M, Carbone KS (2007) Is matching innate? J Exp Anal Behav 87(2):161–199

Goltz SM, Northey JE (1998) Simulating the variability of actual outcomes. Behav Res Methods Instrum Comput 30(4):680–689

Green L, Myerson J (2004) A discounting framework for choice with delayed and probabilistic rewards. Psychol Bull 130(5):769–792

Hantula D (2006) Review of 'copy this! lessons from a hyperactive dyslexic who turned a right idea into one of America's best companies'. J Organ Behav Manage 26(3):79–85

Hantula D, Brockman D, Smith C (2008) Online shopping as foraging: the effects of increasing delays on purchasing and patch residence. IEEE Trans Prof Commun 51(2):147–154

Hantula D, DiClemente DF, Rajala AK (2001) Outside the box: the analysis of consumer behavior. In: Hayes L, Austin J, Houmanfar R, Clayton M (eds) Organizational change. Context Press, Reno, pp 203–223

Herrnstein R (1961) Relative and absolute strength of response as a function of frequency of reinforcement. J Exp Anal Behav 4 (3):267–272

Herrnstein R (1970) On the law of effect. J Exp Anal Behav 13(2):243–266

Herrnstein R, Rachlin H, Laibson D (1997) The matching law: papers in psychology and economics. Russell Sage Foundation, Cambridge

Hills T (2006) Animal foraging and the evolution of goal-directed cognition. Cogn Sci Multidiscip J 30(1):3–41

Jonason P, Cetrulo J, Madrid J, Morrison C (2009) Gift-giving as a courtship or mate-retention tactic? Insights from non-human models. Evol Psychol 7(1):89–103

Kock N (2001) The ape that used email: understanding e-communication behavior through evolution theory. Commun AIS 5(A.3):1–29

Kock N (2004) The psychobiological model: towards a new theory of computer-mediated communication based on Darwinian evolution. Organ Sci 15(3):327–348

Lea SEG (1979) Foraging and reinforcement schedules in the pigeon: optimal and non-optimal aspects of choice. Anim Behav 27(3):875–886

Mazur JE (1984) Tests of an equivalence rule for fixed and variable reinforcer delays. J Exp Psychol Anim Behav Process 10(4):426–436

Mazur JE (1986) Fixed and variable ratios and delays: further tests of an equivalence rule. J Exp Psychol Anim Behav Process 12(2):116–124

Miller G (2000) How to keep our metatheories adaptive: beyond cosmides, tooby, and lakatos. Psychol Inq 11(1):42–46

Pirolli P (2005) Rational analyses of information foraging on the web. Cogn Sci A Multidiscip J 29(3):343–373

Pirolli P (2006) The use of proximal information scent to forage for distal content on the world wide web. Adaptive perspectives on human–technology interaction: methods and models for cognitive engineering and human–computer interaction. Oxford University Press, New York, pp 247–266

Pirolli P (2007) Information foraging theory: adaptive interaction with information. Oxford University Press, New York

Pirolli P, Card SK (1999) Information foraging. Psychol Rev 106(4):643–675

Rachlin H (2006) Notes on discounting. J Exp Anal Behav 85(3):425–435

Rajala AK, Hantula DA (2000) Towards a behavioural ecology of consumption: delay reduction effects on foraging in a simulated online mall. Manage Decis Econom 21 (3/4):145–158

Rode C, Cosmides L, Hell W, Tooby J (1999) When and why do people avoid unknown probabilities in decisions under uncertainty? Testing some predictions from optimal foraging theory. Cognition 72(3):269–304

Rose G, Meuter M, Curran J (2005) On-line waiting: the role of download time and other important predictors on attitude toward E-retailers. Psychol Market 22(2):127–151

Sakai Y, Fukai T (2008) The actor-critic learning is behind the matching law: matching versus optimal behaviors. Neural Comput 20(1):227–251

Sandstrom PE (1994) An optimal foraging approach to information seeking and use. Library Q 64(4):414–449

Szameitat A, Rummel J, Szameitat D, Sterr A (2009) Behavioral and emotional consequences of brief delays in human–computer interaction. Int J Hum Comput Stud 67(7):561–570

Shimp CP (1966) Probabilistically reinforced choice behavior in pigeons. J Exp Anal Behav 9(4):443–455

Smith C, Hantula D (2003) Pricing effects on foraging in a simulated Internet shopping mall. J Econ Psychol 24(5):653–674

Smith C, Hantula D (2008) Methodological considerations in the study of delay discounting in intertemporal choice: a comparison of tasks and modes. Behav Res Methods 40(4): 940–953

Smith EA (2000) Three styles in the evolutionary analysis of human behavior. In: Cronk L, Chagnon N, Irons W (eds) Adaptation and human behavior: an anthropological perspective. Aldin DeGruyter, New York, pp 27–46

Smythe E, Goldstone S (1957) The time sense: a normative, genetic study of the development of time perception. Percept Motor Skills 7(1):49–59

Stephens DW, Brown JS, Ydenberg RC (2007) Foraging: behavior and ecology. University of Chicago Press, Chicago

Stephens DW, Charnov EL (1982) Optimal foraging: Some simple stochastic models. Behav Ecol Sociobiol 10(4):251–263

Stephens DW, Krebs JR (1986) Foraging theory. Princeton University Press, Princeton

Stigler G, Becker G (1977) De Gustibus Non Est Disputandum. Am Econ Rev 67(2):76–90

Strohmetz D (2006) Rebuilding the ship at sea: coping with artifacts in behavioral research. In: Hantula DA (ed) Advances in social and organizational psychology: a tribute to Ralph Rosnow. Lawrence Erlbaum Associates, Mahwah, pp 93–112

White D, Dill L, Crawford C (2007) A common, conceptual framework for behavioral ecology and evolutionary psychology. Evol Psychol 5(2):275–288

Part II
Empirical Research Exemplars

Chapter 5
Surprise and Human Evolution: How a Snake Screen Enhanced Knowledge Transfer Through a Web Interface

Ned Kock, Ruth Chatelain-Jardón, and Jesus Carmona

Abstract It is reasonable to assume that enhanced cognition within the temporal vicinity of animal attacks allowed our hominid ancestors to better build and associate memories related to the animals and their typical habitat markers. This, in turn, increased their survival chances. This may be at the source of an unusual phenomenon with limited but interesting practical uses in the design of human–technology interaction interfaces for learning tasks. The phenomenon is often referred to as "flashbulb memorization" and entails modern humans' short-term memories being instantaneously turned into long-term memories through surprise. This chapter explores this phenomenon in the context of a computer-supported learning task, by testing the prediction that a simulated snake attack will lead to cognition enhancement within its temporal vicinity. In an experiment, those participants who were surprised by a Web-based snake screen did as much as 38% better at answering test questions for Web-based learning modules that were temporally adjacent to the snake screen.

Keywords Biosemiotics · Evolutionary psychology · Surprise · Emotion · Web-based learning · Cognition · Incoterms

N. Kock (✉)
Division of International Business and Technology Studies, Texas A&M International University, 5201 University Boulevard, Laredo, TX 78041, USA
e-mail: nedkock@tamiu.edu

R. Chatelain-Jardón
Division of International Business and Technology Studies, Texas A&M International University, 5201 University Boulevard, Laredo, TX 78041, USA
e-mail: chatelaine@students.tamiu.edu

J. Carmona
Division of International Business and Technology Studies, Texas A&M International University, 5201 University Boulevard, Laredo, TX 78041, USA
e-mail: jcarmona@tamiu.edu

N. Kock (ed.), *Evolutionary Psychology and Information Systems Research*,
Integrated Series in Information Systems 24, DOI 10.1007/978-1-4419-6139-6_5,
© Springer Science+Business Media, LLC 2010

1 Introduction

Human–technology interaction can arguably be understood based on a biosemioti-cal and evolutionary psychological perspective (Barbieri 2006; Cosmides and Tooby 1992; Kravchenko 2006). Certain adaptive mental mechanisms that were evolved to improve reproductive success in our ancestral past may have spread throughout most of the species (Buss 1999; Cosmides and Tooby 1992; Plotkin 1998) and thus would be at the source of observable patterns in human–technology behavior today. Understanding the role of these mental mechanisms today would lead to not only interesting predictions regarding the interaction of humans and technology but also a better understanding of the human mind (Pinker 1997; Trivers 2002; Wilson 2000). Moreover, technology designers could greatly benefit from this understanding as it would enable them to develop technologies that would be more effective in support-ing certain tasks and have greater commercial success. Technology features whose design is motivated by an understanding of evolved brain mechanisms are likely to have universal appeal among users.

The potential of ideas underlying the new fields of biosemiotics and evolutionary psychology to explain human–technology interaction behavior, however, has been largely unexplored among technology design researchers. With a few notable excep-tions (e.g., Hubona and Shirah 2006; Kock 2004; Kurzban and Weeden 2005), the situation is generally the same among researchers in many related fields, such as human evolution and evolutionary psychology. The study presented here aims at bridging this research gap by showing that a biosemiotical and evolutionary psy-chological perspective of human–technology interaction has the potential to lead to counterintuitive predictions that are fairly well aligned with empirical results.

This study discussed in this chapter was the first to look into how simulated ani-mal attacks can be incorporated into computer-based interfaces in order to enhance those interfaces' knowledge communication effectiveness. Underlying the study is the theoretical assumption that animal attacks are surprise events that enhance cog-nition, particularly memorization of contextual information that would allow an individual to recognize the attacker's habitat upon entering it in the future (Nairne et al. 2007). The co-evolution of snakes and our primate and hominid ancestors (Boaz and Almquist 2001; Isbell 2006) likely makes reactions to real or simulated snake attacks particularly strong today. Thus a computer-simulated snake attack is a particularly well-suited surprise event for the purposes of this study.

Investigations of snake attacks and encounters with humans (Hung 2004; Shine and Koenig 2001) allow for the development of a generic and typical scenario involving an unintentional hominid–snake encounter. A schematic representation of a hominid walk where an attack by a venomous snake takes place is shown in Fig. 5.1. It illustrates the point that enhanced cognition in animal attack situations likely contributes to increasing reproductive success. One key assumption here is that the hominid whose footprints are shown in the schematic representation sur-vives the attack after being treated for his or her wounds. Nevertheless, many such attacks in the environment of our evolutionary adaptation were likely fatal, as they are today in non-urban environments and involved individuals who had not reached

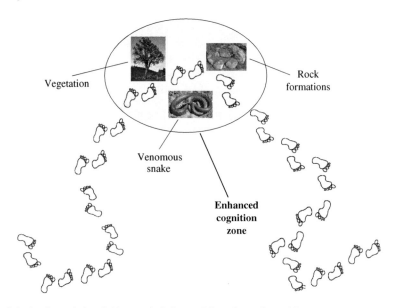

Fig. 5.1   A schematic hominid perambulation and the enhanced cognition zone

reproductive maturity (Hung 2004). These characteristics allow us to conclude that a great deal of evolutionary pressure has been placed in favor of the selection of mental attributes that helped our ancestor effectively avoid fatal attacks. The area near the attack in the schematic representation contains animal habitat markers, such as specific rock formations and vegetation.

Figure 5.1 shows within a shaded oval what is referred to in this study as an enhanced cognition zone. That zone is the temporal area where cognition is likely to be enhanced to generate more vivid and long-lasting mental associations between habitat markers and the attack itself. Given the nature of snake attacks (Hung 2004), and animal attacks in general (Manipady et al. 2006; Sriaroon et al. 2006), this temporal area is hypothesized to start a few minutes before an animal attack and end a few minutes after the attack. Having particularly vivid memories of habitat markers associated with animal attacks is assumed here to have increased the reproductive success of our hominid ancestors.

The rationale for the belief that enhanced cognition associated with attacks by animals, such as venomous snakes, has contributed to increasing the reproductive success of our ancestors is relatively simple. Strong memories of the habitat markers have arguably allowed our hominid ancestors to be more alert when entering the habitats of dangerous animals, or avoid those habitats, thus reducing the probability of death in future attacks.

While the above discussion refers primarily to our hominid ancestors, the related enhanced cognition effect probably has a more remote origin. For example, it is likely that our pre-hominid primate ancestors also had to develop similar mental mechanisms to better deal with attacks by various animals. Snakes in particular must have played a key role in that respect. There is a long documented history of co-evolution of snakes and primates in general, where snakes had been main predators of primates (Barton 1999; Isbell 2006). Primate researchers have suggested that instinctive surprise responses and related brain mechanisms in various primate groups have been developed as a result of that co-evolution (Crockford and Boesch 2003; Isbell 2006).

2 Background and Hypotheses

Past research has provided ample evidence that surprise events in general enhance cognition (Brown and Kulik 1977; Edery-Halpern and Nachson 2004). Nevertheless, the root causes of the phenomenon have been hotly debated (Greenberg 2005; Otani et al. 2005). A brain scan study reported by Michelon et al. (2003) suggests that surprise events are processed by the brain differently than events that do not lead to surprise. Schutzwohl and Reisenzein (1999) studied the responses of children and adults to surprise events and concluded that those responses are age invariant and have a Darwinian evolutionary origin. It seems that surprise events, particularly those that are unpleasant, trigger enhanced memory encoding mechanisms that have arguably been evolutionarily adaptive (Schützwohl and Borgstedt 2005). Enhanced memorization of salient contextual features such as event location has been frequently reported in the literature on the effects of surprise on cognition (MacKay and Ahmetzanov 2005; Schutzwohl 1998).

One difficulty associated with research on surprise effects on cognition is that not all startling events elicit the same degree of surprise from different individuals. For example, Berntsen and Thomsen (2005) studied 140 Danes' contextual memories associated with the news of the Danish occupation and liberation in the 1940s. Their study found that participants who reported having ties to the Danish resistance movement had more vivid, detailed, and accurate contextual memories than did those participants without ties to the movement.

The study by Berntsen and Thomsen (2005) underlies the need for research on surprise and cognition that focuses on events that are less likely to be influenced by the participants' cultural background. Arguably events that are similar to those faced by our hominid ancestors, such as animal attacks, are less likely to elicit different degrees of surprise among different individuals than are events that are very unlike those faced by our ancestors.

If the enhanced cognition effect in animal attack situations has a genetic basis, one would expect to observe it in modern humans facing animal attacks. This opens the door for the conclusion that computer-simulated snake attacks could be used to enhance cognition in a utilitarian way, with the goal of enhancing learning associated with certain topics. Nevertheless, since computer-simulated animal attacks are different from actual attacks, it is reasonable to expect them to have an effect of lower magnitude than actual attacks.

Figure 5.2 shows how a computer-simulated snake attack could be implemented in the context of a Web-based learning task. (This would certainly require informed

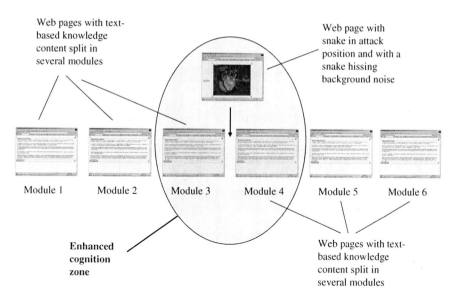

Web pages with text-based knowledge content split in several modules

Web page with snake in attack position and with a snake hissing background noise

Module 1   Module 2   Module 3   Module 4   Module 5   Module 6

Enhanced cognition zone

Web pages with text-based knowledge content split in several modules

Fig. 5.2 A schematic hominid perambulation and the enhanced cognition zone

consent from the participating individuals and, in the case of a research study, Institutional Review Board approval.) The learning task in questions is assumed to be made up of six learning modules, where text-based knowledge is provided in Web pages, one Web page corresponding to each learning module. In between modules 3 and 4, a Web page with a snake in attack position is shown to surprise the individuals viewing the learning modules.

Based on the above discussion, one would expect the enhanced cognition zone to comprise modules 3 and 4, because those modules appear immediately before and after the surprise event elicited by the snake screen. That is, due to the enhanced cognition effect, one would expect the knowledge associated with modules 3 and 4 to be acquired more effectively than that associated with modules 1, 2, 5, and 6. The hypothesized enhanced cognition effect essentially entails the short-term memories acquired for modules 3 and 4 being instantaneously turned into long-term memories (Brown and Kulik 1977; Schacter 2001; Schutzwohl 1998).

Testing the above predictions in the context of a Web-based learning task cannot be easily accomplished if only one condition is used, namely a condition in which the snake screen is included in between modules 3 and 4. The reason is that it is very difficult to design different learning modules with the same degree of difficulty. If modules have different degrees of difficulty, and performance is measured through test scores on questions associated with each of the modules, then differences in the difficulty levels across modules may account for a larger percentage of the variance in test scores than the surprise stimulus.

One way to avoid the above problem is to have two conditions, one treatment and one control condition, with participants randomly assigned to each condition. The two conditions would differ only in that one, the treatment condition, would have the snake screen and the other would not. Variations in knowledge acquisition effectiveness elicited by the snake screen could then be measured based on differences between the two conditions in test scores. Any variations in module-learning difficulty would cancel each other out when performance was compared between conditions. Hypotheses H1 and H2 below provide a formalization of the prediction that knowledge communication effectiveness in the enhanced cognition zone would be increased in the treatment condition.

H1: *The test scores in the treatment condition will be higher than those in the control condition for the module immediately before the snake screen.*

H2: *The test scores in the treatment condition will be higher than those in the control condition for the module immediately after the snake screen.*

One more issue that needs to be explicitly addressed is whether enhanced cognition immediately after the snake screen is likely to be of the same magnitude as that immediately before the snake screen. Different experiences may lead to variations in how effectively knowledge is acquired and vividly recalled (Werkle-Bergner et al. 2006). Memory recall is also affected by the sensorial nature of the knowledge acquisition experience (Winkler and Cowan 2005). Nevertheless, an individual's memories of a topic that he or she studied generally tend to fade over time (Schacter 2001; Waddell 2002; Werkle-Bergner et al. 2006).

Since the knowledge in Module 3 is acquired before the surprise event, our brain is not yet as alert to the need for enhanced cognition as it is for Module 4. That is, while our brain needs to work on memories that are already fading for Module 3, it has advance notice in connection with Module 4. Therefore, one would expect a greater effectiveness in knowledge acquisition for Module 4 than for Module 3. This expectation is formalized through hypothesis H3 below.

H3: *The test scores difference between the treatment and control conditions will be greater for the module immediately after than for the module before the snake screen.*

Figure 5.3 depicts the predictions formalized through hypotheses H1 to H3. It shows a graph with the expected average differences between test scores for each module in the treatment and control conditions. Modules 1, 2, 5, and 6 are outside the enhanced cognition zone, so differences in connection with those modules are expected to be insignificant and are thus represented as zero. Differences for modules 3 and 4 are expected to be significant, hence the two bars protruding out to the right. The difference between modules 3 and 4 is also expected to be significant, which is why the bar for Module 4 is represented as approximately twice the size of the bar for Module 3.

The graph representation in Fig. 5.3 is schematic. Neither the precise sizes of the bars nor the exact magnitudes of the underlying effects are tied to any specific hypotheses. The bars and their relative sizes are used for illustration purposes only.

Fig. 5.3 Expected differences in the test scores for the treatment and control conditions

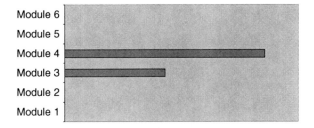

That is, it is not being hypothesized here that the test scores for Module 4 will be on average two times greater than the test scores for Module 3. It is only hypothesized that the test scores for Module 4 will be on average significantly greater than those for Module 3. Our current level of theoretical understanding of the phenomenon does not allow for more elaborate or precise predictions.

3 Research Methods

A Web-based learning experiment was conducted with 186 student participants. Students were promised extra credit for their participation, where the amount of extra credit would be proportional to their performance in the experimental task. Data in connection with each participant's review of six text-based modules were analyzed, with the goal of comparing the participants' performance in the treatment and control conditions. The modules were shown to the participants as Web pages. All participants were business students distributed as follows in terms of their university status: sophomore (6.45%), junior (43.55%), senior (41.94%), and graduate (8.06%). The ages of the participants ranged from 18 to 48, with a mean age of 24. Approximately 53% of the participants were females.

Each of the six modules contained text-based knowledge on Incoterms. The term "Incoterms" is an abbreviation for "International Commercial Terms." They are a body of standard terminology used in international trade contracts. Incoterms are published by the International Chamber of Commerce, an international organization dedicated to the promotion of global trade and global economic growth. Incoterms was a new topic for all of the participants, that is, students reported having no knowledge about Incoterms prior to their participation in this study.

A Web-based screen with the picture of a snake in attack position was used to surprise the participants in the treatment condition (see Fig. 5.4). That screen was absent in the control condition. The snake screen was shown to participants for 10 s in between modules 3 and 4 in the treatment condition. The hissing noise normally made by an attacking snake accompanied the display of the snake screen. Approximately half of the participants were assigned randomly to each of the two conditions. Institutional Review Board approval was obtained, and the study participants signed informed consent forms, prior to the study.

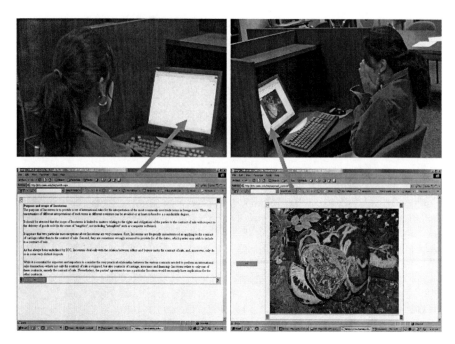

Fig. 5.4 Participant viewing Web-based modules

The participants' review of the modules on Incoterms was timed. That is, each participant reviewed each module during a set amount of time, after which he or she reviewed the next module and so on. The time set for review of each module was 2.35 min and was the same for all of the participants. Each module contained approximately 265 words. Three organizational communication studies suggesting optimal communication unit sizes in different media (Kock 2001; Kock and Davison 2003; McQueen et al. 1999) served as the basis for the decision to design modules with these characteristics – i.e., with approximately 265 words and to be viewed for 2.35 min.

After their review of the modules, the participants took a test covering the knowledge about the Incoterms that they had reviewed. The test contained three multiple-choice questions for each of the modules reviewed by the participants. Each question had four choices and only one correct answer. Shapiro–Wilk normality assessments (Shapiro and Wilk 1965) of the test scores for each of the modules were conducted. The results suggested that no test score distribution was significantly different from the equivalent normal distribution. This in turn led to the conclusion that the test scores could be used as a basis for parametric statistical analysis tests such as ANOVA and generalized linear modeling tests (Hair et al. 1987; Rosenthal and Rosnow 1991).

The test scores obtained in the treatment and control conditions were compared through one-way ANOVA tests where the performance on the test scores for each module was compared across the treatment and control conditions. Additionally, interaction effects between the variable condition (i.e., presence or absence of snake screen) and three demographic variables (gender, age, and grade point average) were assessed through generalized linear modeling tests.

4 Data Analysis Results

Figure 5.5 shows the percentage differences in average test scores obtained by participants in the treatment and control conditions. Each bar refers to a percentage difference, calculated by subtracting, for each module, the average score obtained in the control condition from the average score obtained in the treatment condition and dividing the result by the average score obtained in the control condition. That is, each bar indicates how much greater, in percentage terms, the average score in the treatment condition was when compared with the average score in the control condition.

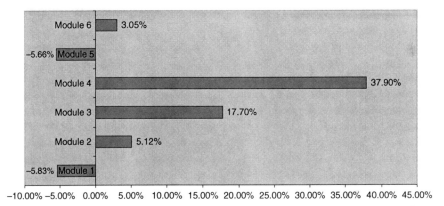

Fig. 5.5 Percentage differences between test scores in the treatment and control conditions

As can be seen from Fig. 5.5, the differences between conditions were less than 6% for the modules outside the enhanced cognition zone, namely the scores for modules 1, 2, 5, and 6. For Module 3, immediately before the snake screen, the average score obtained by participants in the treatment condition was 17.70% greater than the average score in the control condition. For Module 4, that difference in average scores was 37.90%. Table 5.1 shows the results of a one-way ANOVA test comparing those differences. Effect sizes are shown in the column labeled d, which lists Cohen's d standardized effect size statistics associated with each comparison. The last row compares the magnitude of differences between modules 3 and 4.

The results summarized in Table 5.1 suggest that the differences between scores in the treatment and control conditions were statistically insignificant for modules 1, 2, 5, and 6. The 17.70% difference for Module 3 was found to be significant ($F_{1.184} = 2.71$, $p = 0.05$, $d = 0.24$), providing support for hypothesis H1. The 37.90% difference for Module 4 was also found to be significant ($F_{1.184} =$

Table 5.1 One-way ANOVA results

Module	T–C (%)	F	P	d
1	−5.83	0.37	0.27	0.09
2	5.12	0.16	0.34	0.05
3	17.70	2.71	0.05	0.24
4	37.90	9.06	0.001	0.43
5	−5.66	0.53	0.23	0.10
6	3.05	0.09	0.38	0.04
4–3	20.20	4.15	0.04	0.27

T–C (%), percentage difference between treatment and control scores;
p, chance probability of F test statistic; d, Cohen's d standardized effect
size statistic; last row compares differences for modules 3 and 4

0.9.06, $p = 0.001$, $d = 0.43$), providing support for hypothesis H2. Finally, the 20.20% difference in the magnitude of the effects in connection with modules 3 and 4 was found to be significant as well ($F_{1.106} = 4.15$, $p = 0.04$, $d = 0.27$), providing support for hypothesis H3.

In addition to the main effects' results summarized above, three main interaction effects were assessed in connection with modules 3 and 4 through generalized linear modeling tests. Those interaction effects refer to the demographic variables gender, age, and grade point average. The interaction effects between condition (i.e., presence or absence of snake screen) and gender were statistically insignificant for Module 3 ($F_{1.184} = 1.12$, $p = 0.29$, $\eta^2 = 0.006$) and for Module 4 ($F_{1.184} = 2.42$, $p = 0.12$, $\eta^2 = 0.01$). Also, the interaction effects between condition and age were statistically insignificant for Module 3 ($F_{1.184} = 0.96$, $p = 0.49$, $\eta^2 = 0.08$) and for Module 4 ($F_{1.184} = 0.67$, $p = 0.79$, $\eta^2 = 0.06$). Finally, the interaction effects between condition and grade point average were statistically insignificant as well for modules 3 ($F_{1.184} = 0.55$, $p = 0.93$, $\eta^2 = 0.07$) and 4 ($F_{1.184} = 0.60$, $p = 0.89$, $\eta^2 = 0.08$).

5 Discussion

The study reported here was arguably the first to look into whether a computer-simulated surprise event, in the form of a Web-based snake screen accompanied by a hissing background noise, enhanced the performance of participants in a Web-based online learning task. The study compared data collected from 186 individuals who were randomly assigned to a treatment (surprise) and a control (no surprise) condition. The results of the analysis supported the theoretical prediction that computer-simulated surprise does have a significant and positive effect on cognition. The theoretical prediction had three main facets, formalized through three hypotheses (see Table 5.2). All hypotheses were supported by the results.

Individuals who were surprised did approximately 18% better in terms of test scores for the Web-based module immediately before the surprise event and

Table 5.2 Summary of the results vis-à-vis the hypotheses

Hypothesis	Supported?
H1: The test scores in the treatment condition will be higher than those in the control condition for the module immediately before the snake screen	Yes
H2: The test scores in the treatment condition will be higher than those in the control condition for the module immediately after the snake screen	Yes
H3: The test score difference between the treatment and control conditions will be greater for the module immediately after than for the module before the snake screen	Yes

approximately 38% better for the module after the surprise event. A simple analogy may help put these findings into perspective. In a small test, this performance enhancement would be enough to account for a difference in grades from "C" to "A" (that is, from approximately 70 to 90, out of 100), where the individuals that were surprised would get an "A" grade in a test on what they learned and those who were not surprised would get a "C" grade.

The positive effects of surprise on performance for the modules immediately before and after the surprise event occurred regardless of whether the participants were males or females. Or, in other words, both males and females did equally better in terms of test scores for those modules when surprised. The positive performance effects were also observed regardless of the participants' ages (which ranged from 18 to 48 years) and regardless of whether the participants were under or overachievers in their programs of study (measured through the participants' grade point averages). These combined findings provide some support for the notion that surprise-induced enhanced cognition is a rather universal phenomenon. These findings are also fairly consistent with the Darwinian evolutionary basis hypothesized in this study.

Another interesting aspect of the findings is that the performance in the modules outside the enhanced cognition zone was not significantly affected. That is, the variations in performance between those who were surprised and those who were not were statistically insignificant for modules that were not temporally adjacent to the surprise event. This is an interesting finding, because one could expect that surprise would be followed by distraction, and thus decrease in performance, at least for the modules after the module immediately next to the surprise event.

The positive effect in the enhanced cognition zone (modules 3 and 4, in this study), combined with the lack of a negative effect outside that zone (modules 1, 2, 5, and 6), bodes well for possible future applications of the surprise-enhanced learning approach discussed here. Certainly the scope of the applications is limited by the unpleasant nature of the surprise and by the fact that it cannot be ethically used without informed consent. Nevertheless, there are many computer-based training situations in which it makes practical sense to enhance the learning of particular topics, as long as that does not detract from the learning associated with other topics.

An area of application would be training in connection with emergencies, where surprise could be used to create long-term and vivid memories of procedures needed to handle emergency situations. Since emergency situations are rare, related training is likely to be sparse, hence the need for special cognitive enhancement during training. For example, commercial and military aircraft pilots are routinely trained on how to operate airplanes through the use of computer simulators. Airplane control interfaces are among the most complex of all human–technology interfaces. Certain parts of those interfaces are associated with critical situations such as an emergency response to a loss of cabin pressure. Having surprise-induced enhanced cognition associated with those parts of the interfaces, as well as related sequences of actions to be taken by pilots, may significantly enhance the chances of survival in emergencies.

Online training on issues unrelated to emergencies could also benefit from human–technology interfaces incorporating surprise stimuli. In fact, the underlying theoretical basis and the results of this study suggest that the surprise-enhanced cognition phenomenon can be widely applied in the design of online training, as long as ethical considerations make it advisable to do so. Using surprise stimuli of the type employed in this study without the consent of those who will be surprised will in most cases be considered unethical. Nevertheless, human–technology interfaces can be designed so that their users can opt for using surprise or not when employing an interface for online learning purposes. Users can also be allowed to choose the type of surprise to which they are willing to be subjected. In these cases, a certain degree of unpredictability, through randomness and variability in the surprise stimuli used, still needs to be incorporated into the human–technology interface design. Without a certain degree of unpredictability, the stimuli in question will cease to be surprising.

6 Conclusion

This study explores an unusual phenomenon with limited but interesting practical uses in the design of human–technology interaction interfaces for learning tasks. The phenomenon whose underlying basis builds on notions from the fields of biosemiotics and evolutionary psychology involves modern humans' short-term memories being instantaneously turned into long-term memories through surprise in the form of simulated animal attacks. This study explores this phenomenon in the context of a computer-supported learning task, by testing the prediction that a simulated snake attack will lead to cognition enhancement within its temporal vicinity. In an experiment involving student participants, those participants who were surprised by a Web-based snake screen did significantly better (as much as 38% better) in the test questions for Web-based learning modules that were temporally adjacent to the snake screen than were participants who were not surprised.

The potential of ideas from the fields of biosemiotics and evolutionary psychology to explain and predict human–technology interaction behavior has been largely untapped by technology researchers. The field of information systems, of which human–technology interaction is often seen as a sub-field, is an example of this oversight. Information systems researchers are chiefly concerned with the impact that computer technologies have on individuals and groups (Galliers et al. 2006). To this date there are only a handful of published studies in information systems journals that clearly attempted to understand research findings from a biosemiotical or a human evolutionary perspective.

Notable examples of studies that used biosemiotics and/or human evolutionary perspectives to understand information systems phenomena are those by Rajala and Hantula (2000) as well as Smith and Hantula (2003) addressing electronic consumer behavior, by DeRosa et al. (2004) on virtual team leadership, by Hubona and Shirah (2006) on electronic user interface design, and by Spink and Cole (2006) on information search and use behavior. These studies are exceptions, as most information systems studies build on social theories. One influential social theory among information systems researchers has been Anthony Giddens's structuration theory, which served as the basis for DeSanctis and Poole's (1994) widely cited adaptive structuration theory of human–technology interaction. Another influential social theory used by information systems researchers is Jürgen Habermas's critical theory of communication action (Habermas 1987). Te'eni's (2001) excellent review of theories informing information systems research provides not only a good understanding of the influence of Habermas's ideas in that field but also a clear picture of how underutilized Darwinian perspectives have been in the field of information systems.

Human–technology interaction is often seen as an important area of research within the broader field of information systems. Empirical research on human–technology interaction has a long history, arguably dating back to the 1960s. That empirical research led to the development of several theoretical frameworks aimed at summarizing and integrating empirical findings. An extensive review of human–technology interaction frameworks conducted by Kock (2004) suggests that the vast majority of theoretical models of human–technology interaction either build on social theories or adopt a technology deterministic perspective. The technology deterministic perspective assumes that users adopt technologies as intended by the designers of the technologies, which is not often the case in practice (Markus 2005). Kock's (2004) review identified 11 major human–technology interaction models, none of which were built on human evolution notions as a basis for their behavioral predictions.

The study presented here contributes to bridging that theoretical research gap and will hopefully stimulate more research in the future that will follow the same theoretical orientation. This study clearly show not only that biosemiotical and evolutionary psychological perspectives of human–technology interaction can lead to unexpected predictions but also that such perspectives can lead to predictions that are remarkably well aligned with empirical results in connection with technology effects on humans.

Beyond its contemporary applications, this study also goes some way toward providing evidence that having enhanced cognition associated with animal attacks likely improved the survival chances of our ancestors. Evidence of uniform behavioral responses to technology by modern humans, where animal attacks are simulated through technology, can help us better understand our past. Understanding our evolutionary past sheds light on the design of those brain mechanisms that have been shaped by evolution and influence our current behavior. In this sense, this study makes an important contribution to the incipient fields of biosemiotics and evolutionary psychology and hopefully will stimulate further research into the phenomenon of surprise-induced enhanced cognition.

As with any research study, especially one in a new and somewhat unusual topic as this is, the findings and related conclusions must be supported in future research in order to gain increasing credibility. Future research should include variations in research methods and design, one of which could be the addition of conditions where surprise stimuli of different types are used – e.g., non-threatening stimuli. This would allow for a better understanding of the arguably evolutionary nature of the surprise-enhanced cognition phenomenon unveiled through this study.

Acknowledgments This chapter is a revised version of an article by the authors published in 2008 in the *International Journal of Technology and Human Interaction*. The authors would like to thank the students who participated in this study, for their time, and Texas A&M International University, for its institutional support. Thanks are also due to Achim Schutzwohl, Leda Cosmides, and Geoffrey Miller for ideas and suggestions regarding possible links between surprise and cognition, as well as related evolutionary psychological mechanisms.

References

Barbieri M (ed) (2006) Introduction to biosemiotics. Springer, New York

Barton RA (1999) The evolutionary ecology of the primate brain. In: Lee PC (ed) Comparative primate socioecology. Cambridge University Press, Cambridge, pp. 167–203

Berntsen D, Thomsen DK (2005) Personal memories for remote historical events: accuracy and clarity of flashbulb memories related to World War II. J Exp Psychol Gen 134(2):242–257

Boaz NT, Almquist AJ (2001) Biological anthropology: a synthetic approach to human evolution, 2nd edn. Prentice Hall, Upper Saddle River

Brown R, Kulik J (1977) Flashbulb memories. Cognition 5(1):73–99

Buss DM (1999) Evolutionary psychology: the new science of the mind. Allyn & Bacon, Needham Heights

Cosmides L, Tooby J (1992) Cognitive adaptations for social exchange. In: Barkow JH, Cosmides L, Tooby J (eds) The adapted mind: evolutionary psychology and the generation of culture. Oxford University Press, New York, pp 163–228

Crockford C, Boesch C (2003) Context-specific calls in wild chimpanzees, *Pan troglodytes verus*: analysis of barks. Anim Behav 66(1):115–125

DeRosa DM, Hantula DA, Kock N, D'Arcy JP (2004) Communication, trust, and leadership in virtual teams: a media naturalness perspective. Hum Res Manage J 34(2):219–232

DeSanctis G, Poole MS (1994) Capturing the complexity in advanced technology use: adaptive structuration theory. Organ Sci 5(2):121–147

Edery-Halpern G, Nachson I (2004) Distinctiveness in flashbulb memory: comparative analysis of five terrorist attacks. Memory 12(2):147–157

Galliers RD, Markus ML, Newell S (eds) (2006) Exploring information systems research approaches. Routledge, New York

Greenberg D (2005) Flashbulb memories. Skeptic 11(3):74–80

Habermas J (1987) The theory of communicative action: lifeworld and social system. Beacon Press, Boston

Hair JF, Anderson RE, Tatham RL (1987) Multivariate data analysis, 2nd edn. Macmillan, New York

Hubona GS, Shirah GW (2006) The Paleolithic stone age effect? Gender differences performing specific computer-generated spatial tasks. Int J Technol Hum Interact 2(2):24–46

Hung D (2004) Taiwan's venomous snakebite: epidemiological, evolution and geographic differences. Trans R Soc Trop Med Hyg 98(2):96–101

Isbell LA (2006) Snakes as agents of evolutionary change in primate brains. J Hum Evol 51(1): 1–35

Kock N (2001) Asynchronous and distributed process improvement: the role of collaborative technologies. Inf Syst J 11(2):87–110

Kock N (2004) The psychobiological model: towards a new theory of computer-mediated communication based on Darwinian evolution. Organ Sci 15(3):327–348

Kock N, Davison R (2003) Can lean media support knowledge sharing? Investigating a hidden advantage of process improvement. IEEE Trans Eng Manage 50(2):151–163

Kravchenko A (2006) Cognitive linguistics, biology of cognition and biosemiotics: bridging the gaps. Lang Sci 28(1):51–75

Kurzban R, Weeden J (2005) HurryDate: mate preferences in action. Evol Hum Behav 26(3): 227–244

MacKay DG, Ahmetzanov MV (2005) Emotion, memory, and attention in the taboo Stroop paradigm. Psychol Sci 16(1):25–32

Manipady S, Menezes RG, Bastia BK (2006) Death by attack from a wild boar. J Clin Forensic Med 13(2):89–91

Markus ML (2005) Technology-shaping effects of e-collaboration technologies: bugs and features. Int J e-Collab 1(1):1–23

McQueen RJ, Payner K, Kock N (1999) Contribution by participants in face-to-face business meetings: Implications for collaborative technology. J Syst Inf Technol 3(1):15–33

Michelon P, Snyder AZ, Buckner RL, McAvoy M, Zacks JM (2003) Neural correlates of incongruous visual information: an event-related fMRI study. NeuroImage 19(4):1612–1627

Nairne JS, Thompson SR, Pandeirada JNS (2007) Adaptive memory: survival processing enhances retention. J Exp Psychol Learn Mem Cogn 33(2):263–273

Otani H, Kusumi T, Kato K, Matsuda K, Kern R, Widner Jr. R, Ohta N (2005) Remembering a nuclear accident in Japan: did it trigger flashbulb memories? Memory 13(1):6–20

Pinker S (1997) How the mind works. W.W. Norton & Co, New York

Plotkin H (1998) Evolution in mind: an introduction to evolutionary psychology. Harvard University Press, Cambridge

Rajala AK, Hantula DA (2000) Towards a behavioral ecology of consumption: delay-reduction effects on foraging in a simulated Internet mall. Managerial Decis Econ 21(1):145–158

Rosenthal R, Rosnow RL (1991) Essentials of behavioral research: methods data analysis. McGraw-Hill, Boston

Schacter DL (2001) The seven sins of memory: how the mind forgets and remembers. Houghton Mifflin, New York

Schutzwohl A (1998) Surprise and schema strength. J Exp Psychol Learn Mem Cogn 24(5): 1182–1199

Schützwohl A, Borgstedt K (2005) The processing of affectively valenced stimuli: the role of surprise. Cogn Emot 19(4):583–600

Schutzwohl A, Reisenzein R (1999) Children's and adults' reactions to a schemadiscrepant event: a developmental analysis of surprise. Int J Behav Dev 23(1):37–63

Shapiro SS, Wilk MB (1965) An analysis of variance test for normality (complete samples). Biometrika 52(3/4):591–611

Shine R, Koenig J (2001) Snakes in the garden: an analysis of reptiles "rescued" by community-based wildlife careers. Biol Conserv 102(3):271–283

Smith CL, Hantula DA (2003) Pricing effects on foraging in a simulated Internet shopping mall. J Econ Psychol 24(5):653–674

Spink A, Cole C (2006) Human information behavior: integrating diverse approaches and information use. J Am Soc Inf Sci Technol 57(1):25–35

Sriaroon C, Sriaroon P, Daviratanasilpa S, Khawplod P, Wilde H (2006) Retrospective: animal attacks and rabies exposures in Thai children. Travel Med Infect Dis 4(5):270–274

Te'eni D (2001) A cognitive-affective model of organizational communication for designing IT. MIS Q 25(2):251–312

Trivers R (2002) Natural selection and social theory. Oxford University Press, Oxford

Waddell S (2002) Forgetting those painful moments. Neuron 35(5):815–817

Werkle-Bergner M, Müller V, Li S, Lindenberger U (2006) Cortical EEG correlates of successful memory encoding: implications for lifespan comparisons. Neurosci Biobehav Rev 30(6): 839–854

Wilson EO (2000) Sociobiology: the new synthesis. Harvard University Press, Cambridge

Winkler I, Cowan N (2005) From sensory to long-term memory: evidence from auditory memory reactivation studies. Exp Psychol 52(1):3–20

Chapter 6
How Do e-Learners Participate in Synchronous Online Discussions? Evolutionary and Social Psychological Perspectives

Stefan Hrastinski

Abstract Computer-mediated communication (CMC) has been adopted in most e-learning settings. However, few research studies have considered the effect of different CMCs in such settings. This study examined how and why synchronous communication, as a complement to asynchronous communication, affected participation in online discussions. Two online classes that participated in two asynchronous and two synchronous online discussions were examined. The analysis of empirical data was supported by a combination of evolutionary and social psychological theories. Actual and perceived measures of participation indicated that synchronous communication induced personal participation, which should be regarded as a complement to cognitive participation. Personal participation describes more intense interaction better supported by synchronous communication while cognitive participation is a more reflective type of participation better supported by asynchronous communication. In synchronous discussions, the e-learners felt that they worked together and were not restricted to only discuss course content. This was likely to induce arousal and motivation and increased convergence on meaning, especially in small groups.

Keywords Online participation · Computer-mediated communication · Synchronous communication · e-Learning

1 Introduction

e-Learning is an important area for the IS community since more research will be needed to face the emerging knowledge society, in which the need for lifelong learning is emphasized. However, it has been argued that there is a lack of theoretically

S. Hrastinski (✉)
Department of Media Technology, KTH Royal Institute of Technology and Uppsala University, Lindstedtsv. 3, SE-100 44 Stockholm, Sweden
e-mail: stefanhr@kth.se

N. Kock (ed.), *Evolutionary Psychology and Information Systems Research*, Integrated Series in Information Systems 24, DOI 10.1007/978-1-4419-6139-6_6, © Springer Science+Business Media, LLC 2010

grounded and rigorous research on e-learning. There is thus a need to develop theories to support the design and implementation of such environments as they are complex and encompass organizational, administrative, instructional, and technological challenges (Jones and Gregor 2006). The reference discipline of information systems seems uniquely positioned to contribute in this field (Alavi and Leidner 2001). Many IS scholars have focused on the effectiveness of e-learning compared to traditional classroom education. However, Piccoli et al.'s (2001) empirical study and Russell's (2001) major review have not identified significant differences in performance between students enrolled in these two environments. Other IS scholars have aimed to identify the factors that underlie successful use of e-learning by, for example, extending technology acceptance models (e.g., Chiu and Wang 2008; Lee et al. 2005). It seems like it is time to remove the black box of the e-learning artifact and move forward by analyzing the effect of using different e-learning technologies. This question is more complex than introducing sophisticated and novel technologies, as has been empirically showed by Alavi et al. (2002).

Before the widespread use of computer-mediated communication (CMC), Keegan (1980) argued that one of the key elements of distance education is that learners are taught as individuals rather than in groups. The adoption of CMC has resulted in refinements of previous definitions of distance education (Gunawardena and McIsaac 2004). For example, leading scholars in the field of distance education consider CMC to be one of its defining characteristics (Garrison and Shale 1987; Moore and Kearsley 1996). This has led to the introduction of new terms, such as online education and e-learning, to describe new forms of distance education (Harasim 1989).

It is often argued that CMC has transformed learning environments from being teacher-centered to learner-centered (Fåhræus 2003; Kang 1998) since learning with others within a social context has been enabled (Lindberg and Olofsson 2005). In line with social theories on learning (Wenger 1998; Vygotsky 1978), the main advantage of using CMC is that it enables learners to communicate with and learn from each other (Harasim 1989): "More capable peers or adult guides on a computer network might lead students into cognitive processes of writing and communication that they might not independently consider" (Sugar and Bonk 1998, p. 132). It has been empirically showed that the success of e-learning courses depends on providing collaborative learning activities (Fich-Benbunan and Arbaugh 2006).

CMC is commonly classified as asynchronous or synchronous, depending on whether the communication occurs in real time or not. Throughout the years, there has been an ongoing debate on the usefulness of these two types of communication. Asynchronous CMCs have been studied for over 20 years (Hewitt 2003) and have received more attention in research (Orvis et al. 2002; Romiszowski and Mason 2004). Hitherto, most e-learning studies have analyzed asynchronous communication in isolation or in comparison with traditional face-to-face classrooms (Rice et al. 2005). A review of four journals during 2000–2004 on CMC in e-learning settings found that a majority of research papers discussed or evaluated asynchronous communication while research on synchronous communication and mixed approaches have been less common (Hrastinski and Keller 2007). Thus, the debate on the usefulness of asynchronous and synchronous communication seems to be primarily based on studies of asynchronous communication and personal preferences, rather than on studies of media approaches. However, there are some exceptions, which are reviewed in the next section.

The dominance of research on asynchronous communication can, at least, partly be explained by their "anytime, anywhere" feature. Since more time may be spent on refining contributions, asynchronous discussions are generally considered as "deeper" when comparing with synchronous discussions (Hiltz and Goldman 2005). Currently, findings and opinions about synchronous communication in the literature are inconclusive. For example, Palloff and Pratt (1999, p. 47) have argued that synchronous discussions "rarely provides for productive discussion or participation" while Leidner and Jarvenpaa (1995) found that such discussions resulted in increased and more equal communication when comparing with the traditional classroom.

An emerging topic is how synchronous communication should be integrated into asynchronous e-learning (Murphy and Ciszewska-Carr 2006). Many teachers rely on asynchronous communication, by media such as e-mail and discussion boards, but these methods are often not sufficient (Schullo et al. 2005). Researchers can contribute toward a deeper understanding of this topic by investigating how variables, such as learning outcomes, are affected as a consequence of supporting synchronous communication. In this study, the variable of choice is participation, which has been shown to affect learning outcomes positively (e.g., Fredericksen et al. 2000; Hiltz et al. 2000). In these studies, learning has been measured as perceived learning, grades, and quality assessment of assignments. Furthermore, it has been argued that participation positively influences retention rates (e.g., Rovai 2002), satisfaction (e.g., Alavi and Dufner 2005), and sense of community (e.g., Schullo et al. 2005).

More specifically, this study examines how and why synchronous communication by chat, as a complement to asynchronous communication by discussion board, affect participation in online discussions. Various measures of participation for the two types of media will be compared in order to distinguish characteristics of synchronous communication that might complement asynchronous communication. Many practitioners are interested in using synchronous e-learning but simply do not know what the benefits and limitations of this type of communication are. Thus, this study contributes toward a deeper understanding on a topic where guidance is urgently needed.

The plan of the chapter is as follows. Next, a theoretical background is discussed. Then, the underlying method of the study is outlined. This is followed by a presentation and discussion of the results. The concepts of personal and cognitive participation are introduced to explain the benefits and limitations of synchronous and asynchronous communication. Finally, limitations, suggestions for further research, and conclusions are put forward.

2 Theoretical Background

This section provides a theoretical background. First, theories on media choice and use are introduced. Then, comparative studies on asynchronous and synchronous CMC are reviewed. Finally, the concept of online participation and how it may be studied is discussed.

2.1 Theories on Media Choice and Use

In order to bring clarity, researchers have built theories that explain media choice and use. Media richness theory argues that "communication media vary in the capacity to process rich information" (Daft and Lengel 1986, p. 560). Face-to-face communication is an example of a rich medium while numeric documents is an example of a lean medium. The theory proposes that rich media are appropriate for reducing uncertainty, defined as "absence of information," and equivocality, defined as "existence of multiple and conflicting interpretations" (p. 556). However, many studies that have tested the media richness theory have found mixed or conflicting results (for reviews, see Kock 2005; Robert and Dennis 2005). For example, Markus (1994) showed that lean media, such as e-mail, can be used for complex communication and can be used in rich ways, if encouraged by the social context. Moreover, the review of the next section will reveal that asynchronous or lean communication is preferable when discussing complex issues.

In this chapter, two complementary theories will help explain the empirical results. These are Kock's (2005) media naturalness hypothesis and Robert and Dennis' (2005) cognitive model of media choice. The theories were chosen because they have been developed through reviewing and analyzing many years of research on media use. They also address the limitations of the media richness theory by taking better account of social behavior and cognitive-based views of media use.

The media naturalness hypothesis is based on the idea that "human beings evolved a biological communication apparatus through millions of years of Darwinian adaptation and that such apparatus is largely designed for face-to-face communication" (Kock et al. 2007, p. 335). It is concerned with the degree of naturalness of a communication medium (or its degree of similarity to the face-to-face medium). It assumes that natural communication involves the following key elements: (1) a high degree of co-location, (2) a high degree of synchronicity, (3) the ability to convey and observe facial expressions, (4) the ability to convey and observe body language, and (5) the ability to convey and listen to speech (Kock 2005). Synchronous communication is assumed to be more "natural" than asynchronous communication since it closer resembles face-to-face communication. "The media naturalness hypothesis argues that, other thing being equal, a decrease in the degree of naturalness of a communication medium leads to the following effects in connection with communication: (1) increased cognitive effort, (2) increased communication ambiguity, and (3) decreased psychological arousal" (Kock 2005, p. 117).

The cognitive model of media choice argues that individuals need to be motivated and have the ability to process messages (Robert and Dennis 2005). The model argues that "the use of rich media high in social presence induces increased motivation but decreases the ability to process information, while the use of lean media low in social presence induces decreased motivation but increases the ability to process information" (p. 10). Social presence has been defined as the "degree of salience of the other person in a mediated communication and the consequent salience of their interpersonal interactions" (Short et al. 1976, p. 65). Some media are characterized by greater social presence (e.g., videoconferencing) than the other (e.g., e-mail) and enable higher levels of intimacy and immediacy. Robert and Dennis (2005) propose that synchronous communication makes it possible to monitor the receiver's reaction to a message, which leads to the receiver being more committed and motivated to read it. However, when communicating asynchronously, the receiver has more time to comprehend the message since the sender does not expect an immediate answer.

Interestingly, the media naturalness hypothesis and the cognitive model of media choice support and complement each other. While the first theory is based on evolutionary psychology, the latter is based on social psychology. Kock (2005) argues that low synchronicity will lead to increased cognitive effort. Similarly, Robert and Dennis (2005) argue that low synchronicity increases the ability to process information. Kock argues that high synchronicity will lead to increased psychological arousal. Similarly, Robert and Dennis argue that high synchronicity induces increased motivation and decreased ambiguity. Despite criticizing the media richness theory, the cognitive model of media choice is somewhat technologically deterministic. Robert and Dennis do not acknowledge that it is the users, and not the medium itself, that decide whether to use a medium asynchronously or synchronously. As discussed earlier, in some organizations, near-synchronous use of e-mail has been encouraged. Kock acknowledges this when arguing that media naturalness "may or may not lead to certain types of behavior or task outcomes" since users do not always rationally choose the most appropriate medium because of, for example, influences from the social context (Markus 1994). However, a certain medium might better support synchronicity, naturalness, or social presence because of its characteristics.

2.2 Comparative Studies of Asynchronous and Synchronous Communication

As noted in the introduction, most studies on CMC in e-learning settings have analyzed asynchronous communication in isolation or in comparison with traditional face-to-face classrooms. Examples of comparative studies of asynchronous and synchronous communication are summarized in Table 6.1. Most of these studies have compared text-based discussion board and chat in higher education settings. They have mainly relied on social, collaborative, and constructivist learning theories. The

Table 6.1 Comparative studies of asynchronous and synchronous communication in e-learning settings

Source	Type of CMC	Theory base	Data collection	Respondents	Findings
Bonk et al. (1998)	Text-based discussion board and chat	Sociocultural learning theory	Content analysis	Two courses, 65 preservice teachers	Students expressed more complex ideas in asynchronous discussions and interacted more frequently in synchronous discussions
Chou (2002)	Text-based discussion board and chat	Models of interaction	Content analysis	Undergraduate course, number of students not reported	Students were focused on the task in asynchronous discussions but also exchanged socioemotional interactions in the synchronous discussions
Davidson-Shivers et al. (2001)	Text-based discussion board and chat	Not specified	Content analysis, survey	Graduate course, 14 students	Students expressed more reflective statements in the asynchronous discussions and larger number of shorter remarks in the synchronous discussions
Haythornthwaite (2000)	Text-based discussion board, chat, e-mail, and PowerPoint lecture with audio	Social network analysis, computer-supported collaborative learning	Survey, interview	Graduate courses, 52 students	Students who communicated frequently maintained more socially supportive relations and communicated both asynchronously and synchronously
Haythornthwaite (2001)	Text-based discussion board, chat, e-mail, and PowerPoint lecture with audio	Social network analysis, computer-supported collaborative learning	Survey, interview	Graduate course, 14 students	Discussion board was used for class-wide communication, chat more to named others but also for class-wide communication, and e-mail for intra-team communication

Table 6.1 (continued)

Source	Type of CMC	Theory base	Data collection	Respondents	Findings
Hrastinski (2007)	Text-based discussion board and chat	Sociocultural learning theory, cultural differences	Content analysis, surveys, interview	Graduate course, 8 students	It is difficult to get asynchronous discussions started with few students. Combining asynchronous and synchronous communication may enhance participation
Mabrito (2006)	Text-based discussion board and chat	Not specified	Content analysis, survey	Undergraduate course, 16 students	Asynchronous sessions were effective for collaborative writing. Students spent less time focusing on course tasks in synchronous sessions
Malmberg (2006)	Text-based discussion board and chat	Sociocultural learning theory	Content analysis	Undergraduate course, 17 students	Project groups stayed on task in asynchronous discussions while synchronous discussions included private and social talk
Ng and Detenber (2005)	Text-based discussion board and chat	Review of research on online political communication	Survey	Undergraduate course, 153 students	Synchronous discussions were perceived as more informative and persuasive but did not have significant impacts on students' intention to participate
Schullo et al. (2005)	ElluminateLive!™ (synchronous) and WebCT™ (mainly asynchronous)	Review of research on distance education	Surveys, content analysis, interview, observation	Six graduate courses, 7 instructors, 85 students	Synchronous communication allowed educators to build connections with and among students more efficiently

Table 6.1 (continued)

Source	Type of CMC	Theory base	Data collection	Respondents	Findings
Spencer (2002)	Text-based discussion board and chat	Learning (e.g., constructivism) and media theories (e.g., information richness theory)	Content analysis, interview, survey	29 higher education courses, 133 students	Various hypotheses were examined but few were statistically significant. Students found synchronous sessions rewarding
Schwier and Balbar (2002)	Text-based discussion board and chat	Not specified	Not specified	Graduate course, 7 students	Synchronous communication contributed to continuity and sense of community but was less effective in dealing with content and issues

main analysis methods have been content analysis of electronic logs, surveys, and interviews. The large-scale studies have identified few significant differences between asynchronous and synchronous communication. The differences seem to be subtle and have mainly been identified by conducting qualitative content analyses in smaller groups.

The reviewed studies of Table 6.1 indicate that asynchronous communication is more suitable for reflection and discussion of complex ideas. Moreover, the reviewed studies reveal that e-learners have been reported to enjoy synchronous discussions because they are experienced as more social although several of the reviewed studies have found that participation may be more concise and less "deep." The reviewed studies seem to suggest that, when the purpose is to discuss complex ideas, asynchronous communication is preferable. However, the findings are inconclusive on what the benefits and limitations of synchronous communication might be, even though the review reveals that several studies have found that supporting synchronous communication might induce increased communication and social exchanges among e-learners.

2.3 Researching Online Participation

Learning as participation in the social world is at the core of several influential learning theories (Jonassen and Land 2000; Wenger 1998; Vygotsky 1978). Wenger's (1998, p. 55) definition of participation consists of two parts: "a process of taking part" and "the relations with others that reflect this process." Previous research emphasizes that encouraging participation is a central aspect of e-learning (e.g., Bober and Dennen 2001; Hung 2001). Haythornthwaite (2002) argued that in particular three types of exchanges were important in building and sustaining participation in learning communities: information exchange, task support, and social support (see Table 6.2). These three types of exchanges have been addressed in the information systems, social networks, management, social psychology, and online learning literature (Coppola et al. 2002; Haythornthwaite 2002; Münzer 2003).

Table 6.2 Three types of exchanges (adapted from Haythornthwaite 2002)

Type of exchange	Examples
Information exchange	Ask or answer a content-related question
	Share information
	Express an idea or thought
Task support	Plan work, allocate tasks, coordinate joint efforts, or review drafts
	Negotiate and resolve conflicts
Social support	Express companionship, emotional aid, or advice
	Emoticons (e.g., ☺, ☹)
	Support during an upset (e.g., support when having technical difficulties)
	Talk about things other than classwork

First, the importance of sharing information among learners is widely acknowledged. When doing this, learners need to be encouraged to feel comfortable enough to ask questions and share information with as many others as possible. The result of such conversations may be new knowledge, reorganized knowledge, or an awareness of a need for additional understanding (Edelson et al. 1996). There is an insufficiently challenged assumption in research that those who do not contribute are passive recipients even though they may be actively engaged in reading (Romiszowski & Mason 2004). Sutton (2001) argues that e-learners not only benefit by contributing themselves but also by actively processing the interactions of others. In fact, e-learners access many times more messages than they reply to (Goldman et al. 2005). Learning may still occur since participants observe actions of others and the results of these actions. These arguments support an assumption of this chapter: It is important to also include measures of perceived participation when studying online participation.

Second, task support relations are essential, especially when e-learners produce some kind of product, such as an assignment, in collaboration with peers. Therefore, it is important that e-learners gain support to accomplish such exchanges. In some comparative studies of asynchronous and synchronous communication, information exchange and task support have been analyzed as a single entity (e.g., Chou 2002; Davidson-Shivers et al. 2001). Unfortunately, these studies do not acknowledge that task-related interaction may either be related with content or management of a task (Haythornthwaite 2002).

Finally, social support relations are desirable when maintaining relationships to foster knowledge work and collaborative learning (Cho et al. 2005; Kreijns et al. 2003). Such relations are important to create an atmosphere where communication is encouraged. For example, anecdotes and personal experiences encourage trust, which in turn foster receptive and creative learning environments (Hillman 1999; Malmberg 2006). The degree of social bonding that occurs in e-learning settings varies and is probably dependent on many factors. For example, in a study of a 10-week online course, the learners rarely exchanged social and emotional support (Hrastinski 2006) while another study of a 2-year library program identified many examples of such exchanges (Haythornthwaite and Kazmer 2002).

3 Method

Two central questions in case study research are whether to include one or several cases and whether to use several data collection methods. In this study, it was decided to focus two cases. By focusing on two case settings, the cases can still be studied thoroughly but it is also possible to elucidate more general results (Yin 2003). When departing from Wenger's (1998) definition of participation more than "simple" measures, such as the number of messages in discussion boards, are needed. An assumption of this chapter is that participation is a complex phenomenon, which motivates using several data collection methods in order to gain a richer and deeper understanding (Cavaye 1996). Consequently, electronic logs, questionnaires, and interviews were used to collect both actual and perceived measures on participation in two case settings.

3.1 Research Setting

As noted above, it was decided to focus on two cases. Two e-learning courses were selected and deemed suitable since they included asynchronous and synchronous online discussions with geographically dispersed students who mainly communicated by CMC media.

The first case setting is a series of online discussions with students from two courses in knowledge management. A university in Argentina delivered one of the courses and the other course was delivered online at a university in Sweden. Students from the two universities jointly participated in two asynchronous and two synchronous text-based online discussions by discussion board and chat over a 2-week period, where course literature was discussed. Although the Argentinean and Swedish students never met face-to-face, introductory sessions were arranged in both Argentina and Sweden.

The second case setting is an online course in change and knowledge management. It is the first course in a Swedish part-time master program and is the equivalent of a 10-week course of full-time study. The students of the course participated in two asynchronous and two synchronous text-based online discussions, again using discussion board and chat, over a 4-week period. Demographic data for the participants of the two case settings are presented in Table 6.3 and were collected via the questionnaires discussed below. The participants were professionals of a rather high mean age, which suggested that the results may, at least partly, be generalized to e-learning and online collaboration in organizations. A benefit of including groups of different sizes is that tentative results for online groups of different sizes can be discerned.

Table 6.3 Age and gender of the participants

	Mean age	Age range	Males	Females
Case 1 ($n = 8$)	38	23–52	5	3
Case 2 ($n = 19$)	43	28–56	5	14

The online discussions of both classes followed an introductory on-campus sessions to the class and the e-learning environment. The case groups were scheduled to conduct an asynchronous and a synchronous discussion every week or every second week. Most participants did not meet face-to-face, except for two participants. The e-learners participated in the discussions wherever they found convenient, usually at home or work.

In all sessions, the teacher suggested questions for the group to discuss and also asked participants to submit questions on the course literature. The synchronous discussions were scheduled for 3 h and participants worked in small groups while the asynchronous discussions were scheduled over a week. The internal validity of the study may be questioned since the participants were divided into smaller groups in the synchronous discussions but not in the asynchronous ones. However, the decision to configure the two types of discussions differently was informed by research. Asynchronous discussions have been recommended to be conducted in larger groups since this creates a greater potential for interaction (Caspi et al. 2003), while chat discussions are recommended to be conducted in smaller groups since e-learners otherwise find it difficult to maintain a logical sequence of speakers' contributions (Mazur 2004) and to keep message load manageable (Haythornthwaite 2006).

3.2 Data Collection

It is commonly debated whether interpersonal relations should be studied by seeking to measure existing relations or "relations as perceived by actors involved in them" (Marsden 1990, p. 437). Marsden argues that respondents are capable of reporting on their relations in general terms but cannot be expected to "give useful data on detailed discussion topics or the exact timing of interactions" (p. 456). There is evidence from research on e-learning that supports this claim. Picciano (2002) found that e-learners who posted few messages in a discussion board perceived themselves to have made a higher number of postings than they actually did while those that posted many messages perceived themselves to have made fewer postings than they actually did. Similarly, Hrastinski (2006) reported that some e-learners did not feel that they communicated with peers even though they submitted a high number of messages. Since actual and perceived participation may differ (Ng and Detenber 2005; Picciano 2002) it was decided to triangulate measures of actual and perceived participation, in order to gain a deeper understanding.

Actual participation: Electronic logs were used to determine the interpersonal relations that were maintained among participants, i.e., one of the two parts of Wenger's (1998) definition of participation. Quantitative measures such as the number of postings are commonly used when evaluating participation. Such numbers provide too little information about the nature of the interactions (Hillman 1999). For that reason it is also necessary to study the actual interactions to understand what is being discussed. For example, frequency counts of messages or words do not reveal whether e-learners are exchanging information, planning work, or supporting each other socially.

As recommended by Hillman (1999), complete sentences were used as unit of analysis. The author conducted the analysis. Fixed units, such as sentences, are more objectively recognizable as compared with more dynamic thematic units such as "units of meaning" (Henri 1991). Sentences as unit of analysis have been proved to be easy to use and reliable, even though it has also been acknowledged that dividing text into sentences may be inconsistent, especially when communication is informal (Rourke et al. 2000). Synchronous discussions typically contain short and incomplete sentences. Incomplete sentences, which were most commonly found in the synchronous transcripts, were combined to complete ones. For example, the following chat lines were combined to one sentence: "for example... / when you already told your boss you want to leave / and they say 'I [will] give you extra money' or things like that" (Transcript, Synchronous discussion). The sentences of the discussions were classified according to the three types of exchanges described in the previous section, i.e., information exchange, task support, and social support. Table 6.4 contains examples of classified sentences from the electronic logs. Some sentences included more than one type of exchange and were counted in each category.

Table 6.4 Examples of sentences classified as information exchange, task support, and social support

Type of exchange	Synchronous discussion	Asynchronous discussion
Information exchange	"A lack of competence among the employees might explain why the customers are not satisfied"	"A person who is by himself and do not share knowledge is not as attractive in the eyes of the company"
Task support	"OK, I'm not with you now – which question are we discussing?"	"I have created a thread where we can discuss assignment 2"
Social support	"Well done!"	"That's great to hear!"

Perceived participation: Questionnaires and interviews were used to study whether the participants felt that they took part and whether they felt they maintained interpersonal relations with peers, i.e., both parts of Wenger's (1998) definition of participation. The participants were asked to submit a questionnaire after each discussion. A measure on perceived participation was developed in a previous study (reference omitted during review) by combining items adapted from several sources: Gunawardena and Zittle's (1997) social presence scale, Haythornthwaite's (2000) items on sense of belonging, Rovai et al.'s (2004) classroom and school community inventory, and Webster and Hackley's (1997) measure on involvement and participation. There were eight items that were measured on a seven-point ordinal scale. The items that are included in the measure are those that best reflect Wenger's (1998) definition of participation.

Perceived interpersonal relations were studied by using a social network approach, where the most common unit of analysis is the interactions between actors, i.e., relational data (Scott 1991). The approach provides a set of techniques for understanding patterns of relations between and among people (Garton et al. 1999) and has been argued to be a viable tool for evaluating the character of online group dynamics in learning settings (Daugherty and Turner 2003). In this study, two of the most commonly used techniques are relied on network density and sociograms. Network density indicates the number of reported ties relative to the maximum possible number of ties (Wasserman and Faust 1994). Sociograms have been of great illustrative importance ever since the 1930s and is a technique for drawing comprehensible diagrams for smaller sets of actors (Moreno 1934; Scott 1991).

When collecting data for the first case, every participant was asked to what extent information, task support, and social support were exchanged with each other participant on a seven-point ordinal scale after each discussion. The scale ranged from strongly disagree (1) to strongly agree (7). An exchange was noted for respondents that agreed or strongly agreed (6–7) that any of the three types of exchanges had occurred. However, for the second case, it became too complex for respondents to assess the strength of ties with 18 other participants. Therefore, a nominal scale had to be used, i.e., each respondent was asked whether or not information, task support, or social support was exchanged with each other participant after each discussion. Adjustments were made for missing questionnaire data by taking the responses others gave for interaction with the participant during the time period (Haythornthwaite 2001).

The number of participants in each discussion, and the number of them that also submitted a questionnaire, is summarized in Table 6.5. For example, six out of the eight enrolled students (75%) of the first case participated in the first asynchronous discussion. All of them completed the questionnaire. The most common reason for not participating in a discussion was work commitments. For the second case, some participants did not complete the questionnaire despite being reminded.

Table 6.5 Number of participants and response rate for each discussion

	Case 1				Case 2			
	Participants		Respondents		Participants		Respondents	
	n	%	n	%	n	%	n	%
Asynch. 1	6	75	6	100	19	100	16	84
Synch. 1	7	88	7	100	18	95	17	94
Asynch. 2	5	63	5	100	19	100	16	84
Synch. 2	6	75	6	100	16	84	14	88
Total	24	75	24	100	72	95	63	88

Twelve half-hour telephone interviews were recorded and transcribed. In the first case, two Argentinean and two Swedish participants were interviewed. They are referred to as Female #1 and Male #1–3 in the chapter. In the second case, eight interviewees were randomly selected. They are referred to as Female #2–6 and Male #4–6 in the chapter. All interviews were conducted in the month after the discussions were finished and were intended to obtain a richer view of participation in the asynchronous and synchronous online discussions. The interviews were conducted in a conversational mode even though an interview guide was used (Yin 2003). The following is an example of a question from the interview guide: "Did you feel that you had a closer relation with the other participants in the asynchronous (discussion board) or synchronous (chat) online discussions? Why?" The data from the interviews were categorized according to the research questions.

In the next section, a measure on perceived participation in the asynchronous and synchronous settings is revealed. Then, communication patterns, perceived social networks, and participant opinions are presented, which may help to explain why the measure on perceived participation differed when using different media. It is assumed that relying only on one of these measures does not address the complexity of online participation. However, the combination of these measures can give a deeper understanding of online participation by different media.

4 Results

The questionnaire contained a measure of perceived participation consisting of eight items, which were measured on a seven-point Likert scale. The measure was reliable in both the smaller class (Cronbach's $\alpha = 0.90$) and the larger class (Cronbach's $\alpha = 0.93$). Table 6.6 displays descriptive statistics for each item in the measure. It shows that the means for all items were higher when communicating synchronously. When comparing the total means of Table 6.6, the difference in perceived participation between the two types of media was smaller in the larger group. Differences in means of items for both cases indicate that the participants especially felt that the synchronous discussions included social interaction (item 2). However, the high standard deviations of this item show that the participants disagreed about this to quite a large extent. The participants of the smaller class felt more connected to others (item 8) when communicating synchronously.

The eight items were also combined into the categories strong (6–7), intermediate (3–5), and weak (1–2) perceived participation to simplify interpretation. As displayed in Table 6.7, 24 and 63 questionnaires were completed in the first and second cases, respectively. All items were answered by the respondents of the first case ($24 \times 8 = 192$), while one item was left unanswered in the second case ($63 \times 8 = 504$). Drawing on the data, the percentage of items indicating strong perceived participation was higher when communicating synchronously. The percentage of items indicating strong perceived participation was 72–75% in the synchronous setting but 55–57% in the asynchronous setting (see Table 6.7). These findings are corroborated by the interviews where it was found that seven interviewees felt they participated more actively in the synchronous setting. Three interviewees felt they participated in different ways by the two media while the remaining two felt they participated more actively in the asynchronous setting. Next, results that may contribute toward understanding why participants felt they participated more actively in the synchronous setting are presented.

Table 6.6 Perceived participation in synchronous and asynchronous online discussions

	Case 1				Case 2			
	Synch. (n = 13)		Asynch. (n = 11)		Synch. (n = 31)		Asynch. (n = 32)	
	Mean	SD	Mean	SD	Mean	SD	Mean	SD
1. I felt like the participants in the discussion worked together	5.7	1.2	5.1	1.8	5.9	1.3	5.2	1.1
2. I felt that the discussion included social interaction	5.4	1.7	4.1	2.0	5.7	1.4	4.9	1.4
3. As a student, I felt part of the discussion	6.2	0.7	5.5	1.3	6.0	1.0	5.6	1.3
4. I felt comfortable interacting with participant(s)	6.1	1.0	5.4	1.8	5.7	1.4	5.6	0.8
5. As a student, I felt personally involved in the discussion	6.2	0.7	6.1	0.7	5.9	0.9	5.6	1.2
6. I felt that my point of view was acknowledged by others in the discussion	6.2	0.6	5.5	1.8	5.8	1.0	5.3	1.0
7. I felt that students in the discussion cared about each others' opinions	6.0	0.7	5.3	1.6	5.9	1.3	5.6	0.9
8. I felt connected to the others in the discussion	5.8	1.0	4.8	1.8	5.9	1.1	5.5	1.0
Total	6.0	1.0	5.2	1.7	5.7	1.2	5.4	1.1

Table 6.7 Perceived participation by case and media

	Case 1 ($n = 24$)[1]				Case 2 ($n = 63$)[2]			
	Strong n (%)	Intermed. n (%)	Weak n (%)	Total n (%)	Strong n (%)	Intermed. n (%)	Weak n (%)	Total n (%)
Synch.	78 (75)	25 (24)	1 (1)	104 (100)	178 (72)	64 (26)	6 (2)	248 (100)
Asynch.	50 (57)	29 (33)	9 (10)	88 (100)	140 (55)	107 (42)	8 (3)	255 (100)
Total	128 (67)	54 (28)	10 (5)	192 (100)	318 (63)	171 (34)	14 (3)	503 (100)

[1] Chi-square (d.f. = 2) = 11.6, $p < 0.005$.
[2] Chi-square (d.f. = 2) = 15.5, $p < 0.001$.

4.1 Communication Patterns

In Table 6.8, the number and percentage of sentences for the three types of exchanges are presented. The asynchronous discussions were more focused on exchanging information, especially in the smaller class. In the synchronous discussions, less than 60% of the sentences were classified as information exchange. Instead, task support and social support exchanges were more common. Note that higher total frequencies of sentences were produced in the synchronous discussions. This was especially evident in the smaller class. However, in the larger class, the participants wrote a higher number of sentences classified as information exchange in the asynchronous discussions.

Table 6.8 Number of sentences by type of exchange and in total

	Case 1 ($n = 24$)				Case 2 ($n = 72$)			
	Synchronous		Asynchronous		Synchronous		Asynchronous	
	N	%	n	%	n	%	n	%
Information exchange	876	58	369	99	1816	57	2438	93
Task support	507	34	5	1	935	29	131	5
Social support	198	13	2	1	572	18	124	2
All exchanges	1507	100	375	100	3173	100	2608	100

Several interviewees explained that participation in the asynchronous setting was limited by time: "It takes time to write and to read every post and maybe you try to find time to do that … and you start to say: I'll do it tomorrow and I'll do it tomorrow and the days keep on going until you really do" (Male #2). However, in the synchronous discussions, participation could not be postponed. Moreover, some interviewees felt that "much was already said … the first or second day" (Female #3) in the asynchronous discussions and they did not want to repeat what had already been written, while this was not mentioned in relation with the synchronous discussions, probably since the participants discussed questions in smaller groups. Another factor revealed in the interviews was that the interviewees felt they "kept to the subject" (Male #3) in the asynchronous discussions while the synchronous discussions enabled them to maintain more personal relations. For example, most participants exchanged social support in between the group discussions, which several of them acknowledged as important for getting to know other participants better, especially because the classes seldom or never met face-to-face.

Table 6.9 Mean number of sentences per participant and standard deviations

	Case 1 ($n = 24$)				Case 2 ($n = 72$)			
	Synchronous		Asynchronous		Synchronous		Asynchronous	
	n/stud	SD	n/stud	SD	n/stud	SD	n/stud	SD
Information exchange	54	17	20	15	51	18	59	35
Task support	18	6	0	0	23	7	2	2
Social support	13	9	0	0	15	10	3	3
All exchanges	86	30	20	15	84	26	62	36

Table 6.9 displays the mean number of sentences that was submitted by each participant and standard deviations. The high standard deviations for information exchanges in the asynchronous environment and social support exchanges in the synchronous environment show that the number of sentences contributed differed to a large extent between participants. For example, one female said that she is not "the kind of person that can write long texts" and also did not feel like exchanging social support with others: "I try to stick with the tasks. I think it is a bit hard [to exchange social support] since we only met once … I want to meet people several times before I can [do that]" (Female #3).

4.2 Perceived Social Networks

Figure 6.1 displays sociograms and network densities by medium and case, as perceived by the participants. A tie was included if a respondent agreed that an exchange occurred in at least one of the two synchronous or asynchronous discussions. The participants of both classes reported stronger overall network densities in the synchronous setting, especially in the smaller class. This finding underlines the fact that participants not only produced more text in the synchronous discussions, but that they also felt they maintained more ties with peers. This was also evident in the interviews where eight interviewees said they maintained ties with more participants in the synchronous settings. Three interviewees did not feel that was a difference between the two media while one felt that he maintained ties with

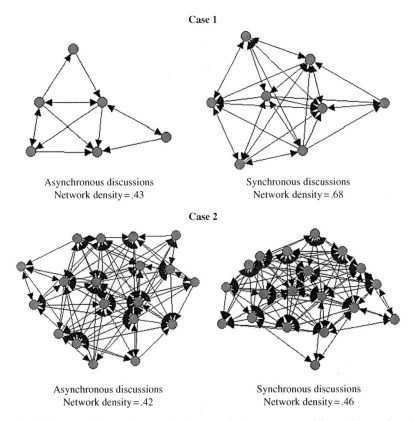

Case 1

Asynchronous discussions
Network density = .43

Synchronous discussions
Network density = .68

Case 2

Asynchronous discussions
Network density = .42

Synchronous discussions
Network density = .46

Fig. 6.1 Sociograms illustrating perceived communication among participants in asynchronous (*left*) and synchronous discussions (*right*). The sociograms were created with Ucinet 6 (Borgatti et al. 2002)

more participants in the asynchronous setting. The synchronous discussions were experienced as more interactive, because discussions were conducted in real time and in smaller groups. This configuration made the participants feel confident that there would be a reply when asking a question.

Most respondents acknowledged that the two types of media promote different kinds of participation. Thus, even though the two sociograms of the second case look similar, they illustrate different kinds of ties. The interviews revealed that the focus of the synchronous discussions was on quantity, i.e., trying to write something fast before "someone else will say what I was going to say" (Female #3). This led to "more of a discussion . . . rather than a monolog" (Female #4), which might have contributed to that a slightly higher number of ties being maintained among participants. However, in the asynchronous discussions, the focus was on quality, which also explains why participants produced fewer sentences in this setting. This was especially appreciated in the larger class.

5 Discussion

In this study it was investigated how and why synchronous communication, as a complement to asynchronous communication, affects participation in online discussions. The results from both cases indicate that synchronous communication has the potential to enhance participation in online discussions. This conclusion was based on the following indications:

- The measure on perceived participation was higher in both settings, especially in the smaller class, when communicating synchronously.
- The standard deviations of sentence counts per participant were smaller for information exchanges when communicating synchronously. This indicates that synchronous communication enabled more equal participation.
- The participants wrote more sentences classified as task support or social support for both classes and a higher number of sentences classified as information exchange in the synchronous discussions of the smaller class. Notably, the participants of the smaller class wrote four times as many sentences in the synchronous discussions.
- The perceived social networks were denser in both settings when communicating synchronously, especially in the smaller class.

Notably, differences in participation were especially evident in the smaller class, which may be explained by the "critical mass" (Markus 1987) to get discussions going in synchronous settings seem to be lower (Caspi et al. 2003; Palloff and Pratt 1999). It should be noted that, even though e-learners seem to communicate more in synchronous environments, it has been found that conversations are more concise and egocentric (Bonk et al. 1998).

The findings from both cases indicated that synchronous use of chat, as compared to asynchronous use of discussion board, induced more social support exchange. The synchronous discussions included quite a number of social support exchanges (13–18%) while the asynchronous ones included very few such exchanges (1–2%). Similarly, Hillman (1999) reported that 2% of the sentences in asynchronous discussions were classified as social support. Moreover, the second item in the measure of perceived participation revealed higher means for the statement "I felt that the discussion included social interaction" when communicating synchronously. It should, however, be noted that both sentence counts per participant and the second item were related with high standard deviations, i.e., some exchanged social support frequently, while others chose not to engage in such exchanges. One reason for the higher levels of social support exchanges in the synchronous setting seems to be that participants feel that it is a more natural medium for communicating and maintaining social support relations (Kock 2005; Malmberg 2006). In line with the results of Orvis et al. (2002), exchanges of social support in the synchronous setting followed temporal patterns. Social interaction usually occurred in the beginning and end of class and in between group discussions. The classes under investigation in this chapter followed a tight schedule, which may be one reason for a lower level of social support compared with some previous studies. For example, Chou (2002) classified 33% of sentences examined as socioemotional in a CMC systems course, Mabrito (2006) classified 33% of communication units as general conversation in a business writing course, and Orvis et al. (2002) classified 30% of chat lines as social in online military training.

The content analyses of both cases also indicated that synchronous communication, as compared to asynchronous communication, induced a higher relative degree of task support exchanges. In the synchronous discussions, the participants had to decide what to discuss and how to sum up and present the results of their discussion within a specific time period. This explains the high percentages of sentences classified as task support exchanges (29–34%). Interestingly, Malmberg (2006) found that self-organizing groups of e-learners who had access to both discussion board and chat chose the latter to support task support relations.

The fact that participants spent more time on task and social support in the synchronous discussions may be interpreted differently depending on the aim of the learning activity. On the one hand, less time is spent discussing content and thus being engaged in what some label substantive communication (Davidson-Shivers et al. 2001). On the other hand, e-learners gain experience in collaborating online and functioning in a group (Haythornthwaite 2006). Also, discussing things other than course literature, for example, supporting each other socially seems to have led to an enhancement of perceived participation (Mabrito 2006). This conclusion is supported by Ng and Detenber (2005) who argue that asynchronous discussions may be experienced as more static and less interactive as compared with synchronous conversations.

5.1 Personal and Cognitive Online Participation

In this section, the media naturalness hypothesis based on evolutionary psychology (Kock 2005) and the cognitive model of media choice based on social psychology (Robert and Dennis 2005) help in providing explanations for the empirical findings. The media naturalness hypothesis predicts that *synchronous communication increases psychological arousal* and, similarly, the cognitive model of media choice predicts that *synchronous communication increases motivation*. Kock argues that each element that characterizes "natural" media (e.g., the ability to convey and observe facial expressions and body language) contribute to psychological arousal. However, if these elements are suppressed, a decrease in psychological arousal can be expected. The interviews revealed that many participants felt that synchronous communication was "more like talking" as compared with asynchronous communication. It seemed more accepted to exchange social support and discuss less "complex" issues. Consequently, the higher level of participation when communicating synchronously can be explained by the fact that participants felt more psychologically aroused and motivated since this type of communication closer resembles natural communication.

Synchronous communication enables monitoring the receiver's reaction to a message. This makes the receiver more committed and motivated to read the message (Robert and Dennis 2005), which leads to increased convergence on meaning

(DeLuca and Valacich 2006; Mason 1998) and decreased communication ambiguity (Kock 2005). Similarly, Woerner et al. (2004) argue that synchronous communication may help create a deeper sense of participation in a conversation and Mason (1998) argues that synchronous communication provides motivation for e-learners to keep up with their peers. These arguments are supported by the interviews of the empirical studies: "Even if I cannot see the person, I write so to speak to the person directly and get an immediate answer" (Female #4). In sum, it can be expected that the sender becomes more psychologically aroused and motivated because he/she knows it is likely that a response will be received.

The media naturalness hypothesis predicts that *synchronous communication decreases cognitive effort* and, similarly, the cognitive model of media choice predicts that *synchronous communication decreases the ability to process information.* From a biological perspective, Kock argues that, because asynchronous communication does not resemble face-to-face communication, extra burden is put on the brain, which has not been designed for asynchronous communication. Robert and Dennis argue that the receiver has more time to comprehend the message since there is not a need to respond quickly. This argument is supported by the interviews of the empirical studies: "In the [asynchronous discussions] it is easier to find some more facts, maybe have a look in a book and do more thorough postings" (Female #6).

As predicted by Robert and Dennis (2005), the participants felt they needed time to process information. This finding is also supported by the media synchronicity theory, which was developed for professional online teams. It stipulates that "virtual teams or largely virtual teams may be improved by using media of low synchronicity for conveying information and media of high synchronicity for convergence on shared meaning and switching media as appropriate" (DeLuca and Valacich 2006, p. 341).

According to Kock's (2005) estimate, an exchange of 600 words requires about 6 min for complex group tasks in face-to-face settings, while exchanging the same number of words over e-mail would take approximately 1 h. In business-to-consumer interactions, asynchronous communication may lead to lower perceived quality and dissatisfaction from customers since they may feel that it is difficult to obtain information about products and services. However, in e-learning settings, it may be interpreted as advantageous to increase cognitive effort since this is expected to enhance learning (Corno and Mandinach 1983). When communicating asynchronously participants discuss a lower number of topics but spend more time on each topic. However, in synchronous settings participants respond quickly since they do not want to disrupt the conversation. In the interviews, it was revealed that the focus of the synchronous discussions was on quantity, i.e., trying to write something fast before "someone else will say what I was going to say" (Female #3). Directly after the discussions, the level of perceived participation was high, which at least partly can be explained by the fact that the participants felt part of a more intense and psychologically arousing experience.

It should be clarified that a medium may be used differently depending on "how it is used, the context in which it is used and the convenience of its use" (DeLuca and Valacich 2006, p. 340). Thus, even though some media seem preferable for supporting certain types of exchanges, they are not necessarily used in that way. A benefit of using the concept of synchronicity is that it can describe the *use* of a medium, rather than inherent characteristics of a medium. For example, in some circumstances e-mail might be used to support communication with a lower degree of synchronicity while it might be used to support communication with a higher degree of synchronicity in other circumstances.

Factoring the above, synchronous communication makes it possible to monitor the receiver's reaction to a message so that the receiver will be more committed and motivated to read it. However, when communicating asynchronously, the receiver has more time to comprehend the message since the sender does not expect an immediate answer. Thus, synchronous communication increases motivation but decreases the ability to process information. The concepts of *personal participation* and *cognitive participation* are introduced to describe the dimensions of participation that are supported by synchronous and asynchronous communication (see Fig. 6.2). Inspired by the media naturalness hypothesis (Kock 2005) and the cognitive model of media choice (Robert and Dennis 2005), it is suggested that, other things being equal, an increase in the degree of synchronicity better support personal participation while a decrease in the degree of synchronicity better support cognitive participation. Synchronous communication better support personal participation because it involves at least the following key elements: (1) increased psychological arousal, (2) increased motivation, and (3) increased convergence on meaning. Personal participation describes the more intense type of participation supported by communication of a higher degree of synchronicity while cognitive participation describes the more reflective type of participation supported by communication of a lower degree of synchronicity. The first type seems to better support less complex information exchanges, including task support and social support exchanges, while the second type seems to better support reflection and discussion of complex ideas.

Fig. 6.2 The concepts of cognitive and personal participation

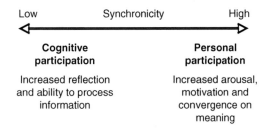

6 Limitations and Further Research

The advantage of examining a small population is asynchronous and synchronous communication could be examined in more depth by adopting several data collection methods. However, a disadvantage is that the results are based on a rather small population of professionals of a rather high mean age. Since the study is exploratory, the results are preliminary and need to be tested in other contexts.

This chapter included two cases, which were studied sequentially. The first case was completed but later yet another case setting was decided to be included with the aim of creating more general results. As mentioned in the method section, different scales (nominal and ordinal) were used when collecting social network data in each case. An implication is that some of the richness of the data on ties between participants from the first case may have been lost when simplifying the data set (Wasserman and Faust 1994). Another issue related with the first case is that both Argentineans and Swedes were included. The results might have been different if a majority of the participants were of the same nationality. For example, the participants might have participated more actively if the online discussions had been conducted using their native language. It should also be noted that this study included professionals of a rather high mean age, which were enrolled in knowledge management courses on master level. The results might have been different if, for example, the population included undergraduate students enrolled in other courses. An advantage is that the results may, at least partly, be generalized to e-learning and online collaboration in organizations. Educational and organizational settings share the challenge of creating positive work and learning environment (Haythornthwaite 2000). However, if and how the findings of this study are valid in other contexts will need to be examined in future research.

This study and most of the reviewed ones, focused on text-based media. However, as more advanced synchronous software become available, audio and video media will become more widely used. For example, in a study of an advanced synchronous system (ElluminateLive!^{TM}) it was reported that the most widely used feature was audio conversations followed by chat (Schullo et al. 2005). Researchers are encouraged to build on the conclusions proposed here when studying other media and settings.

A future research venue that has so far been insufficiently explored is cultural differences in e-learning settings (Hrastinski 2007; Romiszowski and Mason 2004). Since the population was small, it is only possible to reflect on the implications of including Swedes and Argentineans in the study. Hofstede's (1980) constructs for distinguishing national cultures may provide preliminary explanations. Drawing on the construct of uncertainty avoidance, Argentineans are predicted to feel less comfortable with uncertainty and ambiguity. It can be hypothesized that Argentineans might be more likely to prefer synchronous discussions where the activities were scheduled and the teacher gave more specific instructions, while Swedes might be more likely to prefer asynchronous discussions, where the topics and discussions evolved during a longer time period. However, this hypothesis needs to be examined in future research.

7 Conclusions

This study has showed that synchronous communication, as a complement to asynchronous communication, has the potential to affect participation positively in online discussions. This was confirmed by measures on actual as well as perceived participation, which showed that the participants felt they were "taking part" and that they maintained "relations with others" (Wenger 1998). The synchronous discussions enabled higher sentence counts, more dense perceived social networks, and stronger perceived participation. These discussions were more focused on task and social support when compared with the asynchronous discussions. The differences in levels of participation, when comparing participation for the two types of communication, were especially evident in the smaller class. This may be explained by the fact that the "critical mass" (Markus 1987) to get discussions going in synchronous settings seems to be lower (Caspi et al. 2003; Palloff and Pratt 1999). Since these conclusions are drawn from two cases of an explorative character, they need to be interpreted cautiously. The results are nevertheless promising, since participation has been argued to underlie other important variables such as learning outcomes (e.g., Hiltz et al. 2000), retention rates (e.g., Rovai 2002), and satisfaction (e.g., Alavi and Dufner 2005) in e-learning settings.

In the synchronous discussions, the e-learners felt that they worked together, because they were confident that someone would respond to their ideas, and they did not feel restricted to only discussing course content. These seem to be key factors in enabling *personal participation*, which should be regarded as a complement to *cognitive participation*. Personal participation describes the more intense type of participation supported by synchronous communication while cognitive participation describes the more reflective type of participation supported by asynchronous communication. It is suggested that synchronous communication may be used to better support personal participation. This is likely to induce arousal and motivation, and increased convergence on meaning, especially in smaller groups. Synchronous communication seems particularly useful for supporting task and social support relations and to exchange information with a lower degree of complexity. The following quote summarizes well the lessons that can be learnt from this study: "I think that [chat] was needed too because when you post something [in the discussion forum] you are not feeling that the other people are there ... You don't feel like you're talking to someone, it's more like talking to a system. [In the chat] you are feeling that you are talking directly with the people and ... the people on the other side are hearing you and answering you. I like that" (Male #2).

Acknowledgments This chapter is an expanded and revised version of an article by the author published in 2008 in volume 45, issue 7 of the journal *Information & Management*. The work was supported by the Swedish Research School of Management and IT.

References

Alavi M, Dufner D (2005) Technology-mediated collaborative learning: a research perspective. In: Hiltz SR, Goldman R (eds) learning together online: research on asynchronous learning networks. Lawrence Erlbaum, Mahwah, pp 191–213
Alavi M, Leidner DE (2001) Research commentary: technology-mediated learning – a call for greater depth and breadth of research. Inf Syst Res 12(1):1–10

Alavi M, Marakas GM, Yoo Y (2002) A comparative study of distributed learning environments on learning outcomes. Inf Syst Res 13(4):404–415

Bober MJ, Dennen VP (2001) Intersubjectivity: facilitating knowledge construction in online environments. Edu Media Int 38(4):241–250

Bonk CJ, Hansen EJ, Grabner-Hagen MM, Lazar SA, Mirabelli C (1998) Time to "connect": synchronous and asynchronous case-based dialogue among preservice teachers. In: Bonk CJ, King KS (eds) Electronic collaborators: learner-centered technologies for literacy, apprenticeship, and discourse. Lawrence Erlbaum Associates, Mahwah, pp 289–314

Borgatti SP, Everett MG, Freeman LC (2002) Ucinet 6 for Windows: software for social network analysis. Analytic Technologies, Harvard

Caspi A, Gorsky P, Chajut E (2003) The influence of group size on nonmandatory asynchronous instructional discussion groups. Internet High Educ 6(3):227–240

Cavaye ALM (1996) Case study research: a multi-faceted research approach for is. Inf Syst J 6(3):227–242

Chiu CM, Wang ETG (2008) Understanding web-based learning continuance intention: the role of subjective task value. Inf Manag 45(3):194–201

Cho HK, Trier M, Kim E (2005) The use of instant messaging in working relationship development: a case study. J Comp Mediated Commun 10(4)

Chou CC (2002) A comparative content analysis of student interaction in synchronous and asynchronous learning networks. Paper presented at the 35th international conference on system sciences, Hawaii

Coppola NW, Hiltz SR, Rotter NG (2002) Becoming a virtual professor: pedagogical roles and asynchronous learning networks. J Manag Inf Syst 18(4):159–189

Corno K, Mandinach EB (1983) The role of cognitive engagement in classroom learning and motivation. Educ Psychol 18(2):88–108

Daft RL, Lengel RH (1986) Organizational information requirements, media richness and structural design. Manag Sci 32(5):554–571

Daugherty M, Turner J (2003) Sociometry: an approach for assessing group dynamics in web-based courses. Interact Learn Environ 11(3):263–275

Davidson-Shivers GV, Muilenburg LY, Tanner EJ (2001) How do students participate in synchronous and asynchronous online discussions? J Educ Comput Res 25(4):351–366

DeLuca D, Valacich JS (2006) Virtual teams in and out of synchronicity. Inf Technol People 19(4):323–344

Edelson DC, Pea RD, Gomez L (1996) Constructivism in the Collaboratory. In: Wilson BG (ed) Constructivist learning environments: case studies in instructional design. Educational Technology Publications, Englewood Cliffs, pp 151–164

Fich-Benbunan R, Arbaugh JB (2006) Separating the effects of knowledge construction and group collaboration in learning outcomes of web-based courses. Inf Manag 43(6):778–793

Fredericksen E, Picket A, Shea P, Pelz W, Swan K (2000) Student satisfaction and perceived learning with on-line courses: principles and examples from the SUNY Learning Network. J Asynchronous Learn Netw 4(2):7–41

Fåhræus ER (2003) Distance education students moving towards collaborative learning: a field study of Australian distance education students and systems. Educ Technol Soc 7(2):129–140

Garrison DR, Shale D (1987) Mapping the boundaries of distance education: problems in defining the field. Am J Distance Educ 1(1):7–13

Garton L, Haythornthwaite C, Wellman B (1999) Studying on-line social networks. In: Jones S (ed) Doing internet research: critical issues and methods for examining the net. Sage Publications, Thousand Oaks, pp 77–105

Goldman R, Crosby M, Swan K, Shea P (2005) Qualitative and quisitive research methods for describing online learning. In: Hiltz SR, Goldman R (eds) Learning together online: research on asynchronous learning networks. Lawrence Erlbaum, Mahwah, pp 103–120

Gunawardena CN, McIsaac MS (2004) Distance education. In: Jonassen DH (ed) Handbook of research on educational communications and technology. Lawrence Erlbaum Associates, Mahwah, pp 355–395

Gunawardena CN, Zittle FJ (1997) Social presence as a predictor of satisfaction within a computer-mediated conferencing environment. Am J Distance Educ 11(3):8–16

Harasim L (1989) On-line education: a new domain. In: Mason R, Kaye AA (eds) Mindweave: communication, computers and distance education. Pergamon, Oxford, pp 50–62

Haythornthwaite C (2000) Online personal networks: size, Composition and media use among distance learners. New Media Soc 2(2):195–225

Haythornthwaite C (2001) Exploring multiplexity: social network structures in a computer-supported distance learning class. Inf Soc 17(3):211–226

Haythornthwaite C (2002) Building social networks via computer networks: creating and sustaining distributed learning communities. In: KA Renninger & W. Schumar (eds) Building virtual communities: learning and change in cyberspace. Cambridge University Press, Cambridge, pp 159–190

Haythornthwaite C (2006) Facilitating collaboration in online learning. J Asynchronous Learn Netw 10(1):7–24

Haythornthwaite C, Kazmer MM (2002) Bringing the internet home: adult distance learners and their internet, home, and work worlds. In: Wellman B, Haythornthwaite C (eds) The internet in everyday life. Blackwell Publishing, Malden, pp 431–463

Henri F (1991) Computer conferencing and content analysis. In: Kaye A (ed) Collaborative learning through computer conferencing: the Najaden papers. Springer-Verlag, London, pp 117–136

Hewitt J (2003) How habitual online practices affect the development of asynchronous discussion threads. J Educ Comput Res 28(1):31–45

Hillman D (1999) A new method for analyzing patterns of interaction. Am J Distance Educ 13(2):37–47

Hiltz SR, Goldman R (2005) What are asynchronous learning networks? In: Hiltz SR, Goldman R (eds) Learning together online: research on asynchronous learning networks. Lawrence Erlbaum, Mahwah, pp 3–18

Hiltz SR, Coppola N, Rotter N, Turoff M, Benbunan-Fich R (2000) Measuring the importance of collaborative learning for the effectiveness of ALN: a multi-measure, multi-method approach. J Asynchronous Learn Netw 4(2):103–125

Hofstede G (1980) Culture's consequences: international differences in work-related values. Sage, Beverly Hills

Hrastinski S (2006) Introducing an informal synchronous medium in a distance learning course: how is participation affected? Internet High Educ 9(2):117–131

Hrastinski S (2007) Using chat as a complement to discussion board in small-group online seminars: how is student participation affected? Int J Knowl Learn 3(5–6):483–500

Hrastinski S, Keller C (2007) Computer-mediated communication in education: a review of recent research. Educ Media Int 44(1):61–77

Hung D (2001) Theories of learning and computer-mediated instructional technologies. Educ Media Int 38(4):281–287

Jonassen DH, Land SM (2000) Preface. In: Jonassen DH, Land SM (eds) Theoretical foundations of learning environments. Lawrence Erlbaum, New Jersey, pp iii–ix

Jones D, Gregor S (2006) The formulation of an information systems design theory for e-Learning. Paper presented at the 1st international conference on design science research in information systems and technology, Claremont, CA

Kang I (1998) The use of computer-mediated communication: electronic collaboration and inter-activity. In: Bonk CJ, King KS (eds) Electronic collaborators: learner-centered technologies for literacy, apprenticeship, and discourse. Lawrence Erlbaum Associates, Mahwah, pp 315–337

Keegan D (1980) On defining distance education. Distance Educ 1(1):13–36

Kock N (2005) Media richness or media naturalness? The evolution of our biological communication apparatus and its influence on our behavior towards e-communication tools. IEEE Trans Prof Commun 48(2):117–130

Kock N, Verville J, Garza V (2007) Media naturalness and online learning: findings supporting both the significant- and no-significant-difference perspectives. Decis Sci J Innov Edu
5(2):333–355

Kreijns K, Kirschner PA, Jochems W (2003) Identifying the pitfalls for social interaction in
computer-supported collaborative learning environments: a review of the research. Comput
Hum Behav 19(3):335–353

Lee MKO, Cheung CMK, Chen Z (2005) Acceptance of internet-based learning medium: the Role
of Extrinsic and Intrinsic Motivation. Inf Manag 42(8):1095–1104

Leidner DE, Jarvenpaa SL (1995) The use of information technology to enhance management
school education: a theoretical view. MIS Q 19(3):265–291

Lindberg JO, Olofsson AD (2005) Training teachers through technology: a case study of a distance-
based teacher training programme. Unpublished Doctoral thesis, Umeå University, Umeå

Mabrito M (2006) A study of synchronous versus asynchronous collaboration in an online business
writing class. Am J Distance Educ 20(2):93–107

Malmberg C (2006) Kunskapsbygge på nätet: En studie av studenter i dialog. Doctoral dissertation,
Malmö University

Markus ML (1987) Toward a 'Critical Mass' theory of interactive media: universal access,
interdependence and diffusion. Commun Res 14(5):491–511

Markus ML (1994) Electronic mail as the medium of managerial choice. Organ Sci 5(4):502–527

Marsden PV (1990) Network data and measurement. Annu Rev Sociol 16:435–463

Mason R (1998) Globalising education: trends and applications. Routledge, London

Mazur JM (2004) Conversational analysis for educational technologists: theoretical and method-
ological issues for researching the structures, processes, and meaning of on-line talk. In:
Jonassen DH (ed) Handbook of research on educational communications and technology,
Lawrence Erlbaum Associates, Mahwah, pp 1073–1098

Moore MG, Kearsley G (1996) Distance education: a systems view. Wadsworth, Belmont

Moreno JL (1934) Who shall survive? a new approach to the problems of human interrelations.
Nervous and Mental Disease Publishing Company, Washington

Murphy E, Ciszewska-Carr J (2006) Landscape without bearings: instructors' first experiences in
web-based synchronous environments. First Monday 11(3)

Münzer S (2003) An evaluation of synchronous co-operative distance learning in the field: the
importance of instructional design. Educ Media Int 40(1–2):91–100

Ng EWJ, Detenber BH (2005) The impact of synchronicity and civility in online political
discussions on perceptions and intentions to participate. J Comput Mediated Commun 10(3)

Orvis KL, Wisher RA, Bonk CJ, Olson TM (2002) Communication patterns during synchronous
web-based military training in problem solving. Comput Hum Behav 18(6):783–795

Palloff RM, Pratt K (1999) Building learning communities in cyberspace: effective strategies for
the online classroom. Jossey-Bass, San Francisco

Picciano AG (2002) Beyond student perceptions: issues of interaction, presence, and performance
in an online course. J Asynchronous Learn Netw 6(1):21–40

Piccoli G, Ahmad R, Ives B (2001) Web-based virtual learning environments: a research framework and a preliminary assessment of effectiveness in basic IT skills training. MIS Q
25(4):401–426

Rice RE, Hiltz SR, Spencer DH (2005) Media mixes and learning networks. In: Hiltz SR, Goldman
R (eds) Learning together online: research on asynchronous learning networks. Lawrence
Erlbaum, Mahwah, pp 215–237

Robert LP, Dennis AR (2005) Paradox of richness: a cognitive model of media choice. IEEE Trans
Prof Commun 48(1):10–21

Romiszowski A, Mason R (2004) Computer-mediated communication. In: Jonassen DH (ed)
Handbook of research for educational communications and technology. Lawrence Erlbaum,
New Jersey, pp 397–431

Rourke L, Anderson T, Garrison DR, Archer W (2000) Methodological issues in the content
analysis of computer conference transcripts. Int J Artif Intell Educ 12:8–22

Rovai AP (2002) Building sense of community at a distance. Int Rev Res Open Dist Learn 3(1): 1–16

Rovai AP, Wighting MJ, Lucking R (2004) The classroom and school community inventory: development, refinement, and validation of a self-report measure for educational research. Internet High Educ 7(4):263–280

Russell TL (2001) The no significant difference phenomenon. International Distance Education Certification Center, Montgomery

Schullo S, Venable M, Barron AE, Kromrey JD, Hilbelink A, Hohlfeld T (2005) Enhancing online courses with synchronous software: an analysis of strategies and interactions. Paper presented at the national educational computing conference, Philadelphia, Pennsylvania

Schwier RA, Balbar S (2002) The interplay of content and community in synchronous and asynchronous communication: virtual communication in a graduate seminar. Can Learn Technol 28(2)

Scott J (1991) Social network analysis: a handbook. Sage Publications, Newbury Park

Short JA, Williams F, Christie B (1976) The social psychology of telecommunications. Wiley, New York

Spencer D (2002) A field study of the use of synchronous computer-mediated communication in asynchronous learning networks. Unpublished doctoral thesis, Rutgers University, Newark, New Jersey

Sugar WA, Bonk CJ (1998) Student role play in the world forum: analyses of an arctic adventure learning apprenticeship. In: Bonk CJ, King KS (eds) Electronic collaborators: learner-centered technologies for literacy, apprenticeship, and discourse. Lawrence Erlbaum Associates, Mahwah, pp 131–155

Sutton L (2001) The principle of vicarious interaction in computer-mediated communications. Int J Educ Telecommun 7(3):223–242

Wasserman S, Faust K (1994) Social network analysis: methods and applications. Cambridge University Press, Cambridge

Webster J, Hackley P (1997) Teaching effectiveness in technology-mediated distance learning. Acad Manag J 40(6):1282–1309

Wenger E (1998) Communities of practice: learning, meaning, and identity. Cambridge University Press, Cambridge

Woerner SL, Orlikowski WJ, Yates J (2004) The media toolbox: combining media in organizational communication. Paper presented at the Academy of Management Conference, Atlanta

Vygotsky LS (1978) Mind in society: the development of higher psychological processes. Massachusetts: Harvard University Press, Cambridge

Yin RK (2003) Case study research: design and methods. Sage Publications, Thousand Oaks

Chapter 7
Who Is in *Your* Shopping Cart? Expected and Experienced Effects of Choice Abundance in the Online Dating Context

Alison P. Lenton, Barbara Fasolo, and Peter M. Todd

Abstract The advent of the Internet has led to a sizeable increase in the number of options from which humans can choose, in such evolutionarily important domains as housing, food and mates. The level of choice and the amount of information seen on the Internet are well beyond that which would have been found in our ancestral choice environment; so how does it impact our decisions? We describe the results of two experiments in which we examine the influence of increasing online mate choice on expected *and* experienced choice-related affect and cognitions. In Study 1, participants merely expecting an increasing choice of mates believed they would enjoy choosing more from these sets and would have greater satisfaction and less regret with their chosen partner (vs. when they expected to face limited choice), but only up to a point. On the other hand, participants in Study 2 who experienced a supposedly ideal number of potential mates from whom to choose did not have enhanced feelings about the choice process and person selected than did participants experiencing a more limited number of options. Furthermore, the results indicated that having more choice may lead to memory confusion. Together, these studies suggest that while participants anticipate that increasing choice may ultimately yield more downsides than upsides, they underestimate how quickly increasing choice can become overwhelming. We propose that these results may be understood best within the context of an evolutionary–cognitive framework. The chapter concludes by discussing why the error in anticipation may be difficult to overcome

A.P. Lenton (✉)
Department of Psychology, University of Edinburgh, 7 George Square, Edinburgh
EH8 9JZ, Scotland
e-mail: a.lenton@ed.ac.uk

B. Fasolo
Department of Management, London School of Economics and Political Science, London
WC2A 2AE, UK
e-mail: b.fasolo@lse.ac.uk

P.M. Todd
Indiana University, Psychology Building, Room 369, Informatics East, Room 302,
Bloomington, IN 47406-7512, USA
e-mail: pmtodd@indiana.edu

N. Kock (ed.), *Evolutionary Psychology and Information Systems Research*,
Integrated Series in Information Systems 24, DOI 10.1007/978-1-4419-6139-6_7,
© Springer Science+Business Media, LLC 2010

and, further, how the design of dating Web sites could be improved, given people's expectations.

Keywords Affective forecasting · Choice overload · Evolutionary psychology · Mate choice · Online dating · Too much choice · Web site design

1 Introduction

Modern humans in wealthy parts of the globe face resource options of evolutionarily unprecedented magnitudes. For example, while our ancestors had limited food and habitat choices, we have a surfeit of foodstuffs to choose from and the freedom to live in a variety of areas. The "problem" of too much choice is further magnified when one considers the number of options available on the Internet, which has no physical space limitations. For example, a consumer searching for a mountain bike on the Internet is likely to be presented with more than 3000 options from which to choose (Edwards and Fasolo 2001). At the same time, however, our search psychology on the Internet may not be any different from that we employ in foraging for food or other resources in the physical world, as suggested by research on information foraging (Pirolli and Card 1999), as well as by the framework of evolutionary consumer psychology more broadly (Saad 2007; Saad and Gill 2000; Stenstrom et al. 2007). Thus, since the psychological mechanisms that we employ have not changed while our environment has, it may be useful to consider what kinds of information tools may help people deal with the associated decision-making challenges (Fasolo et al. 2007).

Perhaps more so than in any other evolutionarily important domain, the number of options facing us when choosing a mate has become potentially overwhelming. Not only are there simply more people to select among in our local environment than ever before, but modern methods of dating such as speed dating or online dating also present us with more choice than humans have previously dealt with. And this expanding range of options is readily available for inspection; that is, the inspection costs – in terms of option identification and time – are relatively minimal. For example, a typical "speed-dating" event may present singles with as many as 30 potential partners in less than 2 h (Speeddater.co.uk), and one speed-dating event in China comprised as many as 5000 individuals (Haixia 2005). As in consumer choice, the Internet has increased the mate choice challenge even more: Match.com, the leading dating Web site, offers "millions of possibilities" (Match.com 2004). At the same time, the lack of face-to-face cues (e.g., physical presence or ability to hear others' voices) makes dating Web sites a less "natural" and conceivably more cognitively demanding environment in which to acquire information about prospective mates (Kock 2005). Of course, most people do not remain in a state of indecision concerning with whom to partner – 95% of Americans have married by the time they reach age 55 (US Census Bureau 2002) – but recent research in the consumer domain has indicated that all of this choice may have its downsides.

First, however, consider the benefits of having a great amount of choice. Both consumers and manufacturers believe that an abundance of choice is desirable (Chernev 2003; Schwartz 2004). This presumption has long been underpinned by the idea that the more options there are, the more likely it is that the option chosen will closely match the chooser's preferences (Chernev 2003); it has also been supported by research indicating that greater variety brings benefits including enhanced intrinsic motivation (Zuckerman et al. 1978), alertness, well-being (Langer and Rodin 1976), and consumption (Kahn and Wansink 2004).

Moreover, while it may seem as though it will be difficult for a decision maker to wade through many options, large option sets do not necessarily pose a problem if choosers possess well-articulated preferences (Chernev 2003). Having well-articulated preferences is to know what one likes (e.g., "I prefer black cars to green cars") and which attributes are personally important (e.g., "Fuel efficiency is more important than color"). Chernev's research shows that when people with well-articulated preferences are faced with a large option set, they are more likely to "satisfice" (Simon 1955) or choose the first option that is "good enough" along the various criteria that matter to them. As a result, cognitive demand is lowered (Simon), satisfaction is stabilized, and regret is attenuated (Schwartz et al. 2002).

From an evolutionary standpoint, mate choice is a domain in which choosers possess well-articulated (evolved) preferences regarding the qualities that make for a desirable long-term mate (Buss 1989; Buss and Schmitt 1993). For example, men and women prefer partners who possess wealth and status, show family commitment, are attractive, and are likely to be faithful (Buss and Barnes 1986; Buston and Emlen 2003). Importantly for the studies we describe in this chapter – which are situated in the online dating context – research suggests that the mate qualities that are important to people offline are the same as those that are important to people online (Fiore and Donath 2005; Whitty and Gavin 2001).

Despite the appeal of more options, the logic of diminishing returns (e.g., being presented with the 250th option does not add as much benefit as does being presented with the 12th) suggests that ever-increasing amounts of choice may not add much. Indeed, accumulating evidence suggests that the results of having extensive choice are not altogether positive, as it can also lead to decreased satisfaction with the option selected and increased regret toward options not chosen (Iyengar and Lepper 2000), increased decision complexity, and cognitive load (for those with unarticulated preferences; Chernev 2003). Thus, more choice may be worse. In a widely cited set of studies, Iyengar and Lepper found evidence that "less is more" in some standard consumer decisions such as the purchase of chocolate. Despite the fact that people are consistently attracted to situations where they have more options, people choosing from among a couple dozen options found the experience more difficult, they were less confident about their choice, and they made fewer purchases than those choosing from a half dozen (though see Scheibehenne et al. 2009 for consideration of the limits of this effect).

2 From Too Many Products to Too Many Mates

Empirical investigations of the too-much-choice effect to date primarily have been focused on the consumer choice domain. Research on non-human animal mate choice offers reason to believe that there should be some continuity between the consumer choice findings and what we might find in human mate choice. Hutchinson (2005) reviewed research demonstrating the too-much-choice effect in the mating context for animals as diverse as frogs and grouse. While studies show that (female) animals initially prefer greater choice (e.g., they prefer leks – groups comprising numerous advertising males – to solitary males; Bradbury 1981), they may be confused by it (e.g., as with acoustically advertising frogs; Gerhardt 1987; Gerhardt and Klump 1988), and their choice quality may diminish (as with grouse; Kokko et al. 1998).

Dunbar (1992) suggests that primates' neocortex evolved during the environment of evolutionary adaptation (EEA), in part, to deal with the size of their respective social networks, which was itself determined by such things as habitat. A consequence of this is that modern primates may not have the cognitive capacity to maintain social networks larger than that for which their neocortex was designed. Dunbar's regression modeling supports the proposed relationship between neocortex volume and average group size, with neocortex size accounting for approximately 76% of the variance in average group size across 36 primate species. Within a species, social networks greatly exceeding this optimal level tend to become unstable and eventually collapse, fissioning into smaller groups. Dunbar theorizes that the average human social network in the EEA may have contained approximately 148 individuals (with the 95% confidence limits between 100 and 231 individuals), a contention supported by a range of ethnographic, historical, and sociological evidence. Consequently, although too much choice may not have affective downsides (if the chooser possesses well-articulated preferences), there may still be practical costs (e.g., low-quality choice).

How could two contradictory factors – desire for more choice, but detriments in decision making if too much choice is faced – co-exist in our evolved minds? The desire for more options in mate choice is likely to have been adaptive in our evolutionary past. For example, motivation for increasing variety – even within a limited option set – facilitates the avoidance of incest (Grinde 2002), as well as increases the chances of finding an option above a given threshold (Johnstone and Earn 1999), so the wiser among us would have preferred to select a mate from as wide a sample as possible. (Males in particular have a preference for sexual variety; Peplau 2003). Importantly for our purposes, however, in the EEA, the desire for more choice could co-exist with our cognitive limitations for the simple reason that human social network sizes rarely exceeded our cognitive capacity. Our minds are adapted to dealing with few, sequentially presented mate options (Miller and Todd 1998). Given the strong upper limits on the number of options (whether mates, or habitats, or food) that might have been encountered at any one time, our ancestors rarely would have faced the *costs* associated with having "too many" options. But current developments in Internet and e-communication technology have jeopardized the co-existence of desire for choice and the potential to be overwhelmed by choice, by expanding the size of the mate choice environment well beyond our processing capacity. Thus, the two factors can come into conflict. Such theorizing is in accord with the mismatch hypothesis (Eaton et al. 1988; Nesse and Williams 1994; Tooby and Cosmides 1992), which proposes that our minds evolved in past natural environments that do *not* match the structure of modern environments in critical ways. As a result, people may come to experience "Darwinian unhappiness" (Grinde 2002).

More than 600 million people across the world now have Internet access (Manasian 2003), with the vast majority using it to communicate with other people and doing so to maintain interpersonal relationships (Bargh and McKenna 2004). Brym and Lenton (2004) argue that the Internet constitutes a society, with only China and India exceeding it in size. As in any society, mating is a goal possessed by many of the Internet's members: nearly 10 out of every 1000 Internet users log onto dating Web sites (Lenton and Hobaiter 2007, unpublished data). Brym and Lenton suggest that there are four main factors underlying the expansion of Internet dating (vs. "traditional"), including (1) an increasing number of singles; (2) increasing career and time pressures; (3) the increasing mobility of individuals; and (4) a decrease in workplace romance (because of fears surrounding sexual harassment complaints). As we suggested already, however, dating Web sites present people with many more options than they would typically encounter in their local communities. And the average dating Web site user appears to appreciate this variety, as one estimate suggests that they scan as many as 200 profiles each time they log in (Lenton and Hobaiter 2007, unpublished data).

Recently, psychologists have begun to investigate mate choice in dating Web sites, although most of this research concentrates on the decisions that people make (e.g., who people tend to choose and why), rather than focusing – as we do – on subjective perceptions regarding the choice process. The latter is much more likely to differ between online and "real-world" dating situations, because, again, what people look for in mates online and offline does not change (Whitty and Gavin 2001), whereas the online choice context is unique. For example, Bargh and McKenna (2004) argue that the increased anonymity afforded by the Internet leads people to develop closer relationships more quickly, as it facilitates self-expression based on shared interests and values and reduces the potential for physical and non-verbal attraction cues to impede connection. Bargh and McKenna do not consider, however, the effect of one of the most striking features of the Internet social environment: the sheer number of options one encounters.

In this chapter we describe two studies in which we examined the degree to which the number of mate options available online influences people's expectations about (see Study 1) and experience of (see Study 2) the choice situation and option selected. Do people want a multitude of potential partners to choose from and, if they get it, are they as satisfied as expected when they encounter such wealth of choice? We expected that the preference for more choice would be found in the online mating context, given the similarity in people's behavior between the online and offline worlds in terms of their desired mate preferences (as already described) and in terms of their psychological mechanisms for searching and foraging (DiClemente and Hantula 2003; Pirolli and Card 1999). Based on Chernev's (2003) findings regarding the moderating role of well-articulated preferences, we further expected to find that choosers faced with a relatively large set of potential mates are at least as content (if not more so) with their selection than choosers faced with a relatively small set of potential mates. In other words, less may not necessarily be more, at least in terms of choosers' affective experience of selecting a potential mate. At the same time, however, abundant choice may test humans' cognitive capacity, in which case the downsides of "too much choice" may be evident in the choice strategies choosers employ and the quality of the choices they make.

3 Empirical Evidence: Is There Such a Thing as Too Many Mates?

3.1 Expectations

Based on the evolutionary theorizing described above, we anticipated that people would have positive expectations about a larger set of mate options and that the relationship between set size and positive expectations would be monotonic. To examine this proposal, 88 participants (average age = 22.5, 58% female) were given a survey containing questions concerning the role of mate choice set size in preferences and expected choice-related affect and demographic items (including sex, age). Specifically, participants were asked to imagine that they had signed up to a dating Web site with the goal of selecting the one individual with whom they would most prefer to make contact. They were further asked to imagine being presented with a list of potential mates. For each of 10 option set sizes (1, 4, 10, 20, 50, 100, 250, 600, 1000, 5000), participants were asked to rank the sets according to their preferred set size for selection (no ties permitted) and to rate the sets, using seven-point Likert-type scales, along several dimensions: the expected difficulty of making a selection from the set; their anticipated satisfaction with the choice (i.e., the person selected from the set); their anticipated regret concerning their selection from the set; and their expected enjoyment of the selection process in each set. The final page of the survey asked participants to report demographics (e.g., gender, age, sexual orientation).

We examined the effects of participant sex (male vs. female) and set size (vs. 4 vs. 10 vs. 20 vs. 50 vs. 100 vs. 250 vs. 600 vs. 1000 vs. 5000) on the ranks of preference and for the ratings of difficulty, regret, satisfaction, and enjoyment. For each of these five variables, we tested linear and quadratic effects (expecting the former, but open to the latter). We explored whether participant sex moderates these effects, as some evolutionary-based theories suggest that men and women may have different set-size preferences (e.g., sexual strategies theory; Buss and Schmitt 1993), with men supposedly preferring more mating opportunities than do women.

Analysis of stated preferences regarding ideal option set size revealed evidence for reliable linear and quadratic effects. Neither effect depended on participant sex.

Fig. 7.1 Study 1: preferred
number of options (lower
ranks, higher preferences)

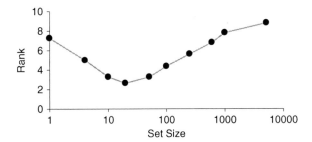

Because the quadratic function yielded the largest effect size, this is the result we interpret. As Fig. 7.1 illustrates, option set size preference is U-shaped, with both men and women expressing strongest preference (lowest rank) for a set size of 20 and decreasing preference for both smaller and larger set sizes.

Analysis of expectations regarding the difficulty of selecting a potential mate from the sets of varying sizes also revealed evidence for reliable linear and quadratic effects, neither of which were moderated by participant sex. We interpret the linear effect, which was stronger. As Fig. 7.2 illustrates, increasing set size is associated with expectations of greater choice difficulty. That is, as the number of potential mates increases, the expected difficulty of making a selection also increases.

Fig. 7.2 Study 1: expected
difficulty and regret by option
set size

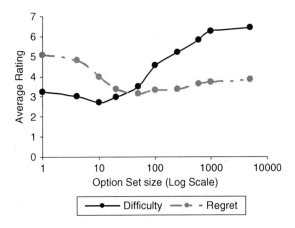

Analysis of expectations regarding anticipated regret with their selection revealed evidence for reliable linear and quadratic effects, neither of which depended upon participant sex. We interpret the stronger quadratic effect. As Fig. 7.2 also illustrates, increasing set size is associated with expectations of experiencing less regret up until the set size reaches approximately 50. After this, regret about one's choice is expected to increase a bit.

Analysis of expectations regarding anticipated satisfaction with their selection revealed evidence for reliable linear and quadratic effects of option set size. Neither

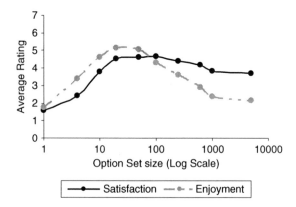

Fig. 7.3 Study 1: expected satisfaction and enjoyment by option set size

effect depended upon participant sex. We interpret the stronger quadratic effect. As Fig. 7.3 shows, increasing set size is associated with expectations of greater satisfaction – but again, only up to a point. After the size of the option set reaches 20–50, expected satisfaction flattens out and may even decrease as the set size reaches 250–600. Both men and women anticipate achieving highest satisfaction if they have had to search through a few dozen options, with diminishing returns obtained thereafter.

Finally, analysis of expectations regarding anticipated enjoyment of selecting a potential mate amongst sets of varying sizes revealed evidence for reliable linear and quadratic effects, neither of which were moderated by participant sex. We interpret the stronger quadratic effect. As Fig. 7.3 illustrates, increasing set size is initially associated with expectations of enjoying the choice process more. After the set size reaches 20–50, however, enjoyment is expected to decrease again. Men and women alike anticipate enjoying making a choice in the presence of some modicum of choice more than very little or very wide choice.

3.2 Experience

Study 1 demonstrated that both men and women expect that they will be more satisfied with their choice, experience less regret over their choice, enjoy the selection process more, and generally prefer to select a mate out of more rather than fewer options – at least up to a point. That point appears to be between 20 and 50. But are these expectations sound – that is, are people well calibrated to the potential challenges of choice in this domain? The primary purpose of our subsequent study was to examine affective responses to the experience of selecting a mate amongst a small vs. a larger option set. To create a strong comparison, we chose the smallest of our set sizes (4 options) along with a set size approximating the presumed "ideal" on the dimensions explored in Study 1 (20 options).

A secondary purpose of this study was to explore the effects of set size on mate search memory in order to assess the presence of potential "cognitive downsides" of greater choice (Jacoby et al. 1974). Information overload is believed to occur when decision quality initially increases with incoming information but then decreases when the incoming information exceeds a point beyond the decision maker's cognitive capacity. Later research confirms the idea that there is a point beyond which information becomes "too much," but indicated that problems may arise only if the decision maker is under time pressure (Hahn et al. 1992) or, again, if the decision maker does not have well-articulated preferences (Chernev 2003). Evidence for information overload in our study would be revealed by poorer memory for the option selected ("mate search memory") among those participants presented with the supposedly "ideal" set size of 20 (vs. those presented with a less-than-ideal set size of 4).

To test these ideas, we recruited 96 individuals (average age = 21.77, 60% female) from the University of Cambridge (UK) community, with approximately 89% self-reported being exclusively heterosexual, 6% reported being bisexual, 3% reported being exclusively homosexual, and 2% did not respond ($n = 2$). In this study, because the methodology assumed attraction to the opposite sex, the results reported below exclude the homosexual and non-reporting participants. The conclusions drawn from these results are generally the same if we do not restrict the sample to exclusively heterosexual participants.

Participants in this study were assigned to one of four conditions: one set of 20 online dating profiles or one of three sets of 4 online dating profiles (sets a, b, and c, which were randomly selected subsets of 20 men or 20 women). The sets of 4 vs. 20 profiles were equivalent, on average, with respect to a separate group of participants' ($n = 88$) ratings of the individuals' physical attractiveness and overall "mate value" (e.g., average of perceived physical attractiveness, physical fitness, socio-economic background, financial power, parental fitness, extroversion, openness, neuroticism, conscientiousness, and agreeableness).

The participants were presented with a mock dating Web site called "DateOnline.com," which was composed of a series of Microsoft® PowerPoint® (2002) slides designed to simulate a Web site (adapted from Lenton et al. 2007). Prior to viewing this mock dating Web site, participants were informed that they would view profiles of people who were hoping to meet a potential romantic partner. Their given goal was to "select the one individual you would most prefer to contact for further communication and, possibly, a meeting."

Each profile provided a variety of information, including the target's age, location, hair color, and 12 other criteria typically mentioned by dating Web sites. The profiles also contained a unique free response text in which, like most dating Web sites, the person had supposedly described him- or herself. All of the pieces of information provided were controlled across the male and female stimulus sets (save sex-related information such as stated sex, height, and pronouns) in order to maintain consistency across these sets and, thus, participant sex. Each profile also contained a black and white photograph of the target individual's head and shoulders.

The first page of DateOnline.com resembled a standard entry page of a dating Web site and asked participants to click on their own sex (man vs. woman). This action directed participants to the first of 4 or 20 profiles of opposite-sex individuals. Participants were instructed to view all of the profiles – one profile per page – in the order presented before making a decision, at which point they could spend as much time as desired looking at any or all the profiles again. When they had decided upon an individual, they wrote his/her screen name on a slip of paper.

Following their choice, participants reported – via seven-point Likert-type scales – their difficulty, regret, enjoyment, and satisfaction with the choice or choice process. This time, of course, they reported choice-related affect based on experience. Additionally, participants were asked to report on the degree to which they desired to choose from more vs. from fewer profiles.

Finally, we presented participants with a cued recall test to assess their recollection of the characteristics possessed by the person they selected. We reminded participants of the 15 criteria comprising a profile (age, location, hair color, height, etc.) and, for each criterion, asked that they recall the relevant characteristic of the selected individual (e.g., "brown"). We also asked that they recall and write down as much as possible from this person's text-based self-description. After completing this task, participants responded to the same demographic items as described previously.

A research assistant (RA) coded the two parts of the recall test separately. For the criteria recollection part, for each criterion the coder distinguished among wholly incorrect responses (0), partially (in)correct responses (0.5), and wholly correct responses (1). The values were summed to obtain an overall criteria memory score (minimum = 0, maximum = 15). For the self-description recall part, the RA counted the number of traits/interests/activities recalled that were contained in the selected profile. The RA also counted the number of confabulations within each self-description recall, i.e., traits/interests/activities recalled, that were not contained in the selected profile.

In the previous study, participants reported a preference to select a mate among 20 rather than 4 profiles. Corroborating this expectation, this study revealed that participants in the 20-profile condition were less likely to want more profiles from which to select than were those in the 4-profile condition. This finding depended, however, on participant sex such that while both men and women wanted more profiles in the 4-profile condition than in the 20-profile condition, the condition difference was smaller for men than for women. Women were more likely than men to perceive a set of 20 as being nearer their ideal option set size, whereas men perceived this same set size as being still somewhat too small.

In Study 1, participants expected that while choosing among 4 vs. 20 would be equally difficult, they also expected to be more satisfied, experience less regret, and better enjoy choosing a potential mate from a set of 20 than a set of 4 options.[1] In accord with this, participants in this study did not find selecting among 20 options to be any more difficult than selecting among 4. And this was equally true among the male and female participants. But contrary to the previously gathered expectations, participants in this study did not find selecting among 20 to be any more satisfying

---

[1] As determined by individual t-tests, not included here; details available upon request.

than selecting among 4, nor did they experience any less regret when choosing from a set of 20 than from a set of 4 options. Participant sex did not qualify either of these results. And finally, participants' enjoyment was not influenced by whether they chose a potential mate from a set of 4 or a set of 20. Again, this effect was the same for both men and women. See Fig. 7.4 for a direct comparison of expected and experience-based choice-related affect.

Fig. 7.4 Expected (Study 1) vs. experienced (Study 2) choice-related affect as a function of choice set size

Set size had an interesting impact on participants' recollection of their chosen mate's characteristics. On average, participants choosing among 4 profiles obtained a significantly higher "criteria memory score" than did those choosing among 20 profiles, but the effect was not equally true of men and women. Set size had no effect on women's recall for the profile criteria, whereas men in the 4-profile condition accurately recalled more criteria than did men in the 20-profile condition.

Both male and female participants in the 20-profile condition were more likely than those in the 4-profile condition to evince memory intrusions (i.e., confabulations) in free recall of the self-descriptions. There were no condition differences, however, with respect to the accurate recall of the self-descriptions' content. Overall, it would appear that having more choice may not necessarily lead to less accurate memory, but it may bring about memory intrusions, which may be an indication of choice overload.

3.3 Summary

Study 1 showed that participants of both sexes *expected* to experience more difficulty in choosing from a set of mates that becomes larger, matching our hypothesized monotonic relationship. However, for all of the other aspects of the choice process – regret, satisfaction, and enjoyment – as well as for what set size they would most prefer, male and female participants' expectations were better fit by quadratic functions. In each of these cases, the *expected* "ideal" or most preferred mate set size was in the range of 20–50 potential mates. Notably, these expectations did not depend on participant sex. But does this match what men and women end up preferring when they actually face such a choice? This is what we tested in Study 2, where we found that, while small (4 options) and larger (20 options) set sizes were experienced as equally difficult to choose from, the expected preference for the larger set size in terms of more enjoyment and satisfaction and less regret did not materialize; an ostensibly "too-small" option set produced the same affective experience as an ostensibly "ideal" option set. Thus, although people *think* they would be more satisfied, less regretful, experience greater enjoyment and, thus, prefer selecting a potential long-term mate from 20 options, their choice experience does not generally confirm these expectations. Instead, the supposedly ideal set size yields no differential affect and some indication of poorer overall memory, compared to the smaller set of four options.

3.4 Limitations

Of course, as is standard in studies investigating the effects of option set size on consumers' choice-related affect (e.g., Iyengar and Lepper 2000), we employed single-item measures of expected and experienced affect. As such, our ability to say something about discrete emotions is limited. Furthermore, our first study presented the 10 option set sizes in an increasing (vs. decreasing or even random) manner, while the second study employed only two of these ten set sizes, and in a between-subjects design – it would be interesting to relax all of these limitations (cf. Shah and Wolford 2007). The experimental instruction of selecting only one person out of the choice set to pursue further allowed our results to be compared with those from other consumer choice studies that similarly imply selection of a single item (e.g., one flavor of jam to purchase), but it may not match what most people are doing when they search for mates online; whether this is the case, and what impact there would be from allowing people to select as many potential mates as they wanted, should be investigated further. Finally, our use of a college population of participants, who may not have been motivated to search for a mate, could have reduced the effects we found; studies using people actually seeking mates, preferably via online sites that could be experimentally manipulated, would provide even more convincing data.

4 Implications

4.1 Theoretical

Our findings contribute to the long-standing body of evidence showing a mismatch between what people think they will feel and what they actually feel (Gilbert and Wilson 2000), as well as adding to more recent research showing that this mismatch holds true in mate choice behavior more specifically (Penke et al. 2007). Because the intention to repeat an experience may depend more on a person's *expectations* of that experience, rather than on the experience itself (Klaaren et al. 1994), however, it is still useful to understand people's expectations. For example, the popularity of

Web sites that advertise "millions of opportunities" (e.g., Match.com) may be based more on people's expectations that more choice is better than on their experience with abundant choice.

Our results also suggest that theorizing about the supposed downsides of too much choice ought to make a distinction between choice-related affect vs. choice process and outcome. We proposed that mate choice is a domain in which people possess well-articulated preferences, in which case extensive choice is dealt with by simpler choice strategies, such as satisficing (Chernev 2003). Satisficing is low in cognitive demand (Simon 1955), thus the chooser with well-articulated preferences *feels* just as good choosing from a large selection as others do choosing from a small selection. The results of Study 2 support this line of reasoning. At the same time that more choice yields similar affective outcomes to less choice, the former may lead to worse actual outcomes. Lenton and Stewart (2008) presented female participants with a small (4) and ideal-sized (24) set of online dating options and included a large option set as well (64), which should have been outside the range of both expected preferences (per Study 1) and humans' natural upper limit on available mates. This study also showed that set size had *no* impact on choice-related affect. The results also revealed, however, that as the option set size increased, participants were more likely to report having used search strategies (e.g., elimination-by-aspects or lexicographic) that are likely to miss options that are "best all around." [Lenton et al. (2009) provide further evidence for this change in choice strategy as number of options increase across speed-dating sessions.] As a consequence, people choosing from extensive online mate options may be less likely to identify partners for whom they are most suited. Notably, the results of our second study were observed with a rather conservative operationalization of "more choice" (i.e., 20 options), suggesting that the potential cognitive-based downsides of abundant choice may be greater in the modern mating game, where it is not uncommon for singles to be confronted with 30 options (speed dating) or even 1000 (Web dating).

It is important to emphasize that our findings indicate that people's expectations concerning the effects of option set size on choice-related affect are not wholly linear (monotonic), as originally hypothesized: people expect increasing choices to result in greater enjoyment, less regret, and enhanced satisfaction, *but only up to a point*. Thereafter, they anticipate that the benefits will decrease. This fits with recent research showing that purchase behavior first increases, then decreases as the set size increases (Shah and Wolford 2007). Our subsequent study indicates, however, that people may misjudge the point at which the costs associated with greater choice outweigh the benefits. Thus, while on the one hand, expectations about the subjective consequences of having too much choice are to some extent "calibrated" (i.e., people accurately anticipate that there is such a thing as too much choice), on the other hand, people mispredict their subjective experience of greater choice at given points in the distribution of choice. In other words, people overestimate the point at which more choice satiates.

Why do men and women *think* they will prefer a relatively large option set in the first place? Such a conundrum could be explained by the mismatch hypothesis (Eaton et al. 1988; Nesse and Williams 1994; Tooby and Cosmides 1992), as described earlier. Extrapolating Dunbar's (1992) theorizing, if the average human group size consisted of approximately 150 people, and we assume that half of these were women and half men and, further, that fewer than half of each sex were fit for reproduction (e.g., age limits, health limits, etc.), then the rough size of the set of local options from which our ancestors could choose (assuming choice) was around 35. Of course, the option set would have been even further constrained because of pre-existing pair bonds between some members of the group. According to this logic, while we are built to be attracted to more options, we are not adapted to deal with the excessive number we see today. This possibility also seems to hold in some domains for other species, such as mating grouse: as option set size increases within a naturally occurring range, mate choice quality is enhanced, but beyond this natural upper limit, choice quality diminishes (Kokko et al. 1998).

We are thus left to wonder if people can be persuaded that having fewer options than they would prefer is a good thing – a view that would be particularly beneficial in online choice domains, where one can spend a great deal of time comparing and contrasting options, only to end up being equally (dis)satisfied or, perhaps worse, less likely to identify someone who is truly suited to them. We believe that it would be difficult to persuade people of such a notion. First, if there are no (affectively) experiential differences between choosing from a smaller vs. a larger set of options (as we found), how could choosers begin to associate the latter situation with negative consequences? Second, if affective downsides of relatively greater choice do exist, but are neither immediate (e.g., choosers may not realize their regret unless they have the time and motivation to reflect upon their post-choice feelings) nor significant (e.g., the chooser selected a jam that was not optimal from a large choice set, as in the studies of Iyengar and Lepper 2000), learning about these disadvantages might only happen after considerable delay and repeated exposure to the choice situation. Third, if decision environments in general are evolving in the direction of offering still more choice, choosers are unlikely to have a point of comparison whereby they can experience the benefits of less choice. Finally, even though expectations of the utility of an event often do not match the actual experience of it (e.g., Kahneman 1994), again, research shows that it is the *expectation* that predicts the likelihood of participating in the same event in the future (Klaaren et al. 1994). Thus, even if people were to eventually recognize lesser enjoyment in having made a selection from a larger option set, their expectation that a larger option set should yield something better might lead them to prefer the large option set again. Future research ought to investigate the impediments to learning that more choice comes with costs, particularly in the online choice context, where the downsides could be as disastrous as divorce or forever being a "lonely heart" as a result of choice deferral or paralysis.

Future research might also examine the role of attribute overload, rather than option-overload, in online mate choice. An abundance of attributes may be more disconcerting to choosers compared to an abundance of options (Fasolo et al. 2007), in part, because humans may not be able to effectively process more than —three to four variables simultaneously (Halford et al. 2005). The average online dating profile contains over 100 items of information available for consideration by the chooser, with one online dating company's profiles containing nearly 500 items of such information (Lenton and Hobaiter 2007, unpublished data). How do online daters deal with this?

Simultaneous presentation of multiple attributes is likely to be especially problematic in a domain (such as mate choice) in which attributes are – until very recently – typically encountered and evaluated sequentially (Miller 1997). Another direction researchers might pursue is investigation of the role of option similarity on choice-related affect and cognitions. For example, research suggests that choice deferral is not due so much to the avoidance of trade-offs but is, instead, the result of small (rather than large) differences between the options in terms of their overall attractiveness (Dhar 1997). Given that larger set sizes necessarily possess smaller average differences amongst the options, it could be that eventual dissatisfaction in larger sets is not due to the set size per se but due to decreasing option differences and the concomitant difficulty in justifying one's choice. In the online dating environment in which choosers are likely to first winnow down to a set of potential mates they already find themselves attracted to, which are likely therefore to be even more similar to each other, this problem may well be exacerbated.

4.2 Practical

Our findings have practical implications for the design of online mate selection aids. Web designers are savvy to the notion that decision makers need help weeding through the multitude of options with which they are presented on the Internet and, to this end, they have developed technology to assist online decision making (Edwards and Fasolo 2001). Decision technology has also been implemented in dating Web sites (e.g., one-way or two-way matching between members based on their profile characteristics and selection criteria; Lenton and Hobaiter 2007, unpublished data). However, dating sites appear to have been designed with the implicit philosophy that the more profiles a user's search yields, the more satisfied the user will be. For instance, dating Web sites do not encourage users to be selective. An example is Yahoo.com, which alerted users to be less selective in their search criteria whenever their search yields fewer than 51–60 profiles. The results of our first study suggest that this alert may backfire, as 50 is about the maximum amount of choice users expect to desire. Similarly, Web sites implement very generous upper limits to users' search results. For instance, users who search for mates on Match.com and Yahoo.com are presented with a non-sortable list of 500 profiles. Our results lead us to expect that on sites with so much choice, users will likely find themselves browsing more profiles in an increasingly superficial way. Hence, online decision aids that can put reasonable limits on choice seem desirable. Such choice-limiting aids have become available (e.g., Chemistry.com – the "frugal" version of Match.com – sends subscribers five new matches a day), but they have not caught on; for instance, the first version of SpeedMatching.com (2004) allowed only four to eight profiles to be "visited," but this Web site was subsequently replaced by a page (http://www.speedmatching.com) that directs users to Match.com's extensive choice universe.

We also note that this ever-expanding list of profiles could be linked to the growing practice of dating sites to compute and display overall "match scores." These scores indicate how well a given mate fits the user's wishes, all criteria considered. This practice implies that Web sites allow users to be "compensatory" (i.e., to trade-off a good value on one criterion with a bad value on another), but in so doing they leave users with very long lists of options (Edwards and Fasolo 2001). It then becomes particularly important to let users "delete" profiles from search lists, as FriendFinder.com allows. Lastly, our results lend psychological support to a design feature that a growing number of dating sites implement: the possibility of "saving" or bookmarking profiles that the user deems interesting during the process of search. This possibility is desirable as it can counteract memory confusions due to information overload and too large sets of profiles. In short, we urge designers of dating Web sites to keep in mind that there is a balance to be maintained between, on the one hand, people's desire for a large number of options (up to a point) and, on the other hand, the fact that more choice will increase the use of simplifying heuristics which may have potentially negative consequences on choice outcome (e.g., a significant mismatch between the chooser's desires and the qualities of the individual or individuals chosen).

Finally, the degree to which a user experiences satisfaction with a dating Web site and the features it possesses may depend on their cultural background, as well as their individual traits (Zahedi et al. 2001). There may even be differences in women's experience of a mate search Web site depending on their current position in their menstrual cycle (Saad and Gill 2000). Thus, research into the impact of cross-cultural, personality-based, and even temporal differences on the effectiveness of online mate search tools is also needed.

5 Conclusions

Even though decision makers understand that the increasing choice so often available in online settings may come at a cost, they overestimate the point at which these costs are likely to be experienced and satiation is likely to occur. A plausible culprit for this effect is the mismatch between the quantity of options available to choose among in our evolutionary past and the far greater numbers made available to us today through our communications technology. Because correction of this misperception is likely to be difficult for the "unaided" decision maker, web designers and e-communication experts should provide some assistance. We highlight some ways in which this correction can take place on dating Web sites, and welcome more research into this important domain.

Acknowledgments This chapter is a revised version of an article by the authors published in 2008 in the journal *IEEE Transactions on Professional Communication*. The authors would like to thank their research assistants for help with data collection (Thea Loch, St John Haw, Albina Shayevich, Martin Bruder, and Joshua Mora) and Kim S. Campbell and Ned Kock for their suggestions in connection with the previous version of this chapter.

References

Bargh JA, McKenna KYA (2004) The internet and social life. Annu Rev Psychol 55:573–590

Bradbury JW (1981) The evolution of leks. In: Alexander RD, Tinkle D (eds) Natural selection and social behavior. Chiron Press, New York, pp 138–169

Brym R, Lenton R (2004) Love at first byte: internet dating in Canada. In: Brym R (ed) Society in question: sociological readings for the 21st century, 4th edn. Nelson, Toronto

Buss DM (1989) Sex differences in human mate preferences: evolutionary hypotheses tested in 37 cultures. Behav Brain Sci 12(1):1–49

Buss DM, Barnes ML (1986) Preferences in human mate selection. J Pers Soc Psychol 50(3): 559–570

Buss DM, Schmitt DP (1993) Sexual strategies theory: an evolutionary perspective on human mating. Psychol Rev 100(2):204–232

Buston PM, Emlen ST (2003) Cognitive processes underlying human mate choice: the relationship between self-perception and mate preference in Western society. Proc Natl Acad Sci USA 100(15):8805–8810

Chernev A (2003) Product assortment and individual decision processes. J Pers Soc Psychol 85(1):151–162

Dhar R (1997) Consumer preference for a no-choice option. J Consum Res 24(2):215–231

DiClemente DF, Hantula DA (2003) Optimal foraging online: increasing sensitivity to delay. Psychol Market 20(9):785–809

Dunbar RIM (1992) Neocortex size as a constraint on group size in primates. J Hum Evol 22(6):469–493

Eaton SB, Konner M, Shostak M (1988) Stone agers in the fast lane: chronic degenerative diseases in evolutionary perspective. Am J Med 84(4):739–749

Edwards W, Fasolo B (2001) Decision technology. Annu Rev Psychol 52:581–606

Fasolo B, McClelland GH, Todd PM (2007) Escaping the tyranny of choice: when fewer attributes make choice easier. Market Theory 7(1):13–26

Fiore AT, Donath JS (2005) Homophily in online dating: when do you like someone like yourself? Paper presented at the 2005 computer–human interaction conference, Portland, Oregon. http://www.ischool.berkeley.edu/~atf/papers/fiore_chi2005_short.pdf. Retrieved 28 May 2007

Gerhardt HC (1987) Evolutionary and neurobiological implications of selective phonotaxis in the green treefrog, *Hyla cinerea*. Anim Behav 35(5):1479–1489

Gerhardt HC, Klump GM (1988) Masking of acoustic signals by the chorus background noise in the green tree frog: a limitation on mate choice. Anim Behav 36(4):1247–1249

Gilbert DT, Wilson TD (2000) Miswanting: some problems in the forecasting of future affective states. In: Forgas J (ed) Thinking and feeling: the role of affect in social cognition. Cambridge University Press, Cambridge

Grinde B (2002) Darwinian unhappiness: evolution as a guide for living and understanding human behavior. Darwin Press, Princeton

Halford G, Baker R, McCredden JE, Bain JD (2005) How many variables can humans process? Psychol Sci 16(1):70–76

Hahn M, Lawson R, Young G (1992) The effects of time pressure and information load on decision quality. Psychol Market 9(5):365–379

Haixia P (2005 Oct. 24) 5,000 turn up at 'meet and mate' mega event. ChinaDaily.com. Retrieved 11 January 2006

Hutchinson JMC (2005) Is more choice always desirable? Evidence and arguments from leks, food selection, and environmental enrichment. Biol Rev 80(1):73–92

Iyengar SS, Lepper MR (2000) When choice is demotivating: can one desire too much of a good thing? J Pers Soc Psychol 79(6):995–1006

Jacoby J, Speller DE, Kohn CA (1974) Brand choice behavior as a function of information overload. J Market Res 11(1):63–69

Johnstone RA, Earn DJD (1999) Imperfect female choice and male mating skew on leks of different sizes. Behav Ecol Sociobiol 45(3–4):277–281

Kahn BE, Wansink B (2004) The influence of assortment structure on perceived variety and consumption quantities. J Consum Res 30(4):519–533

Kahneman D (1994) New challenges to the rationality assumption. J Inst Theor Econ 150(1): 18–36

Klaaren KJ, Hodges SD, Wilson TD (1994) The role of affective expectations in subjective experience and decision-making. Soc Cogn 12(2):77–101

Kock N (2005) Media richness or media naturalness: the evolution of our biological communication apparatus and its influence on our behavior toward e-communication tools. IEEE Trans Prof Commun 48(2):117–130

Kokko H, Sutherland WJ, Lindström J, Reynolds JD, Mackenzie A (1998) Individual mating success, lek stability, and the neglected limitations of statistical power. Anim Behav 56(3):755–762

Langer EJ, Rodin J (1976) The effects of choice and enhanced personal responsibility for the aged: a field experiment in an institutional setting. J Pers Soc Psychol 34(2):191–198

Lenton AP, Bryan A, Hastie R, Fischer O (2007) We want the same thing: projection in judgments of sexual intent. Pers Soc Psychol Bull 33(7):975–988

Lenton AP, Fasolo B, Todd PM (2009) The relationship between number of potential mates and mating skew in humans. Anim Behav 77(1):55–60

Lenton AP, Stewart A (2008) Changing her ways: number of options and mate standard strength impact mate choice strategy and satisfaction. Judgm Decis Mak 3(7):501–511

Manasian D (2003) Digital dilemmas: a survey of the Internet society. Economist 25:1–26

Match.com (2004) Match.com Corporate. From Web site: http://corp.match.com/index/cs_index.aspx. Retrieved 20 September 2004

Miller GF (1997) Mate choice: from sexual cues to cognitive adaptations. In: Cardew G (ed) Characterizing human psychological adaptations, Ciba Foundation symposium 208. John Wiley, New York, pp 71–87

Miller GF, Todd PM (1998) Mate choice turns cognitive. Trends Cogn Sci 2(5):190–198

Nesse RM, Williams GC (1994) Evolution and healing: the new science of Darwinian medicine. Phoenix, London

Penke L, Todd PM, Lenton AP, Fasolo B (2007) How self-assessments can guide human mating decisions. In: Geher G, Miller G (eds) Mating intelligence: sex, relationships, and the mind's reproductive system. Lawrence Erlbaum, New York, pp. 37–76

Peplau LA (2003) Human sexuality: how do men and women differ? Curr Dir Psychol Res 12(2):37–40

Pirolli P, Card S (1999) Information foraging. Psychol Rev 106(4):643–675

Saad G (2007) The evolutionary bases of consumption. Lawrence Erlbaum, Mahwah

Saad G, Gill T (2000) Applications of evolutionary psychology in marketing. Psychol Market 17(12):1005–1034

Scheibehenne B, Greifeneder R, Todd PM (2009) What moderates the too-much-choice effect? Psychol Market 26(3):229–253

Schwartz B (2004) The paradox of choice: why more is less. Harper-Collins, New York

Schwartz B, Ward A, Monterosso J, Lyubomirsky S, White K, Lehman D (2002) Maximizing versus satisficing: happiness is a matter of choice. J Pers Soc Psychol 83(5):1178–1197

Shah AM, Wolford G (2007) Buying behavior as a function of parametric variation of number of choices. Psychol Sci 18(5):369–370

Simon HA (1955) A behavioral model of rational choice. Q J Econ 69(1):99–118

Speeddater.co.uk (n.d.) Frequently asked questions. From Web site: http://speeddater.co.uk/faq/viewfaq.cfm?ID=4. Retrieved 20 September 2004

Speedmatching.com (2004) Online speedmatching. From Web site: http://online.speedmatching.com/. Retrieved 20 September 2004

Stenstrom E, Stenstrom P, Saad G, Cheikhrouhou S (2007) Online hunting and gathering: an evolutionary perspective on sex differences in website preferences and navigation. IEEE Trans Prof Commun Darwinian Perspect Commun 51(2):155–168 (special issue)

Tooby J, Cosmides L (1992) The psychological foundations of culture. In: Barkow J, Cosmides L, Tooby J (eds) The adapted mind: evolutionary psychology and the generation of culture. Oxford University Press, New York

US Census Bureau (2002) Survey of income and program participation. From Web site: http://www.census.gov/population/socdemo/marital-hist/p70-80/tab01.pdf. Retrieved 2 September 2004

Whitty M, Gavin J (2001) Age/sex/location: uncovering the social cues in the development of online relationships. Cyberpsychol Behav 4(5):623–630

Zahedi FM, Van Pelt WJ, Song J (2001) A conceptual framework for international web design. IEEE Trans Prof Commun 44(2):83–103

Zuckerman M, Porac J, Lathin D, Smith R, Deci EL (1978) On the importance of self-determination for intrinsically motivated behavior. Pers Soc Psychol Bull 4(3):443–446

Chapter 8
Cognitive Adaptation and Collective Action: The P2P File-Sharing Phenomenon

Henry F. Lyle and Roger J. Sullivan

Abstract Collective action is a universal characteristic of modern human populations and was likely an adaptive characteristic of our Pleistocene ancestors. Consequently, it has been proposed that selective pressures associated with cooperation favored cognitive adaptations. These adaptations may or may not respond adaptively in novel environments of collective action, such as those created by recent technological innovations. The Internet P2P file-sharing phenomenon is an extraordinary example of collective action that occurs in novel online social environments. In P2P file-sharing networks, altruistic uploaders provide a collective good (i.e., digital media) despite the presence of a large number of non-reciprocating file downloaders. In doing so, uploaders risk prosecution for copyright infringement and are more vulnerable to computer hackers and viruses compared with those who strictly download. In this chapter, we consider the hypothesis that uploading is a costly signal in which males engage in avoidable risk taking as a means to compete for status among their peers on the Internet as well as those they interact with in their everyday social lives.

Keywords Collective action · Costly signaling theory · Evolutionary psychology · Cognitive adaptations · Status seeking · Mismatch theory

H.F. Lyle (✉)
Department of Anthropology, University of Washington, Box 353100, Seattle, WA 98195-3100, USA
e-mail: lyle3@u.washington.edu

R.J. Sullivan
Department of Anthropology, California State University, 6000 J Street, Sacramento, CA 95819, USA
e-mail: sullivar@csus.edu

N. Kock (ed.), *Evolutionary Psychology and Information Systems Research*,
Integrated Series in Information Systems 24, DOI 10.1007/978-1-4419-6139-6_8,
© Springer Science+Business Media, LLC 2010

1 Introduction

With the ubiquitous use of the Internet in the USA and elsewhere, we are becoming increasingly immersed in a social life that depends heavily on online interactions. From finding a job to finding a mate, the Internet is an integral part of many people's lives. The effect modern technologies such as the Internet have on human behavior is particularly interesting from an evolutionary perspective. For example, some incidents of online behavior seem adaptive (e.g., online "foraging"), while others are clearly maladaptive (e.g., online suicide "clubs"). For evolutionary theorists, the Internet is something of a natural laboratory in which to explore the interaction of evolved cognitive adaptations with novel social phenomena. Peer-to-peer (P2P) file-sharing networks, wherein digital media is exchanged among file sharers while online, are venues for studying human behavior in a novel social environment. There are two types of individuals interacting in P2P file-sharing networks: A *downloader* is a file sharer who strictly downloads files without contributing digital data to the network and an *uploader* is a file sharer who also downloads files, but in addition contributes digital media to the file-sharing system. For the downloader, file sharing is convenient and virtually risk-free, since most downloaders simply log on to an online file-sharing program, choose the desired media from uploaders, copy the file to a computer hard drive, and log off. Uploaders, on the other hand, allow other file sharers direct access to their computer's hard drive, which can increase susceptibility to computer viruses and hackers. Most significantly, uploaders are the target of well-publicized attempts by the Recording Industry Association of America (RIAA) to deter infringement of copyright laws and can be fined up to $150,000 for sharing files online (Rainie and Madden 2004). From this intriguing sharing system an evolutionary puzzle emerges: why do uploaders risk prosecution and other tangible costs to provide free digital data to a large number of non-reciprocating downloaders?

1.1 Cooperation and Collective Action

Unconditional generosity among non-kin is widespread in human populations, and thus creates a theoretical conundrum for those who study behavior from an evolutionary perspective. Evolutionary models based on conditional reciprocity, such as reciprocal altruism (Trivers 1971), risk reduction (Cashdan 1985), and tolerated theft (Blurton Jones 1987), have provided valuable insight into the dynamics of non-kin altruism. Although these models sufficiently explain certain types of sharing in small groups under special circumstances, the components that drive conditional reciprocity are not effective in large groups where many examples of altruism occur (Panchanathan and Boyd 2004). A special kind of human generosity involves a subgroup of people who cooperate for the good of the group as a whole, for example, providing meat at a public feast (Smith et al. 2003) or helping build an irrigation canal (Lansing and Miller 2005). These are examples of collective action (CA), which is defined here as any occurrence whereby people cooperate in order to manage or produce something related to the collective good. The ability of humans to engage in CA, such as territorial defense (Wrangham and Peterson 1996), likely has a long evolutionary history in our species and arguably played a role in the late Pleistocene expansion of human populations.

While successful CA can be found in every human society, the presence of under-contributors and free riders (who are also ubiquitous) can challenge the essence of cooperation. These two factors – free riding and overappropriation – define the *CA problem*. Free riding occurs when some people benefit from a public good without paying the costs of producing or maintaining it. Overappropriation occurs when some take more than is fair or sustainable (Ostrom and Gardner 1993). The presence of free riders and the over-appropriation of public goods by some members (even in venues where CA is successful) are of particular interest for those who use an evolutionary approach, since free riders and overappropriators have an adaptive advantage over those who contribute more to CA or consume fewer public goods (Cosmides and Tooby 2005). Over time, free riding should replace alternative strategies (e.g., cooperating), effectively eliminating the benefits of engaging in CA. Yet in many cases of CA, cooperators and free riders coexist in relatively stable sharing environments. The interesting dynamics of common pool resources and the problem of CA have inspired a great deal of interest among social scientists, but our understanding remains incomplete (Ostrom 1990; Agrawal 2003; McCay and Acheson 1987; Smith and Wishnie 2000; Hardin 1982; Acheson 2006). Recent applications of theories that focus on the reputational benefits of unconditional generosity, such as costly signaling theory, may explain why some are willing to contribute to public goods despite the presence of free riders (Lyle and Sullivan 2007; Smith et al. 2003).

1.2 Costly Signaling Theory

Costly signaling theory (CST) has proven to be a useful tool for explicating cases of conspicuous generosity (Gurven et al. 2000; Zahavi and Zahavi 1997) and other forms of wasteful advertising (Neiman 1998). The roots of CST are in the Zahavian theoretical tradition. Zahavi (1975) proposed that the effectiveness of sexual selection lies in its ability to provide information to the selecting sex about the quality of the selected sex. Among mammals, females are more often the selecting sex, since they endure disproportionate costs associated with reproduction (e.g., gestation, parental care). As a result, males in most mammalian species can vie for access to mates by signaling an underlying quality directly to a female or by competing for status among other males. Zahavi's handicap principle (1975 1977) contends that by exhibiting a costly display such as an elaborate physical character or an altruistic behavior, a signaler honestly reveals a hidden quality to potential mates. CST, inspired by the handicap principle, has provided powerful insight into enduring anthropological puzzles, such as unconditional provisioning by hunters in foraging societies (Gurven et al. 2000; Sosis 2000) and risk taking by young men (Farthing 2005; Nell 2002; Wilke et al. 2006). Although sexual selection models focus on signal transmission from male to female, CST also anticipates signals between members of the same sex (Bliege Bird and Smith 2005; Zahavi and Zahavi 1997).

In order for a signaling strategy to achieve evolutionary stability, certain conditions must exist. These are as follows: (1) signalers differ in a quality that is otherwise not readily observable; (2) both the audience and signaler can potentially benefit from the transaction; (3) a link exists between the quality advertised and the cost of the signal; (4) a conflict of interest exists between signalers and the audience in that the signal can be "faked" by low-quality signalers; and (5) the signal provides honest information about the quality advertised insofar as high-quality signalers pay lower marginal costs to signal or receive greater benefits (Bliege Bird and Smith 2005; Grafen 1990).

The unconditional sharing of meat by hunters has been explicated using CST in several cultural contexts (Smith et al. 2003; Sosis 2000; Gurven et al. 2000). Meat sharing at public feasts creates a social arena in which hunters can competitively display their kill to a general audience. The signal in this case is quality-dependent and thus honest – only a skilled hunter can afford to incur the cost of sharing meat that could otherwise be consumed by himself and his family. In this signaling venue, both the hunter and the audience benefit. The audience, by observing differential hunting success, receives adaptive information about the value of each hunter as a reciprocator, ally, competitor, or mate. Using this information, the audience members can make educated decisions concerning how to interact with the signaler in the future (Hawkes and Bleige Bird 2002). The successful hunter potentially receives benefits associated with increased relative status, such as securing coalitional ties and high-quality mates (Smith et al. 2003).

1.3 Cognitive Adaptations for Status Ambition and Resource Exchange

Evolutionary psychologists contend that humans possess cognitive adaptations for seeking *social status*, defined here as an individual's position within a social group relative to peers (Symons 1979). Attaining and maintaining high status in a group can solve myriad adaptive problems. Those of high status have greater influence in social arenas, greater control of resources, more alliances, and their offspring receive better treatment from conspecifics (Symons 1979; Ellis 1992; Buss et al. 1990). There are reproductive benefits to achieving high status as well, and this may be particularly true for males. A wealth of research in a wide range of cultures indicates that females prefer men of high status (Townsend and Levy 1990; Buss et al. 1990). Some have proposed that there was a positive correlation between social status and genetic fitness for men in past human populations (Barkow 1991; Irons 1998), and therefore adaptations likely exist in the human cognitive architecture for status ambition (Symons 1992; Irons 1998).

Risk taking by young men is a kind of status competition that often occurs in specific social contexts among a subset of peers. Risk taking may signal certain traits that an actor possesses (e.g., hand–eye coordination) and can increase the status of the risk taker among his peers. There is conflicting evidence with regard to whom the signal is directed, but it appears that males are more likely to attend to a risky signal compared with females (Farthing 2005; Lyle and Sullivan 2007). Of the three non-heroic risk types – physical risk taking, risky drug use, and financial risk taking – incorporated in a study by Farthing (2005), females *did not* prefer any risk type as a quality in potential mates or friends. Males also did not prefer risk taking in potential mates; however, males *did* prefer physical and financial risk takers as friends compared to risk avoiders. There is no benefit to engaging in signaling behavior if there is no audience (Hawkes and Bliege Bird 2002). Thus, some have hypothesized that women are less likely to participate in many risk-taking behaviors because two important audiences – female friends and potential male mates – appear to be inattentive or displeased by such actions (Lyle and Sullivan 2007; Farthing 2005). On the other hand, risk-taking males have a signal-receptive audience: other males. Sex differences in attentiveness to risk-taking behavior are also supported by a wealth of data indicating that young males are more prone to take avoidable risks, particularly in the presence of other males (Wilson and Daly 1985; Byrne et al. 1999; Daly and Wilson 2001; Nell 2002; Pawlowski et al. 2008). Given this, it is plausible that young males are invoking cognitive adaptations for status seeking when engaging in conspicuous risk taking in the presence of their male peers.

Some have also proposed that specialized cognitive modules have evolved to solve reoccurring adaptive problems associated with resources exchange (Cosmides 1989; Cosmides and Tooby 1992; Sugiyama et al. 2002). Cooperation and economic exchanges can be mutually beneficial if everyone plays by the rules (Trivers 1971). But, as mentioned, free riders and overappropriators are ubiquitous and can disrupt the delicate balance of reciprocal altruism and CA. Our species likely has a long evolutionary history of dealing with these problems and it has been argued that a subroutine for detecting exploiters (termed a cheating-detection module) may be a part of our neurocognitive architecture (Cosmides and Tooby 2005; Sugiyama et al. 2002). Clearly, having a good memory of the past actions of exploiters is a crucial dimension of this adaptation. Facial stimuli have been a focus of studies aiming to understand how past exploiters are recalled and some argue that remembering the faces of cheaters may be part of (or linked to) the psychological architecture of detecting cheaters (Farrelly and Turnbull 2008; Oda 1997).

1.4 Mismatch Theory

A premise of evolutionary psychology is that humans are *adaptation executers*, that is, current/observable human behavior is the result of the interaction between evolved cognitive adaptations and modern environmental stimuli (Tooby and Cosmides 1992). According to mismatch theory, differences between Plio-Pleistocene social environments (the temporal contexts of cognitive evolution) and those of modern environments may cause humans to behave maladaptively (i.e., not in their best reproductive interests). Central to mismatch theory is the concept of the environment of evolutionary adaptedness (EEA), which in its simplest form represents a hypothetical past environment for which a particular species is adapted (Bowlby 1969; 1973; but see Irons 1998); the EEA can also refer to sets of consistent environmental constraints or selection pressures that shaped a specific adaptation. The EEA concept allows researchers to consider the dynamics of past social environment which shaped cognitive adaptations, then consider the possible consequences of these adaptations in modern environments (e.g., are they still adaptive or not?). The EEA does not represent a single time or place, but the environment in which each individual adaptation evolved (Hagen 2005). Mismatch theory and the EEA concept are especially important in the study of humans, since our species has undergone rapid cultural evolution that has radically changed our social environments in short periods of time.

Some have argued that the aforementioned cognitive adaptations for status seeking can reach maladaptive conclusions when coupled with modern reproductive technologies (Symons 1979). For instance, some people in industrialized societies use contraceptives to delay or avoid reproduction in order to establish reputations in highly demanding careers. This scenario represents a mismatch, as the psychological adaptation for status seeking is executed, yet there is no adaptive outcome (i.e., reproduction). There are also differences in the economic exchanges we encounter today compared to those experienced by our Pleistocene ancestors. Reconstructing past social environments is a difficult task, but it is likely that natural selection favored exchange behavior between Pleistocene humans who lived in small, closely related groups (Trivers 1971). Economic exchanges at this time in our evolution involved face-to-face transactions between people who interacted frequently. During the Holocene, large population centers developed, creating novel social environments for economic exchanges. Mismatches between aspects of exchange environments of the past (e.g., face-to-face, repeated interactions) and the present (e.g., disconnected, one-shot interactions) may result in sub-optimal economic exchange behavior.

What does this mean for exchanges that occur over the Internet, where facial recognition and other physical cues are absent? The logic of mismatch theory can be extended to human interactions with modern technologies. Kock (2005 2009) and Kock et al. (2007) devised the media naturalness hypothesis, which contends that the human "biological communication apparatus" (BCA) was designed by natural selection to function optimally in a co-located and synchronous manner. The roles of verbal and body language as well as facial expressions are crucial in the functionality of the BCA, and these elements are absent in most forms of electronic communication, particularly online communication. Simply put, the media naturalness hypothesis argues that human cognition (related to communication) is not perfectly adapted for the types of communication that are associated with modern, novel media, since they do not involve face-to-face, real-time communication. This hypothesis provides explanatory power for some incidences of suboptimal behavior observed online and in other settings that are unnatural with regard to our BCA. From economic purchases to mate choice, people make important decisions in a disconnected and asynchronous manner while online, which in some cases can result in maladaptive outcomes. In this chapter, we draw from the theories reviewed above to explore aspects of the P2P file-sharing phenomenon.

2 Theoretical framework and Hypotheses

Risk taking and unconditional generosity by uploaders may be the result of cognitive adaptations for status seeking, and we explore this prospect framed in CST. First, uploaders differ in quality in terms of their willingness to take risks; the technical skills necessary to avoid litigation and computer viruses; and in the quality, quantity, and variety of media that they provide. Second, there are potential benefits for both signalers and recipients that exist in both online and off-line environments. For signal receivers who observe uploaders online, knowing the status of an uploader via "tags" or "usernames" helps them recognize those file sharers who have the qualities that they prefer (e.g., similar music interests, willingness to upload for extended periods of time, and/or a fast connection speed). These qualities can also be observed by "flesh and blood" peers with whom uploaders interact in their daily lives. Further, peers who observe the display online or off-line may obtain useful information about the signaler such as his ability to incur costs and/or his willingness to share. File uploaders may benefit by increasing social status among off-line peers and/or by enhancing their reputations among the online audience via their username tags. Finally, the signal is honest because only high-quality file sharers can systematically incur the cost and risk of the signal. In other words, it would not pay for low-quality file sharers to fake the signal over the long run. We conducted a study to test these ideas based on the premise that uploaders are executing an adaptation for status ambition by engaging in costly forms of altruism in novel online environments, which may or may not result in adaptive outcomes. Drawing upon current evolutionary signaling theory, we tested the following hypotheses:

H1: *File sharers are selfish (even uploaders)*

This hypothesis is at the core of our perspective on file sharing. There is a split in the evolutionary social sciences regarding the primary level of selection. Some feel that cultural group selection is highly plausible, with group-directed cooperation playing a fundamental role (Henrich et al. 2005). Evolutionary psychologists and human behavioral ecologists for the most part conform to the traditional gene-level selection model (Maynard Smith 1989; Trivers 1971). Given the opportunities for self-interested acquisition of media in P2P networks and the likely status benefits of uploaders, we predict that file sharers are more likely to be motivated by selfish returns than cooperating for the benefit of the group. Put another way, file sharers are executing cognitive adaptations that were selected for in past environments to maximize inclusive fitness (i.e., the reproductive success of the actor and those he/she shares genes with) (Hamilton 1964).

H2: *Uploading is a mostly male endeavor*

Important differences in signaling behavior exist between the sexes regarding level of participation and motivation, but these dimensions are virtually unexplored in the scientific literature. Indeed, Bliege Bird and Smith (2005, p. 235) contend that extrapolating sex differences in signaling behavior is one of the "most significant arenas" for future studies using CST. It is clear that many signaling games, such as those that are subsistence-based, are sex-specific. As is the case with reckless driving, binge drinking, or extreme sports, uploading involves potential risks that are well known among peers. Furthermore, because most file sharers are between the ages of 18–29, P2P file-sharing networks are an ideal arena for competitive signaling among young, risk-taking males (Rainie and Madden 2004). We predict that (a) P2P activity will be gendered with significantly more males uploading than females, while (b) downloading, which is much less risky than uploading, will be comparatively less gendered.

H3: *Uploaders are competing for status*

In P2P file-sharing networks, there are two possible audiences to whom uploaders are signaling: off-line peers and online file sharers. It is plausible that uploaders are competing for status among same-sex peers and we anticipate that uploaders will be concerned with (a) off-line recognition as uploaders among friends. Observable tags such as usernames make it possible for uploaders to increase their online prestige. We also predict that uploaders will be concerned about their (b) online reputation as uploaders among other file sharers.

3 Materials and methods

Institutional review board research approval was obtained from California State University, Sacramento (CSUS) and Sacramento City College (SCC). Focus group discussions were used to obtain information on file-sharing behavior and to identify pertinent research questions and item statements. Four separate focus group sessions were conducted, each containing three to five subjects. A questionnaire was developed and implemented in a pilot study of 52 SCC students (56% male and 44% female) to test focus group-derived items/item clusters and questionnaire structure for the principal research phase.

The primary goal of this research was an initial descriptive analysis of file sharing by university undergraduates based on attitudinal and factual questionnaire data. Consistent with the descriptive objectives of the study, the assessment instrument was not constructed as a unidimensional scale of "file sharing," rather a series of subscales, or item clusters, designed to explore discrete file-sharing dynamics assayed during the pilot interviews. The final questionnaire comprised 36 items in three sections related to file-sharing behavior: one section (18 items) was completed by all file sharers (both uploaders and downloaders) (Table 8.2); a second section (10 items) was completed only by uploaders (Table 8.3); and a final section (8 items) was completed by non-file sharers. For the first section of the questionnaire, file sharers responded to clusters of items assessing the costs of uploading, selfish motivation when file sharing, recognition of uploaders while online, appreciation of uploaders, and differential uploader quality (Table 8.2). Two major risk categories, risk of exposure to viruses/hackers and risk of prosecution, were included among other general statements about the costs of uploading. Selfishness in file sharing was assessed using direct statements about the benefits of file sharing, including saving money and time spent shopping for movies and music. To evaluate online recognition of uploaders by other file sharers, the questionnaire included statements about whether file sharers looked for specific usernames when downloading or used instant messaging to chat with uploaders. Focus group discussions revealed two qualities that file sharers looked for when downloading: uploaders who leave their computers on for an extended period (overnight or while at school or work) and uploaders with a fast connection speed. These two traits were used to measure "signal quality" among uploaders.

The second section, completed by uploaders only, contained groups of items that surveyed attitudes about group motivation, concern with online reputation, and concern with recognition as an uploader among off-line friends (Table 8.3). Group motivation was measured using items that examined an uploader's willingness to contribute to the file-sharing community despite the costs at the individual level. Concern with online reputation was assessed by including a statement about reputation building via usernames. Off-line recognition was determined using items that examined peer identification of file sharers as uploaders. Non-file sharers responded to items that assessed concern with the costs of file sharing, perception of file sharers, and associations with file sharers. The questionnaire employed a five-point Likert scale: (1) strongly agree, (2) agree, (3) undecided, (4) disagree, and (5) strongly disagree. The questionnaire also assayed demographic information: age, gender, and relationship status, and additional factors such as self-rated computer competence, undergraduate focus of study, and preferred file-sharing digital medium (music files, music videos, popular movies, or pornography).

Descriptive statistics of item cluster distributions were generated using 95th-percentile confidence intervals. Relationships between ranked dependent variables and fixed factors were analyzed using Kruskal–Wallis one-way analysis of variance, with Bonferroni adjustment for multiple measurements. The Bonferroni adjustment is used to avoid false positives (type 1 error), but is a conservative method that also increases the risk of false negatives (type 2 error). With this in mind, uncorrected as well as corrected p-values are shown to mitigate the risk of type 2 error in the presentation of results. The underlying structure of the assessment variables was explored using principal components analysis. Two-way demographic comparisons were assessed with the chi-square test. The predictive relationships between uploader/downloader status, computer skill, and gender were tested using logistic regression. Principal components analyses (PCA) were conducted to explore the underlying structure of the questionnaire items and these results can be found in a previous manuscript (Lyle and Sullivan 2007). All statistical tests were two-tailed at the 0.05 level of significance and were carried out in SPSS 16.

4 Results

4.1 Participants

Study participants were recruited from general education courses in anthropology and biology at CSUS. The study population ($N = 331$) was composed of 55% females ($n = 183$) and 45% males ($n = 148$). Fifty percent ($n = 165$) described themselves as single, 44% ($n = 145$) as dating, and 6% ($n = 21$) of the subjects were married. Thirteen subjects returned incomplete questionnaires and were excluded. The average subject age was 20.8 (SD 3.61) years. File sharers ($n = 233$) comprised 70% of the total study population, of whom 53% were male ($n = 123$) and 47% female ($n = 110$). The average age of file sharers was 20.8 years (SD 3.36). Digital music files were the primary shared medium of 94% of file sharers and there were no sex differences among uploaders ($x^2 = 1.74$, $df = 2$, $p = 0.420$) or among downloaders in this regard ($x^2 = 1.32$, $df = 3$, $p = 0.724$).

4.2 Computer Skill

We had subjects self-rate their computer competence by means of a five-point scale in order to assess correlations between computer competence and fixed factors, such as gender and P2P file-sharing activity. Only 5% of the study population reported novice computer competence ($x < 3$), 48% reported *average* skill ($x = 3$), and 47% rated *expert* computer competence ($x > 3$). The mean self-rated computer competence was 3.5 for all subjects. Males rated their computer competence significantly higher than females among all subjects ($x^2 = 30.2$, $df = 1$, $p < 0.0001$). There were similar sex differences among downloaders ($x^2 = 7.63$, $df = 1$, $p = 0.006$) and non-file sharers ($x^2 = 10.9$, $df = 1$, $p = 0.001$); however, among uploaders there were no differences in self-rated computer competence between the sexes ($x^2 = 0.56$, $df = 1$, $p = 0.46$). There were no differences between male uploaders and male downloaders in self-rated computer competence ($x^2 = 0.87$, $df = 1$, $p = 0.351$); in the same regard, there were no differences between female uploaders and female downloaders ($x^2 = 2.46$, $df = 1$, $p = 0.116$).

As anticipated, there were significant gender differences in P2P file-sharing activity ($x^2 = 35.98$; $df = 2$; $p < 0.001$) (Fig. 8.1). Hypothesis 1(a) was supported: significantly more males (72%) than females (28%) uploaded files ($x^2 = 26.48$; $df = 1$; $p < 0.0001$). Hypothesis 1(b), that downloading would not be gendered, was also supported $x^2 = 0.009$; $df = 1$; $p = 0.92$. Although not included as

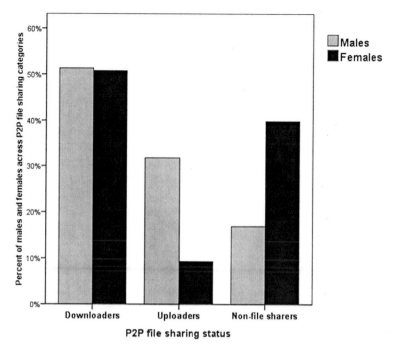

Fig. 8.1 Gender differences in P2P file-sharing activity ($N = 331$)

a study prediction, there were significantly more females (74%) than males (26%) among non-file sharers ($x^2 = 20.77$; $df = 1$; $p < 0.0001$).

A possible confounding factor in our results is that males are more likely to upload as a function of gender differences in computer competence. The relationships between file-sharing activity, gender, and computer skill were further tested using binomial logistic regression, with file-sharing activity as the dependent variable and gender and computer competence as independent covariates. With non-file sharers excluded from the model, male gender significantly predicts file uploading, whereas computer skill had no significant effect on the model (Table 8.1). These results confirm that gender is predictive of file uploading and that file uploaders as a group are not uniquely computer competent.

Table 8.1 The relationships between file-sharing activity, gender, and computer skill were tested using binomial logistic regression, with file-sharing activity as the dependent variable and gender and computer competence as independent covariates

	B	Wald	df	p	Odds ratio
Gender	1.12	11.58	1	0.001	3.06
Computer skill	0.343	2.30	1	0.129	1.41
Constant	−2.89	11.77	1	0.001	0.055

Significant gender differences emerged in attitudes about the costs of file sharing ("concern with costs" item cluster; Table 8.2). While males were more cognizant about the risk of prosecution from uploading ($x^2 = 6.45$, $df = 1$, $p = 0.01$), females were more aware of possible exposure to viruses and hackers ($x^2 = 3.75$, $df = 1$, $p = 0.05$). Females were significantly more likely than males to contend that uploading is riskier than downloading ($x^2 = 4.95$, $df = 1$, $p = 0.03$).

Table 8.3 reports means for items answered specifically by uploaders and reveals differences in attitude between male and female uploaders. Items related to concern with off-line recognition (Table 8.3, C8 and C9) show marked differences between the sexes. Males were significantly more likely to upload in the presence of friends and were more likely to be recognized as uploaders among friends. Regarding concern with group good, males – unlike females – felt strongly that the file-sharing system would collapse if not for their participation as uploaders (Table 8.3, Item A1).

4.3 Motivations for File Sharing

We expected that uploaders would be concerned with increasing online reputation via an observable tag, such as a username. Contrary to this prediction, uploaders were not concerned with online reputation (item cluster mean 2.53, 95% CI 2.3–2.7, $n = 64$) (Fig. 8.2). Furthermore, for an online signal to be effective there must be an audience attending to the signal, but file sharers were not interested in identifying or chatting with uploaders while online (item cluster mean 2.39, 95% CI 2.3–2.5, $n = 233$). Downloaders were also not impressed with items related to "signal quality," indicating ambivalence to a key observable dimension of online performance by uploaders (Table 8.2, Item E16). Thus, the results do not indicate signal transmission from uploaders to other file sharers while online.

We predicted that those file sharers that upload would be concerned with recognition as uploaders among off-line friends at college. The results support this hypothesis and it appears that uploaders, particularly males (Table 8.3, Items C7, C8, C9), are concerned about off-line recognition of their file-sharing activities and are engaging in signaling off-line in social contexts other than the Internet (item cluster mean $= 3.28$, 95% CI 3.1–3.5, $n = 64$) (Fig. 8.2).

The final prediction was that file sharers were motivated by selfish rather than group interests. All file sharers (item cluster mean 3.61, SD 0.68), including both uploaders (item cluster mean 3.70, SD 0.65) and downloaders (item cluster mean 3.58, SD 0.69), stressed selfishness as a primary reason for file sharing and the differences between them were not significant in this regard ($x^2 = 1.57$, $df = 1$, $p = 0.211$). Because uploaders can receive the same benefits (free digital data) as downloaders without incurring the risks, we must also consider whether uploaders were behaving in this manner for the good of the file-sharing community. Whereas uploaders acknowledged selfish motivation as the primary reason for file sharing, they also claimed that they were uploading for the good of the file-sharing community, albeit to a significantly reduced degree (Fig. 8.3). Our

Table 8.2 Items answered by uploaders and downloaders. Corrected mean rank scores (SD) and Kruskal–Wallis H statistics ($N=233$) (5=strongly agree, 4=agree, 3=uncertain, 2=disagree, 1=strongly disagree)

Items	Downloaders n = 169	Uploaders n = 64	H stastistic[a]	All female file sharers n = 110	All male file sharers n = 123	H statistic[b]
A. Concern with costs						
1. Uploading increases the chances a file sharer is prosecuted (+)	3.49 (0.91)	3.44 (0.94)	0.15	3.34 (0.92)	3.59 (0.89)	6.45[*c]
2. Uploading does not increase susceptibility to viruses and hackers (−)	2.08 (0.89)	2.20 (0.88)	0.82	1.98 (0.86)	2.24 (0.90)	3.75**
3. Uploading is riskier than downloading (−)	3.18 (1.00)	3.00 (1.04)	1.71	3.31 (0.96)	2.98 (1.04)	5.00**
4. The potential costs of uploading are not significant (−)	2.84 (0.70)	2.89 (0.80)	0.07	2.95 (0.63)	2.77 (0.80)	4.23**
B. Selfish motivation						
5. I file share in order to get fre stuff (+)	3.24 (1.41)	3.20 (1.27)	0.23	3.12 (1.39)	3.33 (1.35)	1.36
6. Downloading digital data does not save me money (−)	2.20 (0.98)	2.00 (0.99)	2.67	2.21 (0.95)	2.09 (1.02)	1.61
7. The main reason I file share are for the personal benefits (+)	3.77 (1.02)	3.95 (0.93)	2.28	3.83 (0.99)	3.81 (1.01)	0
8. It is easier getting digital data from the store than P2P networks (−)	2.49 (1.01)	2.38 (1.15)	1.56	2.62 (1.06)	2.32 (1.02)	6.12[*c]
C. Appreciation of uploaders						
9. I respect the file sharers that I download from (+)	3.65 (0.94)	3.75 (1.01)	1.04	3.68 (0.95)	3.67 (0.97)	0
10. Uploaders are suckers (−)	2.25 (0.83)	2.02 (1.02)	9.72[**c]	2.32 (0.89)	2.07 (0.88)	4.11**
D. Online recognition of uploaders						
11. I don't care about knowing who I am downloading from (−)	3.46 (1.15)	3.69 (1.14)	2.02	3.25 (1.18)	3.76 (1.07)	11.72[***c]
12. I never chat or send messages to uploaders (−)	3.91 (1.19)	3.67 (1.25)	1.99	3.83 (1.18)	3.86 (1.24)	0.12
13. I look for specific usernames when I am downloading (+)	2.27 (1.00)	2.36 (1.06)	0.45	2.35 (1.01)	2.24 (1.03)	0.89
14. While file sharing, I recognize certain uploaders (+)	2.55 (1.03)	2.83 (1.19)	2.84	2.65 (1.09)	2.60 (1.08)	0.17
E. Signal quality						
15. A "select" uploader does not need a fast computer speed (−)	2.57 (0.88)	2.44 (0.91)	0.7	2.62 (0.75)	2.46 (0.99)	2.32
16. A "choice" uploader leaves his/her computer on for large downloads (+)	3.40 (0.79	3.77 (0.83)	10.18[***c]	3.25 (0.75)	3.72 (0.81)	20.3[***c]

$*p < 0.01$, $**p < 0.05$, $*** p < 0.001$.

[a]Differences between downloaders and uploaders.

[b]Differences between female and male file sharers.

[c]Significant after Bonferroni adjustment.

Table 8.3 Items answered by uploaders only: male vs. female (*N*=64). Corrected mean rank scores (SD) and Kruskal–Wallis *H* statistics (5=strongly agree, 4=agree, 3=uncertain, 2=disagree, 1=strongly disagree)

Items	All uploaders *n* = 64	Female uploaders *n* = 17	Male uploaders *n* = 47	*H* statistic[a]
A. For the good for the group				
1. Without uploaders like me, the file-sharing system will collapse (+)	3.27(1.20)	2.76(1.20)	3.45(1.16)	4.09*
2. I do not upload for the good of the file-sharing community (−)	2.81(1.08)	3.00(1.12)	2.74(1.07)	0.65
3. The benefit to the file-sharing community is greater than the personal cost of uploading (+)	3.27(1.01)	3.06(1.25)	3.34(0.92)	0.65
4. I don't care about helping out other file shares (−)	3.02(1.20)	3.18(1.38)	2.96(1.14)	0.49
B. Concern with online reputation				
5. Uploading does not enhance my reputation among other file sharers while online (−)	3.41(0.97)	3.47(0.72)	3.38(1.05)	0.01
6. I like "tags" such as usernames because they help help increase my online reputation (+)	2.57(0.98)	2.12(0.70)	2.60(1.04)	3.25
C. Concern with off-line recognition				
7. I don't talk about uploading with my friends from college (−)	3.02(1.13)	3.35(1.06)	2.89(1.15)	2.18
8. I have uploaded while hanging out with my friends from college (+)	3.25(1.18)	2.41(1.23)	3.55(1.02)	10.2**[b]
9. Most of my college friends know that I upload (+)	3.08(1.13)	2.59(1.18)	3.26(1.07)	4.34*
10. I'd prefer that my friends did no know that I upload (−)	2.19(0.94)	2.06(1.09)	2.23(0.89)	0.82

*$p < 0.05$, **$p < 0.001$.
[a]Differences between female and male uploaders.
[b]Significant after Bonferroni adjustment.

results indicate, therefore, that both downloaders and uploaders are primarily self-interested, but that they also acknowledge greater than expected group-directed motivation.

5 Discussion

5.1 File Sharing Is a Selfish Enterprise

Our hypothesis that uploaders would endorse self-interest over group motivation was supported, but uploaders also tended to agree with items describing

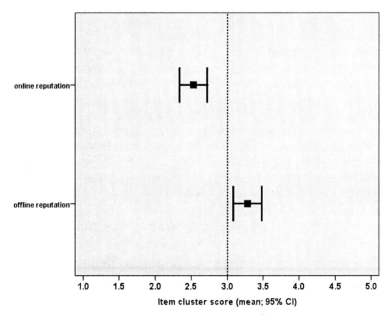

Fig. 8.2 Off-line vs. online recognition of uploaders ($N = 233$). Item cluster means and 95% confidence intervals derived from a corrected five-point Likert scale (5 = strongly agree, 4 = agree, 3 = uncertain, 2 = disagree, 1 = strongly disagree)

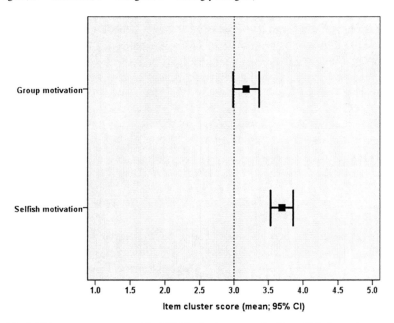

Fig. 8.3 Selfishness vs. group good in P2P file-sharing networks ($N = 233$). Item cluster means and 95% confidence intervals derived from a corrected five-point Likert scale (5 = strongly agree, 4 = agree, 3 = uncertain, 2 = disagree, 1 = strongly disagree)

group-directed motivation (Fig. 8.3). This is an interesting result and suggests that further research is required to parse these apparently conflicting responses from file sharers. However, there are several factors which anticipate the finding that self-interest is the primary motivation in P2P file sharing. First, most P2P networks are anarchic; they are open to anyone who wants to participate, based on an expectation that participants will not necessarily reciprocate, and they operate without administration or rules. This dynamic is in stark contrast to contemporary group-selection models, which predict that cooperation can be maintained in groups if institutional mechanisms exist for reducing within-group phenotypic variation and to limit within-group competition (Gintis et al. 2003). P2P file-sharing networks employ tools that *create* a competitive social environment by displaying phenotypic differences in uploader quality. Second, non-reciprocators greatly outnumber reciprocators in P2P networks. In our study, only 27% of file sharers uploaded. This level of self-interest is very difficult to explain from a group selectionist perspective. Boyd et al. (2003) have demonstrated that group-benefiting behavior that is individually costly can emerge if non-cooperators are punished. Henrich et al. (2006) have also argued that prosocial cooperation can evolve in very large groups in which institutional norms are maintained by the anonymous punishment of individual rule violators. Some file-sharing programs allow uploaders the ability to adjust their settings such that they only share with those who also upload, or upload a minimum number of files. However, in our focus groups with uploaders we discovered that these mechanisms were rarely used, despite knowledge of their existence. Uploaders seemed to be more interested in discussing how they were spiting the RRIA than talking about free riders taking advantage of their generosity or seeking measures to reduce free riding. Other file-sharing protocols, such as Bit Torrent, may be more interesting to cultural group selection practitioners. Such networks are the opposite of the "anarchic" systems we studied: participants are registered members of the network, free riding is punished in various ways, and file-sharing behavior is regulated by system administrators. We strongly recommend subsequent research of file sharing in these networks to test contemporary theories of costly punishment of non-cooperative norm violators (Boyd et al. 2003; Gintis et al. 2003; Henrich et al. 2005; 2006).

5.2 Uploading Is a Predominantly Male Endeavor

Risk taking has always been closely linked to males, but the mechanisms that favor such behavior have yet to be fully explicated within a costly signaling framework (Wilke et al. 2006; Pawlowski et al. 2008). Our findings indicate that a signal's level of risk can be a powerful predictor when extrapolating sex differences in costly signaling behavior. Compared with males, female file sharers felt that uploading was "riskier" than downloading (Table 8.2, Item A3). Interestingly, male and female perceptions of the risks associated with uploading differed significantly. Females were more concerned about exposure to viruses and hackers, whereas males were more concerned with the potential of prosecution (Table 8.2, Items 1 and 2), implying that females and males interpret the costs and thus the information derived from the signal differently.

Exposure to hackers and viruses are real threats to file sharers, but the greatest risk is recording industry litigation, which can cost an uploader many thousands of dollars. A recent survey conducted by *Pew Internet and American Life*, a non-profit organization, reports that the percentage of file sharers were reduced by one-half after the RIAA pursued lawsuits against uploaders in 2003 (Rainie and Madden 2004). Females stopped file sharing more than any other demographic group with a 58% decline in the number of users (Rainie and Madden 2004). In our study, males were more cognizant of the risk of prosecution than females, yet males were significantly more likely than females to engage in risky uploading behavior, an outcome consistent with a CST dynamic in which risky file-uploading behavior by males constitutes the costly signal.

The observed gender differences in file-sharing activities raise important theoretical questions about CST. Cultural restrictions on inter-sex participation can explain many examples of sex-biased signaling (Bliege Bird and Smith 2005), but in many signaling venues, such as P2P file sharing, males and females have equal opportunities to participate. Of the file sharers in this study, there were negligible differences between the sexes concerning participation (53% male, 47% female). In fact, more females (55%) than males (45%) exclusively downloaded files. It is not that females are excluded from or voluntarily do not engage in the file-sharing culture, it is that they choose to participate in the less risky, more immediately profitable file-sharing behavior – downloading.

The efficacy of a signal is dependent upon the attentiveness of the audience, so in order for an off-line signal to be effective, those who upload files must be recognized as uploaders among peers. Female uploaders were not identified as such among friends from college, did not talk about uploading with off-line peers, and were much less likely to upload in the presence of peers when compared with males (Table 8.3, Items C9, C7, C8). Since few females upload, and it is seldom discussed among those who do, there are few, if any, potential benefits for a female signaler. Males, on the other hand, were more likely than females to upload, to talk about uploading, to upload in the presence of peers, and to be identified as uploaders among friends (Table 8.3, Items 7–9). The results also indicated that differences in signal quality are recognized more by males (Table 8.2, Items E15–E16). Sex differences in P2P participation and motivation strongly suggest that risky uploading behavior is an intrasex signal between male uploaders.

5.3 Uploading and the Quest for Status

Veblen (1899) explained how conspicuously consuming material items can be a form of social competition that reliably signals economic status. Conspicuous consumption is a signal strategy involving uneconomical behavior that is observable among peers, including leisurely spending and disinterest in financial profits. Veblen posited that this type of behavior honestly advertises economic status in social environments where information about this quality is unreliable. This same logic has been applied by Mauss (1924) and is mentioned more recently by Zahavi and Zahavi (1997) when considering examples of conspicuous generosity such as public donations. According to the latter, charity donors are concerned with how they are perceived by peers, competitors, and potential mates, rather than with increasing reputations among charity recipients (Zahavi and Zahavi 1997). Our results indicate that uploaders, like donors at charity events, are using their file-sharing activities to impress and compete with their "flesh and blood" social peers off-line and are relatively unconcerned about how they are perceived by those online file downloaders that receive their gift.

In order for a signaling game to be competitive, there must be variations in the cost and/or risk of the signal that logically relate to differential quality among signalers. Based on clues from the study data and the accounts of informants obtained during the pilot interviews, it is clear that all uploaders are not equal. In addition to a general willingness to risk litigation, there are other variable qualities that relate to the cost and the risk of uploading: (1) the degree of financial investment in technology used in file sharing (a high-performance computer and fast Internet connection) and (2) the degree of computer competence that a file sharer may use to mitigate online exposure to risk. These observable differences in quality can be competitively displayed in a manner that signals status among off-line peers while file sharing.

Most file-sharing programs allow downloaders who are searching for digital media to choose among available uploaders by connection speed (T3 or higher, T1, cable/DSL, or 56 K modem). It has become such an important quality in uploaders that many file-sharing programs allow downloaders to filter out low-quality uploaders when searching for digital data. Moreover, some P2P file-sharing networks have icons that display an uploader's connection speed and other qualities on his/her computer screen, and this signal is highly observable when an uploader is file sharing in the presence of friends. The prestige element of connection speed is further evident in the uploader vernacular. When uploaders converse they will commonly ask, "What is your pipe size?" referring to one's connection speed. The size of one's "pipe" is positively correlated with the amount of data that can be transferred between file sharers. For example, the authors downloaded a 6-min song from an uploader with a T4 connection speed (high-speed network) in one-tenth of the time it took to download the same song from an uploader with a 56 K (dial-up) connection speed. Enhancing signal quality using technology is financially expensive – in the vernacular of file sharing, a high quality or "choice" uploader must be equipped with a computer with a fast processor, a "fat" hard drive that is capable of holding large quantities of downloadable data, and a "big pipe" for quickly transferring digital data.

In addition to greater financial investment, some uploaders also take comparatively greater risks. Differences in the level of risk incurred may logically relate to differences in computer expertise among uploaders. The zealous uploader further increases such risks by leaving his/her computer on overnight and while at work or school, which allows other file sharers to download large files such as movies or TV sitcoms, whereas others only upload while downloading files. The former increases the amount of time an uploader is vulnerable to hackers and viruses, while also increasing the chances an uploader is caught for infringing copyright laws. The aforementioned study conducted by *Pew Internet and American Life* illustrates how "time spent uploading" increases risk. Among those surveyed that continued to file share after the 2003 wave of subpoenas, 20% claimed to spend considerably *less* time file sharing due to fear of paying the potential $150,000 fine (Rainie and Madden 2004). This important signal of quality – time spent uploading – is recognized significantly more by uploaders than downloaders and to a greater degree by males when compared to females (Table 8.2, Item E16).

As discussed, many risky signals such as reckless driving are more likely to be performed by males (Nell 2002). Turning to pop culture for an example, Richard Linklater's 1993 film entitled *Dazed and Confused* is rich with examples of competitive status signaling, ritual, and initiation among young adults. In one scene, a young man named Wooderson stands over his 1970 Chevrolet Chevelle SS he called "Melba Toast." Wooderson, with the hood "popped," confidently describes various qualities of his car to a male peer: "I'll tell you what Melba Toast is packing here. I've got a 411 positrac out back, 750 double pumper, Edelbrock intake, bored over 30, 11 to 1 pop-up pistons, turbo-jet, 390 horsepower. We're talking some [expletive] muscle." Later on, the reliability of this verbal display was demonstrated on the highway as Wooderson recklessly races a peer with both cars packed with teenage males. There is a parallel in behavior between the pop-icon car enthusiast and the uploader who muttered to another uploader as they sat down and "popped" open their laptops prior to a focus group discussion: "What do you have there... an Apple G4 Powerbook with a 450 MHz G3 processor? My XPS M170 runs an Intel Pentium 2.26 GHz processor with 2 gigs of dual channel SDRAM. I've got 6 USB connectors and an 80 GB, high speed, 7200 RPM hard drive." P2P file-sharing networks, like the highways where young men race their cars, provide a risky environment for uploaders to show-off their "skills" and "machinery."

5.4 Cognitive Adaptations, Collective Action, and the P2P Phenomenon

As discussed, cognitive adaptations for social exchange evolved under specific conditions: most transactions were repeated, unambiguous, and face-to-face. Social norms likely also played a role in managing cooperation in small Pleistocene groups. This milieu is in stark contrast to those of P2P file-sharing networks, where transactions are not face-to-face, but instead ambiguous and often one-shot. Furthermore, sharing norms in P2P file-sharing networks are relatively nonexistent. Is the generosity of uploaders the result of a mismatch with regard to cognitive adaptations for resource exchange? Does the lack of environmentally relevant cues fail to trigger cheater detection mechanisms? We do not think this is the case. As mentioned, uploaders are well aware of the degree of free riding that occurs in file sharing, but choose to take risks to generously share with non-reciprocators. We feel that the generosity of uploaders is simply a product of the execution of cognitive adaptations for status ambition. But this proposition brings us to a new question regarding mismatch theory and cognitive adaptations in this context: Are there in fact *real* status benefits in these novel signaling venues or can status seeking in online environments be considered sub-optimal behavior? Whether or not the status seeking of uploaders actually pays off is an empirical question that will best be addressed through longitudinal, ethnographic fieldwork. This issue is important to consider since it will provide clues to the adaptiveness (or lack thereof) of the status ambition of uploaders.

The coexistence of contributors and free riders in relatively stable collective action, exemplified in P2P file sharing, is extremely interesting for evolutionary theorists. As mentioned, waste – even in the form of costly generosity – is a common outcome of signal selection. We feel that the generosity of uploaders is simply a product of their quest for status. Like hunters who show off their abilities by sharing meat at public feasts, uploaders who share digital media communicate adaptive information about their quality to peers. The presence of free-riding downloaders is thus not a problem, insofar as the potential for reputational benefits for uploaders exists.

5.5 Conclusions and Future Directions

P2P file-sharing networks are observable, ubiquitous phenomena that involve real-life resource exchange between millions of strangers throughout the world. These dynamic sharing systems – which transcend language, social, and geographic boundaries – provide a unique opportunity to test evolutionary hypotheses about CA and cognitive adaptations in novel social environments. Here, we consider what evolutionary psychology and signaling theory can tell us about the P2P file-sharing phenomenon. Internet uploading behavior appears to meet the criteria for a costly signal. File uploading is an avoidable and risky behavior that is observable among peers and displays variation between uploaders in the costs/risks incurred that logically relate to differences in signaler quality. Both parties potentially benefit from the signal transaction: signalers can compete for enhanced peer-group status and the audience (which is likely composed of other uploaders) gains important information about the differences in quality among members of their peer group.

We feel there is great potential for evolutionarily informed research in other online social environments, such as World of Warcraft, a tremendously popular online game which attracts over 11 million monthly subscribers. In this game, status is sought via observable usernames, and cooperation and deceit are rampant. Rare or unique items, armors, and weapons can be obtained from hard-to-complete quests, which signal the player's skill. So enraptured in the quest for status some play for days on end, even succumbing to heart failure as the result of starvation and dehydration.

Peer-to-peer file sharing constitutes an observable natural experiment and is highly amenable to subsequent research. Future goals include development of methods to parse factors affecting the quality of the communicated signal, such as technology investment and computer competence, and to further understand the motivations for off-line competition among male uploaders. There are several difficulties with deciphering the meaning and significance of gender differences in human behavior (see Kock 2009, Appendix H for a good review), and further investigation of gender differences in uploading behavior using different methods (e.g., ethnographic, economic games) is warranted to help better understand this phenomenon. The nature and target of the signal being sent by female uploaders is unclear. As a group, female uploaders were not concerned with either their reputation online or recognition while off-line and were ambivalent about uploading for the good of the file-sharing community. Further research is required to clarify the motivations for risky uploading among female file sharers. Finally, research of "closed" administered file-sharing systems such as Bit Torrent is recommended to test contemporary group selection theory of costly punishment of norm violators in cooperative groups.

Acknowledgments We would like to thank Richard Sosis, Ed Hagen, Lisa Dunlap, Ben Trumble, and several anonymous reviewers for helpful suggestions on earlier drafts. This chapter is a revised version of a 2007 article by the authors which was published in *Evolutionary Psychology*, Vol 5. Elements of this study were presented at the 2005 Human Behavior and Evolution Society (HBES) conference in Austin, TX and the 2006 HBES conference in Philadelphia, PA.

References

Acheson JM (2006) Institutional failure in resource management. Annu Rev Anthropol 35: 117–134

Agrawal A (2003) Sustainable governance of common-pool resources: context, methods, and politics. Annu Rev Anthropol 32:243–262

Barkow J (1991) Darwin, sex, and status: biological approaches to mind and culture. University of Toronto Press, Toronto

Bliege Bird RL, Smith EA (2005) Signaling theory, strategic interaction, and symbolic capital. Curr Anthropol 46(2):221–248

Blurton Jones NG (1987) Tolerated theft, suggestions about the ecology and evolution of sharing, hoarding, and scrounging. Soc Sci Inf 26(1):31–54

Boyd R, Gintis H., Bowles S, Richerson P (2003) The evolution of altruistic punishment. Proc Natl Acad Sci U S A 100(6):3531–3535

Bowlby J (1969) Attachment and loss, vol 1. Basic Books, New York

Bowlby J (1973) Separation: anxiety and anger, vol 2. Basic Books, New York

Buss DM, Abbott M, Angleitner A, Biaggio A, Blanco-Villasenor A, Bruchon-Schweitzer M et al (1990) International preferences in selecting mates: a study of 37 cultures. J Cross Cult Psychol 21(1):5–47

Byrne JP, Miller D, Schafer WD (1999) Gender differences in risk-taking: a meta-analysis. Psychol Bull 125(3):367–383

Cashdan E (1985) Coping with risk: reciprocity among the Basarwa of Northern Botswana. Man 20(3):454–474

Cosmides L (1989) The logic of social exchange: has natural selection shaped how humans reason? Studies with the Wason selection task. Cognition 31(3):187–276

Cosmides L, Tooby J (1992) Cognitive adaptations for social exchange. In: Barkow JH, Cosmides L, Tooby J (eds) The adapted mind: evolutionary psychology and the generation of culture. Oxford University Press, New York, pp 163–228

Cosmides L, Tooby J (2005) Neurocognitive adaptations designed for social exchange. In: Buss DM (ed) The handbook of evolutionary psychology, Wiley, New Jersey, pp 584–627

Daly M, Wilson M (2001) Risk-taking, intrasexual competition, and homicide. In: French JA, Kamil AC, Leger DW (eds) Evolutionary psychology and motivation, University of Nebraska Press, Lincoln, pp 1–36

Ellis BJ (1992) The evolution of sexual attraction: evaluative mechanisms in women. In: Barkow J, Cosmides L, Tooby J (eds) The adapted mind: evolutionary psychology and the generation of culture, Oxford University Press, New York, pp. 267–289

Farrelly D, Turnbull N (2008) The role of reasoning domain on face recognition: detecting violations of social contract and hazard management rules. Evol Psychol 6(3):523–537

Farthing GW (2005) Attitudes towards heroic and non-heroic physical risk takers as mates and friends. Evol Hum Behav 26(2):205–214

Gintis H, Bowles S, Boyd R, Fehr E (2003) Explaining altruistic behavior in humans. Evol Hum Behav 24(3):153–172

Grafen A (1990) Biological signals as handicaps. J Theor Biol 144:517–546

Gurven G, Allen-Arave W, Hill K, Hurtado M (2000) "It's a Wonderful Life": signaling generosity among the Ache of Paraguay. Evol Hum Behav 21(4):263–282

Hagen EH (2005) Controversial issues in evolutionary psychology. In: Buss D (ed) The handbook of evolutionary psychology, Wiley, New Jersey, pp 145–176

Hamilton WD (1964) The genetical evolution of social behavior. J Theor Biol 7:1–52

Hardin R (1982) Collective action. John Hopkins University Press, Baltimore

Hawkes K, Bliege Bird R (2002) Showing off, handicap signaling, and the evolution of men's work. Evol Anthropol 11(2):58–67

Henrich J, Boyd R, Bowles S, Camerer C, Fehr E, Gintis H et al (2005) Economic man in cross-cultural perspective: behavioral experiments in 15 small-scale societies. Behav Brain Sci 28(6):795–815

Henrich J, McElreath R, Abigail B, Ensminger J, Barrett C, Bolyanatz A et al (2006) Costly punishment across human societies. Science 312(5781):1767–1770

Irons W (1998) Adaptively relevant environments versus the environment of evolutionary adaptedness. Evol Anthropol 6(6):194–204

Kock N (2005) Media richness or media naturalness? The evolution of our biological communication apparatus and its influence on our behavior toward e-communication tools. IEEE Trans Prof Commun 48(2):117–130

Kock N (2009) Information systems theorizing based on evolutionary psychology: An interdisciplinary review and theory integration framework. MIS Q 33(2):395–418

Kock N, Verville J, Garza V (2007) Media naturalness and online learning: findings supporting both the significant- and no-significant-difference perspectives. Decision Sci J Innov Edu 5(2):333–356

Lansing JS, Miller JH (2005) Cooperation, games, and ecological feedback: some insights from Bali. Current Anthropol 46(2):328–334

Lyle III HF, Sullivan RJ (2007) Competitive status signaling in peer-to-peer file-sharing networks. Evol Psychol 5(2):363–382

Mauss M (1924) The gift: forms and function of exchange in archaic societies. Cohen and West, London

Maynard Smith J (1989) Evolutionary Genetics. Oxford University Press, New York

McCay BJ, Acheson JM (1987) The question of the commons: The culture and ecology of communal resources. University of Arizona Press, Tucson

Neiman F (1998) Conspicuous consumption as wasteful advertising: a Darwinian perspective on spatial patterns in Classic Maya terminal monument dates. In: Burton CM, Clark G, Bamforth D (eds) Rediscovering Darwin: Evolutionary theory and archaeological explanation, American Anthropological Association, Arlington, pp 267–290

Nell V (2002) Why young men drive dangerously: implications for injury prevention. Curr Dir Psychol Sci 11(2):79–82

Oda R (1997) Biased face recognition in the prisoner's dilemma game. Evol Hum Behav 18(5):309–315

Ostrom E (1990) Governing the commons: the evolution of institutions for collective action. Cambridge University Press, Cambridge

Ostrom E, Gardner R (1993) Coping with asymmetries in the commons: self-governing irrigation systems can work. J Econ Perspect 7(4):93–112

Panchanathan K, Boyd R (2004) Indirect reciprocity can stabilize cooperation without the second-order free rider problem. Nature 432:499–502

Pawlowski B, Atwal R, Dunbar R (2008) Sex differences in everyday risk-taking behavior in humans. Evol Psychol 6(1):29–42

Rainie L, Madden M (2004) The impact of recording industry suits against music file swappers. Pew Internet and American Life Project. Retrieved online: <pewinternet.org>

Smith EA, Wishnie M (2000) Conservation and subsistence in small-scale societies. Annu Rev Anthropol 29:493–524

Smith EA, Bliege Bird RL, Bird D (2003) The benefits of costly signaling: Meriam turtle hunters. Behav Ecol 14(1):116–126

Sosis R (2000) Costly signaling and torch fishing on Ifaluk atoll. Evol Hum Behav 21(4):223–244

Sugiyama LS, Tooby J, Cosmides L (2002) Cross-cultural evidence of social exchange among the Shiwiar of Ecuadorian Amazonia. Proc Natl Acad Sci 99(17):11537–11542

Symons D (1979) The evolution of human sexuality. Oxford University Press, New York

Symons D (1992) On the use and misuse of Darwinism. In: Barkow J, Cosmides L, Tooby J (eds) The adapted mind: evolutionary psychology and the generation of culture, Oxford University Press, New York, pp 137–159

Tooby J, Cosmides L (1992) The psychological foundations of culture. In: Barkow J, Cosmides L, Tooby J (eds) The adapted mind: evolutionary psychology and the generation of culture, Oxford University Press, New York, pp 19–136

Townsend JM, Levy GD (1990) Effects of potential partners' physical attractiveness and socioeconomic status on sexual and partner selection. Arch Sex Behav 19(2):149–164

Trivers RL (1971) The evolution of reciprocal altruism. Q Rev Biol 46(1):35–57

Veblen T (1899) The theory of the leisure class. Dover, New York

Wilson M, Daly M (1985) Competitiveness, risk-taking, and violence: the young male syndrome. Ethol Sociobiol 6(1):59–73

Wilke A, Hutchinson JM, Todd P, Kruger DJ (2006) Is risk taking used as a cue in mate choice? Evol Psychol 4:367–393

Wrangham R, Peterson D (1996) Demonic males: apes and the origins of human violence. Houghton Mifflin, Boston

Zahavi A (1975) Mate selection – a selection for a handicap. J Theor Biol 53(1):205–214

Zahavi A (1977) Reliability in communication systems and the evolution of altruism. In: Stonehouse B, Perrins CM (eds) Evolutionary ecology, Macmillan Press, London, pp. 253–259

Zahavi A, Zahavi A (1997) The handicap principle: a missing piece of Darwin's puzzle. Oxford University Press, New York

Chapter 9
Studying Invisibly: Media Naturalness and Learning

Ina Blau and Avner Caspi

Abstract This study examines differences between two learning environments: audio-written conferencing and traditional face-to-face instruction. We investigated whether medium richness [media richness theory; Daft and Lengel (Research in organizational behavior. JAI, Greenwich, 1984)], medium naturalness [media naturalness theory; Kock (IEEE Trans Prof Commun 48(2):117–130, 2005)], and invisibility influence students' achievement, satisfaction, and behavior. In two research settings, a field study and a laboratory experiment, students were taught face-to-face and/or via an audio-written conferencing system; subject matter and teacher were constant. We found similar achievement in the two environments. Significant differences, in favor of face-to-face communication, were found regarding learner satisfaction. In addition, invisibility increased certain kinds of students' behavior: participation, risk taking, immediacy feeling, and flaming. These findings were explained in terms of differences in media naturalness and as an effect of invisibility.

Keywords Media naturalness · Media richness · Online disinhibition effect · Invisibility · Visual anonymity · Online learning · Audio-written synchronous conferencing

I. Blau (✉)
Department of Psychology and Education, Open University of Israel, 1 University Road, Ra'anana, Israel
e-mail: ina.blau@gmail.com

A. Caspi
Department of Psychology and Education, Open University of Israel, 1 University Road, Ra'anana, Israel
e-mail: avnerca@openu.ac.il

N. Kock (ed.), *Evolutionary Psychology and Information Systems Research*,
Integrated Series in Information Systems 24, DOI 10.1007/978-1-4419-6139-6_9,
© Springer Science+Business Media, LLC 2010

1 Introduction

Synchronous communication tools, such as textual chat, audio, or video conferencing, have been used in distance education since the late 1970s of the twentieth century (Bates 2005). The main advantages of synchronous tools in education are that they closely simulate the transactions between teachers and students in a contiguous and conventional form of education (Garrison 1989), they may maximize the interactions between students and teachers, as well as among students (Guzley et al. 2001), and they potentially improve the quality of these interactions (Bates 2005). However, dozens of studies found no significant difference in students' achievement between instructional media, mainly when comparisons were made between face-to-face and computer-mediated instructions (Arbaugh et al. 2009; Bernard et al. 2004; Russell 1999). The current study compared learning outcomes resulting from audio-written conferencing and conventional face-to-face instruction. We start by reviewing three theoretical perspectives that compare online and offline communication. Then we present previous findings regarding the differences between audio-written conferencing and face-to-face educational environments, analyzing them through these three theoretical perspectives. Last, we present and test our hypotheses, which were based on both the theoretical background and the findings achieved so far.

1.1 Theoretical Explanations for Differences Between Computer-Mediated and Face-to-Face Communication

Differences between computer-mediated and face-to-face communication can be explained from different perspectives. We present three theoretical frameworks: media richness theory (Daft and Lengel 1984; Daft et al. 1987), media naturalness theory (Kock 2005), and the online disinhibition effect (Suler 2004). Media richness theory and media naturalness theory are frameworks that look for an optimal fit between a medium and a message. The online disinhibition effect is affiliated with psychological theories that try to explain Internet users' behavior.

1.1.1 Media Richness Theory

There are a cluster of theories that differentiate media by their inherent features, in order to predict efficient communication. Each theory selects different features, depending on its theoretical assumptions. One influential theory in this cluster is the media richness theory (MRT; Daft and Lengel 1984; Daft et al. 1987). The theory defined four criteria and ranked different media from "richest" to "leanest" according to their capability (1) to provide immediate feedback, (2) to transmit verbal and non-verbal communication cues, (3) to provide a sense of personalization, and (4) to simulate natural language. The theory assumes that face-to-face communication is the richest medium for transmitting information; this richness can reduce receiver uncertainty (i.e., lack of necessary information) and equivocality (i.e., different interpretations of information). Face-to-face communication is considered the most efficient way to convey complex messages.

Clearly, almost all non-face-to-face communication media involve different degrees of anonymity, especially in the sense of invisibility. *Invisibility* is a type of visual anonymity, the absence of communication cues in the form of facial expressions and body language. Christopherson (2007) noted that it may not be the case that one is truly anonymous in a social context, but the individual perceives himself or herself to be anonymous to others. Thus, on the one hand, identifiable cues may help reduce equivocal messages by supplying relevant information regarding the sender (for example, by eliciting past experience with the sender's perspectives or attitudes). On the other hand, even when communicators know each other, they may behave *as if* they were anonymous (see also Suler 2004), a behavior that may not contribute to reducing equivocality, thus resulting in an inefficient communication. This later state emerges in conditions of invisibility, where the communicators transact information without seeing each other.

The MRT evoked dozens of studies (for recent review, see Donabedian 2006); several, however, criticized its unidimensionality (e.g., Carlson and Zmud 1999; D'Ambra et al. 1998; Shachaf and Hara 2007). In addition, empirical research regarding the influence of media richness on communication provided mixed results (Caspi and Gorsky 2005).

Assuming that learning is a process that aims to reduce learners' uncertainty and information equivocality, it is reasonable to conclude that a richer medium is more appropriate for instruction and learning. Using a lean communication medium may have a negative effect on students' learning and satisfaction. Testing the theory in educational settings has shown that media richness may indeed influence learning. Schultz (2003) found that students who learned an online lesson mediated through a lean medium (textual chat) had significantly lower grades than did students who learned the same lesson with the same tutor through a rich medium (traditional face-to-face instruction). However, other findings pointed to the fact that a rich medium provides distracters that may have a negative effect on learning. Olson et al. (1997) and Sallnäs (2002) found that students using a rich medium (video conferencing) for instructional communication were often distracted and less task focused than were students who utilized a leaner medium (audio conferencing; see also Hampel and Baber 2003; Rosell-Aguilar 2006).

1.1.2 Media Naturalness Theory

A more recent approach to computer-mediated communication, media naturalness theory (MNT; Kock 2005), used "naturalness" (instead of "richness") as a criterion for differentiating media. Similar to MRT, face-to-face communication was ranked highest according to five criteria: co-location, synchronicity, and the ability to convey facial expressions, body language, and speech. According to MNT, a decrease in the degree of media naturalness may lead to (1) an increase in cognitive effort, which is defined as "the amount of mental activity… involved in communication interaction" (Kock 2005, p. 122), (2) an increase in communication ambiguity, and (3) a decrease in physiological arousal (Kock 2005, 2009). Thus, the MNT suggests a compensational mechanism in which performance outcomes may be similar despite differences in naturalness of the media used. For example, learning via textual chat (an unnatural medium in terms of MNT) demands more cognitive effort to decrease communication ambiguity, which may result in outcomes similar to learning face-to-face (the most natural medium according to MNT). However, since using an unnatural medium may decrease physiological arousal, learners may be less satisfied and less exited than may learners who study using a natural medium.

Anonymous communication, either just visual or more extensive, is not a natural way of human interaction. From an evolutionary point of view, anonymous communication evolved only after face-to-face communication had existed. Thus, it seems plausible that the three predictions of NMH are valid for invisible communication.

Kock (2005) interpreted some of the mixed results obtained in MRT studies in terms of media naturalness. Nevertheless, he argued that other factors (like social influence or organizational climate; see: Fulk et al. 1987, 1990) may override media naturalness when selecting a medium for communication.

Some evidences found in educational settings may support media naturalness theory. The prediction of the MNT regarding an increase in cognitive effort using unnatural medium may be referred to as *extraneous load* in terms of cognitive load theory (CLT; Sweller 1998; van Merriënboer and Sweller 2005). Extraneous load is caused by the format of an instruction (as opposed to *intrinsic load* which is associated with the learning task itself). According to CLT, higher extraneous load interferes with learning. Chen et al. (2006) found that satisfaction from cooperative learning tasks in audio conferencing (the more natural communication medium in their study) was significantly higher relative to textual chat (the more unnatural communication medium). However, there was no difference between media in terms of learning outcomes. In the same vein, tutors in Rapanotti et al.'s (2002) study reported feelings of discomfort when teaching through audio conference. This discomfort was caused by the absence of visual cues and body language that characterized face-to-face classes. All these findings may be interpreted as a result of increased cognitive efforts and decreased physiological arousal in less natural media. Recently, Kock et al. (2007) found that while at the middle of a semester, students learning face-to-face achieved significant higher grades than did students who learned online, at the end of the semester this difference disappeared. They did not find support for the compensational mechanism and explained the no-difference effect using Carlson and Zmud's (1999) channel expansion approach, which is not rooted in an evolutionary perspective (Kock 2009).

While MRT assumes that a good fit between a message and a medium will result in better performance and higher satisfaction, MNT assumes that performance and satisfaction depend on inherent characteristics of the medium and are not dependant on the message's attributes. As noted above, the two theories disagree on the criteria that differentiate media and have different predictions regarding the impact of media on learning. Table 9.1 presents examples of predictions from both theories for different media and different messages. Example for a simple message in

Table 9.1 Examples of different predictions of MRT and MNT

Medium	Message	MRT	MNT
Face-to-face	Simple	High outcome High satisfaction	High outcome High satisfaction
	Complex	High outcome High satisfaction	High outcome High satisfaction
Audio conferencing	Simple	High outcome High satisfaction	High outcome Low satisfaction
	Complex	Low outcome Low satisfaction	High outcome Low satisfaction
Chat	Simple	High outcome High satisfaction	High outcome Very low satisfaction
	Complex	Very low outcome Very low satisfaction	High outcome Very low satisfaction

educational context may be "Notify students about a change in deadline for hand-ing in an assignment"; example for a complex message may be "Clarify a complex theoretical issue for a given course unit" (Caspi and Gorsky 2005).

1.1.3 Online Disinhibition Effect

Some communication media afford invisibility, which – as noted above – is a type of visual anonymity. Visual anonymity may disinhibit communicators' behavior, even if the identity of all participants is known (Suler 2004). Suler described the online disinhibition effect as behavior in cyberspace that is not ordinarily done in the face-to-face world. In cyberspace, people may loosen up, feel less restrained, and express themselves more openly. Suler divided the disinhibition effect into positive and negative behaviors. Positive behavior may include exposing personal informa-tion, revealing secret emotions, fears, or wishes, as well as behaving kindly and generously. Negative behavior may include using rude language, harsh criticisms, anger, hatred, even threats, as well as exploring pornography, committing crimes, or using violence. Suler maintained that the distinction between "positive" and "neg-ative" disinhibition might be complex or ambiguous in some cases. One important effect of the online disinhibition is risk taking. Being invisible, people may feel more secure and allow themselves to engage in risky behaviors. For example, prob-lematic behavior may be amplified by the special conditions of Internet surfing, like visual anonymity and illegal content availability (e.g., Quayle and Taylor 2003).

From a learner's point of view, the learning environment may include risks of two kinds: intellectual and social. A student may choose to learn difficult subject matter that might lead to a failure. This is an *intellectual* risk. Tutor or students may criticize the learner for asking questions, or answering incorrectly; thus, participa-tion may involve *social* risk taking. Clifford (1991) reviewed dozens of studies that examined academic risk taking. She found that students preferred moderate risks and believed that risk taking benefits their learning. However, her review focused mainly on intellectual risk taking (i.e., solving a difficult task, learning difficult subject matter) rather than social risk taking (i.e., active participation in class). When students were asked about the reasons they avoid participation in face-to-face classes and in asynchronous conferencing, they mentioned mainly "social" risk (e.g., avoiding social criticism; Caspi et al. 2006b). Such reasons were more disseminated in face-to-face classes than in asynchronous conferencing that afforded invisibility.

Visual anonymity, and even its weaker form – invisibility, may serve as a "shield" for students who are afraid of making mistakes in a face-to-face learning situation (Caspi et al 2006b; Kötter and Shield 2000; Oren et al. 2002; Rosell-Aguilar 2005). Freeman et al. (2006) found that students who interact invisibly expressed more willingness to participate in class. Lobel et al. (2002) reported that students who interact invisibly perceived less risk and more opportunity for self-disclosure. Consequently, they engaged in a larger "windowed" opening to the self, which led them to be more involved in the learning.

There are other consequences of invisible interaction, which might be a result of disinhibited behavior. Eklund-Braconi (2005) argued that synchronous communication created a closer relationship (immediacy) between teachers and students and among students than did face-to-face instructional communication (see also Coghlan 2000; Tosunoglu et al. 2002). Lea et al. (2002) found that interactions among invisible learning group members encouraged them to develop strong identifications with their group, which in turn increased the quality of a group's product.

The "shield" of visual anonymity may allow more equal learner participation, perhaps as another "positive" effect of online disinhibition. Rains and Scott (2007) argued that anonymity in computer-mediated communication diminishes status differences between group members, which encourages more equal participation from all members and allows communicators to focus on the content rather than on the identity of the contributor. Warschauer (1996) studied this "equalization effect" (Dubrovsky et al. 1991; Siegel et al. 1986) in group communication and found more balanced participation between communicators in textual chat relative to face-to-face discussions. Similarly, Blau and Barak (2010) found more equal participation in textual chat than in face-to-face communication. However, in another study (Böhlke 2003), more equal participation in chat was found only in small groups. Christopherson (2007) opined that absolute anonymity is not a necessary condition for the equalization effect to occur. Thus, invisibility may be sufficient to generate equalization.

Positive outcomes of visual anonymity may be accompanied by some negative ones. Sia et al. (2002) found that visual anonymity caused some individuals not only to generate more novel arguments but also to engage in more confrontational behavior. Reinig et al. (1997) found that students in online discussion generated almost five more comments than did face-to-face students, but also transacted more flaming and buffoonery expressions. Nevertheless, percentages of flaming and buffoonery messages were negligible (about 2%). Chester and Gwynne (1998) found a strong sense of community among students who interact invisibly, but also some (minimal) instances of insult and flaming. Freeman and Bamford (2004) reported that some anonymous learners used anonymity to become chronic complainers, and did not help other learners. Additionally, students provided more negative feedback (i.e., dissatisfaction) when anonymity was an option. It is noted that in Freeman and Bamford's study, although students had the option to communicate anonymously, the majority of students did not use this option. In another study, where anonymous participation was an option and manipulated (Kilner and Hoadley 2005), half the participants chose to participate anonymously. Again, more comments were posted under anonymous conditions; anonymity was positively correlated with quality of messages, and only few messages (6%) were classified as flaming.

To summarize, online disinhibition may influence learning in two opposite ways. On the one hand, it may raise the level of participation, may create equalization among participants, may result in a strong sense of community, may allow students to take more risks, and may even elevate the quality of the discussion. On the other hand, although not so common, some negative behaviors such as flaming or unjustified criticism may appear.

As noted above, different media provide different degrees of anonymity. Written communication tools afford both visual and auditory forms of anonymity. These tools also secure other aspects of the communicator's identity, such as name or gender. Audio tools keep visual anonymity but may reveal other aspects of the communicator's identity. A communicator's voice may expose gender or race. In that sense, audio tools afford invisible communication, not the full anonymity afforded by unidentifiable textual communication. If the online disinhibition effect depends on the degree of anonymity, then we may predict that the above listed impacts of the effect on learning may be larger when anonymity is greater.

One criterion of media richness theory indirectly relates to invisibility – the capability of a medium to transmit non-verbal cues. Media naturalness theory has three criteria (out of five) that their combination may define invisibility: co-location, conveying facial expression, and conveying body language (these two may be combined with "transmission of non-verbal cues"). By definition then, media naturalness approach assigns a higher degree to invisibility in its analysis of communication media.

One may argue that comparing face-to-face communication with audio-written communication has a potential confound. A more appropriate procedure would compare audio-written communication with video-written communication. In a pilot study, we tried the video-written communication option and found that it was impossible to keep eye contact between communicators. Eye contact has significant value in human communication (Senju and Johnson 2008), but visibility does not readily mean the existence of eye contact (Barak 2007). In order to be seen as keeping eye contact with the other communicators, one must look directly at the camera. However in the current technological solutions for desktop video communication, the angle at which participants view the screen is different from the angle at which the camera is located. Thus, if the communicator looks directly at the camera, she cannot see the other participants, and when the communicator looks at the screen, it appears that she is not looking at the other participants. The two options are not close to natural conditions of communication.

1.2 Learning via Audio-Written Conferencing Relative to Face-to-Face Class

The current study compares learning outcomes in two environments: the so-called traditional class, in which instruction is done face-to-face, with an audio-conferencing system that embodies textual chat (for a matter of convenience, we use the term audio-written conferencing or AWC). Some studies (Pan and Sullivan 2005; Rapanotti et al. 2002; Tosunoglu et al. 2002) suggested that audio-written conferencing is an effective tool for synchronous discussion that promoted learning. This tool also affords the formation of out-of-class peer support groups that continue the learning (Hampel and Hauck 2004). Hampel (2006) suggested that the use of audio-written conferencing in language courses has the potential to increase students' participation and interaction.

Few studies compare audio-written conferencing and face-to-face learning. Several of those do have methodological weaknesses (e.g., instructional modes were self-selected, different instructors used different tools, etc.). The current study aimed at testing differences in the two environments, in terms of achievements, satisfaction, and students' behavior. We analyzed the two learning environments through the three theoretical perspectives presented above: Media richness theory, media naturalness theory, and the online disinhibition effect.

In terms of media richness theory, face-to-face is a rich communication medium, while audio-written conferencing is a lean one. Although the conveyance of speech may enrich the medium, immediate feedback (not necessarily verbal one), transmission of non-verbal cues, and sense of personalization are lower. According to the media naturalness theory, the two communication modes differ less. They have a similar level of synchronicity and they convey speech to a similar degree. Figure 9.1 depicts the differences. Audio-written conferencing affords visual anonymity, whereas in a face-to-face environment, people are identified.

Our dependent variables are "achievement," "satisfaction," and "students' behavior." Achievement is the difference between pre-learning and post-learning tests. We also measure perceived learning in terms of five possible conceptions of learning (Marton et al. 1993; Marton and Säljö 1976a, b). Satisfaction was measured by students' self-reports vis-à-vis emotions that were evoked during learning (such as enjoyment or interest). Students' behavior was measured by counting risk-taking events (operationalized as answering teacher's questions and offering opinions), counting "public" participation (talking in the class or in the audio-written conference), and counting expressions of immediacy and flaming.

The predictions of the three theoretical perspectives are presented in Table 9.2. Clearly, the three theoretical perspectives have different predictions regarding achievement. MRT predicts better performance in face-to-face settings, since this medium affords exchanging more information that might be more relevant and accurate. MNT predicts that the disadvantages unnatural medium has may be compensated by investing extra cognitive efforts. Thus, achievement may be equal in both settings, unless insufficient cognitive efforts were devoted. The online

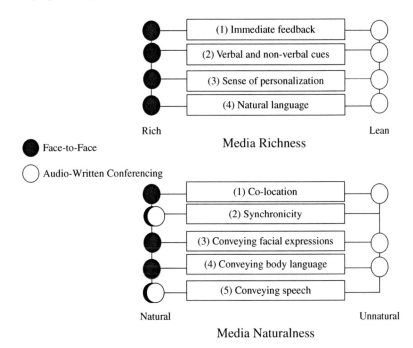

Fig. 9.1 Analyzing face-to-face vs. audio-written conferencing learning setting in terms of media richness (*top*) and media naturalness (*bottom*)

Table 9.2 Predictions of the three perspectives

	MRT	MNT	Online disinhibition
Achievement	FtF > AWC	FtF ≥ AWC	FtF ≤ AWC
Perceived learning	FtF > AWC	FtF > AWC	FtF < > AWC
Satisfaction	FtF > AWC	FtF > AWC	FtF < > AWC
Students' behavior:			
Risk taking			FtF < AWC
Participation			FtF < AWC
Equalization			FtF < AWC
Immediacy			FtF < AWC
Flaming			FtF < AWC

FtF, face-to-face; AWC, audio-written communication

disinhibition effect predicts better performance under visual-anonymous communication, unless levels of negative disinhibited behavior are high.

Regarding satisfaction, both MRT and MNT predict higher levels of satisfaction in face-to-face environments, whereas online disinhibition effect does not have a specific prediction, depending on the actual behavior taken place. Students that communicate invisibly may feel higher levels of immediacy, take more risks, and have higher and more equal participation. At the same time, according to the online disinhibition effect, they may also feel more satisfied than in face-to-face communication. However, if negative events happen, they may feel less satisfied. There are no direct predictions of MRT and MNT vis-à-vis students' behavior.

These predictions were tested in two studies. In the field study, all students alternated between lessons taught face-to-face and lessons taught via audio-written conferencing. In this study, we focused on students' behavior. In the laboratory study, participants were randomly assigned to audio-written conferencing or to a face-to-face lesson. This study measured achievement, learning satisfaction, and students' behavior. In both studies, students were taught by the same teacher in both conditions.

2 Study 1: Field Study

The field study utilized a pedagogical opportunity whereby a teacher could not meet her students face-to-face every week. The solution was audio-written conferencing that took place every even week. Under these conditions, the option to test students every week was unreasonable and might even be unethical. We thus focused on students' behavior: attendance, participation, equalization, risk taking, immediacy, and flaming.

2.1 Method

2.1.1 Participants

Twenty-eight high school students (25% female) from a rural school in northern Israel were studying for a matriculation exam. Participation was mandatory. Two independent groups were formed: 11 eleventh grade students and 17 twelfth graders. Learning through audio-written conferencing was a new experience for all students.

2.1.2 Instruments

Audio conferencing was done using Skype[TM], an Internet application that allows rich synchronous communication. All students knew each other; they were identified by name or nickname. Skype allows video communication, but only in a one-by-one mode. Thus, only two communication channels were available: auditory and textual.

Students' behavior. Participation, risk taking, immediacy, and flaming were checked using quantitative content analysis of the lessons' records. Participation was measured by the frequency of each student's (and of the teacher's) speaking and writing. For oral participation, we regarded a single unit of participation as continuous speaking until another participant started to speak. For written communication, every message was regarded as a single unit of participation. Risk taking was measured by the frequency of answering the teacher's questions and offering opinions regarding the subject matter. Immediacy was measured by the frequency of warmth and confidence expressions, use of humor, and self-disclosure. Flaming was measured by the frequency of potentially offensive expressions. A second rater, familiar with the subject matter but not with the students, analyzed 25% of the records, and a high level of agreement between raters was found (above 90% agreement for each category of analysis, Cohen's $\kappa = 0.88$).

2.1.3 Procedure

Students alternated between face-to-face lessons taught in school and audio-written conferencing lessons taught at a distance. Students participated in the audio-written conferencing lessons from their home and were free to select the mode of communication. The teacher spoke using the audio mode, but also replied to student's input (questions, answers, comments) via the textual chat mode. All lessons were recorded and 12 lessons (6 face-to-face and 6 audio-written conferencing) were randomly selected for the analysis.

2.2 Results

Despite that attendance was mandatory and equal importance was assigned to face-to-face lessons and to audio-written conferencing, students attended significantly more the face-to-face lessons than audio-written conferencing lessons, $t^1(9) = 3.30$, $p < 0.001$, $d' = 2.0$ (STE 0.7). Average attendance is presented in Table 9.3.

Table 9.3 Average (and standard deviation) of students' attendance (number of students attended a lesson)

Lesson mode	11th grade	12th grade	Total
FtF (six lessons)	9.00 (1.65)	13.33 (1.25)	11.60 (2.55)
AWC (six lessons)	5.33 (0.47)	7.33 (2.36)	6.53 (2.09)

Participation was measured in two ways. In terms of average participation per lesson (number of students who participated in a lesson divided by number of attendees), there was no significant difference between the two modes of instruction. In terms of the relative contribution to the lesson (the average proportion of an individual student's oral or written contributions in a single lesson relative to all participants

---

[1] We used a t-test that assumed heteroscedasticity. Note that the unit of analysis is the lesson observation, not the student.

Table 9.4 Average (and standard deviation) of students' participation

	Lesson mode	11th grade	12th grade	Total
Average	FtF (6 lessons)	8.43 (11.27)	7.74 (10.23)	8.03 (10.68)
Participation	AWC (6 lessons)	9.32 (8.66)	12.52 (7.39)	11.14 (8.12)
Relative	FtF (6 lessons)	6.39 (7.15)	5.02 (5.93)	5.57 (6.48)
contribution	AWC (6 lessons)	10.17 (7.34)	9.86 (5.51)	9.99 (6.61)

in that lesson including the teacher), we found that students contributed significantly more in audio-written conferencing lessons, $t(8) = 4.07$, $p < 0.001$, $d' = 0.6$ (STE 0.6). The teacher did not intentionally encourage participation more in one mode of instruction or in the other – there was no significant difference between the two modes of instruction in number of questions referred to students. Table 9.4 presents the average participation. The contribution of the teacher also did not significantly differ between the two modes of instruction. We found no evidence for equalization effect.

Within the Skype mode, we further tested for differences between audio and chat in terms of students' participation. Students talked 111 times; they wrote 218 messages. As Fig. 9.2 shows, a significant difference between classes was found, $\chi^2(1) = 88.19$, $p < 0.001$; eleventh graders used the audio channel more than the text channel, whereas twelfth graders did the opposite.

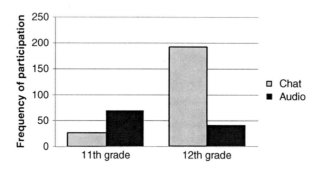

Fig. 9.2 Frequencies of participation

Risk taking, measured as answering teacher's questions and offering opinions regarding the subject, was similar in the two modes of instruction. Comparison of risk taking in audio versus chat revealed that students took more risks in chat (72 events) relative to audio (37 events). A significant difference between classes was found, $\chi^2(1) = 50.03$, $p < 0.001$; this of course resembles the interaction pattern reported regarding participation in the two channels (see Fig. 9.3).

We found 92 expressions of immediacy in audio-written conferencing as opposed to 56 in the face-to-face class. However, the two classes differed significantly, $\chi^2(1) = 16.68$, $p < 0.001$: Amount of immediacy expressions was similar in both

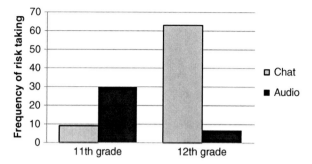

Fig. 9.3 Frequencies of risk taking

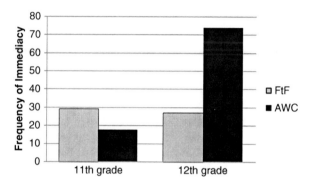

Fig. 9.4 Frequencies of immediacy

eleventh and twelfth grade face-to-face classes, but in audio-written conferencing, we found more than four times the number of expressions of immediacy in the twelfth grade class relative to eleventh grade (see Fig. 9.4).

Flaming expressions were rare. We found 16 flaming in audio-written conferencing (8 in eleventh grade and 8 in twelfth grade) as opposed to 7 in face-to-face classes (5 in eleventh grade and 2 in twelfth grade).

2.3 Discussion

The field study gave initial support for the online disinhibition effect predictions. We found that students participated relatively more in invisible communication; they took more risks in chat than in audio, expressed more immediacy, and at the same time more flaming appeared. We found no evidence for the equalization effect.

These results were moderated by classes. The results found among twelfth grade students were exactly as predicted, while among eleventh grade students they were not. A possible explanation is that twelfth grade students know each other for a longer period of time, thereby making communication easier. Another possible explanation is skill or proficiency in the subject matter. Vetter and Chanier (2006) and Chanier et al. (2006) found significant difference between beginners and advanced students; advanced students communicated through audio conferencing, while beginners used textual chat nearly twice. Our data are exactly the opposite: Twelfth grade students use the chat more than the audio channel and eleventh grade students vice versa. If proficiency matters, then our data suggest that students use a less natural (or less rich) medium more only after subject matter proficiency is accomplished. Another possible explanation is gender distribution. In the eleventh grade, male students were a majority in the class, while in the twelfth grade, gender was evenly distributed. It is possible that males prefer spoken communication and females prefer written communication (for a similar suggestion, see Caspi et al. 2008).

The field study has some limitations. First, we did not measure achievements and satisfaction. Second, students' attendance differed between the two modes of instructions; fewer students attended the audio-written conferencing lessons, but those who showed up participated more. This finding in its own may tell us something about the attractiveness of audio-written communication as a way of studying. While this communication mode is prevalent among teenagers (e.g., Blais et al. 2008; Bryant et al. 2006), they attend these lessons much less than lessons delivered in the traditional teaching mode. We do not know if this attendance pattern is due to the communication features of this technology or due to other factors (such as learning from home instead of in class). To overcome the noted limitations, we designed a laboratory experiment.

3 Study 2: Laboratory Experiment

3.1 Method

3.1.1 Participants

Forty-two undergraduates (71% women) from the Department of Psychology and Education at the Open University of Israel received an academic credit for participation in the experiment. Participants' ages ranged from 14 to 42, average age was 28 years, and the median was 26. The participants' ages did not differ between the two experimental conditions (F2F – average 28.5, SD 6.8; AWC – average 26.9, SD 4). None of the participants had prior acquaintance.

3.1.2 Instruments

Communication media were identical to the field study: face-to-face and audio-written conferencing via Skype.

Post-lesson questionnaire. To measure perceived learning, we administered a questionnaire that related to the five conception of learning (Marton et al. 1993;

Marton and Säljö 1976a, b). Students were asked to self-evaluate their learning along the five conceptions of learning (increasing one's knowledge, memorizing, gaining applied knowledge, understanding, and changing a point of view), using a six-point Likert scale (ranging from "not at all" to "very much").

To measure satisfaction, students used a six-point Likert scale (ranging from "not at all" to "very much") for reporting their emotional states. Six questions related to students' emotional states during learning are the following: losing attention, getting bored, lessening difficulties, enjoying students' interaction, enjoying teacher–students interaction, and feeling that the content is difficult. In addition, students also evaluated their own achievement ("how many answers do you think were correct in the post-test quiz?") and a general question regarding their own learning ("to what degree do you believe that you learned from the lesson?" Answers ranged from "not at all" to "very much" on a six-point Likert scale).

Students' behavior. Participation and risk taking were measured using quantitative content analysis of the lessons' records. Participation was measured by the frequency of verbal actions (speaking and writing) enacted by each student and the teacher; risk taking was measured by testing the frequency of answering teacher's questions and offering opinions regarding the subject.

3.1.3 Procedure

Participants were randomly allocated to face-to-face or audio-written conferencing conditions. Every triad of students received a 20-min music history lesson, taught by the same teacher. This subject matter was unfamiliar to all participants. For a matter of convenience, we set the group size to three students. This size allows testing the behavioral dependent variable (participation, risk taking, and equalization).

Before the lesson started, the students answered a 10-item quiz (pre-test). The same quiz was administered upon completion of the lesson. Additionally, they filled the post-lesson questionnaire. All lessons were recorded for analysis.

3.2 Results

Table 9.5 presents pre- and post-test results. There were no significant differences between the two modes of instruction, either in pre-test, post-test, or the difference between them, but effect size (Cohen's d) was medium for the post-test and the difference between the post- and pre-tests.

Self-evaluated achievement and general evaluation of learning did not differ between the two groups of learners. The correlation between actual and self-evaluated achievement was high ($r = 0.63, p < 0.001$), and no significant difference was found between actual and self-evaluated achievement. There were no significant differences in perceived learning (see Table 9.6). One exception is memorization. Face-to-face learners felt that the lesson helped them memorize the content more readily than did the audio-written conferencing learners and the effect size was large. However, we found significant differences in satisfaction; the effect size was large for all the questions, except the small effect for perceived difficulty. Table 9.7 summarizes the differences.

Table 9.5 Pre-test and post-test averages

	FtF	AWC	t-Test results	d' (STE)
Pre-test	1.6 (0.8)	1.6 (1.2)	n.s.	0.0 (0.31)
Post-test	8.6 (1.0)	8.2 (1.4)	n.s.	0.3 (0.31)
Difference	7.0 (1.3)	6.6 (1.6)	n.s.	0.3 (0.31)

Table 9.6 Achievement, self-evaluated learning, and conceptions of learning averages

	FtF	AWC	t-Test results	d' (STE)
Achievement: self-evaluation	8.5 (1.2)	8.5 (1.4)	n.s.	0.0 (0.31)
Learning: general evaluation	5.2 (0.8)	5.2 (0.7)	n.s.	0.0 (0.31)
Perceived learning:				
Increasing one's knowledge	5.3 (0.8)	5.1 (0.7)	n.s.	0.3 (0.31)
Memorization	5.2 (0.9)	4.6 (1.0)	$t(40) = 2.10^*$	0.6 (0.32)
Implementation	3.1 (0.9)	2.7 (0.9)	n.s.	0.4 (0.31)
Understanding	5.1 (1.0)	4.7 (1.1)	n.s.	0.4 (0.31)
Perspective changing	3.3 (0.8)	3.2 (1.5)	n.s.	0.1 (0.31)

$^* p < 0.05$

Table 9.7 Emotional state averages

	FtF	AWC	t-Test results	d' (STE)
Losing attention (R item)	5.29 (0.90)	4.43 (1.40)	$t(40)= 2.36^*$	0.7 (0.32)
Getting bored (R item)	5.33 (0.80)	4.29 (1.55)	$t(40)= 2.75^{**}$	0.8 (0.32)
Lessening difficulties	5.05 (1.07)	4.33 (1.28)	$t(40)= 1.96^*$	0.6 (0.32)
Enjoying peers' interaction	4.67 (1.02)	3.76 (1.26)	$t(40)= 2.56^*$	0.8 (0.32)
Enjoying teacher interaction	5.29 (0.72)	4.24 (1.30)	$t(40)= 3.23^{***}$	1.0 (0.33)
Perceived difficulty	4.43 (1.21)	4.86 (1.01)	$t(40)= 1.24^a$	0.1 (0.31)

$^* p \leq 0.05;\ ^{**} p < 0.01;\ ^{***} p < 0.001$
^{a} n.s.

Teacher's participation in face-to-face lessons (average 67.4, SD 19.5) was statistically lower than in audio-written conferencing lessons (average 81.6, SD 16.9), $t(6) = 2.87$, $p < 0.05$, $d' = 0.7$ (STE 0.55), but students' participation was statistically not (FtF – average 25.7, SD 14.5; AWC – average 32.6, SD 16.8, $t(40)$ = 1.43, $p > 0.1$, $d' = 0.4$ (STE 0.32). There was no significant difference in teacher's encouragement to participate – the number of questions asked by the teacher was similar in the two modes of instruction (FtF – average 45, SD 4.93; AWC – average 46.57, SD 5, $t(6) = 0.59$, $p > 0.5$, $d' = 0.3$ (STE 0.54).

An equalization effect was not found. In 5 out of 7 groups in each media, one student was dominant and provided more than 50% of the verbal responses.

In terms of risk taking, students in the audio-conferencing groups answered significantly more questions (average 20.6, SD 4.5) than did students in the face-to-face groups (average 13.5, SD 3.7), $t(40) = 2.46$, $p < 0.05$, $d' = 1.69$ (STE 0.36).

3.3 Discussion

The null effect found for achievement supported the media naturalness theory. Achievement was similar under the two conditions. MNT may explain that by arguing that the learner invested more cognitive efforts to compensate for the virtuality of the audio-written conferencing. However, perceived difficulty did not statistically differ between the two conditions, a result that corroborated Kock et al. (2007) but questioned the original MNT assumption. Media richness theory predicts better outcomes in the richest medium (face-to-face), and the online disinhibition effect predicts better performance for invisibility condition, unless the level of negative disinhibited behavior is high. Neither prediction was supported. We found no evidence for negative disinhibited behavior in the current experiment.

Participants were significantly more satisfied with face-to-face instruction, a result that also supports the media naturalness theory. Nevertheless, students did not perceive their learning to be worse (or better) in the audio-written conferencing condition. Regarding risk taking, the results replicated the field study. Taken together, the laboratory study supported the media naturalness predictions to a greater degree, but some evidence for the effect of online disinhibition was also found.

Face-to-face learners felt that the lesson helped them memorize the content more readily than did the audio-written conferencing learners. A possible explanation for this difference is that face-to-face teaching has less distracters or that the audio-written communication has some seductive details (e.g., highly interesting and entertaining information that is only tangentially related to the topic but is irrelevant to the teacher's intended theme; Garner et al. 1992; Harp and Mayer 1998; Mayer 2005). However, the post-tests did not statistically differ. In addition, the theoretical analysis of Robert and Dennis (2005) suggests exactly the opposite: a rich medium may have more distracters than may a lean one. Together, this explanation is ruled out.

An equalization effect was not found. In most of the groups, one student was dominant and provided more than a half of the verbal responses, irrespective of the media used. Blau and Barak (2010) found equalization effect in written communication but not in audio communication, and explained their results by the ability of audio conferencing to clearly transmit social cues (like gender or race), which is an important source of status differences between the participants who interact at zero acquaintance.

Three limitations appeared in the laboratory study. First, it is possible that students were unfamiliar with the audio-written medium. After gaining more experience with this medium, the differences we found may disappear (Kock et al. 2007). Second, we tested the students shortly after the lesson. It is possible that advantages of one mode of instruction or another have a long-term effect that we did not uncover. Third, the pre- and post-tests used mainly factual questions, typified by relatively lower level of thinking. Perhaps higher level questions that call for integration or resolution of details would result in different findings.

4 General Discussion

The effect of two media on three major dependent variables was tested. We found no significant difference in terms of achievement. In addition, we found significant differences between media in emotional satisfaction, but not in perceived learning. Significant differences between media were also found in behavioral variables, such as participation, risk taking, immediacy, and flaming, but equalization effect did not occur.

The no-significant difference in students' achievement that we documented in the laboratory experiment joins hundreds of similar research designs that found non-significant differences between instructional media (Arbaugh et al. 2009; Bernard et al. 2004; Russell 1999). In more natural conditions, when students' actual grades are the dependent variable, one common explanation is that even though mediated communication tools may make learning more difficult, students' motivation may force them to overcome the medium's obstacles by investing more cognitive efforts or by turning to out-of-the-educational-design resources. Clearly, students in our experiment preferred face-to-face instruction over audio-written conferencing; yet their outcomes were similar. Since in contrast to earlier documentations, students in our study could not turn to alternative resources, we may conclude that they invested more cognitive resources to overcome the uncomfortable learning condition. This compensatory process is proposed by media naturalness theory and received some empirical support (Kock 2001; Kock et al. 2007, 2008). This conclusion, however, is somehow weakened by students' report of perceived difficulty. Alternatively, MNT proposed that a medium that supports conveyance of oral speech is considered natural to a higher degree relative to a medium that conveys facial expression and body language without enabling oral speech transactions. In that sense, face-to-face and audio-written conferencing are relatively close to each other in terms of naturalness, and the mental effort required might be similar (see also Graetz et al. 1998 for similar explanation).

A strong matching between perceived- and actual achievement was found. Such compatibility was reported in some studies (Dunlosky and Matvey 2001; Koriat

1997; Koriat and Bjork 2006) when students learned pairs of words from a list. Nevertheless, unlike the current study, in these studies a significant difference was found between perceived and actual learning. A possible explanation for this difference between the studies is that we instructed and tested inter-related, coherent content, not an arbitrary list of words. The more ecological learning condition we had in the current study may help students both recall the learned material and monitor the learning process more adequately, since learning may generate more memory cues that assist the process.

Caspi and Blau (2008) argued recently that perceived learning may rely on two independent sources: cognitive and socio-emotional. The current results support the distinction Caspi and Blau suggested. The difference between the two instructional settings directly influenced the socio-emotional source and perhaps only indirectly, if at all, the cognitive source. The cognitive source reflects the sense that new knowledge has been acquired, that some new understanding has been achieved, and other cognitive-based processes. In the current study, "conceptions of learning" may indicate these sensations. When asked about their perception of learning (using the five conceptions of learning), students rated their perceived learning as high (means about 5 in a scale ranged from 1 to 6) in three out of five concepts (increasing one's knowledge, memorization, and understanding) and as moderate (means about 3) in the remaining two concepts (implementation and change of perspective, two concepts of learning that probably need more time to be attained). Generally, there were no significant differences between media, a result that may strengthen what we found regarding achievement.

The socio-emotional source reflects experience and feelings. These are "peripheral" aspects of learning (Blau and Caspi 2008) that in the present study were measured by the emotional evaluations, such as students' concentration and interest, learning satisfaction, and enjoyment from the interaction with tutor or peers. While conception of learning was similar in both instructional settings, emotional aspects of perceived learning were not. Although perceived difficulty did not statistically differ, after learning via audio-written conferencing, students reported more attention loss, boredom, more difficulties, and less enjoyment. Our participants' emotional report supports media naturalness theory. Kock (2005) suggested that "communication interactions in which certain elements of natural face-to-face communication are suppressed (e.g., the ability to employ / see facial expressions) involve a corresponding suppression of physiological arousal, and, in turn, a consequent decrease in the perceived excitement in connection with the communication interaction" (p. 123).

4.1 The Influence of Invisible Communication on Learning

The behavioral data found in the two studies are summarized as follows: participation was higher in audio-written conferencing than in the face-to-face setting, but an equalization effect did not occur. Students answered more questions in audio-written conferencing, implying more risk taking. Learning via audio-written conferencing resulted in more immediacy and more flaming. We suggest that these results are due to the invisibility afforded by this tool, which instigated the online disinhibition effect. Being invisible while communicating, students loosen their behavior, even when their identity is known. They may feel more secure, less prone to social criticism, and thus participate more and take more risks.

The influence of invisibility on learning is an important result of the two studies. A medium that affords invisibility is regarded as less natural (in terms of MNT) or less rich (in terms of MRT). Together, we may expect a detrimental impact of invisible communication on learning. Clearly, this is not what we found. Students participated more, took more risks, and expressed more immediacy. But these observed behaviors *did not* influence their achievements nor did they become more satisfied. Interacting without being seen (yet being known) may encourage students to be more active, an effort that may render satisfaction.

Some constructivist theories emphasize social learning and suggest active participation as a route to deeper learning (Garrison 1989; Perkins 1991). One interpretation of the current results may be that participation has an immediate price, which does *not* directly cause *better* outcomes. The current study was not designed to test whether this cost has any long-term benefits. If such benefits exist, then invisible communication may be recommended.

Educational practitioners are sometimes worried about the negative consequences of anonymity in online learning. In the field study, students interacted with a weak level of anonymity and some occurrences of flaming were indeed found. It is noted again that we employed only invisibility, a "soft" kind of anonymity, which may reduce the level of negative disinhibited behavior. The trade-off between levering participation and negative disinhibited behavior should be considered when designing learning via communication media. Most evidence so far has suggested that there are more pros than cons for anonymity in educational setting. It seems that further investigation is needed.

5 Summary

Communication media afford different degrees of anonymous interaction. The current studies manipulated invisibility among students that know each other well (in the field study) or have zero acquaintance (in the laboratory experiment). In both cases the behavioral data were similar; students participated more and took more "cognitive" risks in invisible condition, results that are welcomed by constructivist theorizers. However, this type of interaction resulted in lower satisfaction, perhaps because it demanded a higher level of effort invested to compensate for the less natural communication conditions. In turn, achievement was similar in both instructional conditions, which might point to immediate cost (good achievement for low satisfaction). A possible long-term benefit is yet to be tested.

Acknowledgments The authors would like to thank Dr. Paul Gorsky for his helpful comments. An earlier, shorter version of this paper was presented at the Chais conference 2008, in Ra'anana,

Israel, and included in Eshet-Alkalai Y, Caspi A, Geri N (eds) Proceedings of the Chais conference on instructional technologies research 2008: learning in the technological era. Open University of Israel, Ra'anana.

References

Arbaugh JB, Godfrey MR, Johnson M, Pollack BL, Niendorf B, Wresch W (2009) Research in online and blended learning in the business disciplines: key findings and possible future directions. Int High Educ 12(2):71–87

Barak A (2007) Phantom emotions: psychological determinants of emotional experiences on the Internet. In: Joinson A, McKenna KYA, Postmes T, Reips UD (eds) Oxford handbook of Internet psychology. Oxford University Press, Oxford, pp. 303–329

Bates AW (2005) Technology, e-learning and distance education, 2nd edn. Routledge, New York

Bernard RM, Abrami PC, Lou Y, Borokhovski E, Wade A, Wozney L, Wallet PA, Fiset M, Huang B (2004) How does distance education compare with classroom instruction? A meta-analysis of the empirical literature. Rev Educ Res 74(3):379–439

Blais JJ, Craig WM, Pepler D, Connolly J (2008) Adolescents online: the importance of internet activity choices to salient relationships. J Youth Adolesc 37(5):522–536

Blau I, Barak A (2010) Synchronous online participation: the effects of participant's personality and discussion topic on participation in face-to-face versus voice chat, and textual group discussions. Paper to be presented on the 11th annual conference of the Association of Internet Researchers (AoIR): Sustainability, participation, action. Gothenburg, Sweden: University of Gothenburg (October)

Blau I, Caspi A (2008) Do media richness and visual anonymity influence learning? A comparative study using Skype™. In: Eshet-Alkalai Y, Caspi A, Geri N (eds) Learning in the technological era. Open University of Israel, Ra'anana, pp 18–24

Böhlke O (2003) A comparison of student participation levels by group size and language stages during chatroom and face-to-face discussions in German. CALICO J 21(1):67–87

Bryant JA, Sanders-Jackson A, Smallwood AMK (2006) IMing, text messaging, and adolescent social networks. J Comput Med Commun 11(2):577–592

Carlson JR, Zmud RW (1999) Channel expansion theory and the experiential nature of media richness perceptions. Acad Manage J 42(2):153–170

Caspi A, Blau I (2008) Social presence in online discussion groups: testing three conceptions and their relations to perceived learning. Soc Psychol Educ 11(3):323–346

Caspi A, Gorsky P (2005) Instructional media choice: factors affecting the preferences of distance education coordinators. J Educ Multimed Hypermedia 14(2):169–198

Caspi A, Chajut E, Saporta K, Beyth-Marom R (2006a) The influence of personality on social participation in learning environments. Learn Ind Differ 16(2):129–144

Caspi A, Chajut E, Saporta K, Schupak A (2006b) On the reasons for and against participation in class meetings and in online forums. In: Eshet Y, Caspi A, Yair Y (eds) Learning in technological era. Open University of Israel, Ra'anana, Hebrew, pp 91–98

Caspi A. Chajut E, Saporta K (2008) Participation in class and in online discussions: gender differences. Comput Educ 50(3):718–724

Chanier T, Vetter A, Betbeder ML, Reffay C (2006) Retrouver le chemin de la parole en environnement audio-graphique synchrone. In: Dejean-Thircuir C, Mangenot F (Coord.) Les échanges en ligne dans l'apprentissage et la formation, pp 139–150, Available at: http://edutice.archives-ouvertes.fr/docs/00/08/43/88/PDF/FDLM_chanier_060223.pdf

Chen CC, Wu J, Yang SC (2006) The efficacy of online cooperative learning systems: the perspective of task–technology fit. Campus Wide Inf Syst 23(3):112–127

Chester A, Gwynne G (1998) Online teaching: encouraging collaboration through anonymity. J Comput Media Commun 4(2). http://jcmc.indiana.edu/vol4/issue2/chester.html, Retrieved 25 July 2009

Christopherson KM (2007) The positive and negative implications of anonymity in Internet social interactions: "On the Internet, nobody knows you're a dog". Comput Hum Behav 23(6): 3038–3056

Clifford MM (1991) Risk taking: theoretical, empirical, and educational considerations. Educ Psychol 26(3–4):263–297

Coghlan M (2000) An online learning community: the students' perspective. http://www.chariot.net.au/~michaelc/TCC2000.htm, Retrieved 25 July 2009

Graetz KA, Boyle ES, Kimble CE, Thompson P, Garloch JL (1998) Information sharing in face-to-face, teleconferencing, and electronic chat groups. Small Group Res 29(6): 714–743

Daft RL, Lengel RH (1984) Information richness: a new approach to managerial behavior and organization design. In: Staw BM, Cummings LL (eds) Research in organizational behavior, vol 6. JAI, Greenwich, pp 191–233

Daft RL, Lengel RH, Treviño LK (1987) Message equivocality, media selection, and manager performance: implications for information systems. MIS Q 11(3):355–368

D'Ambra J, Rice RE, O'Connor M (1998) Computer-mediated communication and media preference: an investigation of the dimensionality of perceived task equivocality and media richness. Behav Inf Technol 17(3):164–174

Donabedian B (2006) Optimization and its alternative in media choice: a model of reliance on social-influence processes. Inf Soc 22(3):121–135

Dubrovsky VJ, Kiesler S, Sethna BN (1991) The equalization phenomenon: status effects in computer-mediated and face-to-face decision-making groups. Hum Comput Interact 6(2): 119–146

Dunlosky J, Matvey G (2001) Empirical analysis of the intrinsic–extrinsic distinction of judgement of learning (JOLs): effects of relatedness and serial position on JOLs. J Exp Psychol Learn Mem Cogn 27(5):1180–1191

Eklund-Braconi P (2005) Reflections based on empirical experiences during a virtual course in Italian: how is the feeling of presence? How does interaction work? How do students learn? Paper presented at the University of Ulster Centre for Research in Applied Languages UCALL conference: developing a pedagogy for CALL, University of Ulster at Coleraine, Northern Ireland (June)

Freeman M, Bamford A (2004) Student choice of anonymity for learner identity in online learning discussion forums. Int J e-Learn 3(3):45–53

Freeman M, Blayney P, Ginns P (2006) Anonymity and in class learning: the case for electronic response systems. Aust J Educ Technol 22(4):568–580

Fulk J, Steinfield CW, Schmitz J, Power JG (1987) A social information processing model of media use in organizations. Commun Res 14(5):529–552

Fulk J, Schmitz J, Steinfeld CW (1990) A social influence model of technology use. In: Fulk J, Steinfield C (eds) Organizations and communication technology. Sage, Newbury Park, pp 117–140

Garner R, Brown R, Sanders S, Menke D (1992) "Seductive details" and learning from text. In: Renninger KA, Hidi S, Krapp A (eds) The role of interest in learning and development. Erlbaum, Hillsdale, pp. 239–254

Garrison DR (1989) Understanding distance education: a framework for the future. Routledge, London

Guzley RM, Avanzino S, Bor A (2001) Simulated computer-mediated/video interactive distance learning: a test of motivation, interaction satisfaction, delivery, learning and perceived effectiveness. J Comput Mediat Commun 6(3). http://jcmc.indiana.edu/vol6/issue3/guzley.html, Retrieved 25 July 2009

Hampel R (2006) Rethinking task design for the digital age: a framework for language teaching and learning in a synchronous online environment. ReCALL J 18(1):105–121

Hampel R, Baber E (2003) Using Internet-based audio-graphic and video conferencing for language teaching and learning. In: Felix U (ed) Language learning online: towards best practice. Swets & Zeitlinger, Lisse, pp 171–191

Hampel R, Hauck M (2004) Towards an effective use of audio conferencing in distance language courses. Lang Learn Technol 8(1):66–82

Harp SF, Mayer RE (1998) How seductive details do their damage: a theory of cognitive interest in science learning. J Educ Psychol 90(3):414–434

Kilner PG, Hoadley CM (2005) Anonymity options and professional participation in an online community of practice. Proceedings of the 2005 conference on computer support for collaborative learning: learning 2005: The next 10 years! Taipei, Taiwan, pp 272–280

Kock N (2001) Compensatory adaptation to a lean medium: an action research investigation of electronic communication in process improvement groups. IEEE Trans Prof Commun 44(4):267–285

Kock N (2005) Media richness or media naturalness? The evolution of our biological communication apparatus and its influence on our behavior toward e-communication tools. IEEE Trans Prof Commun 48(2):117–130

Kock N (2009) Information systems theorizing based on evolutionary psychology: an interdisciplinary review and theory integration framework. MIS Q 33(2):395–418

Kock N, Verville J, Garza V (2007) Media naturalness and online learning: findings supporting both the significant- and no-significant-difference perspectives. Decis Sci J Innov Educ 5(2):333–355

Kock N, Hantula DA, Hayne SC, Saad G, Todd PM, Watson RT (2008) Introduction to Darwinian perspectives on electronic communication. IEEE Trans Prof Commun 51(2):133–146

Koriat A (1997) Monitoring one's own knowledge during study: a cue-utilization approach to judgment of learning. J Exp Psychol Gen 126(4):349–370

Koriat A, Bjork RA (2006) Illusions of competence in monitoring one's knowledge during study. J Exp Psychol Learn Mem Cogn 31(3):187–194

Kötter M, Shield L (2000) Talk to me! Real-time audio-conferencing and the changing roles of the teacher and the learner in a 24/7 environment. Paper presented on networked learning 2000: innovative approaches to lifelong learning and higher education through the internet, Lancaster, UK, January

Lea M, Rogers P, Postmes T (2002) SIDE-VIEW: evaluation of a system to develop team players and improve productivity in Internet collaborative learning groups. Br J Educ Technol 33(1):53–63

Lobel M, Neubauer M, Swedburg R (2002) Elements of group interaction in a real-time synchronous online learning-by-doing classroom without f2f participation. USDLA J 16(4). http://www.usdla.org/html/journal/APR02_Issue/article01.html, Retrieved 25 July 2009

Marton F, Dall'Alba G, Beaty E (1993) Conceptions of learning. Int J Educ Res 19(3): 277–300

Marton F, Säljö R (1976a) On qualitative differences in learning. I – Outcome and process. Br J Educ Psychol 46(1):4–11

Marton F, Säljö R (1976b) On qualitative differences in learning. II – Outcome as a function of the learner's perception of the task. Br J Educ Psychol 46(2):115–127

Mayer RE (2005) Cognitive theory of multimedia learning. In: Mayer RE (ed) The Cambridge handbook of multimedia learning. Cambridge University Press, New York, pp 31–48

Olson JS, Olson GM, Meader DK (1997) Face-to-face group work compared to remote group work with and without video. In: Finn KE (ed) Video-mediated communication. Erlbaum, Mahwah, pp 157–172

Oren A, Mioduser D, Nachmias R (2002) The development of social climate in virtual learning discussion groups. Int Rev Res Open Dist Lear 3(1). http://www.irrodl.org/index.php/irrodl/article/view/80/155, Retrieved 25 July 2009

Pan C-CS, Sullivan M (2005) Promoting synchronous interaction in an e-learning environment. THE J 33(2):27–30

Perkins DN (1991) What constructivism demands of the learner. Educ Technol 31(10):19–21

Quayle E, Taylor M (2003) Model of problematic Internet use in people with a sexual interest in children. CyberPsychol Behav 6(1):93–106

Rains SA, Scott CR (2007) To identify or not to identify: a theoretical model of receiver responses to anonymous communication. Commun Theory 17(1):61–91

Rapanotti L, Blake CT, Griffiths R (2002) eTutorials with voice groupware: real-time conferencing to support computing students at a distance. Paper presented on the 7th annual conference on innovation and technology in computer science education – ITiCSE2002, University of Aarhus, Denmark, (June)

Reinig BA, Briggs RO, Nunamaker JF Jr. (1997) Flaming in the electronic classroom. J Manage Inf Syst 14(3):45–59

Robert LP, Dennis AR. (2005) Paradox of richness: a cognitive model of media choice. IEEE Trans Prof Commun 48(1):10–21

Rosell-Aguilar F (2005) Task design for audiographic conferencing: promoting beginner oral interaction in distance language learning. Comput Assist Lang Lear 18(5):417–442

Rosell-Aguilar F (2006) The face-to-face and the online learner: a comparative study of tutorial support for open and distance language learning and the learner experience with audio-graphic SCMC. Read Matrix 6(3):248–267

Russell TL (1999) The no significant difference phenomenon. North Carolina State University, Raleigh

Sallnäs EL (2002) Collaboration in multi-modal virtual worlds: comparing touch, text, voice and video. In: Schroeder R (ed) The social life of avatars: presence and interaction in shared virtual environments. Springer-Verlag, London, pp 172–187

Schultz RA (2003) The effectiveness of online synchronous discussion. Proceedings of the informing science and information technology joint education conference, Finland, pp 547–558. Available at http://proceedings.informingscience.org/IS2003Proceedings/docs/077Schul.pdf

Senju A, Johnson MH (2008) The eye contact effect: mechanisms and development. Trends Cogn Sci 13(3):127–134

Shachaf P, Hara N (2007) Behavioral complexity theory of media selection: a proposed theory for global virtual teams. J Inf Sci 33(1):63–75

Sia C, Tan B, Wei K (2002) Group polarization and computer-mediated communication: effects of communication cues, social presence, and anonymity. Inf Syst Res 13(1):70–90

Siegel J, Dubrovsky V, Kiesler S, McGuire TW (1986) Group processes in computer-mediated communication. Organ Behav Hum Decis Processes, 37(2):157–187

Suler J (2004) The online disinhibition effect. CyberPsychol Behav 7(3):321–326

Sweller J (1998) Cognitive load during problem solving: effects on learning. Cogn Sci 12(2):257–285

Tosunoglu C, Rapanotti L, Griffiths RM (2002) Voice groupware to support students at a distance. Paper presented on 4th international conference on new educational environments, Lugano, Switzerland, May. Available at http://iet-staff.open.ac.uk/c.tosunoglu/ICNEE02.pdf

Vetter A, Chanier T (2006) Supporting oral production for professional purposes in synchronous communication with heterogenous learners. ReCALL J 18(1):5–23

van Merriënboer JJG, Sweller J (2005) Cognitive load theory and complex learning: recent developments and future directions. Educ Psychol Rev 17(2):147–177

Warschauer M (1996) Comparing face-to-face and electronic discussion in the second language classroom. CALICO J 13(2):7–26

Chapter 10
Using Evolutionary Psychology to Extend Our Understanding of Fit and Human Drives in Information Systems (IS) Utilization Decisions and Performance

Chon Abraham and Iris Junglas

Abstract This chapter theorizes about the use of evolutionary psychology-based tenets to examine individual characteristics in the context of the innate human drives that compel behaviors oriented toward technology. We examine the phenomenon of mobile information communication technology (MICT) in the context of health care. This chapter reports on a study examining nurses' decisions to utilize MICTs that use the lens of evolutionary psychology to more fully understand individual characteristics, which is an area needing illumination in IS research. A mixed-method approach is used, consisting of both qualitative and quantitative elements, that reveals and empirically tests the significance of novel constellations of fit (i.e., identification, information, patient interaction, physical, time criticality, user comfort, and workflow fit) and individual characteristics, presented as basic human drives (i.e., drive to acquire, bond, defend, and learn). Findings indicate that fit is a multi-faceted construct and that archetypical human drives have an influence on these various notions, which, in turn, impact technology adoption in the health-care context.

Keywords Evolutionary psychology · Human drives · Technology fit · Mobile information communication technology (MICT)

1 Introduction

Understanding how people perceive the fit of a technology requires a holistic approach that extends beyond just evaluating the characteristics of the task and technology. Individual characteristics presumably are also at play in this fit decision,

C. Abraham (✉)
Operations and Information Systems Management Department, College of William and Mary, 101 Ukrops Way, Williamsburg, VA 23187, USA
e-mail: chon.abraham@mason.wm.edu

I. Junglas
Decision and Information Sciences Department, 334 Melcher Hall, University of Houston, Houston, TX 77204-6021, USA
e-mail: ijunglas@uh.edu

N. Kock (ed.), *Evolutionary Psychology and Information Systems Research*,
Integrated Series in Information Systems 24, DOI 10.1007/978-1-4419-6139-6_10,
© Springer Science+Business Media, LLC 2010

but there is a gap in our understanding about how to operationalize these characteristics. Most often, operationalization of individual characteristics takes the form
of constructs derived from social psychology and cognitive psychology (e.g., attitudes, efficacy, and perceived behavioral control) (Ajzen 1991). With some very
notable exceptions (e.g., Kock 2009, 2005, 2004; Pavlou et al. 2007; Hantula et al.
2008; Hubona and Shirah 2006), the IS literature has largely ignored the possible explanatory power of human nature or any biological orientation in explaining
human decision making as expressed in evolutionary psychology, which asserts that
humans are an evolved, social, cognitive species. Traditional frames neglect the
influence of human nature or innate mechanisms that have evolved over time. More
specifically, they neglect that our ancestors came to understand the difference in
positive and negative outcomes that promoted survival in ancient task responses to
certain environmental situations, which have become encoded in the human psyche
as universal human traits (see Kock 2009, Appendix E for a thorough explanation
of universal human traits). These mechanisms are most recognizable in behavior
regarding dire situations that resemble the life and death circumstances, but are
present in mundane behavioral occurrences as well. The aforesaid is the underlying premise of evolutionary psychology and the foundation for models that take
a human nature-oriented approach to explain individual characteristics as drivers
for how people make assessments of situations. "While evolutionary theories can
bridge gaps left by non-evolutionary theories, it is also argued here that evolutionary
theories of information systems generally need to be integrated with other non-
evolutionary theories in order to provide a more precise and testable picture of the
information systems phenomena that they try to explain" (Kock 2009, p. 396). Thus,
it is conceivable that evolutionary psychology and its derivatives can contribute to
our understanding of how people make assessments of the fit of technology – a new
framing in the IS theoretical repertoire for individual characteristics.

We learn from the task–technology fit model that users are motivated to use a
technology because they perceive it to be a better relative fit over and above alternative methods (Goodhue and Thompson 1995). However, the task–technology fit
model does not adequately address the basic, more innate, human drives or motivations that virtually all users possess and that guide users to define the task, determine
its urgency, and then to ascertain not only if the technology fits the task but also how
or on what dimensional levels it most appropriately fits. The evolution of human
drives as motivators of behavior is espoused in the evolutionary psychology literature (Buss 1995). One model, the Four-Drive Model (Nohria et al. 2008; Lawrence
and Nohria 2002), delves into conceptualizing common psychological or instinctive
behaviors and applies them to understanding human decision making in organizational work settings. More specifically, it ascertains underlying motivations of
behaviors in order to categorize sets of behaviors into four different drives that are
shared by all humans. These comprise the following: the drive to acquire material
things to support survival, the drive to bond with others to establish mutual relationships, the drive to defend oneself from threat, and the drive to learn to satisfy
a curiosity. These drives are ever-present in the human psyche and influence how a
person perceives a situation or a task, i.e., a task can cause a drive to become more

salient and dominant in the behavior (Lawrence and Nohria 2002). This is especially true in situations where the task doer is faced with dire situations that embody a strong sense of urgency, such as survival-related tasks. In these situations, our ancestors made assessments about what tools, if any, to use to aid in problem solving, which are assessments influenced by the need to appease certain innate drives (Cosmides and Tooby 2000).

Health care is one such context in which tasks and environments embody a dire sense of urgency reminiscent of ancient circumstances (i.e., marked by life and death situations), provoking the awakening of these human drives to bear influence behavior of the task doer (Abraham et al. 2009). We apply evolutionary psychology to more fully understand the concept of human decision making regarding "fit" with regard to technology within the health-care context. Specifically, mobile computing offers the potential to improve the quality and safety of patient care by decreasing the errors and inefficiencies currently caused by inadequate, and sometimes inaccessible, patient documentation at the point and time of care. To reach that potential, however, the intended users of these technologies must believe applications to be an acceptable match with the task at hand. We learn from the fit literature that users are motivated to use a technology when they perceive it to be a better fit than alternative methods (Dennis et al. 2001; Shirani 1999; Zigurs and Buckland 1998; Zigurs et al. 1999; Davern 1996; Goodhue 1995; Goodhue and Thompson 1995; Thompson et al. 1991). Goodhue and Thompson's (1995) task–technology fit model is the most widely cited model for assessing the interplay between task, technology, and individual in determining technology utilization and the resulting increase or decrease in a user's work performance. The model states that only if the technology provided matches the characteristics of the user as well as those of the task at hand will a performance increase result. However, the same study also showed that task–technology fit alone, and ignoring any individual characteristics, does not predict utilization. Surprisingly, and counter to what was hypothesized, the decision to use the system was not based on how well the technology fits with the task. The authors thus encouraged future research to determine if there are other factors, such as individual characteristics, that would make this relationship significant and, by so doing, better explain what contributes or impairs technology usage (Goodhue and Thompson 1995).

With the emergence of mobile computing, individuals are again confronted with technology acceptance, utilization, and perception issues (Shim et al. 2007). Compared to prior technologies, such as stationary computers, mobile information communication technologies (MICTs) are portable and thus particularly helpful in situations where immediate access to information is vital (Varshney 2007; Junglas and Watson 2003; Lyytinen and Yoo 2002b). In health-care settings, these situations are the norm. MICTs are intended to be used by health-care professionals, particularly nurses, at the point of care with the patient, for information processing and computational needs (Ammenwerth et al. 2001). They are being employed both to help constrain the cost of health care and to improve safety. The US Institute of Medicine has reported that nearly 98,000 people die each year due to medical errors, such as incorrect medication dosages delivered because of poor legibility in manual records, or due to delays in consolidating needed information to determine the proper intervention (Institute of Medicine 2000). Nurses perform the bulk of documentation tasks during the patient care process (Blumenthal 2009; Gururajan et al. 2005; Varcoe 1996); their acceptance is essential for ensuring the success of new MICT applications. From an IS perspective, nurses are at the front lines of patient care confronted daily with life and death situations that can parallel ancient conditions illuminating the existence of the human drives. Nurses perform the bulk of the data-oriented tasks (Varcoe 1996). Accordingly, they benefit the most from having access to information at the point of care via mobile systems (Bove 2006). Unfortunately, nurses are still reluctant to use MICTs (Andersen et al. 2009). Some of the reasons, besides technology characteristics, include fear of being alienated from the patient, loss of patient eye contact, being perceived as unprofessional by the patient (Abraham et al. 2008, 2004; Harris 1990), or because they deem the technology as a foreign tool that slows down their work (Abraham et al. 2008; Farrell 2005). Thus, the application of MICT seems to highlight the need not only for the task and technology to mesh but also to consider some individualistic influences. In our study, we found not only that nurses performed the bulk of the documentation for medical interventions, such as electronic charting, medication administration, and triage with the help of a mobile system, but also the saliency of the human drives that influenced nurses' perceptions of mobile technology fit. These drives, or underlying motivators of behaviors, are surfaced as fundamental characteristics of individuals in a health-care environment. This is not surprising because Goodhue and Thompson (1995) admittedly have noted already that not only the task–technology fit (TTF) model adequately addresses the fit between known characteristics of task and technology but also the influences of an individual's perceptions on that fit assessment need further exploration. Consequently, this chapter applies an empirical and psychometric analysis to determine the validity of the saliency of the drives that we discerned earlier and to ascertain the relationship between human drives and an individual's notion of technology fit perceptions.

The basic premise is that understanding the motivations of how people determine the extent to which a technology fits the task provides a more in-depth understanding of the social and cognitive assessments that take place and that influence technology adoption decisions. As technologies become more pervasive, this understanding about human drives can aid in effectively designing information systems and their supporting mobile technologies to better facilitate an individual's needs and promote intended usage. Health care is one such context where overwhelming benefits are derived from marrying scholarly theory and practice. In particular, the field of nursing informatics seeks to apply concepts concerning some socio-technical aspects to explain, predict, and alter human–computer interaction behavior of nursing personnel. Interestingly, much of health-care improvements via technology initiatives address gaining physician buy-in but do not adequately address engaging nurse buy-in – despite the fact that nurses serve as the frontline caregivers and are a primary user group (Abraham et al. 2008). However, the tide is changing and there is increasing visibility of nurses as information gatherers and processors in the patient care process (Romano 2006). Yet, attaining acceptance by the nurses is an arduous task primarily because the nurses deem the technology as a foreign tool that slows down their workflow (Farrell 2005). Nursing is an aging profession and most that were trained some 15–20 years ago do not possess typing skills and they have never received any formal training in using computers for data access or processing (Abraham et al. 2008, 2004). In light of a severe US nurse shortage (e.g., an estimated 400,000 shortage by 2020; Bass 2002), health-care institutions are employing tactics to improve working conditions and patient safety. They are doing so with the use of mobile technology that affords access to information needed during patient care and electronic documentation that is less laborious and error prone than are manual methods (Breslin et al. 2004). Therefore, the questions asked are: "What are the various notions of fit that determine MICT utilization and performance in a health-care setting?" and "How do individual characteristics or basic human drives map into these types of fit?" These questions are particularly important as we look toward future innovations in mobile health care. For hospitals, intelligent locating systems are on the horizon that can track physicians, nurses, and specialists throughout a building; so they can be found at a moment's notice or automatically re-route phone calls if the recipient cannot be reached directly. Other systems provide comprehensive patient-monitoring capabilities that capture a patient's medical condition and geographic whereabouts in real time. The benefits of these and similar IT-driven innovations in hospital care will be fully realized only if the design and the implementation of these applications adequately reflect the factors that contribute to the utilization of current MICTs.

This chapter is an attempt at information systems theorizing and testing based on "evolutionary psychology in a manner that shows the relationship between an evolved psychological trait (P) and the performance of a modern task (T_M), in a modern environment (Kock 2009, p. 399)." Thus, we uncover the influence of some underlying, basic human drives as evolved psychological traits grounded in the evolutionary psychology literature (i.e., drives to acquire, bond, defend, and learn) (Nohria et al. 2008; Lawrence and Nohria 2002) that make types of fit with modern tasks apparent when researched in conjunction with task and technology characteristics in hospital settings. These novel types of fit pertain to identification, information, patient interaction, physical, time criticality, user comfort, and workflow fit. The types of fit illustrate that various notions of fit must be differentiated as they represent dimensions that are important or obvious to nurses.

In seeking a comprehensive understanding, we have chosen a mixed method approach, consisting of both qualitative and quantitative elements. For the qualitative element, we collected interview data from 50 nurses who were using MICTs across four different medical units (i.e., acute care in-hospital floors, ambulatory care, emergency department, and post-anesthesia care) in three different southeastern US hospitals. This qualitative data revealed the saliency of human drives that influenced nurses' perceptions of MICT fit. These drives, or underlying motivators of behaviors, surfaced as fundamental characteristics of individual nurses; they were also found to have a bearing on how nurses dimensionalized fit, which we present as the novel types of fit. In the quantitative element of the study, we collected survey data from another 107 nurses to further validate our findings concerning the relationship between human drives and fit types in order to determine their impact on performance and utilization decisions for MICTs.

The chapter is structured as follows. We first describe a typical MICT used for patient care and illustrate the nature of health-care tasks. We then dissect the theoretical underpinnings of existing fit research and note the gap in literature regarding individual characteristics. In keeping with traditional presentation of the theoretical underpinnings that either exist at the onset of the study or emerge during the progression of the study as being relevant, we next provide a description of evolutionary psychology and the four-drive model as an instantiation. Evolutionary psychology and the four-drive model became relevant during the qualitative study, which follows the theoretical underpinnings. The various fit notions and the set of underlying human drives that emerge from the qualitative study provide the basis for our quantitative study. We conclude our quantitative study by illustrating how nurses' individual characteristics influence various fit dimensions, which in turn interfere or enhance their utilization and work performance.

2 The Technology Artifact

The typical MICT is mobile (in the sense of movable) and it provides ubiquitous (in the sense of omnipresence) and wireless (in the sense of being untethered) access to an information system within the boundaries of a hospital unit. More specifically, a typical system comprises a mobile workstation with an encased lightweight computer, supplemented by wireless local area networks operated on the 802.11b standard. The size of the workstations (i.e., approximately the same as a laptop) is deemed appropriate by users – unlike personal digital assistants (Krogsie et al. 2004) for which the screens are considered too small for clinical usage tasks such as vital statistics charting. Carts are typically equipped with a full keyboard. Despite its importance, acceptance of an MICT in the health-care context is still a reasonably untapped research area. The field of nursing informatics, however, does seek to apply concepts concerning some socio-technical aspects to explain, predict, and alter the human–computer interaction behavior of nursing personnel. Many efforts to harness technology in health-care environments seek buy-in from physicians but rarely seek buy-in from nurses – though nurses, as frontline caregivers, are a primary user group (Sallas et al. 2007). However, the tide is changing and there is increasing visibility of nurses as information gatherers and processors in the patient care process (Romano 2006). Yet, attaining acceptance by the nurses is an arduous endeavor (Abraham et al. 2008; Harris 1990). In light of a severe US nurse shortage, health-care institutions are employing tactics to improve nurses' working conditions while also increasing patient safety. Among these tactics are mobile technologies that afford access to information needed during patient care and electronic documentation that is less laborious and error prone than are manual methods (Martins and Jones 2005a).

Tasks in health care are peculiar in the sense that they are typically highly inter-dependent (Thompson 1967) and require rich information at the right point in time. They are also, if done incorrectly, life threatening. For example, the activity that a nurse performs during a medical service encounter with a patient determines the characteristics of subsequent caregiving activities (Sallas 2007). Nurses require timely access to documentation in order to assess, diagnose, and treat patients efficiently, effectively, and safely (Sallas 2007). Having no access to the right information at the right time can have detrimental consequences to the extent that it can impair a patient's life and a nurse's career. As all tasks in a health-care environment necessitate actions to be taken at particular locations, times, and by and for specific individuals, understanding the nature of the task as well as the nature of the individual nurse that uses the technology is essential (Abraham et al. 2008, 2004).

3 Theoretical Underpinnings

3.1 Fit Models

The technology-to-performance chain from which the task–technology fit model is gleaned, depicted in Fig. 10.1, combines theories of cognitive fit with theories of attitudes and behaviors (Ajzen 1991; Fishbein and Ajzen 1975); it has been sug-gested that the degree to which the functionality of a technology matches the task as well as the abilities of the individual who performs the task will determine the level of technology utilization (Goodhue and Thompson 1995). Therefore, achieving fit is of utmost importance as it signifies an imperative precursor to the utilization of

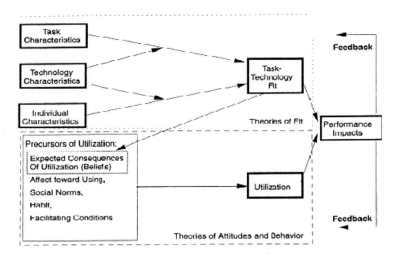

Fig. 10.1 Technology-to-performance chain (Goodhue and Thompson 1995)

technology and consequent performance increase. For time critical environments, such as in health care where inadequate task performance can be life threatening, the fit between task and technology is of utmost importance due to the gravity of error or ignorance.

The original technology-to-performance model identified task, technology, and individual characteristics as three essential components (Davern 1996, Goodhue and Thompson 1995). In this context, a technology is considered to be a tool, such as hardware, software, and data, in addition to user support services, such as training and assistance, which are employed by individuals in carrying out the aforesaid tasks (Dennis et al. 2001; DeSanctis and Poole 1994). Task characteristics, on the other hand, are considered to be the actions carried out by individuals in turning inputs into outputs and may provoke the user to depend more heavily on the information systems capacity to process information (Goodhue and Thompson 1995). Tasks have been analyzed by various means that consider dimensions of their complexity (simple vs. complex) (March and Simon 1958), such as repetitiveness, complexity of cognitive processes (Mintzberg 1973), and ambiguity (Galbraith 1973). Individuals, the third leg of the full model, are those entities that may decide or not decide to utilize technologies to assist them in performing work tasks.

Subsequent studies of the technology-to-performance model have mainly focused on the sole relationship between task and technology and its impact on performance (Goodhue and Thompson 1995). This reduced model, also referred to as the task–technology fit model (TTF), has been applied across differing contexts, such as in the area of group support systems (Zigurs et al. 1999; Zigurs and Buckland 1998), software maintenance (Dishaw and Strong 1999, 1998), and technical support groups (Goodhue et al. 1997; Goodhue 1997), but only sparsely in health-care information systems research (Chau and Hu 2002; Martins and Jones 2005a, b).

By focusing almost exclusively on task–technology fit, the IS field has mostly ignored the influence of individual characteristics – even though proposed early on by researchers such as the originators of the TTF model themselves (Goodhue and Thompson 1995). Suggested characteristics included dimensions, such as past computer experiences, intrinsic and extrinsic motivations, and the level of received computer training, which were said to impact if, how, and to what extent a technology would be utilized (Goodhue 1995; Goodhue and Thompson 1995). Nowadays, with the increasing diffusion of mobile technology, it is expected that individual characteristics will play an even more vital role in the formation of fit constellations. Cellular phones, for example, accompany an individual 24/7 and can be easily customized to personal preference; indeed with each new release, these devices are slowly changing into personal assistants. With little notice, mobile technology has already penetrated our private and professional lives and has caused the fundamentals of social life and structure to shift (Geser 2004). Achieving fit in a mobile context requires that we continue not only to consider the relationship between technology and task but also to incorporate individual preferences and needs.

Other, non-IS related research streams have – less explicitly – examined the concept of fit under a slightly different nomenclature. For example, researchers have tackled fit from a business alignment perspective, such as studies about IT and strategic alignment (Henderson and Venkatraman 1992), that tries to link IT innovation and corporate vision and objectives into a synergistic blend. Other streams, mainly in psychology, approach fit from a dissonance perspective, such as studies about cognitive or identity dissonance (e.g., Compeau and Higgins 1995; Festinger 1957). Cognitive dissonance represents the discrepancy between what an individual currently knows or believes and some new information or impressions that counter this current cognition. Facing two cognitions that are psychologically inconsistent, a person will, according to the theory, always strive to minimize this "misfit" or dissonance. The same strategy applies when an individual tries to reconcile a new identity role with his currently existing identity, thus reducing identity dissonance.

Ecological psychology, a field that argues that human behavior is always situated or highly dependent upon the environment, has approached the concept of fit from a task–person–environment perspective. For example, goal/task fit is considered to bring personal objectives in congruence with what a task or a work requirement imposes on an individual (Gibson 1979). Individual knowledge/ability fit, on the other hand, refers to the gap between insights that are beneficial in problem solving or decision making and the intellectual capacity an individual possesses to process this information (Gibson 1979), and finally, environmental fit refers to matching behavior as a response to particular stimuli in the environment that the person feels is most appropriate for addressing a particular issue or decision (Gibson 1979).

In the marketing literature, the notion of fit can be found in the concept of image congruence (e.g., Hogg et al. 2000). Image congruence, also referred to as self-congruence, describes the match between a consumer's perceived self-concept and the image of a given product, brand, or store. Studies have shown that image congruence has a direct effect on consumer behavior (i.e., the more an individual identifies herself with a product, for example, the more likely she is to purchase it).

Three basic inferences can be drawn by looking across the rich but multi-faceted fit literatures. First, each fit lens describes some sort of interplay between a set of entities that, in an ideal world, should be brought to congruence. This process is often referred to as "gap closing." Failure to close this gap, or not bringing entities in congruence, will likely lead to a bad fit and, in turn, to unwelcome consequences. This implies that fit is contingent (e.g., Davern 1996; Barley 1990) (i.e., depending on the constellation of the set of entities) and differing performance impacts may result. Second, it is a user or a potential user who assesses this interplay between the demands of a task and the provided technological capabilities; each lens stresses the importance of that individual. However, in the IS field, this component has not yet achieved enough attention despite, or even though, we witness technologies, and in this case, mobile technologies, becoming an integral part of our professional work lives. Third, there is not *one* overall fit notion in the adoption of technology; rather, there are multiple notions and they depend on situational factors. With technologies changing, so does the individual that is engaged in a continuous process of adaptation and modification so as to achieve and maintain the best possible fit. As pointed out in prior literature, proposed fit profiles that suggest that one-size fits all approaches are not appropriate (Barley 1990). Instead, organizations have to take a segmented approach in order to achieve desired, or even acceptable, levels of utilization and consequent performance impacts.

3.2 Evolutionary Psychology

IS researchers state that it is entirely possible that we have approached the practical limitations of explanation from these collective frames typically used to explain how people regard technology (Venkatesh et al. 2003). It may be true that we have exhausted our understanding from applying the social psychology and cognitive psychology frames and that we cannot expect these perspectives to lend new insights. Alternative lenses provide new ways of examining a phenomenon. And in the quest of explaining as much as possible in research, scholarship should be open to explore the benefit of applying these lenses. The field of psychology is embracing such an alternative lens (i.e., evolutionary psychology) by incorporating the human nature element of behavior that has been excluded in social psychology and cognitive psychology thus far (Cosmides and Tooby 2000, Cosmides et al. 1992). In fact, evolutionary psychology is being positioned as the third leg to provide a more comprehensive understanding of human behavior especially as research reveals more evidence of the role of innate mechanisms in behaviors such as decision making despite its controversial ties to Darwinism and sociobiology (Burghardt 2009, Buss 2009, Dewsbury 2009; Kenrick et al. 2006). The tenets that we find most relevant from evolutionary psychology is not about the origins of man as a species but rather how the human mind evolved to learn from historical mistakes to provoke behavior that is likely to bring about desired outcomes and survival promotion. The origin of man as a species is also not the primary tenet at the heart of the argument for inclusion of evolutionary psychology in mainstream psychology. Mainstream psychologists acknowledged that many advances in psychology as a discipline can be attributed to evolved psychological mechanisms resulting from innate coding in the brain and thus pre-positioning human behavior under certain situational cues (Dewsbury 2009). This is made evident by the recent special issue dedicated to the attribution of evolutionary concepts appearing in the *American Psychologist*, the authoritative source for the advancement of psychology, which demonstrates that the collective intellect of the most influential scholars in psychology has dramatically shifted from staunch criticism of evolutionary concepts to acceptance of its seminal importance. For example, in a 1974 American Psychologist article, renowned psychologist Ebel condemns the application of evolutionary concepts in psychology as "useless... for understanding of behavioral phenomena" (Ebel 1974, p. 491), whereas in 2009, leading scholars recognize, demonstrate, and celebrate how evolutionary principles over the past 200 years have become an important part of psychology (Dewsbury 2009) and are essential in a comprehensive explanation of functions of the mind and their influence on behavior (Burghardt 2009, Buss 2009; Hess and Pascal 2009).

Over the last 25 years, evolutionary psychology has been framed as a unifying theory that embraces many fields, such as evolutionary biology, cognitive science, anthropology, and neuroscience (Pinker 2007; Tooby and Cosmides 2007; Cosmides and Tooby 2000; Cosmides et al. 1992). Evolutionary psychology is gaining significant recognition as a valuable lens to understand how evolved psychological mechanisms, which are manifested by human nature, relate to motivation and behavior (Nohria et al. 2008; Buss 2004). Evolutionary psychology assumes that human behavior is influenced by a set of evolved psychological mechanisms – sometimes also referred to as domain-specific programs and is nowadays seen as the encompassing theory for both social psychology and cognitive psychology (Tooby and Cosmides 2007; Cosmides et al. 1992). These evolved psychological mechanisms arose as a response to repeated encounters with adaptive problems that constituted reproductive opportunities or challenges (Pinker 2007; Nicholson 1998; Buss 1995; Cosmides et al. 1992). Adaptive problems included activities such as forming social coalitions, gaining and maintaining status, protecting oneself and valuing others from threats, finding and retaining mates, and caring for family members (Pinker 2007; Sundie et al. 2006; Buss 1995). For each of these adaptive problems, mechanisms evolved.

These mechanisms did not necessarily develop in coherence with each other; instead, each so-called domain-specific program developed in response to a particular adaptive problem and is thus functionally specialized (Pinker 2007; Tooby and Cosmides 2007; Cosmides and Tooby 1994). Consequently, evolved psychological mechanisms potentially compete on some dimensions. For example, the tendency to exhibit jealousy in mating situations counters the need to form coalitions that ensure survival and reproduction. The behavioral manifestation of any given evolved psychological mechanism is not fixed but depends heavily on the environment and the cues that activate it (Kaplan 1992). Nonetheless, humans are more prone to exhibit certain patterns of behavior when faced with situations that closely resemble the ones that shaped our evolved psychological mechanisms (Buss 2004).

From an evolutionary perspective, cognition was (and still is) a necessary ingredient in the calibration of evolved psychological mechanisms (Cosmides et al. 1992). Cognition may be viewed as a short-term, phenomenon-driven activity that is necessary to analyze, prepare, and adjust evolved psychological mechanisms for long-term benefits for us to achieve our goals (Kenrick et al. 2006). The evolutionary perspective does not disclaim the influence of cognition. It proposes that, depending on the situation, some underlying evolved psychological mechanisms might also be activated (Kenrick et al. 2006). These deep mechanisms may support or oppose cognition depending on circumstances.

For tens of thousands of years, humankind was exposed to relatively unvarying or slowly varying environmental conditions (Pinker 2007). Evolved psychological mechanisms had sufficient buffer time to adapt to the environmental demands – until recently. Over the most recent few hundred years, the environment has changed dramatically through human intervention (Hess and Pascal 2009). Humans now determine the environment to a greater extent than the other way round. We therefore have a tendency to overlook the impact of evolved psychological mechanisms, as they are camouflaged by daily lives very remote from survival during the era of our ancestors (Hess and Pascal 2009). Evolutionary psychology posits that human nature and the environment are two inseparable forces, which influence each other throughout an individual's life (Ruth 1993). Human cognition has been shaped by evolution but does not completely override our inherent evolved psychological mechanisms. Consequently, the combination of social, cognitive, and evolutionary psychology has the potential to explain more fully human behavior in a wide variety of situations, including regarding the fit of technology.

3.3 The Four-Drive Model: An Instantiation of Evolutionary Psychology

The four-drive (4D) model is a synthesis of research on innate/evolved psychological mechanisms to broadly explain human behavior (Nohria et al. 2008; Lawrence and Nohria 2002). It identifies four drives: the drive to acquire, the drive to bond, the drive to comprehend, and the drive to defend.

The drive to acquire is the need to seek status, take control, and retain objects and personal experiences that humans value (Lawrence and Nohria 2002). Humankind has been (and still is) driven to acquire goods that are either material, such as food, clothing, and shelter, or positional, such as social acknowledgment and recognition (Nohria et al. 2008; Lawrence and Nohria 2002). The likelihood of survival was greater for those who were more apt at acquiring material goods as it elevated their social status and deemed them more capable of caring and providing for others, and thus increased their chances of reproductive success. In turn, their social status and power were based on the continued well-being of their acquired dependents and goods (Wilson 2004, 2000). In the health-care context, the drive to acquire is reflected in the nurses' need to be perceived as legitimate by the patient to gain status as a competent caregiver. If not perceived that way, credibility is at stake and best and safest intervention cannot be guaranteed.

The drive to bond is the need to form social relationships and develop mutual caring commitments with other humans (Nohria et al. 2008). Our ancestors engaged in bonding activities in order to strengthen group cohesion on the inside and to form coalitions against the outside. The premise is that those who bond well had a relative advantage over those who did not. After all, establishing and maintaining groups of individuals that were bonded by a mutual caring relationship improved the odds of surviving environmental threats (Cosmides and Tooby 2000, Cosmides et al. 1992). Bonding and its associated aspects, such as trust, empathy, compassion, loyalty, respect, partnership, and alliance, also manifest themselves in the form of behavioral outcomes altruism and the establishment of moral codes regarding social relationships (Van Vugt and Van Lange 2006; Rusbult and Van Lange 2003; Trivers 1971). Interestingly, many of the strongest reactions, both positive and negative, are linked to belongingness and engagement in a mutually caring relationship (Lawrence and Nohria 2002; Cosmides and Tooby 2000). In the health-care context, the drive to bond is reflected in the nurses' need for mutual assurance. They want to ensure that each participating entity (i.e., caregiver and patient) will act in the best interest of one another.

The drive to defend is the need to defend ourselves and our valued accomplishments whenever we perceive them to be endangered. At the individual level, the drive to defend is activated by perceived threats to one's person, valued objects, status, or beliefs (Lawrence and Nohria 2002). At the collective or organizational level, the drive to defend is triggered when individuals perceive a threat either to the bonds with others in their group, or to the collectively shared resources, or as part of a deviation from socially accepted norms deemed as disloyal (Lawrence and Nohria 2002). The human mind is preconditioned to enact to a variety of threats and the reaction will escalate as the severity of the threat heightens (Buss 2006). In the health-care context, the drive to defend is reflected in the nurses' need to protect oneself, their reputation, and those in their supervision from threats that might be posed from others due to negligent accountability.

Lastly, the drive to learn is the need that pushes humans to collect information, to assess the needs of a situation, to examine their environment, and to make observations about explanatory ideas and theories in hopes of appeasing curiosity and making sound judgments (Lawrence and Nohria 2002). This mechanism encourages individuals to seek out information to resolve problems associated with fulfilling fundamental needs (Kaplan 1992). Individuals seek to learn in order to decrease their uncertainty, to bring about closure to a problem that challenges well-being, to appease curiosity that enhances well-being, or to make situations more consistent with what is perceived as a "normal" behavior (Pinker 2007; Kenrick et al. 2006; Nicholson 1998). In the health-care context, the drive to learn is reflected in the nurses' need to collect information, examine the environment, and make observations about explanatory ideas and theories concerning the patient to assess their condition that aids in decision making concerning medical interventions.

The four drives are not the only human drives, but they are "central to a unified understanding of human behavior" (Lawrence and Nohria 2002, p. 41). The model contends that these drives, shaped by evolution to solve problems humans faced tens of thousands of years ago, remain influential today and have been implicitly reported by scholars for centuries (Lawrence and Nohria 2002). It also contends that all environmental inputs are evaluated in terms of their potential to satisfy or threaten each of the four drives. As described below, we came to discern the drives as an influence on the development of an enriched understanding of fit.

4 Research Design

As MICTs constitute a rather new technology in the health-care context, we decided to apply a comprehensive repertoire of methodological tools in order to gain a deep and rich understanding of the MICT adoption phenomenon. We used a multi-method approach, consisting of qualitative and quantitative elements that allowed us to tackle the phenomenon from varying perspectives. Qualitative methods can provide an in-depth understanding of the phenomenon but are said to lack generalizability; quantitative methods can produce more generalizable results but suffer from limited explanatory power. In combination, the application of both methods potentially achieves what can be termed a "complementary research method circle." Not only are qualitative findings supported by quantitative findings but the opposite applies as well – qualitative findings are further validated through the subsistence of quantitative findings. Research in IS typically uses one or the other but seldom both methodological approaches to study a phenomenon.

4.1 Exploring the Influence of Evolutionary Psychology in Technology Utilization and Performance

We undertook an exploratory effort using qualitative methods to study mobile technology utilization in a health-care context. Fifty nurses across four hospital sites using MICTs participated in this effort. Four sites were chosen so as to be able to observe nurses working in different medical units and attending to different patient care tasks. The four sites afforded enough variation to explain acceptance of MICTs for critical tasks and increased the chances of discerning the influence of different environments. The substantive criteria that we employed required that (1) each site employed similar technological solutions (i.e., MICTs) in use among the target study groups (i.e., nurses) in performing work tasks (i.e., patient care) and (2) the primary work task of the unit varied enough from the other three so that we could discern how different work environments and tasks influenced user behavior.

Site 1 was an emergency department within a 528-bed, not-for-profit hospital in the USA. The IS department implemented MICTs and instituted its mandatory usage for the task of patient triage (i.e., initial assessment) because the IS and managerial staff of the emergency department wanted to standardize the process of triage while providing attending nurses with needed mobility as well as accessibility to historical medical information. The intended benefits for the implementation were to decrease waiting times for patients needing medical care, to improve the quality of the triage assessment, and to promote patient safety. Site 2 was a Post Anesthesia Care Unit in a 124-bed, not-for-profit community hospital. The IS department implemented MICTs and instituted mandatory usage for the task of electronic charting of patients following general surgery. Anesthetized patients upon transfer from the operating room are monitored until they regain consciousness. The primary intended benefit of the implementation was a decrease in laborious manual documentation, a decrease in documentation errors, and improved patient safety. The same anticipated benefits led to the implementation of an MICT at Site 3, an Ambulatory Care Unit in the same hospital. Here the IS department instituted mandatory usage with the objective of enabling electronic charting for nurses preparing conscious patients for day surgery. Site 4 was a Regular Floor in a 478-bed hospital that has 13 regular floor units for inpatients. It was a federally funded veterans' medical center providing inpatient care as well as outpatient care programs, including for those with medical, surgical, and psychiatric needs. The main objective of MICT implementation was to decrease documentation errors associated with validating prescriptions as well as recording medical interventions.

Techniques for data collection at all four sites included interviews, direct observations, and review of documents. Interviews were semi-structured around questions designed to elicit respondents' personal experiences with MICTs in patient care. Overall, 50 interviews were conducted, averaging 45 min each. All interviews were audio-recorded and transcribed. Direct observation was employed to assess actual usage behavior so as to minimize self-report bias. In total, 57 instances of direct observations were conducted across sites. These instances include observations of nurses and registration personnel. Observations were interspersed between interviews in order to provide a holistic picture of the task environment and background for proposing new questions, revising existing questions, and clarifying informant comments. We also solicited and reviewed systems documentation prior to interviews at each site to give us insights into the intended usage and technical characteristics. We also reviewed system documents that interviewees referenced in conversations or used during task performance. In all, we reviewed 250+ pages of written materials inclusive of project proposal description, system requirement documents, end-user manuals, and training manuals. Triangulating the interview, observation, and document analysis was sufficient for attaining theoretical saturation (March and Simon 1958).

Data collection, coding, and data analysis are tightly interwoven in inductive research (Suddaby 2006; Boudreau et al. 2002). Accordingly, the processes for collecting, coding, and analyzing of data were iterative rather than sequential. Through a constant comparative technique, we evaluated and contrasted similar and dissimilar data units, which provided a richer understanding of the research phenomenon (Suddaby 2006). As a result, when data were coded and analyzed, interviews and observations became more focused. We used Atlas.ti, a visual qualitative data analysis tool that provided a means to load and categorize transcripts, count text segments, customize labeling in the coding, automatically assess relationships between text segments based on these customized labels or codes, memo or journal, and query the text segments based on a number of criteria (i.e., associated code, similar memo, etc.).

We elected to use the Straussian coding paradigm (Strauss and Corbin 1998). Accordingly, the analysis of data included three major types of coding – open, axial, and selective – with each type being at a higher, more abstract level of data analysis than the preceding one. In open coding (i.e., the process of breaking down, comparing, conceptualizing, and categorizing data), we created 61 codes related to 553 textual segments attained from the 50 interviews and 57 observations. Axial coding, which necessitates that the data be put back together in new ways by making connections between codes to form categories, resulted in the identification of 12 categories. It led us to uncover the saliency of eight novel fits and four human drives. In selective coding, a conceptualization of the main phenomenon was developed. We used the four-drive model (Lawrence and Nohria 2002), demonstrated in the following, as a means to structure our findings and as a basis for linking human drives with the novel constellations of fit embedded in what we currently know about human MICT acceptance behavior.

4.1.1 Defining Fit Notions

In gathering our qualitative data, we were particularly interested in ascertaining when, how, and in what ways nurses would utilize an MICT as part of their caregiving work. We found nurses exhibiting different forms of utilization, some unanticipated by the designers or the management. For instance, despite managements' entreaties to do otherwise, some nurses used the system on another nurse's behalf. Also, some of the nurses reported that they would not use the MICT at the point of care but in some other location, such as a hallway. Findings of the qualitative study showed that a nurse's decision to use the MICT was influenced by overcoming various "mis-fits" on multiple fronts. As typical of their job description, nurses were faced with a plethora of demands and needs on a daily basis. A nurse's problem-solving behavior therefore became more of a continuous "gap-closing" procedure between specific needs posed by her job and the technology that was intended to support her job. In the present study, we were able to identify eight notions of fit.

Identification fit, for example, describes a nurse's need to identify a patient correctly, to identify the correct associated medical intervention, and to identify herself as the correct caregiver. The degree to which the provided MICT matched one or more of these needs determined her decision to utilize the MICT.

Similarly, we also found that nurses continuously strove to match their need to have the most current information available at the right time with what was provided by the MICT, which we refer to as *information communication fit*. Having access to the most current and updated patients' information is vital, particularly in situations where the patient is unconscious.

Location fit was based on the need to have information access at the right location. This location is most likely at the point of care in which the likelihood of capturing correct data without reliance on either memory or alternative methods of documenting that take the nurse away from the patient's bedside. In essence, being able to document a medical intervention wherever needed was deemed to be most efficient (in terms of computing time savings) and effective in that it was perceived to be less prone to medical mis-specifications.

Patient interaction fit was driven by a nurse's need to bond with patients. Interacting with patients was important to nurses and served multiple purposes. It allowed the nurse to attain data about the patient's physiological condition and psychological state; it also helped to establish a relationship between the nurses and the patient that aided in the patient being agreeable to having the nurse perform care. In some cases it also decreased anxieties associated with providing and receiving care. The MICT supported this need in that the technology was used as a tool to engage patients in their own health-care awareness even while the nurse was providing care. For example, a nurse displaying medical information, such as about the effectiveness of a particular medication regimen, helped to keep the patient compliant.

Physical fit was based on a nurse's need for maneuverability with the MICT to get to the patient's location, especially in physically constrained patient rooms.

Characteristics of the technology in terms of how the hardware was designed to afford mobility determined the physical fit capabilities of the MICT.

Time criticality fit was based on a nurse's need to be informed about urgent medical interventions, such as medication administration. Nurses were typically inundated with activities that became over-engaging and hindered their ability to remember or refer to manual or electronic documents reminding them of interventions. Automatic alerts, as part of the MICT, allayed such problems.

User comfort fit was based on a nurse's need to be and feel comfortable with the MICT in front of a patient. This fit was most analogous to computer self-efficacy (Burk 2006). If the MICT was not designed efficiently, or the nurse was not comfortable manipulating the system, then the MICT was not considered befitting. As nursing is an aging profession (Abraham et al. 2004, 2008), those that were trained 15 or more years ago did not necessarily have sufficient typing skills. We also observed that only few had received formal training in using computers for data access or processing.

Work*flow fit* was based on a nurse's need to streamline work processes and to most efficiently perform work-related tasks in a manner that did not impede the way one is accustomed to performing work. Job fit (Mintzberg 1973) is most analogous to reflecting how the technology characteristics need to improve work or meet a specified goal.

Overall, good fit was achieved if any of these needs were matched through the support of the MICT; bad fit, in contrast, resulted if the MICT met those needs only poorly. Table 10.1 provides a description of the eight notions of fit as well as excerpts of interview data supporting each notion.

4.1.2 Conceptualizing Human Drives as Individual Characteristics

Besides suggesting a richer conceptualization of fit, we also found evidence in our data that suggested a set of psychological factors at play (coded as need for self-presentation, establishing relationship, safety assurance, self-preservation, and information gathering), which added depth to individual characteristics and influence regarding technology fit descriptions and utilization decisions. Traditional fit literature, as pointed out before, does not adequately address this individualistic nature of a user. However, our data led us to see the influence of a set of basic human drives or motivations that guided nurses to define their task, determine their urgency, and then to ascertain not only if the technology fits the task but also how or on what dimensional levels the technology most appropriately fits. We reviewed the psychology literature and discerned that concepts in evolutionary psychology, specifically the four-drive model, parallel our qualitatively derived results and adapted the drives as labels for our themes as they had been previously documented in published literature. Table 10.2 provides the qualitatively derived themes and maps them to a drive that has been adapted in the context of this research and includes excerpts from the qualitative data that revealed the saliency of the drives and their relevance to perceptions of fit regarding the MICT.

Table 10.1 Notions of fit in the health-care context

Fit notion	Description	Excerpt of qualitative data supporting this fit notion
Identification fit	The fit between the need to identify the task doer and the task recipient to determine the unique medical encounter on the one hand and the perceived technological capabilities to support that need on the other hand	"It happened that you might mistakenly chart on the wrong patient with the paper charts or you get your notes mixed up when you went to key it into the EMR. It's less of chance of me getting things mixed up with the wireless, because I'm right there are the patient's bedside and have to scan to make sure that I'm charting on the right patient and giving the right med."
Information communication fit	The fit between the need to have the most current information available at the time of caregiving and the perceived technological capabilities to support that need	"When giving meds, you need to know the most current meds prescribed. You may have had the same patient the day prior, but come on shift and the physician changed the meds in the middle of the night because the nurse on the prior shift told him that meds caused a reaction or weren't effective."
Location fit	The fit between the need to have information access at the point-of-care location and the perceived technological capabilities to support this need	"You may be with a patient and you need to get information about another patient like 'when was the last time I checked if the vitals stabilized' or someone asks you about Mr. So and So and you can't remember. It's so much easier if you can look it up with the wireless system instead of having to leave your patient and go track down another's chart."
Patient interaction fit	The fit between a nurse's need to interact with the patient and the extent to which technology supports or inhibits this need	"The system was so bad and it made me lose eye contact with my patients so I stopped using it in the rooms with me and just went back to making my notes and just use the system in the hallway."
Physical fit	The fit between the need for maneuverability and the perceived ability of the hardware components to support this need in spatially constricted spaces such as patient rooms	"Most of our rooms have three or more beds and the carts aren't slender enough to fit in between the beds so most of the time you end up pushing furniture out of the way or charting at the foot of the bed if you have a cart that has the wireless barcode scanners."

Table 10.1 (continued)

Fit notion	Description	Excerpt of qualitative data supporting this fit notion
Time criticality fit	The fit between the need of being alert of urgent interventions and the perceived technological capabilities to support this need	"The wireless system alerts me when someone needs a pain med effectiveness check or when I have to give a med to make sure that if will be effective. The meds only work the way they are supposed to if we give them when they need to be taken."
User comfort fit	The fit between a nurse's need to display confidence in front of a patient and the perceived technological capabilities to support his need	"... when I tried using the thing in the rooms I always felt like the patient was watching my every move. I think to myself that the patient must think I'm stupid ... As a patient I would get upset seeing my nurse fumble... If a patient's upset we have problems assessing them... then the procedure is delayed and everything slows down."
Workflow fit	The fit between the need to streamline the workflow and the perceived technological capabilities to support this need	"We really needed a way that supported how we work. We do most of our work at the point of care, which can be anywhere really (i.e., in the room, in the hallway/waiting room, in the car or EMS vehicle they arrive in). We can get to the information we need and take the it with us wherever we go ... One thing that may help is being able to print forms right on the carts so we don't have to keep going back and forth to the printers at the nurses' station... I've noticed so much less foot traffic in the halls and I don't forget stuff hardly as much."

As aforesaid, the four-drive model explains decision making from a human nature perspective. Lawrence and Nohria (2002) apply the four-drive model across individuals and groups to explain behavior in and by organizations. They argue that "individuals and social institutions will enjoy adaptive advantage (i.e., advantages in meeting changing business environmental demands) to the extent that they are able to fulfill all four basic human drives" (Lawrence and Nohria 2002, p. 264). The inference that can be drawn from this model is twofold. First, users will decide to utilize technologies only if it aids in appeasing their basic human drives, and second, the influence of drives spurs a richer and broader conceptualization of fit that

Table 10.2 Coded themes and mapping to human drives

Inductively derived theme and abbreviated definition	Excerpt of qualitative data supporting this drive	Human drive from four-drive model
Self-presentation – the need to be perceived as legitimate by the patient to gain status as a competent caregiver	"The patients need to see that I know what I'm doing. They don't have to like me but respect me for what I'm there to do… which in the grand scheme of things is to make them well… My job is just as important as the doc… I'm the one that comes in to see about them at 3am when they are in pain… I can use the wireless [electronic chart available in the MICT] to show them that their meds scripts aren't effective because of the frequency I have respond to their pain calls… I think it helps them to see me as a true professional."	Drive to acquire – desire to seek status, take control, and retain objects and personal experiences that humans value
Establish relationship – the need for the nurse to form and maintain an interpersonal relationship with the patient	"I was happy about getting something [electronic chart available in the MICT] that would help me spend more time with patients…"	Drive to bond – inherent drive to form social relationships and develop mutual caring commitments with other humans
Safety assurance – the need to protect the patient from harm and	"It's [the electronic chart enabled by the MICT] less prone for error and protects you as the nurse as well as the patient. With this technology I can build progress notes, and I can build it with all of the bells and whistles that you need to get everything in your charting that protects you legally….you can do all of that right at the bedside."	Drive to defend[a] – deep-rooted drive for humans to defend themselves and their valued accomplishments whenever they perceive them to be endangered
Self-preservation – the need to protect oneself with information regarding their actions	"In the old days it was just you in that boat, and now there are at least two other people in there with you [the physician and the pharmacists]….You can protect yourself [the electronic chart enabled by the MICT] some 5 years from now when some lawyer got you on the stand [in a court proceeding]."	

Table 10.2 (continued)

Inductively derived theme and abbreviated definition	Excerpt of qualitative data supporting this drive	Human drive from four-drive model
Information gathering – the need to collect information about the patient and what causes the circumstances at hand to provide ample care	"Before [prior to MICTs] I always reviewed the narrative in the paper chart, which may be long... [to answer questions]. I use the mobile system to look at the chart as opposed to asking a nurse or going to the manual file... I can check the chart from any of the mobile system. I don't have to leave my patient."	Drive to learn – pushes humans to collect information, assess the needs of a situation, examine their environment, and make observations about explanatory ideas and theories in hopes of appeasing curiosity and making sound judgments

[a] Safety assurance and self-preservation were collapsed because of the underlying idea of protection either for oneself (e.g., in the case of self-preservation for the nurse) or for another (e.g., in the case of safety assurance for the patient), which mapped to the drive to defend.

goes beyond scrutinizing just the relationship between task and technology. As a result of the selective coding results, we depict the association between the drives, the perceived fits, utilization, and performance using the Strauss and Corbin coding paradigm, which is depicted here (Fig. 10.2).

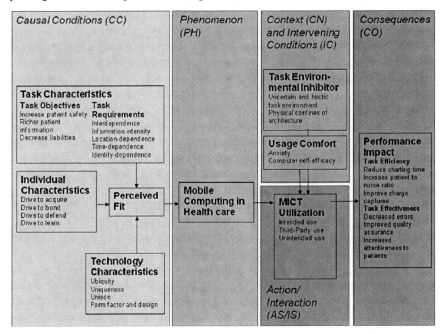

Fig. 10.2 Selective coding results from the qualitative study using Strauss and Corbin coding paradigm

4.2 Testing the Results of the Exploratory Effort

Based on the selective coding results and our literature review of technology fit models, we propose that individual characteristics in the form of four human drives contribute to the saliency of the discrete dimensions of fit perceptions in the context of mobile patient care (Hypothesis 1). Like forecasted in prior literature, the deployment of MICTs to the context of health care is apparently set out to fit the task at hand in a much better way than was traditionally possible (Junglas and Watson 2006). Besides the fact that the IS field has exclusively scrutinized the fitting relationship between task and technology only and has mostly ignored the influence of individual characteristics, it has also predominantly focused on the examination of technology designed to complete a particular organizational task in a structured, non-volatile business environment. This confined perspective seems no longer appropriate. As computing evolves from traditional business (or tethered) computing, to mobile, on to pervasive and ubiquitous computing (Lyytinen and Yoo 2002a, b), technology will become an integral part of an individual's life (Geser 2004).

We also conclude that the plethora of fits found in a health-care setting between task, technology, and the individual influences utilization decisions regarding the MICT (Hypothesis 2a) as well as a nurse's work performance (Hypothesis 2b). MICTs have the capability to improve quality and safety of patient care by decreasing errors that result from the lack of faster, more comprehensive, and more accessible patient documentation at the point and time of care. Nurses perform the bulk of the documentation-oriented tasks in patient care. And nursing documentation is a critical part of clinical documentation, which is a precondition for good patient care and proper communication within the health-care team (Ammenwerth et al. 2003). Yet, documentation is considered a necessary evil in itself, and nurses apply varying levels of utilization and acceptance of computer-based nursing documentation (Abraham et al. 2008, 2004; Ammenwerth et al. 2001; Newton 1995). However, nursing can benefit from access to medical data for medication and patient history to effectively perform work at the point of care (i.e., at the patient's location) (Abraham et al. 2008, 2004). For intended utilization of technology by a target user group, the technology must be deemed a proper fit for the task on multiple dimensions, which we assert should also account for the inherent characteristics that individuals possess. For the health-care context, we therefore propose the following research model (Fig. 10.3).

For the quantitative empirical test, we sought to quantify the various notions of fit and the influence of the human drives identified earlier. Thus, we developed a survey instrument, which we used exclusively to validate our qualitatively derived findings. As we could not rely on the existence of prior measures, it was essential to carefully deploy a consolidated approach to establish valid measures for both: the notions of fit and the human drives. This process was patterned after the one proposed by Moore and Benbasat (1991). A pilot survey was developed that based its measurement items on prior literature and the input received from the nurses across four different hospital sites that participated in the preceding qualitative phase of the

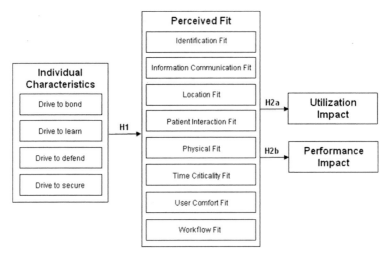

Fig. 10.3 Research model

study. Those four sites were also used to test our survey instrument across 31 voluntary nurses. This process helped us to develop an instrument that displayed solid psychometric characteristics with regard to internal consistency, convergent, and discriminant validities. The survey instrument is detailed in Junglas et al. (2009).

In order to obtain participants for this succeeding quantitative effort, an e-mail invitation was sent to a select group of members of the American Nursing Informatics Association (ANIA) who were not participants in the previous qualitative study. These members were known to perform clinical care with MICTs and information systems management of nursing clinical systems in their respective hospitals. The survey was administered online, containing approximately 50 questions; questions did not seek out any personal information. Respondents were mandatory users of an MICT utilizing the device for any of the following tasks: electronic charting on conscious patients in Ambulatory Care Units (ACUs) (37%) and on unconscious patients in Post Anesthesia Care Units (PACUs) (21%)as, medication administration (24%), patient triage (9%), and patient registration (8%). Overall, 107 nurses participated in the survey, out of which 96% were female (and 4% male). On average, nurses were 45 years old and had on average 20 years experience in the field.

Data were analyzed using structural equation modeling, more specifically partial least square (PLS), version 3 (Gefen et al. 2000; Chin 1998). PLS, as every structural equation modeling technique, differentiates between a measurement and a structural model. Whereas the measurement model analyzes the relationship between the latent constructs and their associated items by scrutinizing their internal, convergent, and discriminant validities, the structural model estimates the strengths of the relationship between latent constructs by providing estimates for path coefficients and variance explained.

Table 10.3 Internal and convergent validities

Construct	Variable name	Factor loadings	t-Statistics	Items per construct	Composite reliability	Average variance extracted (AVE)	Mean	Standard deviation
Drive to learn	DRL1	0.81	1.74	3	0.863	0.677	6.74	0.52
	DRL2	0.83	3.33					
	DRL3	0.83	2.50					
Drive to bond	DRB1	0.75	4.35	3	0.869	0.673	6.52	0.64
	DRB2	0.87	6.80					
	DRB3	0.84	3.90					
Drive to defend	DRD1	0.86	6.69	3	0.877	0.704	6.34	0.85
	DRD2	0.88	7.02					
	DRD3	0.78	4.81					
Drive to acquire	DRS1	0.80	2.14	3	0.864	0.679	6.79	0.61
	DRS2	0.86	4.00					
	DRS3	0.81	2.38					
Identification fit	IF1	0.96	16.92	2	0.952	0.908	6.15	1.21
	IF2	0.94	19.38					
Information fit	IC1	0.91	14.61	4	0.944	0.808	6.27	1.06
	IC2	0.87	14.99					
	LF1	0.92	14.82					
	LF2	0.89	20.91					
Patient interaction fit	PIF1	0.94	14.50	2	0.911	0.836	5.80	1.31
	PIF2	0.89	15.29					
Physical fit	PF1	0.95	12.59	2	0.920	0.853	5.59	1.43
	PF2	0.90	10.00					

Table 10.3 (continued)

Construct	Variable name	Factor loadings	t-Statistics	Items per construct	Composite reliability	Average variance extracted (AVE)	Mean	Standard deviation
Time criticality fit	TCF1	0.95	15.41	2	0.902	0.822	5.72	1.23
	TCF2	0.86	13.16					
User comfort fit	UCF1	0.95	16.91	2	0.923	0.857	5.77	1.25
	UCF2	0.91	16.96					
Workflow fit	WWF1	0.95	17.93	2	0.926	0.862	4.60	1.26
	WWF2	0.90	18.21					
Performance	P1	0.92	28.66	4	0.969	0.886	5.26	1.64
	P2	0.97	35.83					
	P3	0.95	26.40					
	P4	0.92	26.30					
Utilization	UT1	0.91	15.06	3	0.858	0.670	4.84	1.70
	UT2	0.77	7.20					
	UT3	0.77	9.56					

Table 10.4 Structural model with path coefficients

	Identification fit	Information fit	Patient interaction fit	Physical fit	Time criticality fit	User comfort fit	Workflow fit
Drive to learn	0.17*	0.19*	0.00	0.02	-0.09	-0.01	-0.01
Drive to bond	0.02	-0.03	0.07	0.30**	0.23*	0.156	0.14
Drive to defend	0.14	0.24*	0.20*	0.09	0.16	0.23*	0.20
Drive to acquire	0.26*	0.12	0.22*	0.00	0.07	0.07	0.11
Variance explained	0.20	0.18	0.16	0.13	0.13	0.14	0.13

	Performance	Utilization
Identification fit	-0.08	0.21*
Information fit	0.15	0.04
Patient interaction fit	0.12	0.02
Physical fit	0.02	0.00
Time criticality fit	0.17*	0.11
User comfort fit	0.30**	0.14
Workflow fit	0.24**	0.34*
Variance explained	0.70	0.56

* $p < 0.5$; ** $p < 0.01$

Items for the human drives, the eight notions of fit, and both dependent variable performance and utilization were measured using a seven-point Likert scale, ranging from strongly disagree (1) to strongly agree (7). In order to establish internal validity for each construct, we examined item loadings and their respective composite reliabilities. As Table 10.3 demonstrates, each item loads above 0.75 on its respective construct. Further, all constructs display sufficient composite reliabilities. The composite reliability calculated in PLS is equivalent to Cronbach's alpha; however, it does not assume tau equivalency among the measures (Werts et al. 2007). Convergent validity is established if the average variance extracted (AVE) is above a suggested level of 0.5 (Fornell and Larcker 1981); all constructs surpass this criterion (see Table 10.4). As with the human drives, the measurement model of the various notions of fit displayed sufficient internal validity as well as adequate convergent and discriminant validities. However, an initial analysis of the data showed that information communication fit and location fit psychometrically overlapped, indicating insufficient discriminant validity. It became apparent that nurses could not differentiate between having "the most current information at the time of caregiving" and "information access at the point-of-care location." This finding makes sense as mobile technology is exactly about that – it bridges time and space. For subsequent statistical analysis, both information and communication fits were therefore collapsed and analyzed as one construct labeled "information fit" that comprises the notion of "having the most current information available at the time and location of caregiving."

The results of the structural model analysis are displayed in Table 10.4. Overall, the research model explains 70% of the variance in the overall nurses' performance and 56% in their decision to utilize the mobile system. A number of path coefficients between the human drives and the various notions of fit appeared significant. The drive to learn impacts identification and information fits. Further, the drive to bond has an impact on physical fit and time criticality fit; the drive to defend impacts information fit, patient interaction fit, and workflow fit; and the drive to acquire impacts identification fit and patient interaction fit. Three dimensions of fits, namely time criticality, user comfort, and workflow fits, display a significant influence on overall performance; and identification and workflow fits display a significant influence on utilization.

5 Discussing the Relevance of the Human Drives and Fit Notions

We are fortunate to have found environments that illuminate the saliency of human drives and their contribution to a deeper understanding of how people perceive the fit of technology. The findings of this study provide a preliminary test of the viability of archetypical human drives and their influence on various notions of fit to determine individual performance in a health-care setting when using MICT. Our findings extend the traditional TTF model by unfolding a series of nuances in fit perceptions while pointing out the importance of individual characteristics in task–technology fit formations, which are applicable in examining MICT utilization and performance. The evolution of computing toward a ubiquitous nature that organizes and mediates social interaction when and where situations occur has created its own set of organizational work setting issues (Lyytinen and Yoo 2002a). Even though these new computing environments bring formidable advancements, they also pose tremendous challenges to user acceptance and design issues that may not be sufficiently addressed by traditional IS and behavioral theories (Lyytinen and Yoo 2002b). In 2005, nearly 70% of health-care providers (i.e., physicians, specialists, residents, and medical students) used mobile devices, such as personal digital assistants (PDAs), to access catalogued medical information to diagnose patients (Garritty and Emam 2006). While this is improving as of 2009, with the encouragement of health-care information technology reducing errors and curbing costs in health care, perhaps 17% as a generous percentage of all US hospitals actually employ any form of technology to store and access electronic health information (Blumenthal 2009). Despite evidence that usage of electronic health information is beneficial to more timely and more accurate care delivery, promoting acceptance and the desired utilization behavior, which are critical to bring positive performance to fruition, by health-care professionals are still challenging (Blumenthal 2009).

A series of findings can be inferred from the study. Besides varying notions of fit perceptions, the study indicates that some nuances play a more significant role in determining utilization decisions and individual performance than do others. In the health-care context, it seems that identification fit and workflow fit are the most prevalent determinants in MICT utilization considerations. Supporting the identification of the patient, the type of medical intervention, and the nurse as an appropriate caregiver is a necessary pre-requisite that needs to be supported by the MICT in order for nurses to use it. In the same vein, an MICT must also be an integral part of the nurse's workflow. With a proper workflow in place, medical errors are expected to decrease. This finding is in accordance with nurses' comments in the qualitative study, stating that they are much more error prone and forgetful of pertinent information when they cannot document the workflow at the time they perform the medical intervention.

Workflow fit also played a significant role in determining the effectiveness and efficiency of a nurse's work performance. In addition, user comfort fit and time criticality played a significant role as well. Using an MICT in the presence of a patient introduced a new dimension to the patient care process; no longer are there temporal boundaries between a nurse processing information and her physically interacting with the patient. Both activities are intertwined now and require a nurse to display a high level of confidence in doing both. The fact that most nurses have only limited typing skills (Abraham et al. 2004) combined with the degree to which the MICT is easy enough to operate influences a nurse's user comfort level. In the qualitative data, nurses noted that fumbling with the computer in front of a patient increased their anxiety, which, in turn, was perceived as something that patients would undoubtedly view as a lack of professionalism on their part. Nurses did not want to appear incompetent in any manner as any perceived lack of skill potentially can have physiological implications for the patient (e.g., increased high blood pressure, anxiousness). In addition, nurses were confronted with an overwhelming set of tasks that were time critical and highly interdependent. If an MICT, as part of their routine, afforded them with information when and where needed, and they were not afraid of using the MICT, then their overall performance improved.

Another major finding of our study is the viability of underlying human drives that impact perceptions of fit and, in consequence, individual performance. A nurse's *drive to learn* (i.e., the drive to collect information, examine the environment, and make observations about explanatory ideas and theories) seems to be the motivating force behind identification and information fits. The nurse's desire to insidiously identify what needs to be done, by whom and to whom, and at what point in time is a direct result of one's desire to learn and aids in her decision-making process concerning medical interventions. Similarly, her quest to have the most current information available at her fingertips is also a direct consequence of this basic human drive.

The *drive to bond* exhibits significant influences on time criticality and physical fits. Because of the volume of patients and limited resources, medical interventions are typically abbreviated and tasks have to be completed in a timely fashion so as not to impede throughput. Bonding allows for patients to be much more amenable and tolerant of procedures that the nurse must accomplish at designated times. The qualitative data substantiate this in that nurses were more productive and successful in delivering the intended care when they were able to establish a mutually trusting relationship with the patient. Physical fit, or the ability to maneuver an MICT in spatially constrained spaces, such as patient rooms, also appeared to be influenced by a nurse's bonding desire. In accordance with the qualitative study conducted, nurses felt that an ill-designed MICT distracted from their bonding experience and impeded a nurse's ability to prepare the patient for effective care. They noted, for example, that eye contact is a vital ingredient in establishing a trusted nurse–patient relationship and that an MICT, even though it might be considered useful, must not interfere with that. If it does interfere, nurses would decide to use the MICT away from the point of care (e.g., in hallways), which, from an IS research perspective, signifies deviant utilization behavior.

The *drive to acquire*, or a nurse's strive toward gaining status as a competent caregiver, contributed to the perception of identification and patient interaction fit. Achieving legitimacy and professional reputation is possible only if a nurse is able to correctly identify a patient, thus safeguarding that the correct medication or regimen is provided. The better equipped the technology is in ensuring this identification, the more likely a nurse will perceive it as a suitable fit. As for patient interaction fit, it is gravely important for nurses to interact with their patients in order to gain or provide pertinent information. For example, by interacting with a patient, a nurse might not only gather information about the effectiveness of medications or regimens but also use this opportunity to provide educational information to the patient about his compliance with a prescribed regimen.

The *drive to defend*, or the drive of humans to defend themselves and their valued accomplishments wherever and whenever they perceive them to be endangered, exhibits influences on information fit, patient interaction fit, and user comfort fit. Nurses, or caregivers in general, are typically characterized by their imminent drive to preserve patient safety, which apparently also directs the need to ensure a healthy nurse–patient interaction. Preserving patient safety also manifests itself in professional creeds, mission and vision statements, as well as legislation. With the best possible information at hand at the right point in time, nurses try to follow the prescribed medical regimen that causes the least patient distress during the caregiving experience while decreasing the likelihood of medical error and potential legal consequences. However, this is possible only if nurses feel at ease and are able to display confidence in their abilities with the technology in front of the patient.

Even though some of the predicted paths that we hypothesized did not turn out to be significant, we nevertheless think that deciphering the facets of fit in a health-care context as well as deciphering individualistic factors that contribute to (or prevent from) reaching any fit facet is an important contribution as it will help IS designers to develop suitable guidelines for mobile technologies. We do expect that with the level of technology pervasiveness increasing, future studies will find an even more salient connection between all human drives and all fit notions. At present, however, this chapter should be viewed as an attempt to shed light on the influence of individual characteristics as human drives grounded in the evolutionary psychology literature that enriches our understanding of fit and establishes an association with utilization and performance.

The implications here are that our technology acceptance models inclusive of fit that are typically grounded in social and cognitive psychology frames may benefit from augmentation with evolutionary psychology frames. In this regard, we can attain a more comprehensive understanding of how the individual characteristics are formed aside from merely couching it as an attitude or a belief that is cognitively based. This study provides a preliminary test of the viability of human drives and their influence on various notions of fit to determine individual performance in a health-care setting when using MICTs. More specifically, our findings provide insights into the notion of fit by unfolding a series of nuances in fit perceptions while pointing out the importance of individual characteristics in these fit formations that have become salient in light of MICTs.

The basic premise of fit models is that understanding the motivations of how people determine the extent to which a technology fits the task provides a more in-depth understanding of the of the underlying factors that take place regarding decision making about technology utilization. As technologies become more pervasive, this understanding about human drives can aid in effectively designing information systems and their supporting mobile technologies to better facilitate an individual's needs and promote intended utilization. For example, in order to address the drive to bond in the health-care context, an information system should be designed in such a way that it is unobtrusive and does not interfere with the eye-to-eye contact between nurse and patient. Future MICTs, for example, might consider the use of virtual displays instead of physical screens. In the case of the drive to learn, an information system not only should support a high-quality level of information (i.e., it should support information that is most current, cross-linked across different platforms and available in real time at the point of care) but also could potentially provide additional information, such as prophylactic measures that can be taken by the patient as part of his medical recuperation and education in the future. The latter feature would also enhance a nurse's drive to acquire as it would elevate her status in front of the patient as a competent caregiver. To appease the drive to bond, current information systems, for example, already proactively warn about conflicting medications; future systems, however, could possibly raise the level of incidence detection by using, for example, intelligent emergency management systems, or comprehensive patient-monitoring systems [92].

Scrutinizing the characteristics of an individual has received little research attention in the past. This needs to change as future systems become even more pervasive, mobile, and personalizable while having a higher degree of ubiquity. Our study has shown that more fundamental characteristics than the ones identified in the traditional psychology literature are at play in determining technology acceptance. In fact, the four human drives that became salient in the study are rather biological in nature and can even be considered archetypical to any human being.

Besides the fact that designers have to increasingly incorporate individual characteristics, the current study has also demonstrated that technology fit in health-care contexts using MICTs cannot be considered homogeneous but is multi-faceted. In an era of mobile computing – an era in which information systems are portable and not tied to the network outlet of an organization anymore – the perceived fit seems to be highly context driven. Abstracting from spatial and temporal boundaries (Junglas and Watson 2006), mobile devices have to follow design rules that, among other things, make them fit their physical context. For IS designers, this means that information systems have to match the spatial aspects of the context – as reflected, for example, in the location and physical fit notions. Designs of information systems also have to match temporal aspects – as reflected, for example, in the time criticality and information communication fit notions. These findings, even though limited to the health-care context at present, should aid in designing well-suited MICTs for promoting efficiency improvements and reducing laborious manual-laden and error-prone processes while accelerating the delivery of information to the front lines of care or work.

The inclusion of evolutionary psychology as a frame presents opportunities for future research. Even though seven notions of fit and four human drives are crystallized in the health-care environment, this does not necessarily imply that they will also do so in other contexts or that other notions of fit might emerge. Findings are therefore not generalizable and future research therefore needs to explore other environments and roles. One possibility could be looking at training environments to determine the influence of these drivers and the fit of the technology for educational purposes. Also, the exclusive use of online surveys (instead of paper-based surveys) might have introduced a method bias. However, we believe that our multi-method approach paired with the careful attention paid to the development of the survey instrument and its simplistic administration assures a high level of confidence in the results.

Also, the inclusion of the drives in our theoretical repertoires provided a lens for bringing the individual characteristics more in line as being a critical factor in understanding how people regard technology. The implications for future research can be to apply the drives to explain overall technology acceptance as an individual adaptation process, the mediation of communication, and coping mechanisms for use of technology. More importantly, inclusion of the drives or at least an understanding of the tenets of evolutionary psychology regarding evolved psychological mechanisms can help answer why intentions do not always lead to expected use as they are helpful in reconceptualizing organization and individual motivation (Nohria et al. 2008; Spohn 2005). In this regard, we begin to open the discussion about augmenting traditional social and cognitive psychology-based models that serve as seminal IS literature. In the particular case of IS, the Unified Theory of Acceptance and Use of Technology (UTAUT), based on a synthesis of contemporary user acceptance research, explains 70% (adjusted R^2) of the variance in user acceptance (Venkatesh et al. 2003). UTAUT's developers conclude that future research needs focus on identifying constructs that can add to the prediction of intention and behavior beyond current knowledge (Venkatesh et al. 2003). The authors of UTAUT suggest that it is entirely possible that we have approached the practical limitations of explanation regarding human decision making concerning technology from these collective frames *typically* used. It may be true that we have exhausted our understanding from applying the social and cognitive psychology frames to try and understand the individual and with technology becoming more pervasive, we can no longer afford to rest explanation on the dual constellation of task and technology. This suggests that we may need to re-evaluate our seminal IS theories, which is a suggestion by Lyytinen and Yoo (Lyytinen and Yoo 2002b) regarding pervasive technology for which we extend to the inclusion of the human element. At least this research shows how the drives, based in evolutionary psychology, lend new insights and can possibly be the missing piece of the puzzle in explaining the individual's influence in IS research.

6 Conclusion

The aforementioned state is possible only if the IS research community is sensitized and willing to consider the drives, and their influence is having a bearing on utilization and performance, as not an alternative lens but as complementary to collective acumen articulated in our seminal IS theories. This study demonstrates the potential benefits from the use of MICTs in health-care settings and in having a bearing on potential MICT use in similar contexts, which is associated with discerning performance impacts. Technology, and particularly mobile technologies, can be a major factor in improving decision making amongst health-care personnel, cost cutting, and improved safety, but only if these applications are well designed and properly used. Thus, the study provides a template for factors to consider during systems design and implementation that is a richer conceptualization of fit demonstrating the influence of human nature as described by evolutionary psychology tenets. Much can be learned from applying this frame and this study adds to the call of the community to continue theorizing about the role of evolutionary psychology in information systems research. In this chapter, we contribute by not only theorizing but also empirically testing basic tenets that contribute to a new approach to studying the relationships between human behavior and modern technologies.

Acknowledgments   This chapter is a revised version of an article by the authors, published in 2009 volume 46, issue 3, pp. 634–647, of the journal *Decision Support Systems*. The authors would like to thank the individuals and organizations that participated in the study for their time and support. They would also like to thank Dr. Ned Kock, for suggestions for improvement of this chapter.

References

Abraham C, Watson R, Boudreau M-C, Goodhue D (2004) Patient care and safety at the frontlines: nurses' experiences with wireless computing, http://www-935.ibm.com/services/us/gbs/bus/pdf/chm_patientcarereport.pdf. Accessed 10 Jun 2009

Abraham C, Watson R, Boudreau M-C (2008) Ubiquitous access: on the front lines of patient care and safety. Commun ACM 51(6):95–99

Abraham C, Junglas I, Watson R, Boudreau M-C (2009) Studying the role of human nature in technology acceptance. Proceedings of the thirtieth international conference on information systems, Phoenix

Ajzen I (1991) The theory of planned behavior. Organ Behav Hum Decis Process 50:79–211

Ammenwerth E, Eichstadter R, Haux R (2001) A randomized evaluation of a computer-based nursing documentation system. Methods Inf Med 40:61–68

Ammenwerth E, Mansmann U, Iller C, Eichstadter R (2003) Factors affecting and affected by user acceptance of computer-based nursing documentation: results of a two year Study. J Am Med Inf Assoc 10:69–84

Andersen P, Lindgaard A, Prgomet M, Creswick N, Westbrook J (2009) Mobile and fixed computer use by doctors and nurses on hospital wards: multi-method study on the relationships between clinician role, clinical task, and device choice. J Med Internet Res 11(3):e32

Barley S (1990) Technology as an occasion for structuring: evidence from observation of CT scanners and the social order of radiology departments. Admin Sci Q 31:78–108

Bass J (2002) It's not just nurses anymore: Survey of three other health occupations that finds patient safety at risk due to understaffing. http://www.aft.org/press/2002/041102.html. Accessed 5 Feb 2009

Blumenthal D (2009) Stimulating the adoption of health information technology. New Eng J Med 360(15):1477–1479

Boudreau M-C, Gefen D, Straub, DW (2002) Validation in information systems research: a state-of-the-art assessment. MIS Q 25:1–16

Bove L (2006) Implementing a system with clinical transformation in mind. American nursing informatics association conference proceedings, Nashville

Breslin S, Greskovich W, Turisco F (2004) Wireless technology improves nursing workflow and communications. Comput Inform Nurs 22:275–281

Burghardt G (2009) Darwin's legacy to comparative psychology and ethology. Am Psychol 64(2):102–110

Burke P (2006) Identity change. Soc Psychol Q 69:81–96

Buss D (1995) Evolutionary psychology: a new paradigm for psychological science. Psychol Inquiry (6):1–30

Buss D (2004) Evolutionary psychology: the new science of the mind, 2nd edn. Allyn and Bacon, London

Buss D (2006) Evolution of aggression. In: Schaller M, Simpson J, Kenrick D (eds) Evolution and social psychology. Psychology Press, New York, pp 263–286

Buss D (2009) The great struggles of life: Darwin and the emergence of evolutionary psychology. Am Psychol 64(2):140–148

Chau P, Hu P (2002) Examining a model of information technology acceptance by individual professionals: an exploratory study. J Manage Inf Syst 18:191–229

Chin W (1998) Issues and opinions on structural equation modeling, MIS Q 22:vii–xvi

Compeau D, Higgins C (1995) Computer self-efficacy: development of a measure and initial test. MIS Q 19:189–211

Cosmides L, Tooby J (1994) Better than rational: evolutionary psychology and the invisible hand. Am Econ Rev 84(2):327–332

Cosmides L, Tooby J (2000) Evolutionary psychology and the emotions. In: Lewis M, Haviland-Jones JM (eds) Handbook of emotions, Guilford Press, New York, pp 91–115

Cosmides L, Tooby J, Barkow J (1992) Introduction: evolutionary psychology and conceptual integration. In: Barkow J, Cosmides L, Tooby J (eds) The adapted mind. Oxford University Press, New York, pp 3–15

Davern M (1996) When good fit is bad: the dynamics of perceived fit. Presented at proceedings of the 17th international conference on information systems, Cleveland

Dennis A, Wixom B, Vandenberg R (2001) Understanding fit and appropriation effects in group support systems via meta-analysis. MIS Q 25:167–193

DeSanctis G, Poole M (1994) Capturing the complexity in advanced technology use: adaptive structuration theory. Organ Sci 5:121–147

Dewsbury D (2009) Charles Darwin and psychology at the bicentennial and sesquicentennial: an introduction. Am Psychol 64(2):67–74

Dishaw M, Strong D (1998) Supporting software maintenance with software engineering tools: a computed task–technology fit analysis. J Syst Softw 44:107–121

Dishaw M, Strong D (1999) Extending the technology acceptance model with task technology fit constructs. Inf Manage 36:9–22

Ebel R (1974) And still the dryads linger. Am Psychol 29:485–492

Farrell A (2005) Nurses neglecting mobile IT, health data management. http://www.healthdata management.com/news/10601-1.html?type=printer_friendly. Accessed 16 Feb 2005

Festinger L (1957) A theory of cognitive dissonance. Evanston Row, Peterson and Company, Illinois

Fishbein M, Ajzen I (1975) Belief, attitude, intention, and behavior: an introduction to theory and research. Addison-Wesley, Reading

Fornell C, Larcker D (1981) Evaluating structural equations models with unobservable variables and measurement error. J Market Res 18:39–50

Galbraith J (1973) Organizational design: an information processing view. Addison-Wesley, Reading

Garritty C, Emam K (2006) Who's using PDAs? Estimates of PDA use by health care providers: a systematic review of surveys. J Med Internet Res 8:e7

Gefen D, Straub DW, Boudreau M-C (2000) Structural equation modeling and regression: guidelines for research practice. Commun Assoc Inf Syst 4(7):1–70

Geser H (2004) Towards a sociological theory of the mobile phone. http://socio.ch/mobile/ t_geser1.htm. Accessed 15 Mar 2009

Gibson J (1979) An ecological approach to visual perception. Lawrence Erlbaum and Associates, Hillsdale

Goodhue D (1995) Understanding user evaluations of information systems. Manage Sci 41:1827–1844

Goodhue D (1997) The model underlying the measurement of the impacts of the IIC on the End-User. J Am Soc Inf Sci 48:449–453

Goodhue D, Thompson R (1995) Task–technology fit and individual performance. MIS Q 19: 213–236

Goodhue D, Littlefield R, Straub DW (1997) The measurement of the impacts of the IIC on the end-users: the survey. J Am Soc Inf Sci 48:454–465

Gururajan R, Moloney C, Soar J (2005) Challenges for implementing wireless hand held technology in health care: views from selected Queensland nurses. J Telemed Telecare 11:37–38

Hantula DA, Brockman DD, Smith CL (2008) Online shopping as foraging: the effects of increasing delays on purchase and patch residence. IEEE Trans Prof Commun 51:147–154.

Harris B (1990) Becoming de-professionalized: one aspect of the staff nurse's perspective on computerized nursing care plans. J Adv Nurs Sci 13: 63–74

Henderson J, Venkatraman N (1992) Strategic alignment: a model for organizational transformation through information technology. In: Kocham TA, Useem M (eds) Transforming organizations. Oxford University Press, New York

Hess U, Pascal Y (2009) Darwin and emotion expression. Am Psychol 64(2):120–128

Hogg M, Cox A, Keeling K (2000) The impact of self-monitoring on image congruence and product/brand evaluation. Eur J Market 34:641–666

Hubona G, Shirah G (2006) The paleolithic stone age effect? Gender differences performing specific computer-generated spatial tasks. Int J Technol Hum Interact 2(2):24–46

Institute of Medicine (2000) To err is human. http://www.nap.edu/books/0309068371/html. Accessed 15 Mar 2009

Junglas I, Watson R (2003) U-commerce: an experimental investigation of ubiquity and uniqueness. ICIS 2003 Proceedings. Paper 35

Junglas I, Watson R (2006) The U-constructs: four information drives. Commun Assoc Inf Syst 17:569–592

Junglas I, Abraham C, Ives B (2009) Mobile technology at the frontlines of patient care: understanding fit and human drives in utilization decisions and performance. Decision Support Syst 46(3):634–647

Kaplan S (1992) Environmental preference in a knowledge-seeking, knowledge-using organism. In: Barkow J, Cosmides L, Tooby J (eds) The adapted mind. Oxford University Press, New York

Kenrick D, Schaller M, Simpson J (2006) Evolution is the new cognition. In: Schaller M, Simpson J, Kenrick D (eds) Frontiers of social psychology: evolution and social psychology. Psychology Press, New York, pp 1–14

Kock N (2004) The psychobiological model: towards a new theory of computer-mediated communication based on Darwinian evolution. Organ Sci 15(3):327–348

Kock N (2005) Media richness or media naturalness? The evolution of our biological communication apparatus and its influence on our behavior toward e-communication tools. IEEE Trans Prof Commun 48(2):117–130

Kock N (2009) Information systems theorizing based on evolutionary psychology: an interdisciplinary review and theory integration framework. MIS Q 33(2):395–412

Krogsie J, Lyytinen K, Opdahl A, Pernici B, Siau K, Smolander K (2004) Research areas and challenges for mobile information systems. Int J Mobile Commun 2:220–234

Lawrence P, Nohria N (2002) Driven: how human nature shapes our choices. Jossey-Bass, San Francisco

Lyytinen K, Yoo Y (2002a) Issues and challenges in ubiquitous computing. Commun ACM 45: 63–65

Lyytinen K, Yoo Y (2002b) Research commentary: the next wave of nomadic computing. Inf Syst Res 13:377–388

March J, Simon H (1958) Organizations. Wiley, New York

Martins H, Jones M (2005a) Mobility in the rounds: use of wireless laptop PCs in clinical ward rounds. In: Sorenson C, Yoo Y, Lyytinen K, Degross J (eds) Designing ubiquitous information environments: socio-technical issues and challenges. IFIP, New York

Martins H, Jones M (2005b) What's so different about mobile information communication technologies (MICTs) for clinical work practices? A review of selected pilot studies. Health Informatics J 11:123–134

Mintzberg H (1973) The nature of managerial work. Harper and Row, New York

Moore G, Benbasat I (1991) Development of an instrument to measure the perceptions of adopting an information technology innovation. Inf Syst Res 2:192–222

Newton C (1995) A study of nurses' attitudes and quality of documents in computer care planning. Nurs Stand 9(38):35–39

Nicholson N (1998) How hardwired is human behavior. Harv Bus Rev 76(4):134–47

Nohria N, Groysberg B, Lee L (2008) Employee motivation: a powerful new model. Harv Bus Rev 86(7):78–84

Pavlou P, Davis F, Dimoka A (2007) Neuro IS: the potential of cognitive neuroscience for information systems research. ICIS 2007 proceedings. Paper 122

Pinker S (2007) Toward a consilient study of literature. Philos Lit 31(1):162–178

Romano K (2006) Keynote address – improving the health of the nation: the promise of health information technology, American Nursing Informatics Association Conference proceedings, Nashville

Rusbult C, Van Lange P (2003) Interdependence, interaction, and relationships. Annu Rev Psychol 54:351–375

Ruth W (1993) Evolutionary psychology and rational–emotive theory: time to open the floodgates. J Rational–Emot Cogn Behav Ther 11(4):235–246

Sallas B, Lane S, Mathews R, Watkins T, Wiley-Patton S (2007) An iterative assessment approach to improve technology adoption and implementation decisions by Healthcare Managers. Taylor & Francis, Inc., Bristol

Shim J, Varshney U, Dekleva S, Nickerson R (2007) Wireless telecommunication issues: cell phone TV, wireless networks in disaster management, ubiquitous computing, and adoption of future wireless applications. Commun AIS 20:442–456

Shirani A (1999) Task and technology fit: a comparison of two technologies for synchronous and asynchronous group communication. Inf Manage 36:139–151

Spohn M (2005) Organization and leadership theory: an evolutionary, psychology perspective, J Evol Psychol 26(1–2):97–107

Strauss A, Corbin J (1998) Basics of qualitative research: grounded theory methods procedures and techniques, 2nd ed. Sage Publications, Inc., Thousand Oaks

Suddaby R (2006) What grounded theory is not. Acad Manage J 49:633–642

Sundie J, Cialdini R, Griskevicius V, Kenrick D (2006) Evolutionary social influence. In: Evolutionary and social psychology. Psychology Press, New York, pp 287–316

Thompson J (1967) Organizations in action. McGraw-Hill, New York

Thompson R, Higgins C, Howell J (1991) Personal computing: toward a conceptual model of utilization. MIS Q 15:125–143

Tooby J, Cosmides L (2007) Evolutionary psychology, ecological rationality, and the unification of the behavioral sciences. Behav Brain Sci 30(1):42–43

Trivers R (1971) The evolution of reciprocal altruism. Q Rev Biol 46:35–57

Van Vugt M, Van Lange P (2006) The altruism puzzle: Psychological adaptation for prosocial behavior. In: Schaller M, Simpson J, Kenrick D (eds) Evolution and social psychology. Psychology Press, New York, pp 237–257

Varcoe C (1996) Disparagement of the nursing process: the new dogma? J Adv Nurs 23:120–125

Varshney U (2007) Pervasive healthcare and wireless health monitoring. Mobile Netw Appl 12:113–127

Venkatesh V, Morris M, Davis G, Davis F (2003) User acceptance of information technology: toward a unified view. MIS Q 27(3):425–478

Werts C, Linn R, Jöreskog K (2007) Interclass reliability estimates: testing structural assumptions. Educ Psychol Meas 34:25–33

Wilson E (2000) Sociobiology: the new synthesis. Belknap Press, Cambridge

Wilson E (2004) On human nature. Harvard University Press, Cambridge

Zigurs I, Buckland B (1998) A theory of task/technology fit and group support systems effectiveness. MIS Q 22:313–334

Zigurs I, Buckland B, Connolly J, Wilson E (1999) A test of task–technology fit theory for group support systems. Data Base Adv Inf Syst 30:34–50

Chapter 11
The Interaction of Communication Medium and Management Control Systems in the Processes and Outcomes of Transfer Price Negotiations

Penelope Sue Greenberg, Ralph H. Greenberg, and Sakthi Mahenthiran

Abstract Because organizations rely heavily on computer-mediated communication (CMC), it is important to understand the impact of interactions between CMC and the management control system on decision-making behavior and on organizational performance. Management control systems are composed of techniques used by managers to motivate employees to achieve the organization's strategic goals. Because CMC has been shown to impact behavior, CMC has the potential to either support or subvert the goals of the organization. This chapter shows, through the results of two laboratory experiments, that negotiating behavior using CMC leads to lower profits in a transfer pricing scenario. More importantly, this chapter then demonstrates that if organizations are aware of these consequences and design their management control systems using a fundamental concept from evolutionary psychology theory, they can mitigate some of the negative consequences.

Keywords Computer-mediated communication · Transfer pricing · Evolutionary psychology theory

P.S. Greenberg (✉)
School of Business Administration, Widener University, One University Place, Chester, PA 19013, USA
e-mail: psgreenberg@mail.widener.edu

R.H. Greenberg
The Fox School of Business, Temple University, 1801 Liacouras Walk, Philadelphia, PA 19122, USA
e-mail: ralph.greenberg@temple.edu

S. Mahenthiran
College of Business, Butler University, 4600 Sunset Ave., Indianapolis, IN 46208, USA
e-mail: smahenth@butler.edu

N. Kock (ed.), *Evolutionary Psychology and Information Systems Research*,
Integrated Series in Information Systems 24, DOI 10.1007/978-1-4419-6139-6_11,
© Springer Science+Business Media, LLC 2010

1 Introduction

Computer-mediated communication (CMC) is pervasive in organizations. The use of virtual collaboration, instant messaging, document sharing, teleconferencing, telecommuting, and other forms of CMC has been stimulated by lower technology costs, increased accessibility, and user-friendly applications. Network technology, electronic bulletin boards, and e-mail enable rapid exchange of information. Distributed databases and processing along with service-oriented architecture providing interfaces between previously incompatible systems allow processing at multiple locations. Teleconferencing, group decision support systems, and electronic brainstorming systems are being used for idea generation, consensus development, problem solving, coordination, and negotiation. With these varied and versatile capabilities, computer-mediated communication (CMC) technologies possess vast potential that is changing the way in which organizations operate and communicate.

Management control systems are designed to gather and use information to coordinate planning and control decisions throughout the organization. They are intended to guide the behavior of employees and lead them to make decisions congruent with the strategic objectives of the organization. Because many types of CMC technologies have the capability to structure interactions and to capture the contents of the communication, they are often viewed as an integral aspect of control systems.

But the unbridled deployment of CMC can lead to unexpected and undesired impacts on decision-making behavior and organizational performance (Baltes et al. 2002). Behavioral effects of information technologies can be predicted and understood based on a new paradigm that builds on evolutionary psychology (Kock 2004, 2005, 2009). For simplicity, we refer to this new paradigm, in this chapter, generally as "evolutionary psychology (EP) theory." EP theory provides a theoretical framework to explore the interaction of CMC with aspects of management control systems and to identify these impacts. Further, EP theory can guide the design or the re-design of their management control system to appropriately utilize today's communication media.

EP theory is concerned with human mental traits that are assumed to have evolved because they historically enhanced reproductive success. EP theory, when used to examine the level of naturalness of a communication medium, can explain why behavior differs when using different media. EP theory is used in this chapter to develop research questions concerning the main effects and interactions of communication medium with the management control system on the processes and outcomes of intra-organizational transfer price negotiations.

The need for transfer pricing occurs when the output (good or service) of one business unit (division) is an input or resource for another business unit. Because of the unique nature of some outputs, the two units often rely on negotiations to determine the price and quantity of the output to be transferred. Organizations use aspects of their management control system to motivate the transfer of the optimal quantity at the optimal price. The two aspects examined here are arbitration, a common technique for resolving conflict in negotiations, and the incentive pay scheme, which can encourage either competitive or cooperative behavior in the negotiators. The results from laboratory experiments provide evidence that EP can be used to predict the impact that the interaction of CMC with the management control system has on decision-making behavior and on the achievement of organizational goals. EP can also inform the design of a management control system to compensate for the increased cognitive effort required for CMC.

2 Research Background

2.1 Computer-Mediated Communication

The CMC literature has a rich history. It has been informed by theories that are primarily concerned with social aspects of communication, e.g., social presence and social influence, and by theories that are primarily concerned with technological aspects of communication, e.g., media richness and task–technology fit. While these theories recognize the social environment in which communication takes place, much of the empirical research has been concerned with the interaction between the technological aspects of the communication medium and the characteristics of the task (Fjermestad 2004). Myriad tasks (e.g., idea generation, problem solving, and consensus) and various aspects of the medium (e.g., synchronous, asynchronous, structured interactions, and support available) have been examined. The empirical results have been mixed on the relative benefits of CMC versus face-to-face communication (Fjermestad and Hiltz 1998/1999, Baltes et al. 2002, Huang and Zhang 2004). But it is widely accepted that communication medium impacts behavior and outcomes.

More recently, CMC research has been informed by a new theory, EP theory, which not only integrates many aspects of both types of previous theories but also seeks to understand the underlying cognitive processes that lead to differing behaviors (Kock 2004, 2005, 2009). EP theory, exemplified by the media naturalness or psychobiological theory, proposes that there is a negative causal association between the naturalness of a CMC medium and the cognitive effort required for the person using the medium. Media naturalness is based on similarities of a medium to face-to-face communication. The less similar the interactions using a medium are to face-to-face interactions, the more the cognitive effort that is required. Instead of attempting to negate previous theories, EP integrates them and uses the amount of cognitive effort as the reason why face-to-face communication and CMC can lead to different outcomes. The focus is on the cognitive effort required by the difference between "natural" medium (face-to-face) and leaner or richer CMC mediums.

This chapter examines a particular type of task, transfer price negotiations, and develops research questions based on EP theory concerning the interactions between the communication medium and aspects of the management control system.

2.2 Transfer Price Negotiations

Negotiation situations are an interesting task to examine in an organizational setting because the outcomes are of interest not only to the negotiators (managers of the business units) but also to financial stakeholders in the organization. The quantity of the output transferred determines the organization's total profit from the transfer. If the optimal quantity is transferred, the profit to the organization will be maximized, giving the largest profit to be divided between units. The price determines how much of the total profit goes to each of the units. Profit is one measure frequently used for performance evaluation of business units. Thus the organization also has a stake in both the quantity and the price (Solomons 1965; Chalos and Haka 1990; Barkhi et al. 2004; Greenberg et al. 2008/2009).

The challenge to the organization is to design a management control system that balances the integrative and differentiating objectives of transfer pricing (Watson and Baumler 1975; Ackelsberg and Yukl 1979; Grabski 1985). The integrative objective is concerned with inducing both units to transfer the optimal quantity of the good or the service internally in order to achieve the desired economies of scope or scale and/or desirable non-financial benefits such as quality, lead time, or availability. The differentiating objective is primarily concerned with the need for the organization to evaluate the performance of each of the units separately. It is also concerned with maintaining the perceived autonomy of the unit managers. If successful, the management control system for transfer pricing can aid in achieving both objectives. Thus, transfer price negotiations are interesting as a decision-making process and important in organizational coordination and control.

2.3 Management Control Systems

In designing a management control system for transfers of goods or services between two units, a critical question is how to structure the relationship between self-interested, profit-seeking managers in a way that protects the organization's economic interests. The two aspects of the management control system examined in this chapter are arbitration and incentive pay scheme. Arbitration has long been recognized as a factor in the success of transfer pricing when negotiation is used to determine quantity and price. Spicer (1988, pp. 314–316) pointed out that one way to protect the overall economic interests of the firm, yet retain the profit center structure and a measure of divisional autonomy, is through the introduction of a provision for arbitration into the negotiating process. Arbitration that mandates the price and quantity of the transferred good or service can resolve conflicts or overcome impasses in the negotiation between units and serve as a balancing mechanism between the integrating and differentiating objectives of the organization. It can also guard against opportunistic behavior by one of the unit managers.

Incentives have also long been recognized as a factor in the success of a transfer pricing system. Grabski (1985) concluded that it appears that for transfer pricing to perform the integration process, the evaluation of managers must be based on corporate profits rather than division profits (p. 44). Spicer (1988) pointed out that to the extent that rewards of divisional managers are tied to joint (firm) profits, the greater will be the incentive for division managers to cooperate ... (p. 317). The incentive systems examined here are cooperative versus competitive incentive pay schemes.

Incentive schemes can be classified along a continuum from cooperative to competitive. Cooperation and competition refer to the interdependence between goals. With cooperative incentives, the achievement of one unit's goal is positively related to the achievement of the other unit's goal. In transfer pricing, cooperative incentives should lead managers to work together to reach the optimum quantity, which would achieve the goal of integration. With competitive incentives, the achievement of one unit's goal is negatively related to the achievement of another unit's goal. In transfer pricing, competitive incentives should lead managers to negotiate for the price which maximizes the unit's share of total profit, which would achieve the goal of differentiation. Incentives have been shown to affect behavior and to interact with some aspects of CMC such as information sharing (Ravenscroft and Haka 1996) and trust (Ferrin and Dirks 2003).

3 Theory Development and Hypotheses

3.1 Communication Medium

EP theory predicts that there is a negative causal association between the naturalness of a CMC medium and the cognitive effort required for the person using the medium. Media naturalness is based on similarities of a medium to face-to-face communication because, from an evolutionary perspective, we have been using it much longer than CMC. The less similar the CMC is to face-to-face communication, the more the cognitive effort that is required. EP posits that the amount of cognitive effort has the reason why face-to-face communication and CMC can lead to different behaviors and outcomes. The greater the difference between the "natural" medium (face-to-face) and the leaner or richer CMC mediums, the more the cognitive effort required.

Empirical results have shown that, in the absence of arbitration and incentives, face-to-face communication will be more effective than CMC (Mahenthiran et al. 1993). In a group inductive learning task, Daly (1993) found that although CMC was useful in the generation of solutions, CMC was not better than face-to-face communication for deciding among solutions. In a negotiated transfer pricing task with multiple products, Arunachalam and Dilla (1994) found that CMC led to lower outcomes including profit than did face-to-face communication. Stuhlmacher and Citera (2005), in a meta-analysis comparing face-to-face with CMC negotiations found that face-to-face negotiations were less hostile and resulted in higher profit than did CMC negotiations. The theoretical arguments and empirical results support the notion that CMC negotiations require more cognitive effort than do face-to-face negotiations. The increased cognitive effort reduces the effectiveness of negotiations, leading to lower profit. We hypothesize the following:

H1: *CMC negotiations will lead to lower organizational profit than will face-to-face negotiations.*

3.2 CMC and Arbitration

Here we extend the notion of required cognitive effort to two aspects of management control systems, arbitration, and incentive pay. In transfer price negotiations, arbitration mandates the price and quantity of the transferred good or service in order to overcome impasses between business units. If arbitration is not mandated, impasses result in no transfer, leaving the business units and the organization with zero profit from the transfer. If arbitration is not mandated, the ultimate transfer price and quantity are determined by the arbitration rules. We argue that managers will extend increased cognitive effort in the negotiation process when arbitration is not mandated in order to avoid zero profit. If arbitration is mandated, then less cognitive effort is required to earn a profit.

In designing a management control system for CMC negotiations, it may be possible to reduce the cognitive effort of the negotiators by using arbitration. This reduced cognitive effort could lead to increased profit over CMC negotiations without arbitration. We hypothesize the following:

H2: *Arbitration in CMC negotiations will lead to higher organizational profit than will no arbitration.*

3.3 CMC and Incentive Pay Scheme

In incentive pay schemes for negotiated transfer pricing, cooperative pay schemes encourage negotiators to work together to find the optimal price and quantity. Competitive schemes require the negotiators to predict how the trading partner will behave and to react to actual behavior while formulating their own negotiating strategy. We argue that managers will expend increased cognitive effort in the negotiation process when competitive incentive pay schemes are used. If cooperative incentive schemes are used, then less cognitive effort is required during the negotiation process.

In designing a management control system for CMC negotiations, it may be possible to reduce the cognitive effort of the negotiators by using cooperative incentive pay schemes. This reduced cognitive effort could lead to increased profit over CMC negotiations using competitive incentive. We hypothesize that the following:

H3: *Cooperative incentive pay schemes in CMC negotiations will lead to higher organizational profit than will competitive incentive pay schemes.*

4 Method

4.1 Negotiation Task

The experimental scenario had the manager of a buying unit and the manager of a selling unit involved in intrafirm bilateral negotiations for the transfer price and quantity of an intermediate good. The buying unit manager had the marginal revenue schedule for the resale prices of the goods, but did not have knowledge of the costs. The selling unit manager had only the marginal cost schedule for the acquisition costs of the goods. Thus, information asymmetry existed between the managers. The marginal revenue and cost schedules are depicted in Fig. 11.1 and were adopted from DeJong et al. (1989).

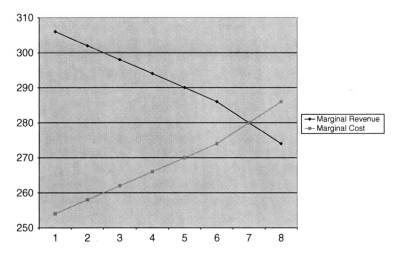

Fig. 11.1 Marginal revenue and marginal cost curves

The optimal quantity was seven units exchanged, which would yield an optimal profit of $280 for the organization. Using marginal revenue and marginal cost functions is useful for experimental purposes because an economic optimal (profit maximizing) quantity can be determined, allowing results to be objective, as opposed to subjective measures of success.

The negotiation support system provided structured interactions in both face-to-face and CMC negotiations. Structuring the interactions has been shown to improve negotiation processes and outcomes.

4.2 Experimental Design

Experiment 1 had a 2 × 2 design with communication medium and arbitration treatments. The two mediums were face-to-face negotiations and CMC negotiations.

Communication in the face-to-face medium followed a similar structured format as in the CMC medium. The structure of the negotiations is described below in Sect. 4.3.

The two levels of arbitration were no arbitration available versus mandatory arbitration if an impasse was reached in the negotiations. Under the "no arbitration available" treatment, if negotiators did not reach an agreement at the end of six rounds (three offer schedules from each negotiator), they were considered to be at an impasse for that period, and no transfer took place. Thus, there were no trading profits for either negotiator for that period.

Under the "mandatory arbitration" treatment, if negotiators did not reach an agreement at the end of six rounds, the arbitration procedures were automatically implemented. These procedures, which are described in detail in the next section, used the negotiators' offer schedules to attempt to determine a transfer price and quantity. Under arbitration, as opposed to mediation, the recommendations are binding. While the traditional transfer pricing literature deals with the problem of information asymmetry between negotiators by allowing an informed arbitrator (Hirshleifer 1956; Ronen & McKinney 1970), here the arbitration procedures rely on the information provided by the negotiators. The arbitration procedures did not rely on the marginal cost and revenue schedules, which are the negotiators' private information. Instead, the arbitration procedures are based on the offer schedules which contain the information communicated between the negotiators. Thus, the arbitration procedure does not reduce the information asymmetry between the negotiators, but only acts as a coordinating mechanism. Further, according to Carnevale and Isen (1986), for the negotiating parties to accept the arbitrated solution as their own, it has to be based on the negotiators' own offers.

In experiment 1, negotiators were paid a flat fee.

Experiment 2 had a 2 × 2 design with communication medium and incentive pay treatments. As in experiment 1, the two mediums were face-to-face negotiations and CMC negotiations. The structure of the negotiations is described below in Sect. 4.3.

The incentive pay scheme treatment had cooperative versus competitive incentive schemes. In both schemes, the divisions earned a trading income from the profits earned from the transfer pricing negotiations and a fixed income. The fixed income served to keep the subjects' cash remuneration from becoming negative in the event of a trading loss. The trading profit was determined by the quantity and the transfer price.

For buying divisions (retailers), the trading profit was the difference between the resale value of the goods and the negotiated amount paid to the seller. For selling divisions (manufacturers or wholesalers), the trading profit was the difference between the negotiated amount received from the buyer and the cost incurred in producing or acquiring the goods.

Under the cooperative pay scheme, negotiators earned 1% of their own division's fixed income plus 1% of one-half of the organization's trading profit, which was determined by the quantity transferred. In the cooperative situation, the buying and selling divisions equally shared the profits from the transfer. This experimental treatment is intended to induce cooperative behavior in both the buyer and the seller.

In the competitive situation, subjects received 1% of their own division's profit, which was their fixed income, plus their division's trading profit from the transfer. In a cooperative situation, the buying and selling division managers received 1% of one-half of the combined profits of both divisions plus 1% of the fixed income.

4.3 Experimental Sequence

One hundred and forty-eight undergraduate students enrolled in accounting information systems and cost accounting classes served as voluntary participants. Subjects were screened prior to the experimental session based on their responses to a utility preference elicitation question. The question was adopted from Greenberg, Greenberg and Mahenthiran (2008/2009) and required the probability assessment for a lottery that stated "If we were willing to give you $5 for certain, or a gamble that pays $10 with probability p or $0 with probability $(1-p)$, what would p have to be so that you are indifferent between receiving the $5 for certain and taking the gamble?" Subjects were assigned a time slot with other subjects who had approximately the same p value. This initial procedure attempted to ensure that participants were paired with trading partners having similar risk preferences.

Time slots were randomly assigned to experiment 1 or experiment 2 and, within each time slot, subjects were randomly assigned to the buyer or the seller position, yielding 73 dyads. Each subject participated in only one set of conditions (experiment 1: face-to-face, arbitration; face-to-face, no arbitration, CMC, arbitration; CMC, no arbitration; experiment 2: face-to-face, cooperative incentive; face-to-face, competitive incentive; CMC, cooperative incentive; CMC, competitive incentive) for the entire experiment.

All participants were given training to ensure that they understood the negotiation and, for experiment 1, the reward process. Subjects in both mediums had to correctly complete the practice calculations before the experiment began. If practice calculations were not correct, oral explanations were given, and the subjects were required to rework the calculations. No subject was allowed to proceed with the experiment until they demonstrated an understanding of the appropriate marginal cost/revenue curve, the negotiation procedures, the business unit profit calculations, and, for experiment 1, the remuneration calculations. We used training rather than ex-post manipulation checks to ensure that subjects understood the experimental procedures and the arbitrations and incentive treatments. We did this because the experiments were costly in terms of money and time to both the experimenters and the participants. Gateway conditions based on training assure that subjects understand the experiment procedures.

The negotiations in both experiments took place over 10 trading periods. Each period lasted up to 12 min. In the CMC condition, the 12 min were divided into six rounds in which the buyer and the seller alternately had an opportunity to accept offers or reject the trading partner's offer and submit their own offers to the trading partner. Offers were made in the form of price and quantity schedules. The schedules contained the quantities available for transfer, i.e., one through eight units. The negotiators listed the average price they were willing to accept for each quantity. The price and quantity schedules were the only information communicated other than acceptance of an offer. The first round of the first period began with the seller entering the prices for each quantity on offer schedule based on the marginal production cost schedule. A 2-min limit was imposed for preparing the schedules. Tripp and Sondak (1992, p. 276) point out that insufficient time to negotiate might lead to uniformly high impasse rates. The pilot had indicated that 2 min was sufficient for each round and that six rounds were sufficient for each period.

In both the CMC and the face-to-face conditions, the seller made the first offer in the first round. The buyer made the first offer in the second round, and they continued to alternate for the remaining rounds. In the CMC condition the computer transmitted the offers. In the face-to-face condition, the participants exchanged written offers.

In the first round, the buyer had two options: (1) accept a given price and quantity combination, and an exchange would take place and the trading period ended or (2) reject all price and quantity combinations proposed by the seller and submit a schedule of price and quantity counter-offers to the seller. The seller then had two options: (1) accept a given price and quantity combination, and an exchange would take place and the trading period ended or (2) reject the buyer's combinations and prepare a new counter-offer schedule for the next round of negotiation. Trading periods ended either when an offer was accepted or at the end of six rounds of offers. If no agreement had been reached at the end of six rounds, the negotiators were considered to be at an impasse. In experiment 1, under arbitration, an impasse led to the implementation of the arbitration procedures, where the price and quantity to be transferred were determined by the arbitration rules. Under no arbitration, an impasse led to no goods transferred and organizational and division profits of zero.

At the end of each period, buyers and sellers in experiment 1 each calculated their division's trading profit, if any, for the period. Under the competitive incentive scheme, the subjects then added their fixed income to the trading profit and used the total divisional profit to calculate their actual cash earnings. Under the cooperative incentive scheme, the buyer and seller each reported their trading profit to the experimenter/computer, who equally divided the total trading profit between the divisions. The subjects then added their fixed income to their share of the trading profit and used that total to calculate their actual cash earnings.

The subsequent periods proceeded in the same sequence. The subjects did not know the number of periods in advance, so there should not have been end of game strategies. At the end of the 10 trading periods, subjects in experiment 1 calculated their total remuneration. The calculations were later audited. All participants were paid by mail. The experimental sessions took approximately 2 h.

5 Results

The optimal quantity of seven units had the highest organizational profit of $192. The average profit for each of the conditions in both experiments is presented in Table 11.1. The results from the ANOVA analyses are presented in Table 11.2.

Table 11.1 Descriptive statistics

	Face-to-face	CMC	Average
Experiment 1			
Arbitration	157.36	127.90	142.63
No Arbitration	139.17	113.84	126.51
Average	148.26	120.87	134.37
Experiment 2			
Cooperative	187.43	158.79	173.11
Competitive	181.56	145.82	163.69
Average	184.50	152.30	168.40

Table 11.2 ANOVA results

Source	df	ANOVA SS	Mean square	F	p
Experiment 1					
Medium	1	71549	71549	22.30	0.0001
Arbitration	1	995	995	0.31	0.56
Med*Arb	1	28684	28684	8.94	0.0031
Error	396	1270556	3208		
Experiment 2					
Medium	1	165640	165640	65.11	0.0001
Incentive	1	5571	5571	2.19	0.1467
Med*Inc	1	16053	16053	6.31	0.0103
Error	336	854784	2544		

Hypothesis 1 predicts that CMC negotiations will lead to lower organizational profit than will face-to-face negotiations. As shown in Table 11.1, in experiment 1, the average profit under CMC was $120.87 and under face-to-face communication was $148.26. In experiment 2, the average profit under CMC was $152.30 and under face-to-face communication was $184.50. As shown in Table 11.2, in both experiments the medium treatment was significant at the 0.0001 level. Thus hypothesis is supported; CMC has a negative impact on profit in this negotiated transfer pricing scenario.

Hypothesis 2 predicts that arbitration in CMC negotiations will lead to higher organizational profit than will no arbitration. As shown in Table 11.1, average profit under CMC and arbitration was $127.90, and under CMC and no arbitration was $113.84. As shown in Table 11.2, the interaction was significant at the 0.0031 level. Although arbitration does not bring profit up the average face-to-face level of $148.26, it does mitigate the negative impact of using CMC.

Hypothesis 3 predicts that cooperative incentive pay schemes in CMC negotiations will lead to higher organizational profit than will competitive incentive schemes. As shown in Table 11.1, average profit under CMC and cooperative incentives was $158.79 and under CMC and competitive incentives was $145.82. As shown in Table 11.2, the interaction was significant at the 0.0103 level. Although cooperative incentives do not bring profit up the average face-to-face level of $184.50, it does mitigate the negative impact of using CMC.

6 Conclusion

Based on the concept from EP theory that our CMC negotiations were cognitively more difficult than face-to-face negotiation, we hypothesized that profit would be lower using CMC rather than face-to-face. Participants assumed the role of buyers or sellers and then negotiated the price and quantity of the transferred goods. In both experiments, the organizational profit using CMC was significantly lower than profit using face-to-face negotiations.

We then theorized that, by using a fundamental concept from EP theory, cognitive difficulty, management control systems could be designed that would mitigate the impact of CMC. We argued that an arbitration policy that enforced transfers when negotiators came to an impasse would be cognitively less difficult than would negotiations without arbitration. In the first experiment, designing arbitration into the management control system led to higher profit when using CMC rather than no arbitration.

We also argued that cooperative incentive pay schemes would be cognitively less difficult than competitive incentives. In the second experiment, designing cooperative incentives into the management control system led to higher profit when using CMC rather than competitive incentives.

Our results support the idea that management control systems can be designed to mitigate the negative impact on profitability in negotiated transfer pricing. These results are also consistent with achieving the integrative goals of transfer pricing by motivating negotiators to make decisions that enhance organizational profit.

Acknowledgments This chapter uses data from experiments used for two articles by the same authors. One appeared in 1993 in volume 3, issue 4 of the journal *Accounting Management and Information Technologies*. The other appeared in 2008/2009 in volume 49, issue 2 of *Journal of Computer Information Systems*.

References

Ackelsberg R, Yukl G (1979) Negotiated transfer pricing and conflict resolution in organizations. Decis Sci 10(July):387–398

Arunachalam V, Dilla W (1994) Computer-mediated communication and structured interaction in transfer pricing negotiation. J Inf Syst 6(2):149–170

Baltes BB, Dickson MW, Sherman MP, Bauer CC, LaGanke JS (2002) Computer-mediated communication and group decision making: a meta-analysis. Organ Behav Hum Decis Process 87(1):156–179

Barkhi R, Jacob VS, Pirkul H (2004) The influence of communication mode and incentive structure on GDSS process and outcomes. Decis Support Syst 37:287–305

Carnevale PDJ, Isen AM (1986) The influence of positive affect and visual access on the discovery of integrative solutions in bilateral negotiation. Organ Behav Hum Decis Process 37:1–13

Chalos P, Haka S (1990) Transfer pricing under bilateral bargaining. Account Rev 65:624–641

Daly BA (1993) The influence of face-to-face versus computer-mediated communication channels on collective induction. Account Manag Inf Technol 3(1):1–22

DeJong DV, Forsythe R, Kim J-O, Uecker WC (1989) A laboratory investigation of alternative transfer pricing mechanisms, accounting. Organ Soc 14:41–64

Ferrin DL, Dirks KT (2003) The use of rewards to increase and decrease trust: mediating processes and differential effects. Organ Sci 14(1):18–31

Fjermestad J (2004) An analysis of communication mode in group support systems research. Decis Support Syst 37:239–263

Fjermestad J, Hiltz SR (1998/1999) An assessment of group support systems experimental research: methodology and results. J Manag Inf Syst 15(3):7–149

Grabski SV (1985) Transfer pricing in complex organizations: a review and integration of recent empirical and analytical research. J Account Lit 4:33–75

Greenberg RH, Greenberg PS, Mahenthiran S (2008/2009) Virtual transfer price negotiations: unintended interactions with incentive systems. J Comput Inf Syst 49(2):18–25

Hirshleifer J (1956) On the economics of transfer pricing. J Bus 29:172–184

Huang W, Zhang PZ (2004) An empirical investigation of the effects of GSS and group process on group outcome in small group decision-makings. J Comput Inf Syst 45(1):23–29

Kock N (2004) The psychobiological model: towards a new theory of computer-mediated communication based on Darwinian evolution. Organ Sci 15(3):327–348

Kock N (2005) Media richness or media naturalness? The evolution of our biological communication apparatus and its influence on our behavior towards e-communication Tools. IEEE Trans Prof Commun 48(2):117–130

Kock N (2009) Information systems theorizing based on evolutionary psychology: an interdisciplinary review and theory integration framework. MIS Q 33(2):395–418

Mahenthiran S, Greenberg PS Greenberg RH (1993) The impact of computer-mediated communication on the processes and outcomes of negotiated transfer pricing. Account Manag Inf Technol 3(4):229–248

Ravenscroft S, Haka S (1996) Incentive plans and opportunities for information sharing. Behav Res Account 8:114–121

Ronen J, McKinney G (1970) Transfer pricing for divisional autonomy. J Account Res 8:99–112

Solomons D (1965) Divisional performance: measurement and control. Richard D. Irwin, Inc., Homewood

Spicer BH (1988) Towards an organizational theory of the transfer pricing process. Account Organ Soc 13:303–322

Stuhlmacher AF, Citera M (2005) Hostile behavior and profit in virtual negotiation: a meta-analysis. J Bus Psychol 20(1):69–93

Tripp TM, Sondak H (1992) An evaluation of dependent variables in experimental negotiation studies: impasse rates and Pareto efficiency. Organ Behav Hum Decis Process 51:273–295

Watson DJH, Baumler JV (1975) Transfer pricing: a behavioral context. Account Rev 50:466–474

Chapter 12
A Research Model for Online Social Behavior Based on an Evolutionary, Social Psychological, and Technological Approach

Ahmed Y. Mahfouz, Antonis Theocharous, and Andreas G. Philaretou

Abstract This study represents an exploratory and quantitative investigation into online dating from evolutionary, psychological, and technological points of view. In the past decade, the relatively inexpensive availability of user-friendly, fast, and reliable Internet technology has appealed to millions of consumers who suddenly found themselves engrossed by this sensational medium of communication, information, consumerism, and service. The majority of Internet users tend to be either recreational or utilitarian oriented, using such medium for a wide variety of tasks ranging from corresponding with friends and significant others, information gathering, purchasing goods and services, and, increasingly so, seeking and securing suitable dating and marital partners. The following research questions constitute the driving force for the current investigation: What are the evolutionary and social psychological intricacies of online dating? What are the technological variants or dimensions that render the consumption of online dating services appealing to users? An online survey was administered to 247 subjects to explore these questions and determine the technological dimensions of virtual social interaction. Exploratory factor analysis was then conducted to analyze the data. Eight technological dimensions emerged as a result of the analysis and served as the basis for the study's technological perspective model of virtual social interactions.

A.Y. Mahfouz (✉)
Department of Management Information Systems, Prairie View A&M University, 1501 Harvey Rd #526, College Station, TX 77840, USA
e-mail: aymahfouz@pvamu.edu

A. Theocharous
Department of Hotel and Tourism Management, Cyprus University of Technology, Saripolou 2-8, 3036, Lemesos, Cyprus
e-mail: antonis.theocharous@cut.ac.cy

A.G. Philaretou
Department of Social & Behavioral Sciences, European University Cyprus (formerly Cyprus College), 6 Diogenes Street, Engomi; PO Box 22006, 1516, Nicosia, Cyprus
e-mail: aphilare@hotmail.com

N. Kock (ed.), *Evolutionary Psychology and Information Systems Research*,
Integrated Series in Information Systems 24, DOI 10.1007/978-1-4419-6139-6_12,
© Springer Science+Business Media, LLC 2010

Keywords Online dating · Virtual environment · Evolutionary psychology · Experience · Social interaction

1 Introduction

From online shopping to electronic bill pay to booking travel and lodging all the way to online dating, we, as individuals living in the twenty-first century, are becoming increasingly identified by online usernames, passwords, and code names (Lohse 1998). Even though there does exist a lag between technology and culture, the sudden availability of inexpensive, fast, reliable, and user-friendly personal computers and Internet technology to mainstream consumers has changed our lives drastically and possibly irreversibly (Chen et al. 1999). From the occasional to the everyday online user lies a spectrum along which we all find ourselves.

The current investigation attempts to identify the technological and social psychological variants of online dating by providing an exploratory and quantitative analysis of the conceptual intricacies of this virtual medium of interpersonal attraction. The resulting theorizations and conceptualizations are based on the detailed and methodical distilling of literature compiled and analyzed from various studies in the fields of management information systems, psychology, and social psychology, as well as the administration of an online survey to 247 subjects to determine several technological factors related to online dating, based on exploratory factor analysis. Results are contextually situated within the overarching umbrella of evolutionary psychology and contested in terms of their future viability and applicability.

It is noteworthy to mention that the treatment of evolution of dating in this present study refers to dating as a form of cultural and social evolution, and not a mimetic one, consistent with relevant work involving natural selection and mathematical formalizations of the evolution of behavioral patterns (Kock 2009; McElreath and Boyd 2007).

2 Evolutionary and Social Psychological Perspectives

Evolutionary psychology is a broad topic concerned primarily with the study of mind and behavior (Buss 1995, 2003, 2004; Buss and Schmitt, 1993; Cosmides and Tooby 1987; Crawford and Krebs 1998; Jones 1999; Simpson and Kenrick 1997). Evolutionary psychology could be conceptualized in terms of evolutionary theory (Alexander 1989; Buss 1999, 1995; Caporael 1997, 2001; Depew and Weber 1996; Lewin 1998; Richards 1987), sociobiology (Brewer and Caporael 1990; Crawford and Anderson 1989; Crawford et al. 1987; Kaye 1986; Kitcher 1985; Wilson 1975), inclusive fitness theory (Buss 1995; Caporael 2001; Cosmides and Tooby 1987; Crawford and Krebs 1998; Hamilton 1964; Simpson and Kenrick 1997), and general selection theories (Campbell 1997; Cziko 1995; Darwin 1965; Donald 1991).

Natural selection constitutes a powerful driving force that ensures the survival and success of living things. However, the principles of evolution do not necessarily have to be applied to biological entities but could also be applied to social psychological processes, such as those of interpersonal attraction in mate selection. In fact, in the past several decades, the evolutionary psychological perspective on interpersonal attraction and mate selection has gained increased attention and postulates that cross-culturally, human beings are governed by principles of attraction and mate selection that prioritize the conception, birth, and survival of their offspring. Evolutionary psychology, thus, utilizes principles of biological evolution and natural selection to understand human social behaviors.

Evolutionary or Darwinian-based theories are determined by three interacting principles of change, primarily those of variation, selection, and retention (Caporael 2001). In the social psychological process of interpersonal attraction and mate selection, variation is defined in terms of getting oneself exposed to a pool of available mates, either directly – in face-to-face interaction settings, such as those of work, school, and leisure – or virtually, through an artificial/symbolic medium, such as online dating. The process of successfully selecting an appropriate partner, from the large number that is available in either a natural or a virtual setting, takes place through the learning of courting mechanisms, through various socialization processes, in order to maximize rewards and mate's level of physical attractiveness and, in the case of online dating, to capitalize on the many advantages offered by virtual nearness. Finally, retention refers to the initiation of viable strategies for ensuring the successful carrying out of the dating process, first virtually – by capitalizing on the many advantages offered by virtual nearness – and then in face-to-face interactions. The ultimate purpose of retention is long-term commitment in the form of marital union.

2.1 Rewards and Physical Attractiveness

Humans, being social beings, are drawn to each other and are motivated to initiate social contact for various reasons, primarily out of an innate need for affiliation. We often seek others for companionship, play, and commitment and tend to be drawn to different kinds of individuals. Exchange reward hypotheses postulate that we are also attracted to those individuals with whom a rewarding relationship, or the promise of one, exists (Byrne et al. 1986; Lott and Lott 1974). There are two kinds of rewards: (1) direct, such as attention, emotional/psychological support, money, status, power, information, material things, sex, and other valuable commodities; and (2) indirect, such as feeling good by associating with, or being in the company of, a person who is attractive, intelligent, or humorous (Brehm et al. 2005).

Just like other individuals involved in the dating scene, virtual dates are out to establish and maintain online contacts with others – through the creation and maintenance of personal profiles – by promising an immediate or a near-future rewarding relationship. However, a big part of the online dating process involves the modification of online personal profiles, which are sometimes intentionally or unintentionally falsified, thereby misleading other online daters as to the viability of a rewarding relationship or the extent of its potential reward.

Most individuals in most social settings respond more favorably to those who are viewed as physically attractive. One reason for the beauty bias is because most people find it rewarding to be in the company of physically attractive others. Such others are often perceived as more popular and socially skilled, even though this may not be so.

The technological sophistication of user-friendly Internet technology has rendered online dating a viable avenue for meeting potential romantic partners, especially through its utilization of an interactive user interface with high-quality photographic images and video clips. Through subscriptions to online dating services, virtual daters have the opportunity to not only create their customized Web sites but also upload their best pictures and video clips, thereby manipulating their projected level of physical attractiveness and appeal.

2.2 Evolution of Dating: Historical and Social Aspects

According to Donald (1991), there exist four major phases in the evolution of human cognition: (1) episodic culture, whereby memory is dependent on environmental cues; (2) mimetic culture, whereby the body is utilized as a medium for representation and memory; (3) mythic culture, where language development allows the construction, deconstruction, and reconstruction of narratives, which enable the expression of the fine intricacies of everyday human life, as well as the description of past and anticipation of future events; and (4) symbolic culture, characterized by hard and electronic copy storage manipulation of codified information as exemplified in the use of print and personal computers.

The evolution of the dating process could be traced through its developmental sequence, cross-cultural communicative competence, and culture-specific contexts in which dating could take on different meanings (Caporael 2001; Eibl-Eibesfeldt 1971, 1989). Hence, the dating process progresses from a relatively simple to a more complex state. Extrapolating Donald's (1991) categorization to the process of interpersonal attraction, dating, and social union formation, it can be argued that such process started out on a more temporal and instinctual basis as purely a reflection of individuals' instinctual concerns for sexual gratification, procreation, and pairing. Prehistoric hunting and gathering living was largely nomadic in nature and survival oriented. As such, the process of interpersonal mating developed on an episodic basis whereby individuals paired merely for the satisfaction of their instinctual drives (Gowdy 1998; Janicki 1998).

With the passage of time, however, and as stable agrarian-oriented cultures and societies evolved, episodic mating turned mimetic whereby the focus of attention evolved from the environment to the physical body and personhood. Agrarian living was more stable in terms of its physical locale, increased probabilities for individual survival and success, and, therefore, allowed more time for bodily concerns. Mimetic mating was primarily achieved through bodily representations, which took precedence over the much simplistic environmental concerns. For instance, individual mating was not indiscriminately determined based on the environmental availability of mates but rather was organized around ritualistic practices, involving elaborate props, dance, body paints, costumes, and artifacts. Such mating ceremonial practices were, in turn, encoded in memory and intergenerationally transmitted. This can be thought of as the beginning of the evolution of the culture of mating and the ancestor of contemporary dating (Donald 1991; Griffiths and Gray 1994; Janicki 1998).

Prototypical mimetic agrarian cultures evolved to mythic kingdoms, empires, and civilizations, which culminated in the evolution of highly complex industrial societies organized around an elaborate division of labor. The primary determinant of such mythic societies was predicated on the social construction of highly sophisticated communicative systems of shared meanings known as languages (Deacon 1997). Such written and oral language systems of shared meaning allowed not only the systematization of cultural processes, such as mating, marriage, and family, but also, and more importantly, their codification in narratives, which were continually defined, redefined, and transmitted from one generation to the next. The evolution of detailed cultural systems of mores, norms, and folkways provided an array of proscriptions and prescriptions concerning all matters related to interpersonal relationships in general and mating and dating in particular (Axelrod 1986; Brehm et al. 2005). For example, in the cases of the latter, various spoken and unspoken rules and regulations evolved, such as who, when, and how to date/marry, the intricacies of the marital ceremonial procession and contract, the nature of the couple's sexual repertoire, the birth and raising of children, inheritance rules, relationships with in-laws, relatives, and friends, etc. The mating, dating, and marital processes were no longer left to the probabilistic and environmental whims of physical presence/availability and satisfaction/satiation of instinctual drives (as in prehistoric episodic clans), neither were they left to the mere enactment and reproduction of simplistic rituals of the body (as in primitive mimetic tribes) but, instead, evolved to codified and highly regulated ritualistic systems that were constructed, deconstructed, and reconstructed through language (as in ancient and historic mythic cultures) (Donald 1991; Janicki 1998).

Mythic cultures and societies evolved to present-day postmodern postindustrial service-oriented symbolic cultures characterized by an almost exponential increase in both hard and electronic copy informative knowledge (Deacon 1997). The widespread and relatively inexpensive availability of reliable mechanical and electronic machinery and devices, coupled with the presence of effective and efficient transportation systems, reduced work hours, disposable income, and material comforts and luxuries, has significantly contributed to the evolution of highly individualistic pleasure-oriented cultures of painless problem resolution and short-term gratification. In such cultures, impersonal communication through such means as telephones, cell phones, text messages, e-mails, chat rooms, message boards, and webcams initially started out as viable tools to meet the demanding ends of fast-pace modern living. Such impersonal communicative avenues, however, evolved from being mere means to an end to an end in themselves, where individuals could satisfy their emotional and psychological needs for interpersonal relatedness and sexual desires virtually and sometimes even anonymously somewhere in on the Web. Here begins the evolution of the culture of online dating with technology as its major determinant (Donald 1991; Griffiths and Gray 1994; Janicki 1998).

3 Technological Perspectives

What are the technological variants or dimensions that render the consumption of online dating services appealing to users? To answer this question, a pilot study, followed by the present study, was undertaken. First, the pilot study was conducted with open-ended type questions to ascertain and categorize important technological factors that users deem important in online dating services. Based on the pilot, an online survey was then administered to 247 subjects to explore this question further along the technological dimensions of virtual social interaction. Exploratory factor analysis was then conducted to analyze the data. Eight technological dimensions emerged as a result of the analysis. A discussion of the analysis, including sample, questionnaire, reliability, validity, and the various dimensions, is outlined.

3.1 Sample and Questionnaire in the Study

The subjects of the study were undergraduate college students in a university. Each individual had basic Internet skills to be able to browse the Web. The sample consisted of 247 subjects. The sample was 59% female and 41% male, with ages ranging from 18–28 years old. An online questionnaire was given to each subject in a computer laboratory. The laboratory environment facilitated tighter control and reduced distractions and interruptions. The scales used in the study were taken from and based on Schmitt (1999) and Novak et al. (2000), following the results of the pilot study which pointed to mutual and relevant constructs of interest. Each item had a seven-point Likert scale, with the following anchors: 1, strongly disagree; 4, neutral; and 7, strongly agree. Any subject who has never visited a dating or an online social interaction site was dropped from the data. Hence, there were only 247 usable responses.

3.2 Statistical Reliability and Validity of the Study

Reliability is the extent to which an item, scale, or instrument will produce the same values when given in different times, places, or populations (Cronbach 1951;

Nunnally and Bernstein 1994). Internal consistency reliability is the degree to which individual scale items correlate with one another or with the entire scale (Nunnally and Bernstein 1994). A scale is internally consistent if each item in a scale measures the same concept or construct. The most widely used index of internal consistency reliability is Cronbach's (1951) alpha or coefficient alpha. A calculation of Cronbach's alpha was used to assess the reliability of the study. The conventional standard is that Cronbach's alpha should be 0.70 or higher for a scale to be considered reliable (Nunnally and Bernstein 1994). Cronbach's alpha for the present study was 0.83.

To ensure validity, the study used previously validated and reliable scales. The scales used in the study were taken from and based on Schmitt (1999) and Novak et al. (2000). Researchers should strive to use existing and already validated scales as much as possible (Straub et al. 2004). Moreover, exploratory factor analysis was used to interpret and categorize the variables, as well as ascertain construct validity (Kerlinger and Lee 2000). Construct validity deals with whether the variables are true constructs of the phenomenon under observation (Cook and Campbell 1979). In essence, validity assesses whether a study measures what it intends to measure through the operationalization of the variables (Kerlinger and Lee 2000).

Exploratory factor analysis with maximum likelihood extraction method with equamax rotation was used to assess construct validity. The criteria used in determining how many interpretable factors to retain are the scree test and highest contribution to the proportion for variance accounted for by a given factor. Related variables tend to group together under and load on the same factor. Within a retained factor, these variables or items in a scale are retained if the absolute value of their factor loadings is at least 0.50 or higher. Otherwise, an item or a question is dropped from the scale. In addition, two other criteria resulted in dropping items: items loading on a factor other than the original factor as reported in the scale from the literature or items (known as complex variables) loading on multiple factors simultaneously (a clear violation of criteria for validity; Straub et al. 2004). The variables or scale items that are retained after conducting factor analysis are shown in Appendix.

The interpretation of the factors, based on exploratory factor analysis, was consistent with the original scales on which they are based, as reported in the literature. Hence, the factors matched and corresponded to the factors in the original scales. For example, the first factor was interpreted as *sensory experience,* based on variables or scale items: Sn1 (engaging site for the senses), Sn2 (perceptually interesting site), and Sn3 (site lacking sensory appeal, a reverse-coded item), as shown in Appendix. The second factor was interpreted as *emotional experience*. Both factors are consistent in interpretation with Schmitt's (1999) scale. This was the case for the remainder of the scales: cognitive experience, behavioral experience, collaborative experience, multimedia, customization, and telepresence. A detailed discussion of the interpretation and meaning of each dimension is outlined below.

For a more logical grouping of the technological variables, the first five are grouped under two headings: virtual nearness experience (sensory, emotional, cognitive, behavioral, and collaborative experiences) and interactivity level (multimedia, customization, and telepresence).

3.3 Virtual Nearness Experience

Physical proximity or nearness constitutes an important factor in interpersonal attraction. In recent decades, with virtual interaction patterns gaining increasing importance, it is not unusual for individuals to attempt romantic connections through various non-traditional dating means, such as subscribing to online dating sites and using e-mail, chat rooms, and message boards. However, such avenues of virtual nearness require prospective dating partners to coordinate their online exchanges by being in the same place (near their computer) at the same time (Latane et al. 1995). In the online dating labyrinth, romantic partners are thus more likely to initiate and sustain online dating relationships with those message posters not only whose dating profile appeals to them but also who respond to their romantic invitations. An appealing but unresponsive online dater is of no use to anyone who wants to meet prospective dating partners on the Internet (Wallace 1999).

Virtual nearness tends to increase the frequency of contact between prospective online daters and, by extension, the degree of their exposure to one another. In turn, the more their online exposure, the more likely for them to exchange positive online dating interactions and evaluations (Bornstein 1989).

The online dating virtual nearness experience is defined in terms of the following: sensory, emotional, cognitive, behavioral, and collaborative or social identification with a group. The ultimate goal of such experience is to integrate all five of the aforementioned components into a holistic virtual nearness experience for the online user (Schmitt 1999, 2003).

Sensory online dating experiences include how a Web site engages the senses, as well as the extent to which it is perceptually interesting and appealing to virtual daters (Schmitt 1999, 2003). Such attributes result in high-quality sensory immersion, which is an important factor in virtual dating environments – other factors also include well-designed software and highly enthusiastic and interested online daters (Whitton 2003). For example, various online dating sites may provide an appealing online dating experience via the site (Schmitt 2003).

Emotional online dating experience has to do with the emotional aspect of online behavior. This includes how an online dating Web site aims at placing virtual daters in a certain mood, encourages them to respond in an emotional fashion, and appeals to their feelings (Schmitt 1999, 2003). Online daters' range of feelings can vary from being somewhat positive to real joy and excitement when they find themselves interacting with a user-friendly pleasing Web site and its product/service offerings. Restrictive or user-unfriendly Web site navigation results in negative emotions and reduces the likelihood of future site revisits (Dailey 2004). Therefore, emotional responses toward a Web site or a virtual environment, such as navigation enjoyment and convenience, are of outmost importance to virtual daters (Agrawal and Venkatesh 2002; Lee et al. 2003).

In a state of heightened concentration and joy during an online task, Web navigation results in increased user learning about site content, and in turn that learning leads to changes in online behavior, such as increased Web site visits (Skadberg and Kimmel 2004). Cognitive experiences, characterized by rich online interactions, engage online daters in creative and provocative ways. These experiences include how a Web site intrigues them, stimulates their curiosity, and appeals to their creative cognition and result in the elicitation of cognitive absorption and engagement in online daters (Agrawal and Venkatesh 2002; Schmitt 1999, 2003).

Behavioral experiences show users' alternatives to using or interacting with sites, including changes in lifestyles and behaviors (Schmitt 1999, 2003). Behavioral experiences include experiences outside the physical body, as in virtual reality or navigating a Web site that takes the online dater on a virtual dating experience. In terms of the interface, Li et al. (2001) define behavioral simulation as animation, spatial navigation, and social simulation as the process of using agents and avatars to interact with others.

Online communication is one of the major tenets of Internet experience (Kim et al. 2002). Collaborative experiences contain elements from the aforementioned experiences (sensory, emotional, cognitive, and collaborative) but expand to a broader perspective, beyond the individual user, to include a group or a community (Schmitt 1999, 2003). For example, this includes how an online dating Web site enables online daters to relate to and communicate with others through the Web site, such as via e-mail, discussion forums, chat rooms, instant messaging, and/or e-groups. These applications employ social simulation, which is online socialization using personas, agents, or avatars for communication purposes (Li et al. 2001).

3.4 Interactivity Level

In the case of online dating, interactivity with respect to digital media is the direct communication and involvement between users and an online dating system interface, in order to bring about some on-screen changes (Palmer 2002; Zhu and Kraemer 2002). Such changes can include bringing up the following: (a) personal profiles of all the online daters that subscribe to that particular site, (b) personal profiles of a restricted range of virtual daters accordingly depending on their initial tastes and preferences, and (c) different text, pictures, and video clips of the same virtual dater for closer inspection and final choosing. All of the aforementioned are done so as to meet the initial online dater's goal of finding a likable, viable, and suitable date.

In the present investigation, interactivity deals with high interactivity level, since such rich sites provide more stimulation and engagement to users (Coyle and Thorson 2001; Palmer 2002; Teo et al. 2003). Traditionally, interactivity is defined in terms of two levels: low and high. These two levels are categorized based on the following dimensions: multimedia (which includes textual and graphical elements, sound, video, and 3D capabilities in a Web site), customization, and telepresence. Low interactivity level is interactivity that utilizes only two elements that are fixed or static: multimedia textual and graphical elements (and no customization or telepresence). The textual element involves text descriptions of the personal profiles of online daters, such as static descriptions of their personal characteristics and attributes, whereas the graphical element includes the static descriptions of their various pictures and movie clips. Hence, the low interactivity level is low in terms of multimedia and has no customization options or telepresence. These latter three dimensions are associated with a high level of interactivity. The high interactivity level includes the low interactivity level elements of multimedia (textual and graphical) and expands beyond those elements to include richer multimedia (sound and video clips), customization, and telepresence.

E-commerce online dating companies recognize that higher levels of interactivity and content lead to a Web site's success (in terms of the number of subscribers and hits), as well as to higher levels of virtual users' perceived satisfaction, effectiveness, efficiency, value, and positive attitudes toward the Web site (Coyle and Thorson 2001; Palmer 2002; Teo et al. 2003). Hence, a highly interactive online dating user interface tends to enhance the online dating experience. Three aspects of high interactivity level of relevance and interest to this research are multimedia, customization, and telepresence. These were the variables interpreted from the factor analysis of the data.

Multimedia is the degree of media richness in a site, such as text, images, sound, video, and 3D simulations. Online daters perceive multimedia content to be important to a Web dating site's success. Dealing with how an environment conveys sensory data, multimedia helps to create a sense of presence (or being there in an environment) through breadth and depth (Steuer 1992). Sensory breadth is the amount and scope of information presented in a sensory dimension or channel at the same time, while depth is the resolution within the presentation of that information. Coyle and Thorson (2001) conclude that increased levels of multimedia, based on Steuer's (1992) definition of interactivity, result in more positive attitudes toward a Web site, more hits, and, therefore, more subscriptions. This constitutes the primary reason for the increased technological sophistication of online dating sites in recent years.

Customization is a very important user-centric function in a Web site's success that permits users to make unique interface changes to create individual user experiences through tailor-made products and services (Palmer 2002; Wind and Rangawamy 2001). Hence, the user, and not the Web site, is behind the choices and decisions – although in many cases these choices are generally made from a menu of possible selected options.

Customization includes custom-design products and the selection of different components and characteristics in a site (McKinney et al. 2002; Williams and Larson 2000). For example, many online dating sites allow customers to individually tailor the various aspects of their online personal profiles, according to their own tastes and dating preferences.

When users find themselves in a virtual dating environment, they may feel as if they are transported to a real-life dating scene with all its associated characteristics of front-stage/backstage behaviors and impression management techniques, a sensation known as telepresence (Goffman 1959, 1974; Steuer 1992). Since the senses of smell and taste are hard to simulate in a virtual environment, visual, auditory, and tactile simulations are the three senses that are utilized the most by online dating site creators to attract customers and increase their satisfaction. Tactile sensations can be induced via feelings of telepresence in a virtual dating environment, sensory substitution, or force feedback sensations against an input device, such as a joystick during a computer game (Sherman and Craig 2003).

Telepresence lends itself to another cognitive concept: body boundary. Body boundary describes how individuals see the limits of their physical body, and it spans two dimensions: location and permeability (Fisher 1986). The location refers to the boundary set by skin and outlines of body extremities, and permeability refers to barriers that prevent entry from outside elements. For example, these concepts underscore important issues in the online dating experience, such as the lack of tactile sensations against the skin of a potential dating partner (the actual feeling of touching someone) (Rosa and Malter 2003). However, the relative anonymity, convenience, and lack of embarrassment afforded by the online dating environment are important trade-offs that are worth forgoing some elements of reality.

While browsing the Internet, virtual daters may have sensations of time distortion, enjoyment, and heightened telepresence. Such heightened telepresence can, in turn, incite a flow experience, such as those immersive feelings users get when interacting with 3D games and simulations (Chen et al. 1999; Csikszentmihalyi 1975, 1990, 2000; Novak et al. 2003, 2000; Skadberg and Kimmel 2004). Losing oneself in the online dating labyrinth is an experiential activity whereby virtual daters become considerably taken by the flow of their romantic consciousnesses and sub-consciousnesses. Individuals who are regular subscribers to online dating sites report that they find themselves entering this state of heightened telepresence at peak moments of their browsing routine (Cooper 2002). In order to facilitate a sense of flow, online dating site creators go to great lengths to make their Web sites appealing, stimulating, and responsive to virtual daters.

3.5 Technological Perspective Model of Virtual Social Interactions

Based on the results of factor analysis of the online survey of 247 subjects and interpretation of the factors, the present study determined a model of eight dimensions, from a technological perspective for virtual social interactions that render the consumption of online dating services attractive to users. The dimensions were sensory experience, emotional experience, cognitive experience, behavioral experience, collaborative experience, multimedia capabilities of a Web site, Web site customization, and telepresence feelings induced while interacting with a dating site.

4 Conclusion

During the million-year long evolutionary period of the human species, interpersonal communication processes – both verbal, such as sounds and speech, and non-verbal, such as signs, facial expressions, and body language – have evolved in increasing complexity. For example, gradual refinement in interpersonal communication behavior had led to our ability to express thoughts facially, as well as to communicate symbolically through complex languaging systems of meaning of oral, written, and pictorial variety (Kock 2004).

The recent explosion in the symbolic use of the personal computer for initiating and sustaining effective and efficient interpersonal relationships may be also conceptualized as a sophisticated written and pictorial communicative means to our evolutionary end of emotional, psychological, and reproductive survival. For instance, online dating allows individuals to search for and secure emotionally and psychologically satisfying relationships with potential dating partners, thereby increasing their chances for reproductive survival.

Hence, the present study explored evolutionary, social psychological, and technological perspectives of virtual social interactions in terms of online dating. Based on the results of factor analysis of an online survey of 247 subjects, the present study determined a model of eight dimensions, from a technological perspective, that render the consumption of online dating services appealing to users. The dimensions were sensory experience, emotional experience, cognitive experience, behavioral experience, collaborative experience, multimedia capabilities of a Web site, Web site customization, and telepresence feelings induced while interacting with a dating site.

Furthermore, as personal computers (PCs) are becoming increasingly more technologically advanced and individuals more and more accustomed to their basic operations, we anticipate an even greater use of PCs for leisure and entertainment, as well as utilitarian activities. Recent advances in PC artificial intelligence, greater portability (afforded by larger battery capacities, smaller sizes, and more ergonomic structures), user-friendly software, faster processing, larger memories, higher quality in-screen images, etc. will ultimately lead to a new generation of "smart but also humane" computers with enhanced sensory, emotional, cognitive, behavioral, and collaborative features, which will better cater to the average person's social, psychological, material, and entertainment needs.

In fact, we anticipate that in the near future, there would not only be an exponential increase in both the quantity and the quality of virtual social interactions, made possible by the aforementioned PC technological advances, but, more importantly, also begin to emerge a new breed of "PC human surrogate machines," which, armed with sufficient and workable artificial intelligence features, will begin to perform many interactive functions previously reserved only for humans (Kurzweil 2000, 2006). In other words, PCs will act not only as just another technologically advanced medium of communication and interaction that brings people together by reducing physical distance, computes thousands of calculations, and executes hundreds of exchanges in only fractions of a second, seconds, or minutes but also as intelligent human-like entities with sufficient thinking, feeling, and acting capacity to mimic many of the functions an average human performs in the context of his/her personal and interpersonal life, such as providing social support and advice to others, keeping friendly company, acting as playmates, etc.

We are already witnessing the considerable breakthrough of PCs in the recent phenomenon of secondlife.com whereby although the person–computer interaction is still limited on the PC as a technologically advanced sensory, emotional, cognitive, behavioral, and collaborative medium – and not as the intelligent human surrogate entity mentioned above – still, the emotional, cognitive, psychological, and behavioral effects such an interaction has on those who aspire to it (as a "second life" and by extension as an escape valve from their personal lives to a make-believe world) are indeed tremendous. Consider the millions of individuals who have recently "plugged themselves into" the virtual world of second life and the millions more to do so in the near future. Therefore, we would argue the following: if second life has been having such an appeal and impact amongst individuals, imagine what "PC human surrogate machines" will do. Just like stem cell research, however, now is the time to begin pondering about all the controversies, legalities, and ethics that would be involved in the "PC human surrogate machine" debate.

Acknowledgments This chapter is a revised version of a journal article by Ahmed Y. Mahfouz, with Antonis Theocharous and Andreas G. Philaretou, published in 2008 in volume 24, issue 6 of the journal *Computers in Human Behavior*.

Appendix: Scales, Factors, and Factor Loadings of Items After Factor Analysis

Factor 1: Sensory
Sn1. The site tries to engage my senses (0.81).
Sn2. The site is perceptually interesting (0.76).
Sn3. The site lacks sensory appeal for me* (0.72).
Factor 2: Emotional
Em1. The site tries to put me in a certain mood (0.62).
Em2. The site makes me respond in an emotional manner (0.71).
Em3. The site does not try to appeal to feelings* (0.79).
Factor 3: Cognitive
Cg1. The site tries to intrigue me (0.69).
Cg2. The site stimulates my curiosity (0.70).
Cg3. The site does not try to appeal to my creative thinking* (0.73).
Factor 4: Behavioral
Bv1. The site tries to make me think about my lifestyle (0.67).
Bv2. The site reminds me of activities I can do (0.77).
Bv3. The site does not try to make me think about actions and behaviors* (0.73).
Factor 5: Collaborative
Cl1. The site tries to get me to think about relationships (0.76).
Cl2. I can relate to other people through this site (0.59).
Cl3. The site does not try to remind me of social rules and arrangements (0.74).
Factor 6: Multimedia
Mm1. This site provides good multimedia features (0.72).

Mm2. The site has pictures, sound, and video capabilities (0.73).

Mm3. The site does not provide adequate user interaction* (0.67).

Factor 7: Customization

Cu1. The site makes recommendations based on my specific search criteria (0.67).

Cu2. I feel I am a unique user when I interact with the site (0.78).

Cu3. I believe this site is not tailor-made to my needs* (0.56).

Factor 8: Telepresence

Tf1. I forget about my immediate surroundings when I use the site (0.59).

Tf2. In the site, I feel like I come back to the "real world" after a journey (0.63).

Tf3. I do not feel I am in a world created by the site I visit* (0.65).

Note: *, Reverse-coded

References

Agrawal R, Venkatesh V (2002) Assessing a firm's Web presence: a heuristic evaluation procedure for the measurement of usability. Inf Syst Res 13(4):168–186

Alexander RD (1989) Evolution of the human psyche. In: Mellars P, Stringer C (eds) The human revolution. Princeton University Press, Princeton, pp 455–513

Axelrod R (1986) An evolutionary approach to norms. Am Polit Sci Rev 80(4):1095–1111

Bornstein RF (1989) Exposure and affect: overview and meta-analysis of research, 1968–1987. Psychol Bull 106(2):265–289

Brewer MB, Caporael LR (1990) Selfish genes versus selfish people: sociobiology as origin myth. Motiv Emot 14(4):237–242

Brehm SS, Kassin S, Fein S (2005) Social psychology, 6th edn. Houghton Mifflin, New York

Buss DM (1995) Evolutionary psychology: a new paradigm for psychological science. Psychol Inquiry 6(1):1–30

Buss DM (1999) Evolutionary psychology. Allyn and Bacon, Boston

Buss DM (2003) The evolution of desire: strategies of human mating, rev. edn. Basic Books, New York

Buss DM (2004) Evolutionary psychology: the new science of the mind, 2nd edn. Allyn and Bacon, Boston

Buss DM, Schmitt DP (1993) Sexual strategies theory: an evolutionary perspective on human mating. Psychol Rev 100(2):204–232

Byrne D, Clore GL, Smeaton G (1986) The attraction hypothesis: do similar attitudes affect anything? J Person Soc Psychol 51(6):1167–1170

Campbell DT (1997) From evolutionary epistemology via selection theory to a sociology of scientific validity. Evol Cogn 3(1):5–38

Caporael LR (1997) The evolution of truly social cognition: the core configurations model. Pers Soc Psychol Rev 1(4):276–298

Caporael LR (2001) Evolutionary psychology: toward a unifying theory and a hybrid science. Annu Rev Psychol 52(1):607–628

Chen H, Wigand RT, Nilan MS (1999) Optimal experience of Web activities. Comput Hum Behav 15(5):585–608

Cook TD, Campbell DT (1979) Quasi-experimentation design and analysis issues for field settings. Houghton Mifflin Company, Boston

Cooper A (2002) Sex and the internet: a guidebook for clinicians. Brunner-Routledge, New York

Cosmides L, Tooby J. (1987) From evolution to behaviour: evolutionary psychology as the missing link. In: Dupre J (ed) The latest on the best: essays on evolution and optimality. MIT Press, Cambridge, pp 277–306

Coyle RJ, Thorson E (2001) The effects of progressive levels of interactivity and vividness in Web marketing sites. J Adv 30(3):65–77

Crawford CB, Anderson JL (1989) Sociobiology: an environmentalist discipline? Am Psychol 44(12):1449–1459

Crawford CB, Krebs DL (1998) Handbook of evolutionary psychology. Erlbaum, Mahwah

Crawford CB, Smith M, Krebs D (1987) Sociobiology and psychology. Erlbaum, Hillsdale

Cronbach LJ (1951) Coefficient alpha and the internal structure of tests. Psychometrika 16(3): 297–333

Csikszentmihalyi M (1975) Beyond boredom and anxiety: experiencing flow in work and play. Jossey-Bass, San Francisco

Csikszentmihalyi M (1990) Flow: the psychology of optimal experience. Harper and Row, New York

Csikszentmihalyi M (2000) Beyond boredom and anxiety: experiencing flow in work and play. Jossey-Bass, San Francisco

Cziko G (1995) Without miracles: universal selection theory and the second Darwinian revolution. MIT Press, Cambridge

Dailey L (2004) Navigational web atmospherics: explaining the influence of restrictive navigation cues. J Bus Res 57(7):795–803

Darwin C (1965) The expression of the emotions in man and animals. Chicago University Press, Chicago

Deacon TW (1997) The symbolic species: the co-evolution of language and the brain. Norton, New York

Depew DJ, Weber BH (1996) Darwinism evolving. MIT Press, Cambridge

Donald M (1991) Origins of the modern mind. Harvard University Press, Cambridge

Eibl-Eibesfeldt I (1971) Love and hate. Methuen, London

Eibl-Eibesfeldt I (1989) Human ecology. Aldine, New York

Fisher S (1986) Development and structure of the body image. Lawrence Erlbaum Associates, Hillsdale

Goffman E (1959) The presentation of self in everyday life. Doubleday, New York

Goffman E (1974) Stigma: notes on the management of spoiled identity. Jason Aronson, New York

Gowdy J (1998) Limited wants, unlimited means: a reader on hunter–gather economics and the environment. Island, Washington

Griffiths PE, Gray RD (1994) Developmental systems and evolutionary explanation. J Phil 91(6):277–304

Hamilton WD (1964) The genetical evolution of social behaviour (vols I and II). J Theor Biol 7(1):1–52

Janicki MG (1998) Evolutionary approaches to culture. In: Crawford C, Krebs DL (eds) Handbook of evolutionary psychology. Erlbaum, Mahwah, pp 163–207

Jones D (1999) Evolutionary psychology. Annu Rev Anthropol 28(1):553–575

Kaye HL (1986) The social meaning of modern biology: from social Darwinism to socio-biology. Yale University Press, New Haven

Kerlinger FN, Lee HB (2000) Foundations of behavioral research, 4th edn. Wadsworth Thomas Learning, Belmont

Kim J, Lee J, Han K, Lee M (2002) Business as buildings: metrics for the architectural quality of Internet businesses. Inf Syst Res 13(3):239–254

Kitcher P (1985) Valuing ambition: sociobiology and the quest for human nature. MIT Press, Cambridge

Kock N (2004) The psychobiological model: towards a new theory of computer-mediated communication based on Darwinian Evolution. Organ Sci 15(3):327–348

Kock N (2009) Information systems theorizing based on evolutionary psychology: an interdisciplinary review and theory integration framework. MIS Q 33(2):395–418

Kurzweil R (2000) The age of spiritual machines: when computers exceed human intelligence. Penguin Group, New York

Kurzweil R (2006) The singularity is near: when humans transcend biology. Penguin Group, New York

Latane B, Liu JH, Nowak A, Bonevento M, Zheng L (1995) Distance matters: physical space and social impact. Person Soc Psychol Bull 21(8):795–805

Lee J, Pi S, Kwok RC, Huynh MQ (2003) The contribution of commitment value in Internet commerce: an empirical investigation. J Assoc Inf Syst 4(2):39–62

Lewin R (1998) Principles of human evolution. Blackwell Science, Malden

Li H, Daugherty T, Biocca F (2001) Characteristics of virtual experience in electronic commerce: a protocol analysis. J Interact Market 15(3):13–30

Lohse GL (1998) Electronic shopping: the effect of customer interfaces on traffic and sales. Commun ACM 41(7):81–87

Lott AJ, Lott BE (1974) The role of reward in the formation of positive interpersonal attitudes. In: Huston TL (ed) Foundations of interpersonal attraction. Academic Press, New York, pp 171–189

McElreath R, Boyd R (2007) Mathematical models of social evolution: a guide for the perplexed. The University of Chicago Press, Chicago

McKinney V, Yoon K, Zahedi, F (2002) The measurement of Web-customer satisfaction: an expectation and disconfirmation approach. Inf Syst Res 13(3):296–315

Novak TP, Hoffman DL, Yung Y (2000) Measuring the customer experience in online environments: a structural modelling approach. Market Sci 19(1):22–42

Novak TP, Hoffman DL, Duhachek A (2003) The influence of global-directed and experiential activities on online flow experiences. J Consum Psychol 13(1/2):3–16

Nunnally JC, Bernstein IH (1994) Psychometric theory, 3rd edn. McGraw-Hill, New York

Palmer JW (2002) Web site usability, design, and performance metrics. Inf Syst Res 13(2):151–167

Richards RJ (1987) Darwin and the emergence of evolutionary theories of mind and behaviour. University of Chicago Press, Chicago

Rosa JA, Malter AJ (2003) E-(Embodied) knowledge and ecommerce: how physiological factors affect online sales of experiential products. J Consum Psychol 13(1/2):63–73

Schmitt BH (1999) Experiential marketing: How to get customers to sense, feel, think, act, and relate to your company and brands. The Free Press, New York

Schmitt BH (2003) Customer experience management: a revolutionary approach to connecting with your customers. Wiley, Hoboken

Sherman WR, Craig AB (2003) Understanding virtual reality: interface, application, and design. Morgan Kaufmann Publishers, San Francisco

Simpson JA, Kenrick DT (eds) (1997) Evolutionary social psychology. Erlbaum, Mahwah

Skadberg YX, Kimmel JR (2004) Visitors' flow experience while browsing a web site: its measurement, contributing factors, and consequences. Comput Hum Behav 20(3): 403–422

Steuer J (1992) Defining virtual reality: dimensions determining telepresence. J Commun 42(4):73–93

Straub DW, Boudreau M, Gefen D (2004) Validation guidelines for IS positivist research. Commun Assoc Inf Syst 13(24):380–427

Teo H, Oh L, Liu C, Wei K (2003) An empirical study of the effects of interactivity on Web user attitude. Int J Hum Comput Stud 58(3):281–305

Wallace P (1999) The psychology of the Internet. Cambridge University Press, New York

Whitton MC (2003) Making virtual environments compelling. Commun ACM 46(7):40–47

Williams T, Larson MJ (2000) Creating the ideal shopping experience: what consumers want in the physical and virtual store. Trustees of Indiana University-KPMG, Bloomington

Wilson EO (1975) Sociobiology. Harvard University Press, Cambridge

Wind J, Rangawamy A (2001) Customerization: the next revolution in mass customization. J Interact Market 15(1):13–32

Zhu K, Kraemer KL (2002) Ecommerce metrics for net-enabled organizations: assessing the value of ecommerce to firm performance in the manufacturing sector. Inf Syst Res 13(3):275–295

Part III
Emerging Issues and Debate

Chapter 13
Costly Traits and e-Collaboration: The Importance of Oral Speech in Electronic Knowledge Communication

Ned Kock

Abstract It is argued here that oral speech is a costly trait evolved by our human ancestors to enable effective knowledge communication. Costly traits are phenotypic traits that evolved in spite of imposing a fitness cost, often in the form of a survival handicap. In non-human animals, the classic example of costly trait is the peacock's train, used by males to signal good health to females. This chapter argues that, because oral speech is a costly trait, it should be a particularly strong determinant of knowledge communication performance, an effect that generally applies to e-collaborative tasks performed by modern humans. The effects of oral speech support in e-collaborative tasks are discussed based on empirical studies and shown to be consistent with the notion that oral speech is a costly trait. Specifically, it is shown that the use of e-collaboration technologies that suppress the ability to employ oral speech, when knowledge communication is attempted, leads to the two following negative outcomes: (a) a dramatic decrease in communication fluency and (b) a significant increase in communication ambiguity. These effects are particularly acute in e-collaborative tasks of short duration.

Keywords Human evolution · Costly traits · Handicap principle · Oral speech · Electronic communication · Electronic collaboration · Media naturalness · Compensatory adaptation

1 Introduction

One phenomenon that has often puzzled computer science and information systems researchers over the years, particularly researchers interested in e-collaboration issues, is the high importance of having an audio channel for communication in the

N. Kock (✉)
Division of International Business and Technology Studies, Texas A&M International University, 5201 University Boulevard, Laredo, TX 78041, USA
e-mail: nedkock@tamiu.edu

N. Kock (ed.), *Evolutionary Psychology and Information Systems Research*, Integrated Series in Information Systems 24, DOI 10.1007/978-1-4419-6139-6_13, © Springer Science+Business Media, LLC 2010

context of e-collaborative tasks (Graetz et al. 1998; Kock 2004; Kock and DeLuca 2007; Wainfan and Davis 2004). Whenever audio is available (e.g., teleconferencing, telephone conference calls, face-to-face meetings), tasks seem to be performed more easily and with fewer misunderstandings. Moreover, adding video to an already present audio channel typically adds little to the e-collaboration medium's ability to support group tasks (Burke and Aytes 2001). While this is not a universal phenomenon (see, e.g., Daly-Jones et al. 1998; Baker 2002), its frequent appearance in the empirical research literature merits a more robust theoretical analysis.

An evolutionary explanation of the importance of oral speech is proposed here, as a new theoretical contribution to the e-collaboration literature. It is argued that the high importance of oral speech is restricted to knowledge-intensive tasks. The reason for that, which is advanced in more detail in the subsequent sections, is that oral speech evolved among our hominid ancestors as a costly trait to enable efficient and effective knowledge communication.

As a costly trait, oral speech is analogous to the large train used by male peacocks to attract mates (often incorrectly called the peacock's tail). That is, like the male peacock's train, oral speech is (a) a survival handicap that only evolved because of its strong indirect effect on reproductive success, which counteracts its negative effect on survival, and (b) particularly important in the context of the task for which it evolved, namely communication of knowledge.

Finally, it is argued here that even in knowledge-intensive tasks, the negative effect caused by suppression of oral speech may be countered by compensatory adaptation, whereby individuals adapt their communicative behavior to overcome the limitations posed by the suppression of oral speech.

2 Costly Traits, Survival, Fitness, and the Handicap Principle

Costly traits are phenotypic traits that evolved in a species in spite of having a negative impact on survival performance (Gillespie 2004; Maynard Smith 1998; Rice 2004). Survival performance is the performance of an individual in the general task of survival, which can be measured by the age of the individual at the time of death. The older an individual of a species is, the more successful it is at surviving in spite of survival threats (e.g., disease, predators, and accidental falls).

Costly traits evolve because they have a positive impact on reproductive success (normally referred to as "fitness" by evolutionary biologists), generally measured as the number of surviving offspring or grand-offspring of an individual (Gillespie 2004; Hartl and Clark 2007). The positive impact on fitness results from the competing effects of a costly trait on (a) survival performance, a negative effect, and (b) a task performance attribute, a positive effect. The net effect of these competing effects on fitness is positive, leading to an increase in the frequency of the genotype associated with the costly trait in the species.

One example of task performance attribute that could lead to such a positive net effect on fitness is the number of lifetime copulations an individual participates in, a performance attribute associated with the task of mating. A classic example of costly trait that evolved due to having increased the number of lifetime copulations individuals possessing the trait participated in, which in turn offset the survival cost of that trait, is the male peacock's train (Maynard Smith and Harper 2003; Zahavi and Zahavi 1997). The male peacock's train is frequently referred to, incorrectly, as the peacock's tail (Petrie et al. 1991; Zahavi and Zahavi 1997). Both males and females in the peacock species have tails, but only males have the tail appendages known as trains.

Costly traits may also exist that have competing effects on survival, and that are unrelated to mating, through intermediate effects on other variables that themselves directly affect survival. For example, propensity toward aggressive behavior among our ancestors might have increased their chances of being the target of violent behavior by other individuals, which contributed to a decrease in survival, but might also have increased their access to nutritious food obtained through hunting (for which aggressiveness is important), which in turn contributed to an increase in survival. In this sense, propensity toward aggressive behavior might have evolved as a costly trait, where the positive indirect effect on survival, mediated by increased access to nutritious food, was stronger than the negative indirect effect on survival from attracting violent behavior (Boaz and Almquist 2001; Dobzhansky et al. 1977).

Costless traits are defined here as phenotypic traits that have no negative impact on survival performance. Most costless traits are actually associated with enhanced survival performance and may be observable indicators of unobservable underlying traits that enhance survival performance (Hamilton and Zuk 1982; Kokko et al. 2002). The ability of males of the fruit fly species *Drosophila subobscura* to engage in a rapid courtship dance with females is an example of trait that fits this definition (Maynard Smith and Harper 2003). Males increase their success at the task of mating by demonstrating to females that they possess the ability to dance vigorously in response to lead movements by the females. This trait is a costless trait because it has no negative impact on the survival success of males. In other words, the dance itself has no negative effect on the survival of males. The ability to dance is in fact positively correlated with survival performance, since it is an indicator of health.

The most widely cited theoretical framework in connection with the evolution of costly traits was proposed by Zahavi (1975), centered on what is known as the handicap principle (Walker 2008; Zahavi and Zahavi 1997). This framework is not only ingenious but also intuitively appealing. These qualities have led to its becoming widely used in research not only by evolutionary biologists (Hausken and Hirshleifer 2008) but also by researchers in relatively new disciplines that build on evolutionary ideas, such as evolutionary psychology (Griskevicius et al. 2007; Walker 2008).

The handicap principle focuses on costly traits used for signaling and is founded on the notion that those traits are honest indicators of the signalers' fitness. For example, the large train displayed by the males of the peacock species is a survival handicap, making them more vulnerable to predation (Maynard Smith and Harper 2003; Zahavi and Zahavi 1997). Thus males with large trains and who are still alive at the age of reproductive maturity also must possess other traits that make them particularly good at survival, such as vitality and speed. The tails are a reliable indicator of fitness, exactly because they are costly.

3 Costly Traits' Commonalities: Rarity, Late Evolution, and Strong Effects

The discussion presented here expands on and refines the handicap principle to cover any costly trait, in connection with the performance of any organism in any task that influences fitness, not only signaling tasks. Three key conclusions are reached, which are that costly traits should be rare in nature, generally evolve late, and be costly not to use. While these conclusions are consistent with the handicap principle, they allow for predictions and explanations that go well-beyond signaling tasks. As such, they provide the basis for the analysis of the evolution of oral speech and its importance in the task of knowledge communication.

Costly traits should be rare in nature: The survival handicaps imposed by costly traits create obstacles for their evolution, eventually making those traits significantly rarer in nature than costless traits. These obstacles can be seen as "thresholds" for the evolution of the traits, where the thresholds are proportional to the survival cost of the traits (Gillespie 2004; Hartl and Clark 2007; Maynard Smith and Harper 2003).

New traits (e.g., high intelligence, long legs, and slow fat metabolism) usually appear in populations of organisms as a result of random genetic mutations, a general rule that applies to all organisms, including our hominid ancestors (Hartl and Clark 2007; Boaz and Almquist 2001; Mayr 1976). Therefore, the effects of new traits on fitness are also random, whether those traits are costly or costless. Evolution is not an engineering process; it is a wasteful process of continuous tinkering, where the vast majority of new traits are in fact detrimental to fitness (Hartl and Clark 2007; Wilson 2000). Traits that have a positive net effect on fitness are far and few in between (McElreath and Boyd 2007; Wilson 2000).

Given that costly traits must overcome obstacles, or thresholds, to evolve in a species, fewer costly traits than costless traits are likely to evolve. That is, the probability of evolution of costly traits in any species is generally lower than that of costless traits. Moreover, the higher the cost of the trait, the lower the probability of evolution. Thus, costly traits should be rarer in nature than costless traits; the more costly, the rarer.

Costly traits should generally evolve late: Lower probability events tend to take longer to happen than higher probability events. For example, let us assume that two people, PA and PB, randomly throw darts on two walls, WA and WB, each with a total area of 100 square feet. Both people throw one dart every minute, each time hitting a random spot on WA or WB. Either person receives an award if a dart falls within a target area of only 50 square feet, for WA, and 10 square feet, for WB. The target areas are hidden; that is, both PA and PB are unaware of where their target areas are. This example is analogous to the evolution of new genetic traits, since genetic mutations are believed to appear largely at random in populations (Gillespie 2004; Hartl and Clark 2007).

Since the probability that PA will hit the target in each throw is 50%, which is higher than the 10% probability for PB, one can reasonably expect that PB will hit the target later than PA. Of course, it is possible that PB will hit the target in the first throw, but that is much less likely than PA hitting the target in the first throw. Analogously, since the probability of evolution of any costly trait is generally lower than that for a costless trait, with that probability decreasing with increases in the survival costs imposed by the costly trait, then it follows that costly traits should generally appear later in the evolutionary history of a species than costless traits.

Costly traits should be costly not to use: Costly traits must have had a strong effect on the performance of the task for which they evolved in order to make up for the survival costs imposed by those traits. Today this would translate into a higher correlation between costly traits' measures and performance attributes for the task than between costless traits' measures and the same task performance attributes. That is, not using a costly trait would be more costly, so to speak, than not using a costless trait in the context of the task for which the traits evolved.

The above conclusions seem to be true when we look at the classical example of costly trait, the peacock species. Petrie et al. (1991) found that the costly ornamental train of the male peacock, and especially the number of eyespots on the train, are far more attractive traits for the peahens than other apparently costless traits. Costless ornamental traits are more numerous in the peacock species than costly ones, of which the only known one is the train, and their relative importance in the context of the mating task is dwarfed by the importance of the train. Examples of costless ornamental traits likely evolved for mating in the male of the peacock species are the crest atop the male's head, the brightly colored feathers on the male's chest, various color patterns around the eyes, various feather patterns occurring in different parts of the male's body, and the level of bilateral (i.e., left–right) symmetry of these ornamentations (Darwin 1871; Zahavi and Zahavi 1997).

4 The Evolution of Oral Speech in Humans: A Costly Trait Associated with Choking and Illnesses

Modern oral speech was enabled by the evolution of a larynx located low in the neck (Lieberman 1998). The evolution of oral speech is one of the most important landmarks in the evolution of the human species, having happened relatively recently in our evolutionary history (see Fig. 13.1). However, the new larynx design also significantly increased our ancestors' chances of death by choking during ingestion of food and liquids and of suffering from various aerodigestive tract diseases such as gastroesophageal reflux (Laitman and Reidenberg 1997), among other survival-related problems. Oral speech must have been particularly important for effective communication in our evolutionary past, and effective communication must have

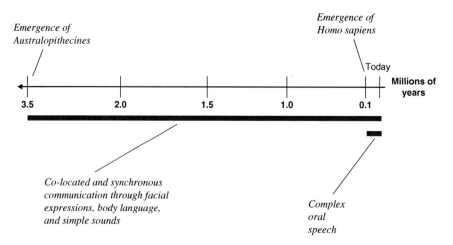

Fig. 13.1 The evolution of oral speech in humans

been important for fitness enhancement (Pinker 2003), otherwise its survival cost would have prevented complex speech from evolving.

Oral speech seems to exhibit the three common characteristics of costly traits. Oral speech is a rare costly trait among human traits involved in the transfer of communicative stimuli. By all accounts, it is the only such trait that obviously imposed a survival cost as it evolved among our ancestors. In addition to increasing our ancestors' chances of death by choking and of developing aerodigestive tract diseases, it also hampered our ancestors' ability to breathe while drinking water. Water sources are likely to have been a preferred site for predators to ambush prey (Boaz and Almquist 2001), as they are today, and the oxygen depletion caused by having to hold their breath while drinking created yet another survival cost for our ancestors. Other communication-related traits, such as the ability to use body language and facial expressions, do not seem to have imposed a similar survival handicap on our ancestors.

Oral speech also appeared late in the evolutionary history of hominids, in the last 100,000 years of that 3.5 million year history, or approximately the last 3% (Cartwright 2000; Laitman 1984; Lieberman 1998). This is consistent with it being a costly trait, since the evolution of a costly trait is a low probability event, and low probability events take more time to happen than high probability events. In fact, the evolution of oral speech coincides with the evolution of our species, *Homo sapiens*, likely from another species within the genus *Homo*, namely *Homo erectus* (Boaz and Almquist 2001; Lieberman 1998). Many human evolution researchers believe that it was the evolution of oral speech, with the complexity of human interactions that it enabled, that made us truly human (Cartwright 2000; Dunbar 1993; Lieberman 1998).

Finally, empirical research on the effects of electronic communication media that suppress the ability to use oral speech suggests that it is very costly not to use oral speech in communicative interactions. This is reflected in as much as a 10-fold reduction in communication fluency, coupled with a significant increase in communication ambiguity and perceived cognitive effort (Graetz et al. 1998; Kock 2005; Kock and DeLuca 2007; Kock et al. 2007; Simon 2006). Communication fluency is defined here as the number of ideas effectively conveyed per unit of time and has been somewhat imprecisely measured as the number of words conveyed per unit of time (Kock 2005; Kock and DeLuca 2007). It seems that, when oral speech is removed from a communication medium, communication becomes rather cumbersome (Crowston et al. 2007; Graetz et al. 1998; Kock 2005).

If the use of oral speech is enabled by an audio channel, adding a video channel typically has little impact on the effectiveness or ease with which communication takes place (Burke and Aytes 2001; Daly-Jones et al. 1998; Simon 2006). In this sense, oral speech could be seen to the communication task as analogous to what the peacock's train is to the mating task (Petrie et al. 1991); both are costly traits that have an effect that dwarfs the effects of other costless traits evolved in connection with the same task. There are exceptions to this general rule regarding the importance of a video channel (see, e.g., Daly-Jones et al. 1998), such as modern tasks in which shared and real-time visualization of an object or situation is important for the task completion. Examples would be a surgical intervention involving two or more geographically distributed doctors and a real-time collaborative design of a car engine.

5 Oral Speech and Knowledge Communication: Fitness Enhancement and Evolution

The notion that oral speech is particularly important in modern human communication, as discussed so far, needs further theoretical elaboration and refinement. Simple observation of modern human communication practices suggests that oral speech is not equally important for all types of communication interactions. For example, if one person is trying to communicate his/her home or work address to another, to be used on a letter, then probably an e-mail will be just as effective as a phone call. Also, web-based social communication tools that enable human interaction through short text messages and provide no audio channel, such as Twitter, would probably not be as successful as they are if the theoretical framework put forth here applied to all types of communicative interactions.

This takes us back to a review of why oral speech evolved in the first place. More specifically, how did oral speech affect fitness among our ancestors? As discussed earlier, only if oral speech had a net positive impact on fitness, by enhancing the performance of a fitness-relevant task, it would have overcome the survival handicap associated with our customized vocal tract. The answer is that oral speech enabled the exchange of knowledge among our ancestors, which indirectly increased their reproductive success by allowing them to occupy what Pinker (2003) refers to as the "cognitive niche."

A common characteristic of the simple exchanges illustrated above (communication of a home or work address and interaction through short text messages) is that these types of exchanges involve little or no knowledge transfer. Therefore, if we assume that oral speech was evolved by our ancestors primarily to enable the communication of knowledge, its effect should not be particularly strong in communication interactions with little or no knowledge content. There are other factors that may induce modern humans to communicate electronically through text only and with no audio – e.g., via e-mail without audio file attachments. Among those factors is the ease with which e-mail can be sent to many individuals at the same time. Video and audio blogs can be used for the same purpose, incorporating oral speech, but their use is still not as widespread and embedded in communication practices as is the use of e-mail.

Knowledge about "something" is defined here in a way analogous to how it is defined by many cognitive psychologists: as a set of mental schemas that allow one to predict the future or find out more about a present situation based on information about the present or the past (Gardner 1985; Kock 1999; Lee and Holyoak 2008; Waldmann et al. 1995). As noted by artificial intelligence researchers, with knowledge, one can build mental rules that can be expressed in the form of "if . . . then . . ." statements (Luger and Stubblefield 2008; Russel and Norvig 2002) or reworded as statements that contain linguistic elements that express causality such as "the reason for . . . is . . .," "this is . . . because . . .," and "the cause for . . . is . . ." (Kock 1999; Waldmann et al. 1995). For example, the statement "the temperature in room 118, where 100 people are attending a lecture, is now 78 degrees Fahrenheit" contains only information, whereas the following statement contains knowledge: "if the temperature in room 118 reaches 80 degrees Fahrenheit, most of the 100 people attending a lecture there will feel uncomfortable."

Our ancestors faced survival threats on a regular basis – exposure to pathogens, attacks by predators or territorial animals, encounters with venomous insects or snakes, and ingestion of toxins, among others. These events often occurred in specific contexts. For example, territorial animals would attack when their habitat was invaded by our ancestors and venomous insects and snakes occur in higher quantities in certain areas (Hung 2004; Kock et al. 2008; Manipady et al. 2006). Without the ability to vicariously obtain knowledge linking contexts with survival threats, our ancestors would have to experience the survival threats or observe someone experiencing them at a close distance, in order to build that knowledge. Oral speech enabled vicarious knowledge acquisition regarding survival threats, and thus significantly increased our ancestors' chances of survival, easily overcoming the extra survival costs associated with our vocal tract.

Costly traits evolved by our human ancestors must have had a strong effect on the performance of the task for which they evolved, in order to make up for the survival costs imposed by those traits. In the case of oral speech, a strong candidate for the task in question is the knowledge communication task, where oral speech evolved in part to increase the performance with which knowledge about survival threats was communicated among our ancestors. Oral speech may also have influenced fitness in other ways, although avoidance of survival threats must have been an important element in the selection of this costly trait. For example, vicarious knowledge about survival-enhancing elements, such as seasonal availability of food, was likely also enabled by oral speech (Cartwright 2000; Dunbar 1999). So probably was the ability to build social relationships and court potential mates (Dunbar 1993; Miller 2000, 2002). This type of knowledge communication likely required reciprocal altruism to have evolved before, which mathematical formalizations and empirical evidence strongly suggest was the case in the human species (Fletcher and Zwick 2007; Henrich 2004; McElreath and Boyd 2007; Trivers 2002).

Knowledge communication performance refers to both the effectiveness and efficiency with which knowledge is communicated (Kock 1999; Russel and Norvig 2002; Waldmann et al. 1995). Effective knowledge communication between two individuals occurs when the knowledge possessed by one individual is comprehensively and unambiguously conveyed to the other individual. Efficient knowledge communication occurs when the knowledge possessed by one individual is quickly and effortlessly conveyed to the other individual.

6 Oral Speech in e-Collaborative Tasks: The Effects on Communication Fluency and Ambiguity

It follows from the theoretical discussion presented in the previous section that removing the ability to convey speech from an electronic communication medium is likely to impair communication performance much more strongly than removing the medium's ability to convey other communicative stimuli – e.g., facial expressions, body language, olfactory cues, and tactile stimuli. However, this effect is moderated by the extent to which knowledge is being communicated. This conclusion is consistent with the results of various studies that compare the impact of various media on communication performance (Graetz et al. 1998; Kock 2004; Kock and DeLuca 2007).

Graetz et al. (1998) compared the performance in four-person groups across three communication media conditions: face-to-face, telephone conferencing, and electronic chat. The experimental task required exchange of knowledge to be successfully accomplished and the participants were given a limited amount of time (approximately 30 min) to review the information provided to them by the researchers and to discuss it with the other group members. Group outcome quality was about the same through the face-to-face and telephone conferencing media, slightly higher in the latter, a statistically insignificant difference. Group outcome quality was significantly lower through the electronic chat medium. Measures of perceived cognitive effort and frustration were about the same for the face-to-face and telephone conferencing media and significantly higher for the electronic chat medium. In summary, the medium that did not enable oral speech was the least conducive to effortless and unambiguously knowledge communication. This is consistent with the view that oral speech is a costly trait that is "costly not to use" in the context of knowledge communication.

Particularly noteworthy is the finding by Kock and DeLuca (2007), in a study of individuals in two different countries, that the use of an electronic communication medium that suppressed the ability to convey speech (a version of e-mail) dramatically reduced communication fluency. In this study, communication fluency was measured as the number of words conveyed per unit of time, a surrogate measure. The reduction in fluency observed by Kock and DeLuca (2007) was estimated to have been more than 10-fold; that is, e-mail users' fluency was less than 1/10 of their expected fluency communicating over the phone or face-to-face. This is too drastic a reduction to be explained by the known fact that typing is mechanically more cumbersome than speaking, which would normally lead to a twofold reduction in fluency (Kock 2004; McQueen et al. 1999). Again, it appears that our brain was designed by evolution to rely heavily on oral speech for effective and efficient knowledge communication, because oral speech was costly to evolve. As a result, it is costly not to use oral speech in modern human communication whenever a significant amount of knowledge must be exchanged.

7 Compensatory Adaptation as a Moderating Effect

A possible conclusion based on the arguments presented thus far is that a decrease in communication fluency and an increase in ambiguity, caused by the suppression of oral speech in an electronic medium, may lead to a decrease in the quality of the outcomes accomplished by a group using the medium for most of its communication. Indeed, this seems to frequently be the case in short duration tasks (Graetz et al. 1998; Kahai and Cooper 2003; Warkentin et al. 1997), but not necessarily in long duration tasks (Burke and Chidambaram 1999; Carlson 1995; DeLuca 2003; Kock 2005; Kock and DeLuca 2007). The reason is that, in long duration tasks, it is common to observe a phenomenon known as compensatory adaptation (Kock 2002). This phenomenon may counteract the problems associated with the suppression of oral speech (Kock 2005; Kock et al. 2007).

Compensatory adaptation seems to be one of the reasons why groups performing knowledge-intensive tasks over a relatively long period of time (e.g., days, weeks, or months), using an e-collaboration medium that suppresses oral speech, often have the same or even better performance than groups where oral interaction is not suppressed (Kock 2005). As long as there is motivation among group members to expend additional compensatory effort, which may be strongly influenced by social factors (Bandura 1986; Fulk 1993), group members are likely to adapt their communicative behavior in order to compensate for the obstacles posed by the e-collaboration medium's suppression of oral speech (Short et al. 1976; Ulijn et al. 2001).

Compensatory adaptation can be understood as a moderating effect. That is, the effects of oral speech suppression on communication fluency and ambiguity are moderated by compensatory adaptation, whose moderating effect is in turn positively correlated with e-collaborative task duration. In short duration tasks, the negative effects of oral speech suppression on communication fluency and ambi-guity are likely to be particularly acute, as there is no time for compensatory adaptation to take place. In long duration tasks, the e-collaborators may adapt their behavior to compensate for the cognitive obstacles caused by the suppression of oral speech. This phenomenon has been referred to as compensatory adaptation to e-collaboration media of low naturalness (Kock 2004).

8 Conclusion and Implications

The arguments presented in the previous sections can be summarized into three main predictions. The first refers to the effects of oral speech suppression on communica-tion fluency and ambiguity in the context of e-collaboration. The second refers to the moderating effect that the amount of knowledge communicated is likely to have on these effects. The third prediction refers to the moderating effect that compensatory adaptation is likely to have on the effects of oral speech suppression on communica-tion fluency and ambiguity. Compensatory adaptation itself is correlated with task duration and may take place even when a large amount of knowledge is being com-municated. These predictions are outlined below and followed by recommendations for the use of e-collaboration tools in organizations.

Communication fluency and ambiguity: A key prediction based on the discussion put forth here is that removing the ability to convey speech from an e-collaboration medium used by modern humans is likely to decrease communication fluency and increase communication ambiguity much more strongly than removing the medium's ability to convey other communicative stimuli such as facial expressions and body language. The reason is that the ability to use speech for communication evolved at a much higher survival cost among our human ancestors than the ability to use any other communicative stimulus.

The moderating effect of knowledge communication: The negative effects of oral speech suppression on communication fluency and ambiguity are moderated by the amount of knowledge communication taking place in an e-collaborative task. Due to the context in which oral speech evolved among our ancestors, oral speech is not equally important for all types of communication interactions among mod-ern humans; it is particularly important in knowledge-intensive communication. Communicating one's home address to another person, for example, can be eas-ily and effectively accomplished through e-mail. Conversely, if one engineer wants to communicate knowledge about how to design a new car engine to a production manager, then the suppression of oral speech may make the communication much slower and ambiguous.

The moderating effect of compensatory adaptation: Another moderating effect, similar to but of a different kind than knowledge communication, is compensatory adaptation. Compensatory adaptation, or the degree to which individuals adapt to a communication medium that is unnatural (e.g., one that suppresses oral speech), seems to moderate the negative effects of oral speech suppression on communication fluency and ambiguity. Compensatory adaptation to media that suppress oral speech typically happens over time (e.g., days, weeks or months), as individuals modify their communicative behavior to make up for the shortcomings of the medium. This may be one of the reasons why compensatory adaptation is not normally observed in short duration tasks requiring intense knowledge exchange. For example, groups performing knowledge-intensive tasks through text-based e-collaboration technologies, and where the tasks last from a few minutes to a few hours, generally tend to produce task outcomes of inferior quality. These groups would be better off either (a) performing the task face-to-face or using an e-collaboration technology that provides an audio channel or (b) performing the task using a text-based e-collaboration technology, but over a long time period (e.g., a few days) so that compensatory adaptation can take place.

The increasingly distributed nature of organizational processes (e.g., sets of activities that are repeated over and over again) and projects (e.g., sets of activities that are carried out once or a few times) requires tasks to be accomplished by groups of individuals who are not only geographically distributed but also distributed across multiple time zones. Given this, it is impractical to try to ensure that all activities in a process or project are performed face-to-face or even through e-collaboration involving synchronous oral speech interactions. Sometimes ubiquitous text-based asynchronous communication such as e-mail must be used for part of the process or project, due to cost constraints. It is also possible that asynchronous oral speech interactions will be used (e.g., voice messaging or e-mail with attached audio messages) for part of the process or project, due to group members having to work from different time zones.

A more practical piece of advice to managers, which follows from the theoretical discussion, is the following: (a) break organizational processes and projects into component collaborative activities; (b) rank those activities in terms of the perceived amount of knowledge exchange involved; (c) make sure that highly knowledge-intensive activities are performed through media that incorporate synchronous oral speech (e.g., face-to-face or teleconferencing interaction), which may mean that certain group members will have to make special accommodations to participate in group discussions (e.g., attend a meeting at 3 a.m., local time); (d) make sure that moderately knowledge-intensive activities are performed through media that incorporate some form of oral speech, even if asynchronous (e.g., voice messaging or e-mail with attached audio messages); and (e) encourage the use of text-based e-collaboration media for activities that involve little or no knowledge exchange among participants, as this is likely to be the cheapest and most widely available organizational communication medium.

Acknowledgments This chapter is a revised version of an article by the author published in 2009 in the journal *Electronic Markets*. A mathematical formalization of the key predictions of this chapter is presented in that article and has not been included here. The author discussed several of this chapter's core biological and evolutionary ideas in a presentation at the 2008 Annual Meeting of the Human Behavior and Evolution Society in Kyoto, Japan. The presentation argued, through a mathematical formalization based on the Price equation and the method of path analysis, that costly mate choice traits should be rare and particularly attractive to the members of the opposite sex. The author is grateful for the comments and questions from the audience at that presentation.

References

Baker G (2002) The effects of synchronous collaborative technologies on decision making: a study of virtual teams. Inf Res Manag J 15(4):79–94

Bandura A (1986) Social foundations of thought and action. Prentice Hall, Englewood Cliffs

Boaz NT, Almquist AJ (2001) Biological anthropology: a synthetic approach to human evolution. Prentice Hall, Upper Saddle River

Burke K, Aytes K (2001) Do media really affect perceptions and procedural structuring among partially-distributed groups? J Syst Inf Technol 5(1):10–23

Burke K, Chidambaram L (1999) How much bandwidth is enough? a longitudinal examination of media characteristics and group outcomes. MIS Q 23(4):557–580

Carlson JR (1995) Channel expansion theory: a dynamic view of media and information richness perception. Doctoral dissertation. Florida State University, Tallahassee

Cartwright J (2000) Evolution and human behavior: Darwinian perspectives on human nature. The MIT Press, Cambridge

Crowston K, Howison J, Masango C, Eseryel UY (2007) The role of face-to-face meetings in technology-supported self-organizing distributed teams. IEEE Trans Prof Commun 50(3): 185–203

Daly-Jones O, Monk A, Watts L (1998) Some advantages of video conferencing over high-quality audio conferencing: fluency and awareness of attentional focus. Int J Hum Comput Stud 49(1):21–58

Darwin CR (1871) The descent of man, and selection in relation to sex. John Murray, London

DeLuca DC (2003) Business process improvement using asynchronous e-collaboration: testing the compensatory adaptation model. Doctoral Dissertation. Temple University, Philadelphia

Dobzhansky T, Ayala FJ, Stebbins GL, Valentine JW (1977) Evolution. W.H. Freeman and Company, San Francisco

Dunbar RIM (1993) Coevolution of neocortical size, group size and language in humans. Behav Brain Sci 16(4):681–735

Dunbar RIM (1999) Culture, honesty and the freerider problem. In: Dunbar RIM, Knight C, Power C (eds) The evolution of culture. Rutgers University Press, New Brunswick, pp 194–213

Fletcher JA, Zwick M (2007) The evolution of altruism: game theory in multilevel selection and inclusive fitness. J Theor Biol 245(1):26–36

Fulk J (1993) Social construction of communication technology. Acad Manag J 36(5):921–938

Gardner H (1985) The mind's new science. Basic Books, New York

Gillespie JH (2004) Population genetics. The Johns Hopkins University Press, Baltimore

Graetz KA, Boyle ES, Kimble CE, Thompson P, Garloch JL (1998) Information sharing in face-to-face, teleconferencing, and electronic chat groups. Small Group Res 29(6):714–743

Griskevicius V, Tybur JM, Sundie JM, Cialdini RB, Miller GF, Kenrick DT (2007) Blatant benevolence and conspicuous consumption: when romantic motives elicit costly displays. J Pers Soc Psychol 93(1):85–102

Hamilton WD, Zuk M (1982) Heritable true fitness and bright birds: a role for parasites? Science 218(4570):384–387

Hartl DL, Clark AG (2007) Principles of population genetics. Sinauer Associates, Sunderland

Hausken K, Hirshleifer J (2008) Truthful signalling, the heritability paradox, and the Malthusian equi-marginal principle. Theor Popul Biol 73(1):11–23

Henrich J (2004) Cultural group selection, coevolutionary processes and large-scale cooperation. J Econ Behav Organ 53(1):3–35

Hung D-Z (2004) Taiwan's venomous snakebite: epidemiological, evolution and geographic differences. Trans R Soc Trop Med Hyg 98(2):96–101

Kahai SS, Cooper RB (2003) Exploring the core concepts of media richness theory: the impact of cue multiplicity and feedback immediacy on decision quality. J Manag Inf Syst 20(1): 263–281

Kock N (1999) Process improvement and organizational learning: the role of collaboration technologies. Idea Group Publishing, Hershey, PA

Kock N (2002) Compensatory adaptation: understanding how obstacles can lead to success. Infinity Publishing, Haverford

Kock N (2004) The psychobiological model: towards a new theory of computer-mediated communication based on Darwinian evolution. Organ Sci 15(3):327–348

Kock N (2005) Compensatory adaptation to media obstacles: an experimental study of process redesign dyads. Inf Res Manage J 18(2):41–67

Kock N, DeLuca D (2007) Improving business processes electronically: an action research study in New Zealand and the U.S. J Global Inf Technol Manag 10(3):6–27

Kock N, Verville J, Garza V (2007) Media naturalness and online learning: findings supporting both the significant- and no-significant-difference perspectives. Decis Sci J Innov Educ 5(2):333–356

Kock N, Chatelain-Jardón R, Carmona J (2008) An experimental study of simulated web-based threats and their impact on knowledge communication effectiveness. IEEE Trans Prof Commun 51(2):183–197

Kokko H, Brooks R, McNamara JM, Houston AI (2002) The sexual selection continuum. Proceedings of the Royal Society of London: Biol Sci 269(1498):1331–1340

Laitman JT (1984) The anatomy of human speech, Natural Hist 20(7):20–27

Laitman JT, Reidenberg JS (1997) The human aerodigestive tract and gastroesophageal reflux: an evolutionary perspective. Am J Med 103(5):2S-8S

Lee HS, Holyoak KJ (2008) The role of causal models in analogical inference. J Exp Psychol Learn Mem Cogn 34(5):1111–1122

Lieberman P (1998) Eve spoke: human language and human evolution. W.W. Norton & Company, New York

Luger GF, Stubblefield WA (2008) AI algorithms, data structures, and idioms in prolog, Lisp, and java for artificial intelligence: structures and strategies for complex problem solving. Addison-Wesley, Reading

Manipady S, Menezes RG, Bastia BK (2006) Death by attack from a wild boar. J Clin Fore Medicine 13(2):89–91

Maynard Smith J (1998) Evolutionary genetics. Oxford University Press, New York

Maynard Smith J, Harper D (2003) Animal signals. Oxford University Press, New York

Mayr E (1976) Evolution and the diversity of life. Harvard University Press, Cambridge

McElreath R, Boyd R (2007) Mathematical models of social evolution: a guide for the perplexed. University of Chicago Press, Chicago

McQueen RJ, Payner K, Kock N (1999) Contribution by participants in face-to-face business meetings: implications for collaborative technology. J Syst Inf Technol 3(1):15–33

Miller GF (2000) The mating mind: how sexual choice shaped the evolution of human nature. Doubleday, New York

Miller GF (2002) How did language evolve? In: Swain H (ed) Big questions in science. Jonathan Cape, London, pp 79–90

Petrie M, Halliday T, Sanders C (1991) Peahens prefer peacocks with elaborate trains. Anim Behav 41(2):323–331

Pinker S (2003) Language as an adaptation to the cognitive niche. In: Christiansen M, Kirby S (eds) Language evolution: states of the art. Oxford University Press, New York, pp 16–37, NY

Rice SH (2004) Evolutionary theory: mathematical and conceptual foundations. Sinauer Associates, Sunderland

Russel S, Norvig P (2002) Artificial intelligence: a modern approach. Prentice Hall, Upper Saddle River

Simon AF (2006) Computer-mediated communication: task performance and satisfaction. J Soc Psychol 146(3):349–379

Short JA, Williams E, Christie B (1976) The social psychology of telecommunications. John Wiley & Sons, London

Trivers R (2002) Natural selection and social theory. Oxford University Press, Oxford

Ulijn JM, Lincke A, Karakaya Y (2001) Non-face-to-face international business communication: how is national culture reflected in this medium? IEEE Trans Prof Commun 44(2):126–138

Wainfan L, Davis PK (2004) Challenges in virtual collaboration: videoconferencing, audioconferencing and computer-mediated communications. RAND Corporation, Santa Monica

Waldmann MR, Holyoak KJ, Fratianne A (1995) Causal models and the acquisition of category structure. J Exp Psychol Gen 124(2):181–206

Walker T (2008) Could sexual selection have made us psychological altruists? Stud Hist Phil Sci C: Stud Hist Phil Biol Biomed Sci 39(1):153–162

Warkentin ME, Sayeed L, Hightower R (1997) Virtual teams versus face-to-face teams: an exploratory study of a web-based conferencing system. Decis Sci 28(4):975–996

Wilson EO (2000) Sociobiology: the new synthesis. Harvard University Press, Cambridge, MA

Zahavi A (1975) Mate selection—A selection for a handicap. J Theor Biol 53(1):205–214

Zahavi A, Zahavi A (1997) The handicap principle: a missing piece of Darwin's puzzle. Oxford University Press, Oxford

Chapter 14
Homo Virtualensis: Evolutionary Psychology as a Tool for Studying Video Games

Zack Mendenhall, Gad Saad, and Marcelo Vinhal Nepomuceno

Abstract Video games represent a growing new trend in entertainment. The majority of research conducted regarding video games suffers from problems endemic to the standard social sciences model (SSSM). Chiefly, these problems are the result of presuming that all observed variation in mental traits is due to social learning and not innate differences. This chapter examines this body of work critically and provides evolutionary explanations for three largely unexamined or incompletely explained phenomena in the research area: game content; sex differences in gaming; and the link between gaming and play behavior. It is concluded that the literature on gaming can benefit from an infusion of evolutionary-based theorizing.

Keywords Video games · Evolutionary psychology · Sex differences · Content analysis · technology · Interactive entertainment · Play

1 Introduction

Technology has given *Homo sapiens* a veritable stranglehold over the environment. The suburbs have been purged of predators, and grocery stores minimize the costly risks and efforts of hunting and gathering. Air-conditioned housing keeps us safe

Z. Mendenhall (✉)
John Molson School of Business, Concordia University,
1455 de Maisonneuve Blvd. West, Montreal, QC, Canada H3G 1M8
e-mail: z_mend@jmsb.concordia.ca

G. Saad
Department of Marketing, John Molson School of Business, Concordia University,
1455 de Maisonneuve Blvd. West, Montreal, QC, Canada H3G 1M8
e-mail: gadsaad@jmsb.concordia.ca

M.V. Nepomuceno
John Molson School of Business, Concordia University, 1455 de Maisonneuve Blvd. West, GM
1002-03, Montreal, QC, Canada H3G 1M8
e-mail: m_nepomu@jmsb.concordia.ca

N. Kock (ed.), *Evolutionary Psychology and Information Systems Research*,
Integrated Series in Information Systems 24, DOI 10.1007/978-1-4419-6139-6_14,
© Springer Science+Business Media, LLC 2010

from wind, rain, and other mild discomforts, and automobiles enable us to travel vast expanses of land without so much as breaking a sweat. Medicine has proven more effective than exorcisms at curing the sick. Thanks to the Internet, knowledge is now diffusing at a tremendous pace. We use technology to maximize the salience of fitness-promoting cues and to reduce the threat of fitness-reducing cues. The modern technological environment is the result of our ancestral minds unleashed: We delight in being over-sanitized, overfed, and over-stimulated. As if this masterful environmental manipulation were not enough, humans have also developed the ability to create and interact with completely artificial environments that are optimally designed to excite and activate our evolved psychology in ways that reality does not allow. In the parlance of contemporary culture, we call these artificial environments "video games." Video games have given humans the ability to create and explore *completely artificial* worlds. The properties of these worlds (and their subsequent success or failure in the market) should reveal much about the species that created them. After all, millions of users worldwide are paying for the emotionally stimulating experiences that video games provide. This chapter investigates, from an evolutionary stance, why the market for such experiences is so ripe. In other words, we seek to answer the following question: What in our evolved human nature makes virtual reality worth paying for?

In building our case, we will critically examine contemporary works in the video game literature, where evolutionary theory is conspicuously absent. We suggest that evolutionary theory provides key and unique insights on three levels: (1) when considering sex differences in video game preferences; (2) in exploring the design of video game content; and (3) in the manner by which video games elicit our evolved penchant to play. To motivate our discussion, we begin with a demonstration of the commercial might of our target industry.

The commercial import of the video game industry has increased tremendously in recent years. For instance, despite being a relatively new form of entertainment (the original Nintendo Entertainment System was released in the USA in 1985), video games have now overtaken the movie industry in sales figures (Entertainment Software Association (ESA) 2007; Motion Picture Association of America 2007). The ESA (2007) report illustrates the impact of video games on modern day lives. Sixty-five percent of American households play computer or video games. The average gamer has been playing for 13 years, which suggests that gamers are quite loyal to the pastime. We investigate some of these demographic realities from an evolutionary perspective in subsequent sections.

Despite their growing commercial might, video games are under-researched in general and very rarely are considered from an evolutionary perspective (a point recently acknowledged regarding all Internet behavior by Piazza and Bering 2009; but see Cherney and Poss 2008; Kock 2008; Mazur et al. 1997; Ohler and Nieding 2006a, b). Much of the existing literature pertaining to video games fails to provide ultimate-level explanations for the phenomena in question and often relies on social constructivist accounts (Gee 2007; Yee 2008) rooted in the standard social science model (SSSM). The SSSM is the conceptual framework under which the great majority of social scientists have operated (Tooby and Cosmides 1992). The SSSM is critically wrong (or, at best, incomplete) for the following reason: It presumes that all of human nature is the result of a general learning mechanism. The primary implication of such an assumption is that intelligence, pathology, personality, gender, and any conceivable mental trait observable in adulthood is the result of idiosyncratic childhood experiences. In his treatise against the SSSM, Pinker (2002) provides an excellent rationale for the intuitive appeal of such an assumption. He suggests that, prior to knowledge of genetics, researchers noticed that kids had psychological traits in common with the people with whom they grew up. Since we had virtually no knowledge of the heritability of mental traits, it was easy to assume that children acquired their personhoods via learning. Pinker then argues that, when one controls for heritability (as we now can with twin studies), most of these so-called learning effects dwindle away.

SSSM-based thinking is pervasive in video game research, as well. Many video game researchers presume that, since video games often feature violence, they are "teaching" the children who play them to be more violent. We will posit that the exact *opposite* causal link explains the relationship between violence and video games. Humans have evolved to deploy aggression and violence under certain ecological conditions, and the design of violent games is a process of recreating those conditions. So it is not games that make us violent, it is we (and our evolved appetites) who make games violent. But it is not just violence that we are concerned with. Our objective in this chapter is to demonstrate the relevance of evolutionary theory in understanding a plethora of gaming phenomena. We begin by reviewing some of the work done on video games rooted in non-evolutionary theorizing and then proceed to prospective ways in which evolutionary theory could inform the study of video games.

2 A Review of Non-evolutionary Research

The literature on video games has traditionally focused on the effects that playing games have on any number of variables (with a conspicuous emphasis on aggression). As mentioned, the majority of these studies are perfunctorily SSSM-based, leaving their findings inadequately explained, and their theory incomplete if not erroneous. We provide a brief recapitulation of representative studies in the area and then offer an evolutionarily informed critique.

There is evidence that playing violent games increases aggression (Bartholow and Anderson 2002; Konijin et al. 2007), decreases helping behavior (Anderson 2004), increases aggressive self-views (Uhlmann and Swason 2004), and desensitizes individuals to violence (Bartholow et al. 2006). Recent research has also shown that customizable characters provoke more aggressive behavior, as players feel more committed to the game, increasing the intensity of the psychological effects of video games (Fischer, Kastenmüller and Greitemeyer, 2010). However, there appears to be some dispute as to the validity of these findings.

Some authors have provided evidence for a publication bias that yearns to find a positive relationship between playing video games and violent behaviors. For instance, in a meta-analysis, Ferguson (2007) found that articles reporting positive relations are more likely to be published than the ones that report negative relations. Also, there are reports of potential methodological issues, which could dampen many findings (Ferguson and Kilburn 2009), such as the use of non-standardized and unreliable measures of aggression, the lack of control of mediating variables (such as personality), and the use of instruments that do not measure aggression and violent behavior directly. Moreover, Ferguson and Kilburn (2009) observed that these studies failed to control for sex. Thus, the inclusion of females, who are both less aggressive and play violent video games less frequently, may have been a confounding variable in many of the findings. Incidentally, Greitemeyer and Osswald (2009) found that prosocial games (wherein game play promotes actions that benefit others, as is the case with *Lemmings*) may actually reduce aggressive cognitions when compared to neutral ones (which do not promote antisocial or prosocial behavior, such as *Tetris*). These results hold true even though both games are perceived by subjects as similar in terms of aggressive content. These authors found that after playing prosocial games, participants reported fewer aggressive behaviors, thoughts, and feelings when completing ambiguous stories. These findings, and their SSSM-laden nature, lead us to question the validity of the body of work that struggles to create a causal link from playing video games to aggressive thoughts or behavior.

Non-aggression-related video game research has also been conducted. Studies have shown that video games can improve the performance of old adults in executive control functions, such as task switching, working memory, visual short-term memory, and reasoning (Basak et al. 2008). Moreover, video games can improve spatial skills, especially for those lacking in this ability (Subrahmanyam and Greenfield 1994). Similarly, Lowery and Knirk (1982/1983) also suggested that video games can increase eye–hand coordination. Hence, far from strictly yielding deleterious effects, video games can generate a wide range of tangible benefits to those who play them.

Occasionally, the non-evolutionary literature has explored our motivations to play video games. For instance, Olson et al. (2007) showed that, compared to boys, girls declared that they play electronic games because they are bored or because they have nothing else to do. On the other hand, boys find the games much more exciting and fun; they play to compete and win; enjoy the challenge of figuring the game out; use the game as a relaxing source; use the game to get anger out; and play because they like guns and weapons. Additionally, Sanger et al. (1997) suggested that video games allow children, especially boys with low self-esteem and confidence, to have a sense of control, gain respect from others, and operate as experts. In an investigation of cultural differences in gaming, Chou and Tsai (2007) showed that, while Taiwanese boys like playing video games for slightly different reasons than the US boys, one commonality across both cultures was that competition between males was a primary motivator, reinforcing the findings of Olson et al. (2007). All of the works that have been cited thus far in this section did not incorporate evolutionary theorizing, even in instances when it was ripe to do so. Accordingly, we shift our attention to the ways in which an evolutionary approach can shed new light in this area.

The quality and quantity of work in evolutionary psychology regarding sex differences in aggression are impressive (for books on the evolution of aggression, see Buss 2005; Ghiglieri 2000; Keeley 1997; Rosen 2007; Smith 2007; Thayer 2004; Wrangham and Peterson 1996; and for evolutionary explanations of human sex differences, see Geary 2009). We suggest that the association between violent games and males might be parsimoniously explained by this cogent evolutionarily informed argument: Men are predisposed toward aggression and warfare because it was genetically advantageous for them to be so, under certain conditions. Hence, they are more likely to enjoy simulations of those experiences than are females (Mendenhall et al., 2010; Nepomuceno et al. 2009). Next, we continue our exploration of how evolutionary theory can contribute to our understanding of gaming phenomena. The following section proposes evolutionary explanations for cultural products in general, and then specifically analyzes video game content.

3 Evolutionary Perspectives on Video Games

Cultural products come in many forms. Examples include songs, literature, art, and television shows. An evolutionary-informed analysis of cultural products can take one of several approaches. One might investigate whether the creation of a cultural product is itself an adaptation that confers survival benefits. This is the approach taken by Ellen Dissanayake in her exploration of the evolutionary origins of art (cf. Dissanayake 1992). A second approach argues that the production of cultural products yields a reproductive advantage to their creators via an enhancement of their social status (Miller 2000). A third approach posits that some cultural products are exaptations namely byproducts of adaptations that were selected for other purposes. This is the approach taken by Boyer (2001) in his exploration of the evolutionary roots of religion. A fourth approach for studying cultural products is to conduct content analyses on said products (Saad 2007, Chap. 5). In so doing, cultural products can be construed as fossils of the human mind. For example, song lyrics from around the world and across temporal periods can be analyzed to gauge the common themes that are addressed in this particular form of expression. Not surprisingly, one finds that the great majority of songs deal with mating. Furthermore, the attributes that men and women sing about regarding prospective mates are universally similar. Other approaches for investigating culture from an evolutionary perspective include gene–culture coevolution models (Boyd and Richerson 1985; Richerson and Boyd 2005) and memetic theory (Aunger 2002; Blackmore 1999; Dawkins 1976). Next, we explore how video games, similar to songs, are cultural products that offer a rich impression of the phylogeny of their creators.

3.1 An Evolutionary Explanation for Video Game Content

This section discusses four broad aspects of video game content: characters, environments, tasks, and mechanics (the tools that a player is provided in order to complete tasks). Given that players of video games have minds that have been forged by the forces of natural and sexual selection, the stimuli they are most likely to attend to will be indicative of their phylogeny (i.e., evolutionary history). Features that make video game content rich and compelling correspond to features that are rich and compelling in the real world. Since what our minds perceive to be boring (or exciting) is the result of evolutionary pressures, game stimuli must bear some relevance to our fitness-conscious objectives in order for us to feel compelled to spend money on them. For instance, being attacked by a lion, seduced by a member of the opposite sex, or attacked by a rival group are decidedly *not boring* experiences *because* these are challenges that humans have recurrently faced in their evolutionary history. One might imagine that it was terribly maladaptive to yawn apathetically on such occasions. So, in order for video games to be compelling, they must deliver stimuli that we have been evolutionarily selected to attend to. We begin our content analysis by linking recurrent player preferences for certain features of video game characters to an ultimate evolutionary explanation.

3.2 The Evolutionary Origins of Virtual Character Preferences

We expect that the design of characters by both game developers and players alike will reflect our evolved psychology. Specifically, characters should exhibit features that possess fitness-relevant characteristics. We suggest that players are likely to prefer avatars (a character that a player controls) that exude high-fitness cues. This assertion assumes that players are willing to "believe in" the high-fitness cues of virtual avatars, a point that we address shortly.

Avatars will vary on sexual attractiveness, one of the most robustly investigated topics by evolutionary behavioral scientists. We now know that men consider physical attractiveness more important in prospective mates than do women (Buss 1988). Furthermore, women's fashions tend to accentuate their fertility-revealing physical features such as their waist-to-hip ratio (Hill et al. 2005) or the shape of their buttocks (Saad 2007), whereas men's fashions tend to signal personal wealth and/or high social status (as women are attracted to such cues). These are two of the defining universal laws of attraction, namely men select mates based on cues of fertility (observable through their bodily form) and women choose men based on their ability to invest in offspring (observable through their access to resources). Using this evolutionarily informed framework, we posit that the design of characters will feature if not exaggerate these evolved cues of attractiveness because gamers "internalize" the fitness-relevant information of their avatars as if it applied to them.

Prior to investigating the ways in which character design reflects evolved preferences, an essential issue needs addressing. Do players actually "internalize" (or "believe in") the stimuli that they are provided in video games? If they do not, then our hypothesis (that video games are played because they provide *believable* fitness-promoting cues) would be moot. The evidence suggests that such "internalization" does indeed occur, as discussed below.

There is evidence in the literature to support the claim that the use of virtual characters influences real-world behaviors. For instance, when a person takes control of an attractive avatar their real-life behavior becomes similar to that of a person who is *actually* attractive. Yee and Bailenson (2009) tested the effects of controlling an attractive versus an unattractive avatar on real-life behavior. They found that participants who were aware that they controlled attractive avatars later selected more attractive partners from an artificial dating web site and were more likely to exaggerate their self-reported height than those who were aware of their avatar's unattractiveness. Yee and Bailenson (2007) called the tendency for avatars to influence real-world behavior the "Proteus effect," after the Greek God who assumed many physical forms (for discussion see Yee et al. 2009). Yee et al. (2009) found that subjects who were assigned taller avatars negotiated more aggressively with a confederate in face-to-face (non-virtual) interactions. Additionally they found that the height and attractiveness of an online avatar predicted player performance. These findings are supportive of our premise that players "internalize," at some level, the information that is being communicated to them in virtual worlds regarding their own fitness. We hereby dub the tendency to internalize the fitness-relevant aspects of an avatar *virtual vanity*.

Since it appears that players are disposed to virtual vanity, we anticipate that players' avatar preferences will be congruent with sex-specific mating preferences. For instance, there is some preliminary evidence that players prefer to adorn their avatars with items that serve as conspicuous signals of avatar wealth. Mendenhall and Miller (in preparation) found that *World of Warcraft* players charged other players a very large price premium (in the virtual currency of *WoW*) for weapons that were conspicuously rare. Such a finding is consistent with the notion that modern humans use technological products as signaling devices (Miller 2009; Saad 2007; Saad and Vongas 2009) and is well aligned with Mendenhall et al.'s (2010) notion that males play to acquire cues of social status. In fact, the acquisition of signaling items often serves as the impetus for males to play (Yee 2006). These findings are all consistent with the evolutionary expectation that men are compelled to signal their wealth.

Researchers have found that players prefer physically attractive, sex-typified characters albeit evolutionary theory was absent as an explanatory framework. For example, Yee and Bailenson (2009, p. 12) noted, "most [players] are using avatars that are attractive, powerful, youthful, and athletic." Note that these descriptors are congruent with evolved mating preferences. When choosing male avatars, males will prefer characters that convey *power* and *athleticism* because these traits signal to females that the male has access to, or can acquire and defend, resources. On the other hand, females will prefer avatars that convey *youth* and *attractiveness* because these traits signal fecundity and fertility. According to Yee's online reports (www.nickyee.com/daedalus), players tend to prefer avatars that are slightly taller and more attractive than they are, regardless of the player's sex. Men were about equally likely to select an "average" avatar, as they were an "attractive/graceful" one whereas women were twice as likely to prefer an "attractive/graceful" avatar to an average one. Men were also more likely to prefer characters that are "dark, menacing," "large, hulking," "normal, human," and "short, aged." With the exceptions of "normal, human" category and the "short" descriptor (which is only present because the typical fantasy setting in such games includes mythical dwarves), this makes sense in light of the previously discussed evolved preferences. Men prefer avatars that signal dominance and status. Being wise (as captured by age), large, and/or ominous are traits that are correlated to one's ability to acquire and maintain social status. Of note, Kaplan et al. (2000) show that male access to resources (measured in the caloric value of hunted meat per day) peaks at about age 35, which may help explain why "aged" (which we take to mean "middle aged" and not "elderly") characters might be preferred by males. This finding again aligns with Mendenhall et al.'s (2010) assertion that men often play games in order to immerse their minds with cues of high social status. Females, by contrast, prefer "cute" (small, nubile) and "lithe" avatars more than men do, suggesting that women often play to signal physical attractiveness (which is easier to accomplish vicariously through a customizable avatar in a virtual life than by rigorous diet and exercise in real life).

Once players have selected their optimally attractive avatars, they are projected into a virtual world, full of fitness-reducing threats and fitness-promoting opportunities. Since every species is selected to survive and reproduce under particular ecological conditions, virtual environments ought to cater to the evolved environmental preferences of the species they are designed for. In the following section we look at human landscape preferences and how these predict the environmental content of various games.

3.3 Virtual Environments and Evolved Landscape/Habitat Preferences

In this section we discuss how the design of virtual environments reflects our innate preferences and aversions to certain ecological conditions. We first explain how evolutionary theory has informed the study of landscape preferences and then proceed with a discussion of how different games utilize these innate preferences to communicate a meaningful experience to the user.

In order to understand how virtual environments are congruent with evolutionary principles, one must explore how habitat preferences are formed. Silverman and Choi (2005, p. 190) write, "[habitat preferences] were selected for on the basis of their capacity to meet the ecological requirements of the animal. These include food, water, shelter, weather, and protection from predators." For example, despite having plenty of water and no man-eating predators, Antarctica's lack of shelter and brutally frigid weather make it an unsuitable environment for human life. On the other hand, emperor penguins are expressly adapted to exploit such an environment during their mating season. Our distaste for frozen wastelands coupled with our longing for lush temperate plains with fresh running water are indeed adaptive landscape/habitat preferences corresponding to the environmental conditions in which we have evolved.

Appleton (1975) suggested that humans prefer landscapes based upon how well they allowed us to (1) *prospect* for predators, prey, resources, and enemies at a distance and (2) seek *refuge* from predators, conspecific enemies, and violent weather. Additionally, Kaplan and Kaplan (1989) suggested that preferences should be highest for landscapes that are of relatively low risk to explore and for which an exploration has the potential to confer useful information. For a recent investigation of the evolutionary roots of landscape preference, see Falk and Balling (2009). It follows then that preferences for virtual landscapes with ecologically useful features would match the evolutionary-based likings as described both by Appleton and by Kaplan and Kaplan. But sometimes an ecologically harsh environment should be utilized in order to create a compellingly fear-inducing ambiance. In the next paragraph, we compare how various game genres utilize different environmental designs in accordance with the type of fitness-relevant stimuli they promise to deliver.

Perhaps the most dramatic example of a ferociously hostile virtual environment is that of *Doom 3*. In *Doom 3,* the player is submerged in complete darkness and must choose between using a flashlight and a weapon (and cannot use both at the same time, making target tracking very difficult). There are no lush, beautiful sunset vistas in *Doom 3* – only pitch-black anfractuous metallic hallways infested with mutated, bloodthirsty enemies that make ghoulish, growling noises. The game is effective because the player feels genuinely threatened by the absence of the ecological advantages inherent to prospect-refuge theory, and each exploratory step leads to a life-threatening encounter with a flesh-hungry predator. In sharp contrast to *Doom 3*, players of *The Sims* are treated to a pleasant suburban environment with lush green grass and no predators. This provides an optimally peaceful setting from which the player can pursue the game's primary objectives (build a house, manage a family, get a job, and maintain social relations). Other games provide both safe and threatening environments within their repertoire of possible surroundings. *World of Warcraft (WoW)* offers players a wide range of landscapes, usually ripe with both predators *and* prey. Some landscapes in *WoW* are designed to be appreciably aesthetic (e.g., players are perched atop a hill from which they can see a path into the horizon, fresh running water, and a friendly settlement in the distance), while others are designed to evoke fear and excitement (such as dark, winding caves and dungeons that are full of powerful, hostile entities). Such settings are appropriate for what this game seeks to simulate: a variety of thrilling adventures in a fantasy setting.

Playing as an attractive and interesting character in compelling environments is insufficient to make a game appealing. In order for the game to elicit an enriching experience, it must motivate players with titillating and challenging objectives while providing them with interesting tools for achieving these. In the next section, we turn to how the objectives and mechanics of a game must be synchronized with our evolved motivations and sensorial apparatus in order to provide the player with a believable and exciting experience.

3.4 Game Objectives and the Means to Achieve Them

Beyond the visual stimuli (characters and environments) that games feature, they also provide users with things to do (e.g., "save the princess") and the means to do them (e.g., "press A to attack"). Objectives in games can be said to constitute the game's plot. So, virtual game objectives have much in common with fictional literary plots. Accordingly, we briefly discuss the evolutionary underpinnings of literary plots and then meld that analysis into our perspective of the evolutionary origins of gaming objectives. The objectives that designers program into games need to carry fitness consequences, lest they seem austere. Escaping from the police in a stolen helicopter is decidedly *not* a boring experience precisely *because* it has plenty of fitness-relevant stimuli, including the threat of punishment if not death. We argue that game objectives, and the tools used to achieve them, are only exciting if they tickle our evolved motivational systems.

Sherman (1997) suggests that video games are digital recreations of folkloric tales. She compares the story of Mario (the famous Nintendo character, who is called upon to rescue Princess Toadstool from the evil clutches of King Koopa) in *Super Mario Brothers* to that of other literary heroes (including Agamemnon, who was called upon to liberate Helen from the evil clutches of Paris of Troy). Sherman's essential point is that video games are yet another way in which literary archetypes emerge. Whereas for Sherman this constitutes a cultural phenomenon that reinforces gender stereotypes, we consider the re-emergence of prototypical (compelling) plot-lines across mediums, cultures, and time to be evidence of an evolved, universal psychology. In his evolutionary analysis of literature, Carroll states that "[characters and situations] must operate within the range of behaviors that are intelligible and meaningful to our evolved psychology" (2005, p. 944). In other words, if the plot does not involve fitness gains or fitness losses of some sort, it is unlikely to be interesting or motivating, and thus it is doubtful that the game will garner much market share. Seen from this perspective, it is no surprise that the most popular games often feature plot objectives that are exaggerations of what we may wish to achieve in real life.

As an example of how games utilize evolved emotional systems to motivate players via specific tasks, we discuss how *Deus Ex*, a story-driven shooter game, bases most of its plot on the ancestral urge to punish cheaters (see Cosmides and Tooby 1992, 2005, for a discussion of the Darwinian module dedicated to cheater detection). Players begin the game by being sent on a mission to neutralize a group of terrorists who have threatened to attack the Statue of Liberty. In time, the US government betrays the player. Because punishment for such transgressions (including homicide) is an adaptive means for ending such exploitation, players become highly motivated to seek revenge upon the corrupt individuals. In *Deus Ex*, revenge is compulsory, but players do not mind: The game is widely hailed as a classic *precisely for* its storyline. Players experience a strong sense of justice and power over the course of a complex and coherent plot by satisfying their evolved motives to avoid exploitation and to punish it when it occurs. But success in the game does not come easily. In order to beat *Deus Ex* (or any game) players must make good use of the tools that the game provides them with. These usually include various forms of equipment and character abilities (which we previously called "mechanics"). Next, we tackle how the design and subsequent implementation of the mechanics of a given game is also revelatory of our evolved psychology.

If any of the aforementioned game objectives had been too easily met, they would have failed to be reliable signals of a player's underlying ability. Game mechanics must be delicately calibrated to be both easy enough for new players to understand, but difficult or complex enough to make one's in-game achievements credible signals of one's skills and abilities. So, whereas video games are appealing for their capacity to amplify fitness-promoting information, they still must be at least minimally challenging in order to be stimulating. So, a game's tools must tread a fine line between simplicity and complexity, careful to never be too easily mastered, or too inaccessibly obtuse. Video game designers have just as much power over the range of behaviors that are possible in a game as they do over the visual representation of characters and environments. That which they choose to include as possible behavioral decisions should coincide with what our native psyches would anticipate in the game's setting. Since different game genres have sharply contrasting fitness-granting objectives (e.g., kill members of a rival out-group versus successfully raise a high-status family), the mechanics built into each game can (and must) differ drastically.

Let us compare the mechanics of two vastly different games. When playing a fast-paced, competitive game (such as *Call of Duty 4*) where players shoot each other, to only have the ability to move and to fire a weapon would be banal and accordingly the game would be too easily mastered. It is much more interesting when the player can opt to move quietly (enabling stealthy attacks), duck, sprint, jump, fall to a prone position, and use "flash-bang" grenades to blind and deafen opponents prior to attacking them. Conversely, in *The Sims* one has the ability to perform more routine tasks such as using a toilet, taking a shower, kissing one's spouse, or changing diapers. Because these two games mimic sharply contrasting fitness-granting *objectives*, their *mechanics* are completely different from one another. In *Call of Duty 4*, nobody can stop to blend a smoothie, and in *The Sims*, one cannot flash-bang one's guests in the living room before breaching the skylight with platefuls of fresh hors d'oeuvres.

Another way in which these two games diverge is the perspective from which the player interacts with the game. *Call of Duty 4* is played from the first-person perspective, while *The Sims* is played from a third-person perspective (or bird's-eye view). Any mother will corroborate that having an extra set of eyes would be an invaluable aid in the management of her offspring. *The Sims* acknowledges this fact by putting the player in the perspective of an all-seeing arbiter of family affairs. A player can simultaneously track three different children in three different rooms, her husband's interaction with their seductive neighbor in a fourth, and the progress of her turkey dinner in the kitchen. In *Call of Duty 4* a player controls only one avatar, and so the camera is placed directly behind the "eyes" of the avatar. This perspective requires that players have expert three-dimensional spatial rotation abilities, lest they become lost. As an adaptation to hunting (Gurven and Hill 2009;

Marlowe 2001), males have excellent three-dimensional spatial rotation (Stenstrom et al. 2008). In many games (e.g., shooter games) eye–hand coordination plays an important role (Lowery and Knirk 1982/1983). According to Binsted et al. (2001) such coordination aids in goal-directed aiming (using a mouse to hit targets on a screen), a relevant skill in hunting situations and shooting games, but not in diaper changing or vegetable foraging.

In this section we have highlighted how game objectives and mechanics tap into our evolved mental apparatus. For instance, men are more interested in heroic objectives regarding the successful liberation of (not-so-coincidentally) fertile-looking damsels whereas females are more interested in social or nurturance objectives such as raising a family or organizing social gatherings (Nepomuceno et al. 2009). Additionally, we discussed how the mechanics in video games could be interpreted via an evolutionary lens. It is no coincidence that many of our observations are consistent with documented sex-specific adaptive behaviors. Sex differences have been one of the most consistent findings within the video game research stream (ESA 2007, 2009; Nepomuceno et al. 2009; Yee 2006, 2008). Naturally, that most of these findings were discussed within the SSSM rubric, explanations are assumed to be due to socialization and learning. In the following section we explore these findings and proffer evolutionary explanations for the sex gap across several facets of gaming.

3.5 An Evolutionary Perspective on Sex Differences in Gaming

This section addresses the robust sex differences that have been uncovered within the video game literature. After discussing some of these differences, we suggest ways in which evolutionary theory can clarify why sex differences are so prominent in the following three genres: first person shooters (FPSs), massively multiplayer online role playing games (MMORPGs), and life simulators. We begin the discussion by providing some telling statistics about sex differences in the proclivity to play video games in general.

Men constitute the great majority of players of video games. The Entertainment Software Association (2009) report indicated that 60% of gamers, across all game genres, are men. This is an aggregate statistic, and gender distribution does vary wildly based on the game genre. Nepomuceno et al. (2009) reported that, compared to females, males have more positive attitudes toward FPS games (such as *Halo*), and real-time strategy games (such as *Starcraft*). On the other hand, females evaluate party games (like *Mario Party*), life simulators (*The Sims*), and platformers (*Super Mario Brothers*) more positively. On a related note, Ducheneaut and Yee (2006) reported that 85.4% of *WoW* players are males. What is at the root of these robust sex-specific game preferences? We tackle this issue using some of the most popular and most sexually differentiated genres on the market as examples, including the FPS, the MMORPG, and the life simulator. Note that these genres are the ones most often studied in the literature, thus further justifying our decision to focus on these game types.

In FPS games the player's objectives invariably involve the killing of enemies and/or monsters using a wide variety of weapons (such as rifles, chainsaws, pistols, and shotguns). Put simply, the game's objective is to kill enemies in order to achieve specific goals, as set for each mission. In these games, the player uses hand–eye coordination, timing, projectile analysis, theory of mind, and three-dimensional rotational memory to flank, surprise, ambush, and ultimately kill hostile entities. As such, much of what FPS games seek to emulate is the thrill of the hunt or the raid: tasks that, in the overwhelming majority of hunter-gatherer societies, males have been responsible for (Kaplan et al. 2000). Males still retain the suite of evolved solutions to the adaptive problems of hunting and resource defense, which predisposes them to violence and aggression (Buss 2005; Keeley 1997; Ghiglieri 2000; Rosen 2007; Smith 2007; Thayer 2004; Wrangham and Peterson 1996). Evolutionary psychologists have construed males' superior three-dimensional object rotation abilities as a likely adaptation for hunting (for a discussion regarding possible implications of such sex-specific abilities in online mediums, see Stenstrom et al. 2008). In an FPS, players must navigate complex three-dimensional spaces and anticipate the trajectories of weapons and the movements of other players. Thus, having strong three-dimensional rotation skills is an invaluable aid in such a game. In sum, men have a pronounced preference for FPSs because these cater to the male penchant for violence, which tended to confer fitness benefits in the ancestral task environment (Ea) (Kock 2009).

Another game genre with a strong male inclination is the MMORPG. Recall that Ducheneaut and Yee (2006) reported that 85.4% of *WoW* (an MMORPG) players are male. Mendenhall et al. (2010) surmised that the content of MMORPG games was male-biased. Such games track avatar progress and display it publicly, allowing players to quickly organize themselves into status hierarchies; they allow for the acquisition of rare, conspicuous avatar equipment (enabling wealth signaling); they encourage inter-factional warfare and even simulate the cooperation needed for big-game hunting. All of these primary modes of play in MMORPGs closely resemble activities that are pursued largely, if not exclusively, by males in the real world. Thus, the substantial over-representation of males in this gaming genre makes sense when viewed through an evolutionary lens. In sum, men prefer MMORPGs because they provide a setting in which competition, hierarchical social dominance, and cooperative hunting and warfare situations are recreated.

Life simulators are played by a very different audience. Recall that females evaluate life simulators (such as *The Sims* and *Second Life*) more positively than do males (Nepomuceno et al. 2009). In these games, the avatar is sent to work, to buy food, to make friends, to build and furnish a house, and to get married and raise offspring in a virtual world. It is important to note that we are neither condoning nor justifying supposed sexist stereotypes. We are, in fact, merely suggesting that the activities that likely occupied the time and attention of females throughout evolutionary history did so for adaptive reasons (see Kaplan et al. 2000), and it is accordingly plausible that these activities would be recreated in video games. Cooperative and competitive forces are at play in ways similar to those found in modern life (e.g., cooking dinner with friends as a cooperative activity and "keeping up with the Joneses" as a competitive one). One can have a very successful avatar with a respectful job, a new house, and an expansive roster of friends. These games are particularly alluring to women, because they simulate the sort of social networking and offspring rearing activity that women have done throughout evolutionary history. As pointed out by Di Leonardo (1987), women are generally more involved than men with housework and childcare. Kaplan et al. (2000) discuss the division of labor among hunter-gatherers and found that females do more childcare than males. So, in the same manner that males use MMORPGs to signal hierarchical social status via virtual wealth and rank, life simulators may be used by females to signal cues of fitness via their ability to successfully manage a family that grows in size and prestige. In other words, a physically attractive female who has an exemplar family, a luxurious house, and several friends is providing cues of her adequacy as a mate. Life simulators allow females to achieve female-specific fitness goals much more easily than in real life, thus explaining their greater preference for such games.

This section has explored how FPSs, MMORPGs, and life simulators are specialized in the fitness cues that they provide, as a function of the sex of the target market. Being a sexually reproducing and sexually dimorphic species, it is intuitive to first focus on evolutionary hypotheses that tackle sex differences, albeit it is important to reaffirm that there are evolutionary applications within the gaming context that are not related to sex. One such way to investigate video games from an evolutionary lens is to examine how video games resemble our evolved penchant to play. Our final section deals with the ways in which gaming appears to be related to play behavior.

3.6 The Evolutionary Roots of Play Behaviors

Thus far, we have asserted that video games are emotionally compelling because they tap into our evolved sensory and emotional systems. Since video games provide fitness-relevant stimuli, and consumers often respond to such stimuli as if they were real, we are arguing that, in a sense, video games "fake out" consumers (recall the earlier discussion of "virtual vanity" and the Proteus effect). One implication of such a perspective is that game playing is time spent acquiring or defending "artificial" fitness in an artificial world and thus represents time that was *not spent* acquiring and defending *real* fitness in the *real* world (i.e., virtual bowling can be said to confer less fitness than actual bowling and virtual status confers less fitness than actual status). Some might argue then that video game playing is *maladaptive*, in the evolutionary sense of the word, because it offers all of the fitness feedback with none of the true fitness benefits. However, it is important to note that humans are not equipped with a domain-general fitness-maximizing objective. Our current behavior is calibrated to the ancestral environment in which we evolved. Kock (2009) distinguishes between an "ancient task environment" (Ea) and a "modern task environment" (Em). Elements of the Em (such as video games) may trigger responses that were selected for in the Ea. As such, it is perfectly conceivable to engage in behaviors that do not translate into clear fitness benefits (Buss 1995). However, gamers' responses to video game stimuli are not as dramatic as they would be if the simulated situations on screen were real. They probably do not experience the same parasympathetic activation to a virtual predator attack that they would to an actual attack. This suggests that players understand that they are playing (and not living) the experience at a preconscious, emotional level. The evolutionary roots of play help us to explain why the human mind has this capacity to experience emotionally salient simulations without needing to activate a full-fledged fight-or-flight response. Additionally, if video games were just a modern tool for engaging in play behavior (a mammalian universal), then they might actually confer important benefits rendering them useful on several levels. Playing games might constitute a perfectly normal behavioral tendency and *not* a maladaptive misfiring of psychological mechanisms. In the remainder of this section, we investigate ways in which video games share characteristics with play behavior.

The evolution of play has been addressed in many different ways, and as such the field is far from having reached consensus. It is beyond the scope of this chapter to provide a thorough treatise of the evolutionary roots of play behavior. Rather, we restrict our discussion to how evolutionary forces (including our innate desire to play) influence modern entertainment, how "training for the unexpected" may have been the adaptive impetus for the evolution of play, and how our childhood tendency to engage in pretense may be related to our creativity in adulthood.

Ohler and Nieding (2006a, b) provide summaries of the research that connects play, modern entertainment (including video games), and EP. In Ohler and Nieding (2006a), the authors discuss the three dominant evolutionary perspectives on play. Play can be construed as entertainment, and as such as a solution to boredom (the leisure-time theory); it can also be viewed as a sexually selected trait meant to serve as a fitness-revealing ornament (Miller 2000); and finally, it might have been naturally selected for survival value. The latter two of these theoretical positions are the most relevant to our purposes. The first, which proposes that our attempts at entertaining one another were selected for because they were costly signals, seems especially consistent with the arguments we have laid out here. In many games, players interact via an avatar that grows in social and material status during the course of play, in ways that are consistent with costly signaling theory. In online games, it is easy to make the case that real humans are signaling meaningful characteristics to one another via their avatars. That natural selection might have forged our penchant for play (i.e., that those of us who played were better at hunting, gathering, and evading predators) is also relevant to our context. Earlier in this chapter we discussed some of the positive effects that individuals experience when playing a video game including that gaming improves performance in task switching, working memory, visual short-term memory, and reasoning (Basak et al. 2008); spatial skills (Subrahmanyam and Greenfield 1994); and hand–eye coordination (Lowery and Knirk 1982/1983). It is plausible to suggest that these effects might improve one's skills in areas that would have yielded positive fitness consequences in the ancestral environment. It is also reasonable to call them "practice" effects, as the individuals being measured are simply getting better at things that the game requires them to do as the result of repeated trials. This notion of "practicing" leads us into our discussion of another play perspective called "training for the unexpected."

Spinka et al. (2001) provide a thorough review of the four most commonly examined hypotheses regarding mammalian play, as well as offering their own, fifth hypothesis. Since Spinka et al.'s "training for the unexpected" hypothesis is the most consistent with the existing findings in the area, and reconciles the sexual ornament and survival benefit theories into one parsimonious theory, we favor it over the competing theories in the area.

Spinka et al.'s (2001) training for the unexpected hypothesis suggests that animals will self-handicap during play behavior (by "playing the victim," for instance), in order to simulate a lack of control in decision making. For instance, by intentionally head-tilting, falling, and bumping into each other, species can practice their emotional and behavioral routines when facing an uncontrolled (or unexpected) situation (e.g., accidentally bumping into a conspecific during flight from a predator or losing a dominance competition). This is the reason that predatory mammals are often seen "play fighting" whereas the mammals that they feed on are often seen "play fleeing," and why, during play, both predators and prey will commit clumsy, play-acted "mistakes." Such self-handicapping translates well into video games. For instance, selecting the highest difficulty setting in a game constitutes a form of self-handicapping, as players are making a conscious decision to reduce their own likelihood of success, and inevitably leads to a more challenging experience, but a (perhaps) more satisfying completion of the game.

Game content also seems to be well aligned with the "training for the unexpected" hypothesis. As previously discussed, such content tends to favor characters, environments, and objectives that possess fitness relevance. So, although few players of military-style FPSs *actually* expect to be recruited into the United States Marine Corps or the British Special Air Services, in playing these online games against other humans, they may develop a robust, fast-acting theory of mind by being rewarded for successfully anticipating the actions of others. On a similar note, a young woman might be exposed to the incessant needs of offspring by having a virtual baby in *The Sims* and thus learning that diligence is a prerequisite to successful parenting. Commercial and military pilots train on simulators for the express purpose of "training for the unexpected." Thus, one could plausibly argue that by playing video games, individuals are engaging the psychological mechanisms that have evolved for training for the unexpected.

Carruthers (2002) provides a somewhat different perspective on human play behavior. He limits his scope to "make-believe" or "pretend" play. This type of play is cerebral and includes talking to dolls or invisible friends. As far as we know, "The young of no other species of creature on earth behaves like this in natural circumstances – not even the other great apes..." (Carruthers 2002, p. 228). Carruthers makes the case that "pretend play" is an ontogenetic phase that enables human infants to develop a strong creative capacity. He further argues that, given human social complexity, those with the greatest ability to work out social problems ahead of time (via creative fantasy) would be predisposed to survive and reproduce better than those without such an ability. Thus, the degree to which one could accurately re-create the imagined social situation would serve as a predictor of one's ability to successfully maneuver similar real-life situations. Carruthers surmises (p. 225), "…essentially the same cognitive resources are shared by adult creative thinking and problem-solving, on the one hand, and by childhood pretend play, on the other – namely, capacities to generate and to reason with suppositions (or imagined possibilities)."

Carruthers' central premise is consistent with our theorizing regarding video game stimuli. Both exciting gaming and exciting play behavior require that one react as though the experience is authentic, while consciously understanding that it is not (as in pretending to flee, pretending that a banana is a telephone, and pretending that a growling, three-legged extraterrestrial has identified you as prey). However, a major difference between gaming and pretend playing is that the stimuli in pretend playing are the product of the players' creative imaginations whereas video game stimuli come "pre-packaged." Thus, the "creative faculty" to which Carruthers refers may not be getting activated in video gaming and the subsequent effects on social maneuvering are not expected to be operative. In fact, time spent gaming online has been correlated with social anxiety and dissatisfaction with physical interpersonal relationships (Lo et al. 2005), suggesting that video games do not encourage users to "train up" their creative social problem solving. For more on the adaptive nature of pretense and entertainment, see Steen and Owens (2001).

Video games diverge from Carruthers' "pretend play" behavior in another very important way: the age of the participants. Pretend play is defined as an activity that is engaged in by juveniles in preparation for adulthood whereas video gamers can be significantly older. In proclaiming that pretend play is absent in adults, Carruthers has overlooked some of the rather elaborate pretending that adults engage in. Examples of such behaviors include sexual role playing and various other subcultures that are founded on various forms of "pretend play" (e.g., the Society for Creative Anachronism, Furry Fandom, and Star Wars reenactors, to name but a few). In this sense, video games appear to constitute play behavior as enunciated by Spinka et al. but not so from the more restricted perspective of Carruthers.

Whereas the evolutionary underpinnings of play have yet to be fully determined, it is plausible that video gaming is not rooted in any adaptive process but rather it might serve as an exaptation (i.e., a byproduct) of a more fundamental adaptation. In other words, humans might have evolved the capacity to play as a means of addressing specific evolutionarily relevant problems and video gaming is a modern invention for engaging that capacity.

At present, video games constitute a growing cultural phenomenon whose implications (both societal and theoretical) are dubiously understood, at best. Fortunately, avenues for inquiry are vast and largely unexplored. Similar to play, video games allow us to immerse ourselves in characters, environments, and tasks limited only by the state of our hardware, software, and imagination.

4 Future Research and Conclusions

The cultural impact of video games is rapidly expanding. Games continue to encompass ever-larger audiences and are ever-more engrossing. Players can travel to settings of lush medieval fantasy, post-apocalyptic rubble, or among the stars. Players are provided with opportunities to act with heroic altruism or lecherous villainy. They can save the world or dominate it. They can help other players in need or ruthlessly pummel them into submission. With the unabated increases in computing power, game stimuli are becoming more complex, making games more immersive and real. The effect of gaming on minds has only begun to be documented by researchers, the key results of which can be quite contentious (as in the violence literature). In an attempt to better understand the existing literature and provide new insights in the study of this fascinating new cultural phenomenon, we have examined video games through an evolutionary lens. Such a lens renders the flaws of the SSSM clear: By assuming that humans are born with empty minds, the predominantly SSSM-based research is at best incomplete and at worst erroneous. We posit that an understanding of the innate workings of the mind, shaped by the dual forces of natural and sexual selection over eons of time, can inform video game researchers in unique and novel ways.

In this chapter we addressed non-evolutionary streams of video game research and argued for the importance of an evolutionary perspective in future work. Specifically, we began with a discussion of how evolutionary psychology can be used to study all cultural products (of which video games are but one category). From this position, we postulated that the content of video games simulates fitness-relevant stimuli and then proposed that sex differences in gaming are well explained by fitness-informed evolutionary theory. We concluded our treatise by highlighting the manner by which video game playing is both similar to and different from play behavior.

The future research opportunities at the nexus of video games and evolutionary theory appear highly promising. As laid out in Mendenhall et al. (2010), some possible avenues include the following: examining how the differences between games in the design of their economic systems differentially activate our mental module for cheater detection; how anonymity allows gamers to experiment with personality signaling through multiple avatars; and how the tendency of players to work together and form "guilds" match evolutionary perspectives on group formation and cooperation.

Earlier, we discussed how the innate predisposition to detect and then avoid or punish cheaters was used in *Deus Ex* to motivate that game's plot. In order for altruism to have evolved, the ability to detect and punish selfish non-reciprocators was a necessary precedent (Trivers 1971). Treachery was scripted in *Deus Ex,* but in many MMORPGs, cheating is simply the inevitable consequence of interacting with self-interested conspecifics. In these online worlds, players often trade with one another, and each trading event has the potential for one party to acquire unfair gains, rendering the intrinsic vulnerabilities of altruism salient (i.e., defection from cooperative behaviors). In reality, there is no objective force which prevents would-be defectors from violating the implicit rules of trading. In the judicial system, we pass laws to punish defectors, but in games, objective rules are explicitly arbitrated in the design. Developers can choose to program trading interfaces in ways that delimit exploitation. This decision is likely to shape the behavior of players, especially in regard to how they communicate and interpret signals of trustworthiness. An illustrative example can help clarify the following: In *WoW*, if two players wish to trade with one another, they can open a "trade window." In the trade window, prospective trading partners can see what each has offered. If player A finds the trade attractive, they click the "trade" button, and their offer is highlighted in bright green, signaling to player B that they have accepted the terms of the transaction and are willing to trade. If player B agrees, by also hitting "trade," the goods are transferred and the window is closed. In an early version of *WoW*, player B could modify his half of the deal *after* player A had accepted the terms. Thus, if player B wanted something for nothing, he could wait for player A to agree to the deal and, moving quickly, pull all of his goods off of the table and hit the trade button. The program simply presumed that player A had agreed to magnanimously donate his goods to player B, when player A did not have any such intention. When exploitation of this interface bug became widespread, the makers of *WoW* changed the rules of the trade window. Since then, when either player changes the terms of the trade, existing agreements are dropped, so neither player can be tricked. *WoW's* trade rules actually reduce the amount of cheater detection one has to engage in by limiting cheaters' ability to cheat via the improved design of the trade interface. *WoW* has many more systems in place that generally preserve an equal distribution of resources and prevent exploitation of naïve (or nice) players.

This is starkly different from the economic system in *EVE Online*. The major premise of *EVE Online* is to simulate a highly competitive free market economy amid a science-fiction backdrop. As such, no holds are barred, and trickery and deceit are considered part of the experience of playing *EVE*. Players can profit through cooperation, but the mechanics of the game do not insure or uphold the interests of each party (as they do in *WoW*): One player could run off with the other's goods. In fact, players hire one another to spy on, sabotage, and steal from rival groups. In *EVE*, cooperation hinges on the delicate trust between the parties, a situation far closer to that found in our evolutionary past. We posit that the variance in "cheating potential" between games will be correlated to several social perception dimensions related to cheater detection. In *WoW*, we expect a dampened concern over trustworthiness in cooperative settings relative to *EVE*, because the objective rules of *WoW* protect players from exploitation. However, managing trust can be difficult given that a single player can control multiple avatars, and other players are not privy to the number of avatars that are under the control of a given player. As such, another avenue of inquiry could explicitly explore how the ability to change identities via multiple avatars influences gamer behavior.

Avatars act like identities. MMORPG players repeatedly interact with other players via their avatars, developing friendships and rivalries along the way. Strictly speaking, the relationships exist on an avatar-to-avatar basis and not a player-to-player one. To illustrate, let us take two imaginary players and their avatars. Mike plays two avatars in some imaginary online game: *Milli,* an attractive female healer, and *Grunt,* a new (and thence, weak) male barbarian. Stan also plays two avatars: *Gallahad,* a noble male knight, and *Pest,* an aggressive but sneaky assassin. *Milli* and *Gallahad* often cooperate together on quests. Mike allows Stan to believe that he is, in the real world, a female (i.e., that *Milli* is controlled by a flesh-and-blood female), because Stan often gives him a generous portion of the resources they find. Stan (as *Gallahad*) often tries to flirt with Mike (as *Milli*), but his stronger advances are rebuffed, as Mike is merely using the pretense of being a woman in real life for profit in the online world. To alleviate his frustration, Stan occasionally plays as *Pest* and kills weaker avatars, one of whom happened to be named *Grunt.* Mike is not aware that Stan killed him, and Stan is not aware that he killed Mike, so the consequences of the action will not be held against them when they play as *Gallahad* or *Milli.*

Since the owner of an avatar is not explicitly known, players can lead entirely different playing careers with different characters. Only with clever observation or explicit information (such as a personal relationship with the player) can one learn that the two avatars are played by the same person. Players may have one avatar that is the fearless leader of a respected guild and another, less important avatar that they play when they need a break from guild duties.

Another implication of the ability to switch avatars is that players can pretend that one of their avatars is the alternative avatar of a *different* player. This would be the case if Mike, playing as *Grunt,* tells another player (say Alex, who is holding goods that belong to Stan) that he (Mike) is Stan by saying, "I have grown tired of playing as *Gallahad,* so I started this new avatar. Please give me everything you owe me." If the resources are construed as being owed to the *player* (and *not* the avatar), and Stan is entitled to resources from Alex, Mike may be able to intercept those resources by playing as "Stan's new avatar." Such tales of multiple avatar abuse pepper gaming forums and provide a rich set of data for exploring reputation effects. So far, we have discussed potential investigations of social phenomena that involve, at most, only a few individuals. However, social interactions in online worlds occur in greater magnitudes as well. Another social behavior with exciting research potential is the tendency for players to form and join groups in various online games.

In many games, players choose to form new groups and/or join existing groups. These groups can be formally arranged within the game (a group of avatars) or informally arranged outside of the game (a group of players). Groups are referred to by different names (e.g., "guilds," "clans," and even "corporations" in the ultra-capitalistic *EVE*). A game can have built-in systems for acknowledging group membership (i.e., each avatar's guild name is displayed beneath the avatar name) or not (in which case, players usually put a "tag" in front of their name to signal group membership). Groups vary in their size, exclusivity, and interests. Some are casual collections of friends, whereas others are very large and highly organized, requiring militant observation of strict rules of participation. These various group types can be analyzed from an evolutionary point of view. Essentially, the more seriously a given player views his/her virtual status (i.e., the extent to which he/she "internalizes" the status-promoting cues they perceived from playing the game), the more likely he/she is to pledge allegiance to a highly selective group with the prestige, presence, and organization necessary to improve that status. For instance, the most powerful equipment in any given MMORPG can usually only be acquired through the careful, determined cooperation of 25–40 players investing several hours a day, several times per week. Those who are heavily invested in acquiring such equipment have little patience for tardiness or careless mistakes. Players that "play for fun" might be more likely to enjoy casual, fluid groups with far fewer obligations, but far fewer benefits as well.

To conclude, whereas an understanding of the ultimate (evolutionary) causes of human behavior is imperative for a consilient scientific worldview, it would be fatuous to claim that evolutionary explanations are operative for all phenomena. In fact, it is perhaps as silly as proclaiming that all human behavioral phenomena are explained by social construction (i.e., the inherent flaw of the SSSM). In establishing robust knowledge of any phenomenon, it is essential that both proximate and ultimate explanations be utilized. We hope that our evolutionary analysis of video games has shed new light on the previously held presuppositions regarding their connection to violence, sex, play, and culture. With the dissemination of evolutionary theory throughout the social sciences, it is inevitable that a complete and accurate understanding of video games will require that the evolutionary lens be injected within this research stream.

References

Anderson CA (2004) An update on the effects of playing violent video games. J Adolesc 27(1):113–122

Appleton J (1975) The experiences of landscapes. William Clowes and Sons, London

Aunger R (2002) The electric meme: a new theory of how we think. The Free Press, New York

Bartholow BD, Anderson CA (2002) Effects of violent video games on aggressive behavior: potential sex differences. J Exp Soc Psychol 38(3):283–290

Bartholow BD, Bushman BJ, Sestir MA (2006) Chronic violent video game exposure and desensitization to violence: behavioral and event-related brain potential data. J Exp Soc Psychol 42(4):532–539

Basak C, Boot WR, Voss MW, Kramer AF (2008) Can training in a real-time strategy video game attenuate cognitive decline in older adults? Psychol Aging 23(4):765–777

Binsted G, Chua R, Helsen W, Elliot D (2001) Eye-hand coordination in goal-directed aiming. Hum Mov Sci 20(4/5):563–585

Blackmore S (1999) The meme machine. Oxford University Press, Oxford

Boyd R, Richerson PJ (1985) Culture and the evolutionary process. University of Chicago Press, Chicago

Boyer P (2001) Religion explained: the evolutionary origins of religious thought. Basic Books, New York

Buss DM (1988) The evolution of human intrasexual competition: tactics of mate attraction. J Pers Soc Psychol 54(4):616–628

Buss DM (1995) Evolutionary psychology: a new paradigm for psychological science. Psychol Inq 6(1):1–30

Buss DM (2005) The murderer next door: why the mind is designed to kill. Penguin, New York

Carroll J (2005) Literature and evolutionary psychology. In: Buss DM (ed) Handbook of evolutionary psychology. Wiley, Hoboken, pp 931–952

Carruthers P (2002) Human creativity: its cognitive basis, its evolution, and its connection with childhood pretence. Br J Philos Sci 53:225–249

Cherney ID, Poss JL (2008) Sex differences in nintendo Wii[TM] performance as expected from hunter-gatherer selection. Psychol Rep 102(3):745–754

Chou C, Tsai MJ (2007) Gender differences in Taiwan high school students' computer game playing. Comput Hum Behav 23(1):812–824

Cosmides L, Tooby J (1992) Cognitive adaptations for social exchange. In: Barkow JH, Cosmides L, Tooby J (eds) The adapted mind: evolutionary psychology and the generation of culture. Oxford University Press, New York, pp 163–228

Cosmides L, Tooby J (2005) Neurocognitive adaptations designed for social exchange. In: Buss DM (ed) Handbook of evolutionary psychology. Wiley, Hoboken, pp 584–627

Dawkins R (1976) The selfish gene. Oxford University Press, London

Di Leonardo M (1987) The female world of cards and holidays: women, families, and the work of kinship. Signs 12(3):440–453

Dissanayake E (1992) Homo aestheticus: where art comes from and why. The Free Press, New York

Ducheneaut N, Yee N (2006) Building an MMO with mass appeal: a look at gameplay in World of Warcraft. Games Cult 1(4):281–317

Entertainment Software Association. (2007) Industry facts. http://www.theesa.com/facts/index.asp, Retrieved 15 Jan 2009

Entertainment Software Association. (2009) Industry facts. http://www.theesa.com/facts/index.asp, Retrieved 27 July 2009

Falk JH, Balling JD (2009) Evolutionary influence on human landscape preference. Env Behav DOI: 10.1177/0013916509341244

Ferguson CJ (2007) Evidence for publication bias in video game violence effects literature – a meta-analytic review. Aggress Violent Behav 12(4):470–482

Ferguson CJ, Kilburn J (2009) The public health risk of media violence: a meta-analytic review. J Pediatr 154(5):759–763

Fischer P, Kastenmüller A, Greitemeyer T (2010) Media violence and the self: the impact of personalized gaming characters in aggressive video games on aggressive behavior. J Exp Soc Psychol 36(1):192–195

Geary DC (2009) Male, female: the evolution of human sex differences, 2nd edn. American Psychological Association, Washington

Gee JP (2007) What video games have to teach us about learning and literacy. Palgrave Macmillan, New York

Ghiglieri M (2000) The dark side of man: tracing the origins of male violence. Perseus Books, Reading

Greitemeyer T, Osswald S (2009) Prosocial video games reduce aggressive cognitions. J Exp Soc Psychol 45(4):896–900

Gurven M, Hill K (2009) Why do men hunt? a reevaluation of "Man the Hunter" and the sexual division of labor. Curr Anthropol 50(1):51–74

Hill RA, Donovan S, Koyama NF (2005) Female sexual advertisement reflects resource availability in twentieth-century UK society. Hum Nat 16(3):266–277

Kaplan R, Kaplan S (1989) The experience of nature: a psychological perspective. Cambridge University Press, New York

Kaplan R, Hill K, Lancaster J, Hurtado M (2000) A theory of human life history evolution: diet, intelligence, and longevity. Evol Anthropol 9(4):156–184

Keeley LH (1997) War before civilization: the myth of the peaceful savage. Oxford University Press, Oxford

Kock N (2008) E-collaboration and e-commerce in virtual worlds: the potential of Second Life and World of Warcraft. Int J e-Collab 4(3):1–13

Kock N (2009) Information systems theorizing based on evolutionary psychology: an interdisciplinary review and theory integration framework. MIS Q 33(2):395–418

Konijin EA, Bijvak MN, Bushman BJ (2007) I wish I were a warrior: the role of wishful identification in the effects of violent video games on aggression in adolescent boys. Dev Psychol 43(4):1038–1044

Lo S-K, Wang C-C, Fang W (2005) Physical interpersonal relationships and social anxiety among online game players. Cyberpsychol Behav 8(1):15–20

Lowery BR, Knirk FG (1982–1983) Micro-computer video games and spatial visualization acquisition. J Educ Technol Syst 11(2):155–166

Marlowe F (2001) Male contribution to diet and female reproductive success among foragers. Curr Anthropol 42(5):755–760

Mazur A, Susman EJ, Edelbrock S (1997) Sex difference in testosterone response to a video game contest. Evol Hum Behav 18(5):317–326

Mendenhall Z, Miller G (in preparation) Conspicuous consumption in world of warcraft: auction versus vendor prices reveal the price premium for conspicuously cool weapons

Mendenhall Z, Nepomuceno MV, Saad G (2010) Exploring video games from an evolutionary perspective. In: Lee I (ed) Encyclopedia of e-business development and management in the digital economy. IGI Global, Hershey, pp 734–742

Miller GF (2000) The mating mind: how sexual choice shaped the evolution of human nature. Doubleday, New York

Miller GF (2009) Spent: sex, evolution, and consumer behavior. Viking Adult, New York

Motion Picture Association of America (2007) Entertainment industry market statistics. http://www.mpaa.org/USEntertainmentIndustryMarketStats.pdf, Retrieved 15 Jan 2009

Nepomuceno MV, Saad G, Stenstrom E, Mendenhall Z (2009) Finger length ratio and attitudes towards several product categories. Human Behavior and Evolution Society Meetings. California State University, Fullerton, May 27–31

Ohler P, Nieding G (2006a) An evolutionary perspective on entertainment. In: Bryant J, Vorderer P (eds) Psychology of entertainment. Lawrence Erlbaum, Hillsdale, pp 423–433

Ohler P, Nieding G (2006b) Why play? an evolutionary perspective. In: Vorderer P, Bryant J (eds) Playing computer games: motives, responses, and consequences. Lawrence Erlbaum, Hillsdale, pp 101–113

Olson CK, Kutner LA, Warner DE, Almerigi JB, Baer L, Nicholi AM, Beresin EV (2007) Factors correlated with violent video game use by adolescent boys and girls. J Adolesc Health 41(1):77–83

Piazza J, Bering JM (2009) Evolutionary cyber-psychology: applying an evolutionary framework to Internet behavior. Comput Hum Behav 25(6):1258–1269

Pinker S (2002) The blank slate: the modern denial of human nature. Viking, New York

Richerson PJ, Boyd R (2005) Not by genes alone: how culture transformed human evolution. University of Chicago Press, Chicago

Rosen SP (2007) War and human nature. Princeton University Press, Princeton

Saad G (2007) The evolutionary bases of consumption. Lawrence Erlbaum, Mahwah

Saad G, Vongas JG (2009) The effect of conspicuous consumption on men's testosterone levels. Organ Behav and Hum Decis Processes 110:80–92

Sanger J, Wilson J, Davies B, Whitakker R (1997) Young children, videos and computer games: issue for teachers and parents. Falmer Press, Bristol

Sherman S (1997) The perils of the princess: gender and genre in video games. West Folk 56(3/4):243–258

Silverman I, Choi J (2005) Locating places. In: Buss DM (ed) The handbook of evolutionary psychology. Wiley, Hoboken, pp 177–199

Smith DL (2007) The most dangerous animal: human nature and the origins of war. St. Martin's Griffin, New York

Spinka M, Newberry RC, Bekoff M (2001) Mammalian play: training for the unexpected. Q Rev Biol 76(2):141–168

Steen FF, Owens SA (2001) Evolution's pedagogy: an adaptationist model of pretense and entertainment. J Cogn Cult 1(4):289–321

Stenstrom E, Stenstrom P, Saad G, Cheikhrouhou S (2008) Online hunting and gathering: an evolutionary perspective on sex differences in website preferences and navigation. IEEE Trans Prof Commun 51(2):155–168

Subrahmanyam K, Greenfield PM (1994) Effect of video game practice on spatial skills in girls and boys. J Appl Dev Psychol 15(1):13–32

Thayer BA (2004) Darwin and international relations: on the evolutionary origins of war and ethnic conflict. University Press of Kentucky, Lexington

Tooby J, Cosmides L (1992) The psychological foundations of culture. In: Barkow J, Cosmides L, Tooby J (eds) The adapted mind: evolutionary psychology and the generation of culture. Oxford University Press, New York, pp 19–136

Trivers R (1971) The evolution of reciprocal altruism. Q Rev Biol 46: 35–57

Uhlmann E, Swason J (2004) Exposure to violent video games increases automatic aggressiveness. J Adolesc 27(1):41–52

Wrangham R, Peterson D (1996) Demonic males: apes and the origins of human violence. Houghton Mifflin, New York

Yee N (2006) Motivations for play in online games. Cyberpsychol Behav 9(6):772–775

Yee N (2008) Maps of digital desires: exploring the topography of gender and play in online games. In: Kafai YB, Heeter C, Denner J, Sun JY (eds) Beyond barbie and mortal kombat: new perspectives on gender and gaming. MIT Press, Cambridge, pp 83–96

Yee N, Bailenson J (2007) The Proteus effect: the effect of transformed self-representation on behavior. Hum Commun Res 33(3):271–290

Yee N, Bailenson JN (2009) The difference between being and seeing: the relative contribution of self perception and priming to behavioral changes via digital self-representation. Media Psychol 12(2):195–209

Yee N, Bailenson JN, Ducheneaut N (2009) The Proteus effect: implications of transformed digital self-representation on online and offline behavior. Commun Res 36(2):285–312

Chapter 15
The Modern Hunter–Gatherer Hunts Aliens and Gathers Power-Ups: The Evolutionary Appeal of Violent Video Games and How They Can Be Beneficial

Christopher J. Ferguson

Abstract Video game violence has been the focus of much recent concern among politicians, activists, and some social scientists. Evolutionary psychology can help explain the origins of fascination of many individuals, particularly males, with violent games. Interest in violent video games can be viewed as an extension of normal and adaptive aggression instincts, in which video games provide a safe arena in which individuals can express aggression and manage mood without actually causing harm to others. An evolutionary model of violent game interest, the Catalyst Model, is presented and contrasted with traditional social learning models of video game violence use. It is argued that the harmful effects of violent game exposure on the majority of players are negligible whereas violent games may provide a useful platform for positive development in education, visuospatial cognition, and social networking.

Keywords Mass media · Computer games · Violence · Aggression · Evolutionary psychology

1 Introduction

Humankind's fascination with violent entertainment has been noted during virtually every historical period (Kutner and Olson 2008; Trend 2007) as well as among most cultures. Such entertainment has varied in form and intensity, ranging from actual deaths for entertainment during Roman games or medieval executions to more modern forms of entertainment such as television and video games, where the injuries and deaths are largely fictional (excepting those occurring during sporting events

C.J. Ferguson (✉)
Department of Behavioral Sciences, Applied Sciences and Criminal Justice, Texas A&M International University, 5201 University Boulevard, Laredo, TX 78041, USA
e-mail: cferguson@tamiu.edu

N. Kock (ed.), *Evolutionary Psychology and Information Systems Research*,
Integrated Series in Information Systems 24, DOI 10.1007/978-1-4419-6139-6_15,
© Springer Science+Business Media, LLC 2010

perhaps). Media violence has historically had its critics as well ranging from moral philosophers such as Tertullian (200) and Augustine (397) to modern politicians and anti-media lobbyists. However, whatever one's feelings are about media violence, there can be little doubt that such entertainments are ubiquitous, popular, and a constant element of the human condition. As new media have developed quickly in the twentieth and twenty first centuries, cycles of "moral panics" have broken out regarding new media (Kutner and Olson 2008; Trend 2007). In most of these cases, society "elders" who do not use the new media complain that this new media (whether novels, comic books, jazz, rock and roll, movies, television, Elvis Presley, Betty Boop, Harry Potter, etc.) will corrupt or "harm" youth. In retrospect, most of these concerns seem absurd with media that previously caused great alarm now recognized as harmless, yet this does not stop the cycle from continuing with emerging media. In recent years, video games have been at the center of some of the most recent concerns (Anderson 2004; Ferguson 2008). This chapter concerns itself with understanding the use and impact of violent video games from the standpoint of evolutionary psychology. The chapter will be divided into two main parts: first, discussing the appeal of violent video games from an evolutionary standpoint and second, discussing ways in which this appeal can be harnessed to use violent video games for positive outcomes.

2 Understanding Aggression

Much of the discussion of aggression in the social sciences began with an assumption that aggression is an inherently bad thing, both for the individual and for society at large. This trickles down into news reports of scientific studies. For instance, when people hear something along the lines of "Scientists conclude that eating pomegranates causes aggression," this is often met with considerable hand-wringing among politicians, activists groups, parents, etc. about the deleterious effects of pomegranates, the moral turpitude of those who dare to farm pomegranates, and self-righteous questions about how anyone, particularly the youth of today, could possibly get any pleasure out of eating pomegranates. Some will call for the restriction of sale of pomegranates, particularly to minors. This all assumes that aggression is necessarily a bad thing. Certainly, in the extreme, when heightened aggression results in extreme violence likely to cause harm to oneself and others, this can be the case (Ferguson and Beaver 2009). However, aggressiveness may also have positive benefits and indeed be evolutionarily adaptive, particularly in moderate amounts. Moderate aggressiveness may aid us in defending ourselves and our family, standing up for our beliefs, seeking high-status positions in society, developing leadership, excelling in sports and many careers, enduring hardships, etc. These are behaviors that increase social status and reproductive success. Indeed, some scholars have recognized that aggressiveness, particularly when allowed to be defined broadly, may have more positive qualities than negative (Hawley and Vaughn 2003; Smith 2007). Aggression measures used in many social science studies do not adequately distinguish between healthy adaptive aggression and extreme violent behaviors (Ferguson and Rueda 2009; Ritter and Eslea 2005). Thus, much of the hand-wringing may be premature.

Aggression is defined in this paper as a "behavior that is intended to increase the social dominance of the organism relative to the dominance position of other organisms" (Ferguson and Beaver 2009). Aggressiveness is a ubiquitous human trait across societies and historical periods (Ferguson and Beaver 2009). Archeological evidence from pre-historical human cultures reveals evidence of the use of fatal violence in these cultures (McCall and Shields 2008). The evolutionary roots of aggression can be observed by examining humans' closest genetic relative, the chimpanzee. Chimpanzees have been observed engaging in mass intergroup fatal violence (Goodall 1979) and fatal abuse of infants (Goodall 1977). Given that greater sexual competition exists among males (Gottschalk and Ellis 2009), and that females are more invested in the care of young (Buss and Duntley 2006), males engage in greater levels of aggression than do females, as is the case with most other mammalian species (Gottschalk and Ellis 2009; Okami and Shackelford 2001). This *sexual selection* of male aggression and violence may also be related to the division of labor between males and females in prehistoric hunter–gather societies in which males typically undertook the riskier activity of hunting (Morris 1999).

The observation that aggression is an evolutionary adaptation which provides a selective advantage to those individuals who possess a moderate level of the trait is at odds with much of the lingo and dogma of the social sciences across the latter twentieth century. Historically it had been assumed that aggression and violence were learned behaviors, shaped largely by environmental influences including family and peers, but also media effects (e.g., Berkowitz 1993). Increasingly, evidence has demonstrated that this tabula rasa (i.e., blank slate) view of aggression has been mistaken and that there are strong genetic roots to aggressive and violent behaviors (Caspi et al. 2002; Ferguson 2010; Rhee and Waldman 2002). Thus too often in the social sciences, the presumed causal arrow between aggression and its correlates may have been misdirected.

3 Violent Video Games and Aggression

As noted earlier, complaints that various media forms would spark waves of rebelliousness, violence, and moral turpitude are nothing unique to the twentieth century. However the latter half of the twentieth century saw a considerable emphasis on media violence research guided by the "social learning" theoretical tradition. Briefly, this tradition, attributed largely to Albert Bandura, suggests that individuals learn through imitating or modeling the behavior of others. Arguably over time, modeling morphed, in the view of many social scientists, from something that humans *can* do to something that they *must* do without volition or consideration of the benefits and costs of doing so.

Bandura's "Bobo doll" studies in particular provided much guidance for the media effects tradition of the latter twentieth century (Bandura et al. 1961, 1963). There are actually numerous variations on these sets of studies, but in brief they had children (males and females) watch adults (also males and females) either in real life or in filmed sequences engage in a series of highly novel acts against a Bobo doll (an inflatable toy doll which is designed to be boxed or hit). So, for instance, the models would sit on the Bobo doll and punch it in the nose, or whack it with a mallet. The researchers then irritated the children by showing them a host of toys that they were not allowed to play with before bringing them to the test room with the Bobo doll. Children who had seen an adult model these behaviors (either in real life or in film) were more likely to engage in similar behaviors. Although the Bobo doll studies are not media violence studies per se, they purport to demonstrate that aggression can be imitated by children. Presumably, these results would potentially be generalizable to television and other media forms.

However, there are limitations to the Bobo doll studies that are important to acknowledge (see Gauntlett 1995). First, the effects appear to be small overall and evaporate very quickly. Second, the "aggression" in the study was directed at an object, not another person, and it remains unclear if the studies' results can be generalized to real-life aggression against people. Related to that is the concern that the entire situation is contrived; after all, one might ask, what else are you supposed to do with a Bobo doll other than hit it? Third, it is unclear whether the children were necessarily more motivated to engage in aggression in general, as opposed to mimicking *specific* aggressive acts. In other words, overall aggressive behaviors may not have changed much, but the style of the aggressive behaviors might have been altered due to the novel kinds of aggressive behaviors presented. Fourth, it is unclear whether the children were necessarily motivated by aggression, as opposed to aggressive play or even the desire to please the adult experimenter. Children are quite used to being given instructions by adults and they may arguably have simply viewed the models (who were adults) as instructors telling them what to do. In other words, the children may have even believed that they might be scolded or punished if they did not follow the model's lead. Lastly, in a subsequent paper, Bandura (1965) found that showing the model being punished for attacking the Bobo doll decreased modeled behaviors in child participants. Yet the punishments themselves appeared to involve considerable aggressive behavior. As described in the original text:

> For children in the model-punished condition, the reinforcing agent appeared on the scene [this occurs after the children watched the model hit the bo-bo doll] shaking his finger menacingly and commenting reprovingly, "Hey there you big bully. You quit picking on that clown. I won't tolerate it." As the model drew back he tripped and fell, and the other adult sat on the model and spanked him with a rolled up magazine while reminding him of his aggressive behavior. As the model ran off, cowering, the agent forewarned him, "If I catch you doing that again, you big bully, I'll give you a hard spanking. You quit acting that way" (Bandura 1965. p. 591).

From this description it is reasonable to wonder what we can conclude when it appears that children are willing to imitate non-violent aggression against an object, but viewing violence against an actual person inhibits their aggression. However one interprets the meaningfulness of the Bobo doll studies, there is little doubt that they had considerable impact on the media violence debate.

The media effects tradition continued more or less along the same lines, testing the hypothesis that viewed violence produces increased aggression (although notice the slip in terms between violence and aggression. . .with the assumption once again that aggression is inherently pathological). The meaningfulness, and even size of this body of research, has been debated for decades. For instance, the American Academy of Pediatrics has infamously claimed upward of 3500 studies on the topic of media violence, although an actual careful examination of the literature field found closer to 200 studies with mixed results (Freedman 2002). Like the Bobo doll studies, studies of media violence have oftentimes been limited by poor methodology, inadequate aggression measures, poor control of extraneous variables, and an almost desperate effort to "prove" the theory rather than to meaningfully test hypotheses (Ferguson 2009; Olson 2004; Pinker 2002; Savage 2004). Indeed, in many studies, the study abstracts are worded so as to imply a meaningful connection between media violence viewing and aggression, whereas a careful perusal of the results finds non-significant or contradictory results (e.g., Anderson and Dill 2000; Malamuth and Ceniti 1986; see Ferguson 2009 and Savage 2004 for complete discussions).

Not surprisingly, this research tradition has continued with the advent of video games. Research on video games began soon after the development of early video games, with "violent" video games oftentimes represented by games such as *Pac-Man*, *Asteroids*, and *Zaxxon* (e.g., Anderson and Ford 1987; Dominick 1984). That games such as these are an important source of youth violence today would likely be considered absurd to most individuals familiar with games (or youth violence for that matter). Indeed this highlights the very nature of the media violence moral panic cycle. . .that past panics appear absurd, yet new media continues to incite new panics (Gauntlett 1995). As video game technology has improved, some newer games have "pushed the envelope" on good taste, including considerable violence and sometimes lewd sexual content. However, recent meta-analyses have indicated that such content is unlikely to increase violence risk among players (Ferguson and Kilburn 2009; Savage and Yancey 2008; Sherry 2007).

Although the furor over video game violence effects is unlikely to die down soon, from a scientific view, it is probably time to reduce our focus on video games as an important causal contributor to youth violence. Instead of looking at how video game violence causes an increase in aggression, it may be more fruitful to examine the reverse. Namely, how aggressiveness among the human species promotes an interest in violent media including violent video games. Given that players of violent video games do not randomly stumble upon such games, this causal directionality arguably makes more sense. Why, though, do many humans find violent video games enjoyable to play?

Humans, perhaps like many other creatures, find violent acts to be intrinsically rewarding and pleasurable. There are exceptions to this, of course (and perhaps those exceptions go on to become social scientists wedded to tabula rasa views of aggression); however there is little argument that violent media and violent video games are overwhelmingly popular. Recent research on mice has suggested that engaging in violent behavior activates reward centers of the brain (Couppis and Kennedy 2008) and some have suggested that similar mechanisms may exist among humans (Taylor 2009).

Although it is hardly a new idea to state it here, rather than humans becoming aggressive because of exposure to violent media, it is likely more true that humans like violent media because of an inherent aggressive streak in our species (Ferguson 2002). Thus many individuals, particularly males, may be inclined to enjoy violent video games due to natural interests in aggression and competitiveness. Females may have used "sex selection" to promote aggressiveness in males (Okami, and Shackelford 2001) as such traits are useful for hunting and protection of the family unit (Morris 1999). Thus it should not be surprising to find that young males, in particular, almost universally play violent video games (Ferguson et al. 2008a; Griffiths and Hunt 1995; Kutner et al. 2007). Violent video game playing among females, although certainly not unheard of, is considerably less universally. Play of such game may relate to pre-existing needs for and enjoyment of aggressive and competitive stimuli. Indeed recent research has suggested that, far from stimulating antisocial behavior, video game play may relate to increased social behavior and civic engagement (Lenhart et al. 2008). Thus aggressiveness may play an essential role in male bonding and dominance hierarchies. Violent game playing, like sports and competitive hobbies, may be merely a consequence of such pre-existing motivations, not a cause of them.

4 An Evolutionary Model of Violent Video Game Playing

Ferguson (Ferguson 2009; Ferguson et al. 2008a) has proposed a model, called the Catalyst Model, to explain the interaction between genes and evolution, environmental determinants of aggressiveness, and violent video game playing. It should be noted that the term "violent video game," like aggression, is rather broad, encompassing a wide variety of games, not only those such as *Grand Theft Auto* which tend to receive the most negative attention. As noted above, games such as *Centipede*, *Pac Man*, *Space Invaders*, and *Asteroids* have been labeled as "violent" games. Although this is technically accurate (all of those games involve one thing attempting to destroy other things), it does point to the degree to which some of this debate has become absurd. Such notions are dependent upon the view that the human mind is naturally devoid of aggressive inclinations, that humans *must* model behaviors that they witness, and that even the slightest hint of violence potentially carries risks of deleterious outcomes.

The Catalyst Model, presented in Fig. 15.1, approaches the relationship between video game playing and aggression from a different view than the traditional tabula rasa social science view. Briefly, this model suggests that excessive aggressiveness and a proneness to extreme violence (Ferguson and Beaver 2010) are the product of

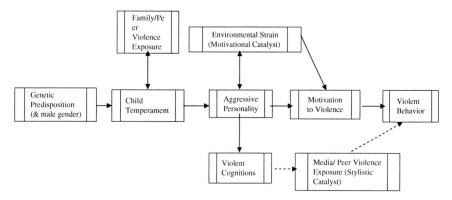

Fig. 15.1   The catalyst model of aggression

a combination of genetic effects and exposure to violence in the family and among peers. This observation has been supported by existing literature (Beaver et al. 2009; Caspi et al. 2002). The Catalyst Model suggests that aggression (and eventually violence) increases in proportion to the amount of stress that the organism experiences. Increased stress results in increased violence risk. For individuals already prone to acts of extreme violence due to genetic or family of origin influences, the amount of stress required to "catalyze" aggression is less than that for individuals with a normal or healthy genetic profile or background.

Related to violent media and video games, individuals with aggressive tendencies (relatively speaking) may have more aggressive thoughts and may be more prone to seek out violent media than may other individuals. Violent media may, at times, serve as a "stylistic catalyst." In essence, a stylistic catalyst may influence the form that a violent act takes, but not the motivation to be violent itself. For instance, a criminal who watches *CSI* or plays the video game spin-off may use bleach to destroy evidence of a violent crime where they would not have done so before. However, whether or not the individual watched *CSI* or played a violent video game, the violent act still would have occurred. Thus, exposure to violence in video games may influence the *style* of a violent act, but not the frequency or motivation of violent acts. An offender might repeat a phrase from a game, dress like a character, or reference the game after being caught (offenders blaming video games after being caught is obviously self-serving and should be taken with a large grain of salt). Aside from these minor details, the game had no real influence on the offender's motivation or intention to commit a violent act in the first place. Initial data on the Catalyst Model have suggested that it is superior to existing social learning-based models in explaining the interaction between video game violence and aggressive behavior (Ferguson et al. 2008a).

A further evolutionary point is worth considering. Namely humans, with some variation and particularly among males, are intrinsically aggressive, and thus, to varying degrees, drawn to aggressive stimuli. It thus follows that humans and males particularly will be drawn to violent stimuli, including those in the media. Although this issue is often referenced in regard to heinous violent crimes such as mass shootings (see Ferguson 2008 for a discussion), evidence makes clear that even healthy non-pathological young males (and some females) enjoy consumption of violent media (Ferguson et al. 2008a; Griffiths and Hunt 1995; Olson et al. 2007). In condemning this reality, which is probably unchangeable no matter how much social critics might rant against it, are we missing an opportunity to use such media for positive outcomes?

5 Using Violent Video Games for Positive Purposes

In the above sections I have argued that humans are intrinsically aggressive, that aggressive behavior in moderate doses can be adaptive, and that as an aggressive species, humans and males in particular are likely to be drawn to violent media. Further I have argued that the evidence suggests that, for most consumers at least, violent media does not have a deleterious effect on viewers. I am well aware that other social scientists have advocated the opposing view, but I feel that such arguments are not based on data, but rather on scientific ideology, politics, and emotion (see Grimes et al. 2008 for an excellent discussion of this issue).

One unfortunate element of this debate, which persists in a vacuum of evidence, is that the utility of an intrinsically attractive media is being missed. I am not advocating that the most savagely and offensively violent games be employed in these contexts. However, I do argue that scientists might consider a balance involving incorporating educational elements into games with a moderate amount of violence that will be interesting and fun for students to play. Some games have already done this with considerable success (Kato et al. 2008). One difficulty that educational games traditionally have is in competing with commercial games. Frequent gamers might find educational games "lame" in comparison to the sophisticated and action packed games that they are used to playing. As a related issue, the "shelf life" of many games, including educational games, can be limited. Some games such as *World of Warcraft* have exhibited remarkable staying power, however, and individuals interested in designing games for educational purposes would do well to learn some of the lessons of commercial games rather than trying (and perhaps failing) to reinvent the wheel.

In the following sections I will discuss some of the existing research on the use of games, both commercial and "serious games" (i.e., games that are specifically developed for purposes related to human enhancement or development, rather than as entertainment only), for "positive" purposes. Specifically I focus on the "unintended" consequences of violent video game playing on visuospatial cognition and the "intended" use of games, including both commercial and educational games with violent content in education.

Visuospatial cognition. Put simply, visuospatial cognition refers to a set of intellectual abilities related to the mental manipulation of and memory for objects and relationships between objects. Such abilities may provide advantage in careers ranging from art to engineering to surgery. Generally it is acknowledged that males tend to perform higher on tasks related to visuospatial cognition than do females (Collaer and Hill 2006; Livesey and Intili 1996; Parsons et al. 2004), although there may be some degree of task specificity in these differences (Ferguson et al. 2008b; Halpern and Collaer 2005). From an evolutionary perspective it is hypothesized that these differences may relate to a division of labor in early human hunter–gatherer societies in which males were involved in the hunting role, which benefited to a greater degree from high visuospatial cognition (Silverman and Eals 1992; Morris 1999).

Just as it makes sense that males who are more aggressive than females may be drawn to violent games, so too males high in visuospatial cognition relative to females (who, by contrast, excel in verbal skills) may be drawn to video games for their involvement with visuospatial cognition. Thus, any relationship between video game playing and gender might only be a gender effect, and thus gender should be carefully controlled in all research on this topic.

Nonetheless, evidence has emerged to suggest that individuals who play video games generally, and violent games specifically, tend to have better visuospatial cognition than do non-gamers. Ferguson et al. (2008b) found that gamers, and those who play violent games specifically, outperformed non-gamers on visual memory tasks, even when gender was controlled. Similar results were found by De Lisi and Wolford (2002), although Sims and Mayer (2002) found that playing non-violent games such as *Tetris* did not translate to better visuospatial performance. As such there may be something particular about *violent* video games that relates to visuospatial cognition. It may not be the violence per se but rather the type of fast action found in such games.

The results described above are largely correlational, however. Even though gender is controlled, it may still be true that those with better inherent visuospatial cognition are more attracted to video games and violent games specifically. However, more recent experimental research has confirmed that a causal pathway exists between violent video game play (these research articles typically refer to such games as "action" games, whereas aggression articles refer to "violent" games, despite that these two groups of scholars use the same games...itself an interesting observation in how science is marketed for audiences) and improved visuospatial cognition (Feng et al. 2007; Green and Bavelier 2003 2006). Further research has also suggested that practice with violent video games is even related to improved performance in surgery for medical doctors (Rosser et al. 2007). Lastly, a recent meta-analytic review has noted that the effect size for the relationship between playing violent games and improved visuospatial cognition is many times greater than for that seen between violent game playing and aggression, which was negligible (Ferguson 2007).

This last finding raises the question of why violent games would function reasonably well at improving visuospatial cognition, despite that they do not increase aggression. Isn't all learning the same? The answer, obviously, is "no," and the question assumes a rather simplistic and naïve version of "learning." Behaving aggressively (or violently) requires intrinsic motivation. One must "decide" to engage in such behavior. Although innate genetic tendencies influence an individual's level of aggression, the influence of environment on aggression is correspondingly small (Ferguson 2010). That is not to say that environment has *no* impact on violence, but the largest environmental predictors appear to be related to stress, family violence, and peer delinquency, as predicted by the Catalyst Model (Ferguson et al. 2009). After those factors are controlled, video game violence (or television) has no impact on violent behavior. Thus individuals are, to varying degrees, predisposed to violence, but ultimately "decide" to act violence, particularly when under stress. Violence is an act of volition and a personality trait that is not easily changed by environmental influences.

By contrast, visuospatial cognition is an automatic cognitive task, not a volitional personality trait. Automatic cognitive tasks do not require volition to function and improve with practice. Thus the difference between visuospatial cognition and aggression (or violence) is in the nature of the outcome...a volitional personality trait versus an avolitional, automatic cognitive task. Cognitive tasks respond to practice, while personality traits do not.

6 The Use of Violent Games in Education

The benefits of violent games on visuospatial abilities are probably not terribly controversial as such influences are *accidental*. In other words, gamers become better at visuospatial tasks due to practice at those tasks, but that was never their intention. Violent games were not particularly developed for those tasks. Using violent games in education may be considerably more controversial as, in many instances, this would involve purposely designing a violent game for use by children in schools, a notion that schools and parents may be uneasy about, even as kids are exposed to violence in the books they read in literature classes. The use of video games directly in educational settings faces several practical constraints, including time commitment limitations and teacher prejudices against video games (Rice 2007). Nonetheless, as such games have inherent appeal to many children, there is potential for such games to make educational material more appealing.

In this context, there are two research sets. One avenue considers the "accidental" educational value of commercial games, with considerable attention focusing on *World of Warcraft* in particular. The other focuses on games purposely developed for educational purposes, games that may be included under the heading of "serious games."

In regard to commercial games it has been found that the use of violent video games in informal settings may promote some cognitive development, although this is usually an unintended element of game play. For instance, research in this area has typically focused on *World of Warcraft* (WoW), an MMORPG (massively multiplayer online role-playing game) that has enjoyed an unusually long active life. WoW is a fantasy role-playing game with violent content, for which many players actively participate in message boards and blogs related to the game. Some early research has suggested that WoW may promote reading and writing achievement, including among boys who previously had little interest in such activities (Steinkuehler, in press; Steinkuehler and Duncan 2009; Steinkuehler and Williams 2006). Similarly VanDeventer and White (2002) found that children who displayed expertise at mildly violent games were likely to display higher ordered thinking skills. Durkin et al. (2009) have found that frequent use of video games and other electronic media is associated with improved social and language development in children with language disorders.

Research on games purposely designed for use in education remains in its infancy. Some of the most promising research in this regard has come out of health psychology, where specifically targeted video games have promoted the health of young medical patients. In one remarkable recent study, researchers found that a first-person shooter game *Re-Mission* improved self-efficacy, cancer knowledge, and treatment adherence in teen and young adult cancer patients (Kato et al. 2008). In the game *Re-Mission*, players play as a microscopic female robot that is injected into the bodies of cancer patients and blasts cancer cells and infections with a variety of weapons. Arguably the game succeeds because it presents a lively action-oriented platform that holds players' attention, allowing the educational components of the game greater opportunity for impact. *Re-Mission* takes advantage of the existing, popular first-person shooter format and applies this format for a pro-social purpose. Both non-violent and mildly violent educational games have demonstrated short-term efficacy for specific educational goals in controlled settings (Asakawa and Gilbert 2003; Reiber et al. 1998), yet little research has expanded outcomes to longer term, global, and ecologically valid results.

Research on the use of violent video games in promoting educational agendas remains in infancy. Yet the promise of *Re-Mission* directly, and *World of Warcraft* somewhat indirectly, has led to calls for increased use of video games, including those with violent content, to promote educational agendas. For instance, NASA has begun development of an MMO to promote science education (NASA 2008). The adoption of violent games as potential educational tools will naturally need to take place in the framework of a larger discussion of positive and negative effects of violent games. Yet, given the appeal and staying power of violent games, it may be worth having this discussion.

References

Anderson C (2004) An update on the effects of playing violent video games. J Adolesc 27(1): 113–122

Anderson C, Dill K (2000) Video games and aggressive thoughts, feelings and behavior in the laboratory and in life. J Pers Soc Psychol 78(4):772–790

Anderson C, Ford C (1987) Affect of the game player: short term effects of highly and mildly aggressive video games. Pers Soc Psychol Bull 12(4):390–402

Asakawa T, Gilbert N (2003) Synthesizing experiences: lessons to be learned from internet mediated simulation games. Simul Gaming 34(1):10–22

Augustine (397) Confessions. http://www.ccel.org/ccel/augustine/confessions.toc.html, Retrieved 10 Jan 2008

Bandura A (1965) Influence of models' reinforcement contingencies on the acquisition of imitative response. J Pers Soc Psychol 1(6):589–595

Bandura A, Ross D, Ross SA (1961) Transmission of aggression through imitation of aggressive models. J Abnorm Soc Psychol 63(3):575–582

Bandura A, Ross D, Ross SA (1963) Imitation of film-mediated aggressive models. J Abnorm Soc Psychol 66(1):3–11

Beaver KM, Shutt JE, Boutwell BB, Ratchford M, Roberts K, Barnes JC (2009) Genetic and environmental influences on levels of self-control and delinquent peer affiliation: results from a longitudinal sample of adolescent twins. Crim Justice Behav 36(1):41–60

Berkowitz L (1993) Aggression: its causes, consequences, and control. McGraw-Hill, New York

Buss D, Duntley J (2006) The evolution of aggression. Evolution and social psychology. Psychosocial Press, Madison, CT, pp 263–285

Caspi A, McClay J, Moffitt T, Mill J, Martin J, Craig I, et al (2002) Role of genotype in the cycle of violence in maltreated children. Science 297(5582):851–854

Collaer M, Hill E (2006) Large sex difference in adolescents on a timed line judgment task: attentional contributors and task relationship to mathematics. Perception 35(4):561–572

Couppis M, Kennedy C (2008) The rewarding effect of aggression is reduced by nucleus accumbens dopamine receptor antagonism in mice. Psychopharmacology 197(3):449–456

De Lisi R, Wolford J (2002) Improving children's mental rotation accuracy with computer game playing. J Genet Psychol 163:272–282

Dominick J (1984) Videogames, television violence and aggression in teenagers. J Commun 34(2):136–147

Durkin K, Conti-Ramsden G, Walker A, Simkin Z (2009) Educational and interpersonal uses of home computers by adolescents with and without specific language impairment. Br J Dev Psychol 27(1):197–217 (March)

Feng J, Spence I, Pratt J (2007) Playing an action video game reduces gender differences in spatial cognition. Psychol Sci 18(10):850–855

Ferguson CJ (2002) Media violence: miscast causality. Am Psychol 57(6–7):446–447

Ferguson CJ (2007) The good, the bad and the ugly: a meta-analytic review of positive and negative effects of violent video games. Psychiatr Q 78(4):309–316

Ferguson CJ (2008) The school shooting/violent video game link: causal link or moral panic? J Investig Psychol Offender Profiling 5(1–2):25–37

Ferguson CJ (2009) Media violence effects: confirmed truth, or just another X-File? J Forensic Psychol Practice 9(2):103–126

Ferguson CJ (2010) Genetic contributions to antisocial personality and behavior (APB): a meta-analytic review (1996–2006) from an evolutionary perspective. J Soc Psychol 150(2):160–180

Ferguson CJ, Beaver KM (2009) Natural born killers: the genetic origins of extreme violence. Aggress Violent Behav 14(5):286–294

Ferguson CJ, Kilburn J (2009) The public health risks of media violence: a meta-analytic review. J Pediatr 154(5):759–763

Ferguson CJ, Rueda S, Cruz A, Ferguson D, Fritz S, Smith S (2008a) Violent video games and aggression: causal relationship or byproduct of family violence and intrinsic violence motivation? Crim Justice Behav 35(3):311–332

Ferguson CJ, Cruz A, Rueda S (2008b) Gender, video game playing habits and visual memory tasks. Sex Roles J Res 58(3–4):279–286

Ferguson CJ, San Miguel C, Hartley RD (2009) A multivariate analysis of youth violence and aggression: the influence of family, peers, depression and media violence. J Pediatr 155(6):904–908

Freedman J (2002) Media violence and its effect on aggression: assessing the scientific evidence. University of Toronto Press, Toronto

Gauntlett D (1995) Moving experiences: understanding television's influences and effects. John Libbey, Luton

Goodall J (1977) Infant-killing and cannibalism in free-living chimpanzees. Folia Primatol 28:
   259–282

Goodall J (1979) Life and death at Gombe. Natl Geogr 155:595–621

Gottschalk M, Ellis L (2009) Evolutionary and genetic explanations of violent crime. In: Ferguson
   C (ed) Violent crime: clinical and social implications. Sage, Thousand Oaks

Green S, Bavelier D (2003) Action video game modifies visual selective attention. Nature
   423(6939):534–537

Green S, Bavelier D (2006) Enumeration versus multiple object tracking: the case of action video
   game players. Cognition 101(1):217–245

Griffiths M, Hunt N (1995) Computer game playing in adolescence: prevalence and demographic
   indicators. J Commun Appl Soc Psychol 5(3):189–193

Grimes T, Anderson J, Bergen L (2008) Media violence and aggression: science and ideology.
   Sage, Thousand Oaks

Halpern D, Collaer M (2005) Sex differences in visuospatial abilities: more than meets the eyes.
   In: Shah P, Miyake A (eds) Cambridge University Press, New York

Hawley P, Vaughn B (2003) Aggression and adaptive function: the bright side to bad behavior.
   Merrill Palmer Q 49(3):239–242

Kato P, Cole S, Bradlyn A, Pollock B (2008) A video game improves behavioral outcomes
   in adolescents and young adults with cancer: a randomized trial. Pediatrics 122:e305–e317,
   http://pediatrics.aappublications.org/cgi/content/full/122/2/e305, Retrieved 10 Jun 2008

Kutner L, Olson C (2008) Grand theft childhood: the surprising truth about violent video games
   and what parents can do. Simon & Schuster, New York

Kutner L, Olson C, Warner D, Hertzog S (2007) Parents' and son's perspectives on video game
   play: a qualitative study. J Adolesc Res 23(1):76–96

Lenhart A, Kahne J, Middaugh E, MacGill A, Evans C, Mitak J (2008) Teens, video games
   and civics: teens gaming experiences are diverse and include significant social interaction
   and civic engagement. http://www.pewinternet.org/PPF/r/263/report_display.asp, Retrieved 10
   Feb 2008

Livesey D, Intili D (1996) A gender difference in visual–spatial ability in 4-year-old children: Effects on performance of a kinesthetic acuity task. J Exp Child Psychol 63(2):
   436–446

Malamuth N, Ceniti J (1986) Repeated exposure to violent and nonviolent pornography:
   Likelihood of raping ratings and laboratory aggression against women. Aggress Behav
   12(2):129–137

McCall G, Shields N (2008) Examining the evidence from small-scale societies and early prehis-
   tory and implications for modern theories of aggression and violence. Aggress Violent Behav
   13(1):1–9

Morris D (1999) The naked ape: A zoologist's study of the human animal. Delta, New York

National Aeronautic and Space Association (2008) NASA MMO game.
   http://ipp.gsfc.nasa.gov/MMO, Retrieved 10 Jul 2008

Okami P, Shackelford T (2001) Human sex differences in sexual psychology and behavior. Annu
   Rev Sex Res 12:186–241

Olson C (2004) Media violence research and youth violence data: why do they conflict? Acad
   Psychiatry 28(2):144–150

Olson C, Kutner L, Warner D, Almerigi J, Baer L, Nicholi A, Beresin E (2007) Factors correlated
   with violent video game use by adolescent boys and girls. J Adolesc Health 41(1):77–83

Parsons T, Larson P, Kranz K, Thiebaux M, Bluestein B, Buckwalter G et al (2004) Sex differences in mental rotation and spatial rotation in a virtual environment. Neuropsychologia 42(4):
   555–562

Pinker S (2002) The blank slate: the modern denial of human nature. Penguin, New York

Reiber L, Smith L, Noah D (1998). The value of serious play. Educ Technol 38(6):29–36

Rhee S, Waldman I (2002) Genetic and environmental influences on antisocial behavior: a meta-
   analysis of twin and adoption studies. Psychol Bull 128(3):490–529

Rice J (2007) New media resistance: barriers to implementation of computer video games in the classroom. J Educ Multimed Hypermed 16(3):249–261

Ritter D, Eslea M (2005) Hot sauce, toy guns and graffiti: a critical account of current laboratory aggression paradigms. Aggress Behav 31(5):407–419

Rosser J, Lynch P, Cuddihy L, Gentile D, Klonsky J, Merrell R (2007) The impact of video games on training surgeons in the 21st century. Arch Surg 142(2):181–186

Savage J (2004) Does viewing violent media really cause criminal violence? A methodological review. Aggress Violent Behav 10(1):99–128

Savage J, Yancey C (2008) The effects of media violence exposure on criminal aggression: a meta-analysis. Crim Justice Behav 35(6):1123–1136

Sherry J (2007) Violent video games and aggression: Why can't we find links? In: Preiss R, Gayle B, Burrell N, Allen M, Bryant J (eds) Mass media effects research: advances through meta-analysis. L. Erlbaum, Mahwah, pp 231–248

Silverman I, Eals M (1992) Sex differences in spatial ability: evolutionary theory and data. In: Barkow J, Cosmides L, Tooby J (eds) The adapted mind: evolutionary psychology and the generation of culture. Oxford Press, New York, pp 531–549

Sims V, Mayer R (2002) Domain specificity of spatial expertise: the case of video game players. Appl Cogn Psychol 16:97–115

Smith P (2007) Why has aggression been thought of as maladaptive? In: Hawley P, Little T, Rodkin P (eds) Aggression and adaptation: the bright side to bad behavior. Lawrence Erlbaum, Mahwah, pp 65–83

Steinkuehler CA (in press) Cognition and literacy in massively multiplayer online games. In: Leu D, Coiro J, Lankshear C, Knobel K (eds) Handbook of research on new literacies. Erlbaum, Mahwah

Steinkuehler C, Duncan S (2009) Informal scientific reasoning in online virtual worlds. J Sci Educ Technol, DOI: 10.1007/s10956-008-9120-8

Steinkuehler C, Williams D (2006) Where everybody knows your (screen) name: online games as "third places". J Comput Mediat Commun 11(4):article 1

Taylor K (2009) Cruelty: human evil and the human brain. Oxford University Press, New York

Tertullian (200) De spectaculis. http://www.tertullian.org/lfc/LFC10-13_de_spectaculis.htm, Retrieved 10 Jan 2008

Trend D (2007) The myth of media violence: a critical introduction. Blackwell, Malden

VanDeventer S, White J (2002) Expert behavior in children's video game play. Simul Gaming 33(1):28–48

Chapter 16
Three Roads to Cultural Recurrence

Robert Aunger

Abstract Social scientists have long remarked that there is consistency in what people believe and value over time, especially within definable groups. Anthropologists call this body of information "culture." There are (at least) three causal mechanisms that can explain the recurrence of cultural traits. Recurrence can occur through (1) strong individual learning biases; (2) population-level normalizing effects on what is adopted; and (3) replicator-based inheritance. Each of these mechanisms is favored by a particular brand of evolutionary theorizing about human society. Evolutionary psychologists (EPs) advocate the first option, which emphasizes the ability of universal structures in the evolved mind to come up with the same responses to environmental conditions time and again. What explains cultural consistency over time, then, is evolved psychological decision-making processes in the face of common environmental challenges. A group I call "cultural selectionists" (CSs) prefer the second option, which notes that even poor social learning abilities can still produce consistently shared features at the level of the group if there are widely shared psychological preferences for traits or the types of individuals from whom to acquire culture. The third option, based on replication of the same information from generation to generation, is the memetic position. In this scenario, the cultural features that keep popping up are the phenotypic expressions of memes, or cultural replicators, disseminating through the population via social communication or mediated transmission via information machines such as computer networks. This variety in the possible explanations for cultural evolution is not generally recognized nor do advocates of one position generally acknowledge the validity of others. But I will argue in this chapter that all three of these possibilities are viable in our present state of ignorance about the means through which cultural traits reappear each generation; any one of them may account for a particular aspect of cultural inheritance.

R. Aunger (✉)
Disease Control and Vector Biology Unit, Department of Infectious & Tropical Diseases, London School of Hygiene & Tropical Medicine, Keppel Street, London, WC1E 7HT, UK
e-mail: robert.aunger@lshtm.ac.uk

N. Kock (ed.), *Evolutionary Psychology and Information Systems Research*, Integrated Series in Information Systems 24, DOI 10.1007/978-1-4419-6139-6_16, © Springer Science+Business Media, LLC 2010

Keywords Cultural evolution · Memes · Evolutionary psychology · Dual inheritance

1 First Road

Getting ideas into other people's heads is a problem. People are like islands, isolated in space. Neither bits of brain (neurons) nor infobits of "brain code" (the action potentials neurons use to communicate to one another) survive in the environment outside the brain. All human communication is thus mediated in the sense that a "public" code must be created that two brains can share (Sperber and Wilson 1986; Sperber 1996, 2000). Social communication is thus always achieved through the use of signals, acting as intermediaries. These signals can be generated by bodily movements like hand-waving or the movements of lips and palate accompanied by the forceful expression of air (speech "behavior"), and so on. In modern Western societies, signaling is also increasingly made more complex by the intervention of artifacts: the signals we consume have been modified through interaction with books or computers. People make the artifact; the artifact in turn modifies "ambient" signals (such as reflected sunlight) or generates new ones (such as electricity through wires), which become what we interact with.

From an evolutionary viewpoint, the problem is that information is constantly being reconstructed in the course of communication – by receiver's minds, and possibly by interaction with artifacts prior to reception; what we eventually acquire as a message has been through a suite of transformations. As widely acknowledged in the literature on human communication, signals are "impoverished" in informational terms – not everything that the sender wants to communicate is present in the signal itself; there is a difference between message and meaning. In effect, successful communication depends on the receiver's ability to correctly *infer* meaning from message. Why are messages impoverished? Analogy can be made to the "translator's problem" of recreating a poem written in another language: meaning and nuances of implication are almost inevitably "lost" in the process. Similarly, we can assume that the mere act of translating from brain code to public code results in some loss of information. Second, we simply are not aware of everything we wish to communicate; some of our message remains subconscious. Part of this subconscious information no doubt gets communicated through non-verbal means – bodily attitudes, tones of voice – but presumably there are intrinsic limits to the kinds of information that any given channel can bear.

But it is commonly observed that similar traits tend to pop up generation after generation, particularly within groups that communicate with one another and which often identify themselves as sharing a "culture." If we are to explain the recurrence of cultural features in the face of this sloppy transmission of information, we need to postulate another factor that keeps culture "on track." For prominent evolutionary psychologists such as Steven Pinker (1997) and Geoffrey Miller (1999), this mechanism is tightly channeled individual learning. Shared, evolved mental routines for processing environmental stimuli assure regularized responses to recurrent events. EPs thus argue against the commonly held conception that culture is largely transmitted through social learning from individual to individual. Instead, it is the universal ability to derive the proper response from features of the environment that ensures the similarity of beliefs and behaviors within the groups that share those environments. If social transmission is unreliable and cannot guarantee that individuals have the information they need when a dangerous occasion or important opportunity arises, then evolution would have opted for a more secure option. It would have placed the relevant information inside each of our heads from the beginning, through genetically inherited content and structures for judiciously ascertaining just what kind of situation any given state of affairs represents. "Culture" is thus "evoked" in people from a repertoire of stored memories by their similar surroundings and common mental algorithms. These mechanisms evolved over time for their ability to produce optimized responses in evolutionarily important situations.

In particular, EPs have little use for cultural dynamics. Steven Pinker is scathing on the idea that cultural evolution introduces a new kind of evolutionary force into human life. He says (1997, p. 210) "Nothing in culture makes sense except in the light of psychology. Evolution created psychology, and that is how it explains culture." For Geoffrey Miller (1999), culture is not a system of inheritance in which useful knowledge and group-benefiting traditions are passed through the generations, rather cultural behaviors constitute courtship displays in which individuals try to attract and retain sexual partners. In neither case is there an admission that culture can lead to emergent phenomena such as social institutions that can feed back on human psychology. Tooby and Cosmides (1992, pp. 121–122), however, are somewhat more eclectic; they admit that social institutions and maladaptive traditions can emerge at the group-level through epidemiological processes of information exchange, although they tend to argue that "evoked culture" (i.e., that which emerges from individual psychological responses to local environmental conditions) is more important in human life than "transmitted culture" (the information acquired from others).

2 Second Road

However, the EPs are mistaken in their belief that because transmission is inherently error ridden, it cannot underlie cultural evolution. The EPs' mistake is to think that only a gene-style approach to transmission will guarantee accumulated advances, as well as fidelity to valuable past traditions – cultural recurrence, in effect. All of the virtues we find so admirable in genetic evolution derive from the accurate, unbiased replication of genetic material. Mutations rarely occur as DNA molecules are copied, thanks to multiple safe-guards on the process, and individuals are just as likely to get their mother's as their father's autosomal genes, so there is little intrinsic sorting of genes as they are inherited (Henrich and Boyd 2002). If cultural evolution is to have these qualities, the EP thinking goes, then it will have to be based on the same mechanism as the genetic case: unbiased, error-free replication.

However, Robert Boyd and his colleagues (Henrich and Boyd 2002; Boyd and Richerson 2000; Gil-White 2001) have recently shown that cultural evolution need not exhibit unbiased, error-free replication for that process to exhibit cumulative adaptive outcomes. There is in fact more than one way to skin a cat, more than one road to Rome. Adaptive culture can evolve even if transmission is sloppy. The key to accumulating adaptations is the possibility that cultural traits are *non-randomly sorted*: individuals can use their minds to preferentially adopt particular variants from among the traits circulating in the population. This gives a kind of directionality to cultural evolution missing from its genetic cousin, with its Mendelian rules of inheritance. Any such predilection to adopt particular variants we can call a psychological "bias." These biases may themselves be just the sort of thing that EPs talk about: universally shared, evolved modules for processing information in certain substantive domains in specific kinds of ways. The bias can be "direct" in the sense of depending on the content of the trait or "indirect" in the sense of reflecting a preference for other features of the trait, such as who is harboring it. If we assume that there is a bias toward imitating individuals with high social prestige, for example, or even just a predilection toward adopting the most common trait in the population, cultural "inertia" can be exhibited by the population – there is a strong tendency for the dominant trait to remain dominant, and to continue to characterize the population, even in the face of a very high rate of error in transmission (that is, a relatively low likelihood that a given individual will infer the correct trait value from his/her learning experiences). In effect, many instances of the same bias lead to a cumulative reduction in the measured error of transmission at the population level; error is absorbed by being consistently biased in one direction because everyone shares the same cognitive bias. This gives a directionality to changes in the frequency of traits that would not be apparent from looking only at the apparently random errors that individuals in that population are making.

So cultural evolution can be both error ridden and biased and still accumulate adaptations, cultural selectionists assert. Highly biased transmission can effectively compensate for a high rate of mutation in cultural inheritance. Even if the trait is characterized as a quantitative distribution rather than as having discrete values, this tendency holds true: the population can maintain a cultural tradition despite strong proclivities among individuals to make mistakes about what they should be learning from others in the group. As long as the psychological bias is sufficiently strong relative to selective forces, representing cultural variation as a continuous spectrum of values has no effect on the outcome: the weak selective component determines the equilibrium values of the population (Henrich and Boyd 2002). As Henrich and Boyd note, population genetic models were providing insights into the nature of biological evolution before anyone knew anything about DNA discreteness or replication. Further, genetic models of quantitative characters, like height, still ignore these "units." So adaptation occurs even if you characterize cultural variants along a gradient. Further, mathematically speaking, the outcome is the same as if the process had been that of replication in discrete traits. That is, the population winds up with the same cultural configuration as would occur had memes been replicating through communication between individuals all along.

Henrich and Boyd (2002) also find that cumulative adaptive evolution is facilitated when the social group is larger – as might be expected when they are basically aggregating over errors to achieve their desired result. Things also work out better when individuals tend to make independent "mistakes" in their learning, so that there is no consistent pressure working in a direction other than that of selection. No matter how poor individuals are at imitating one another, cumulative evolution can still be generated for some combination of error-proneness and selective pressure. Cultural selectionists conclude that we must consider both the social environment and individual cognition in our thinking about cultural change because both influence the conditions for cultural adaptation.

We can thus conclude that it is an error to equate evolution with replication – even though one of the premier contemporary evolutionary theorists, Richard Dawkins (1976, 1982, 1999), continues to assert that evolution depends on replicators. As Lewontin (1970) pointed out, a process need only exhibit inheritance, selection, and variation in order to qualify as evolutionary. You therefore cannot argue, as the EPs do, that cumulative cultural evolution is not possible because cultural transmission leads to different representations in each individual's mind. Replication is but one mechanism of inheritance, so evolutionary theory encompasses a larger universe of possibilities than the example of DNA suggests. Culture can evolve through other means than genes do.

Dan Sperber and his colleagues have suggested a specific mechanism that produces cultural recurrence without replication and which is therefore consistent with the CS position. They begin with the need to reconstruct meaning from messages, as pointed out at the beginning of this chapter. In particular, mental representations in person A give rise to behaviors (which Sperber calls "public representations") that are observed by person B, who must then infer A's mental representation from that public version of the information. Sperber (1996) has encapsulated this perspective, with its sequence of translations from private to public representations, in the phrase "the epidemiology of ideas." Further, because individuals differ and public representations provide incomplete information, this inferential process can be highly inaccurate (Sperber 1996, pp. 103–118; Atran 2001). However, in some cases, psychological attractors work to ensure that sender and receiver meanings are sufficiently similar to call them replicas of one another (Sperber 1996, p. 104). In effect, variations introduced into a message, as inferencing mechanisms to ascertain the meaning of a communication, must either stay close to "home" or cancel each other out. Cases of attraction, where similarity of mental representations *does* result from communication, may reflect the operation of evolved modules, as postulated by EPs. In other cases, these modules can themselves be the products of the cultural exchange of information. But replication is just the limiting case in which no transformation of meaning takes place during communication. In general, we need a social science of culture that takes the special features of cultural recurrence into account – particularly the different possible outcomes of signaling, which range from replication to great disparity between mental representations. What needs explaining is how mental representations can sometimes recur stably over generations in a considerable proportion of a group's population, to constitute their "culture," given the tendency for inferencing modules to go astray.

Sperber thus agrees with the cultural selectionists that replication is not the only road to cumulative adaptation. Like CSs, he also fully accepts the modularity hypothesis of EP. His difference from these other positions arises in his commitment to the hypothesis that psychological attractors help cultural lineages persist in the face of messy social transmission.

3 Third Road

There is a third road which none of the parties discussed thus far care to travel and that is the memetic road. Although perhaps the least traveled, I believe it still remains a viable way of winding up in Rome. The cultural selectionists have saved the idea of cultural transmission from the onslaught of the evolutionary psychologists, but at the cost of losing the possibility of replication as a consequence of that transmission. My argument is that there is a way to save both the baby and the bathwater, a way to mix heavy-duty mental reconstruction with the social replication of information. This may seem an impossible combination, given the arguments I have just rehearsed, but let me attempt to justify this position in the following.

Sperber suggests that communication is about the sharing of thoughts, about the recreation of a particular message or meaning in the minds of others (Sperber and Wilson 1986, p. 1). But to an evolutionist, this is only a proximate goal for communicators; the ultimate goal of communication is to manipulate the mind and hence behavior of others through the manufacture or display of signals or signal-generating artifacts (Dawkins and Krebs 1979). For example, the sender may need help to achieve some goal that can only be achieved through cooperation, like moving a piano or raiding an enemy's camp. But inducing cooperation may not depend on a duplicate of the sender's thought being produced in the receiver's mind. Instead, deception or irony may be involved, in which case the speaker may not want his/her true intention to be inferred, and hence duplicated in the receiver's mind. People depend on their mutual abilities to mind-read to help achieve this goal. Mutual mind-games are a major part of sharing culture. So replication is not a prerequisite to successful communication, just as the EPs and CSs claim.

But at the same time, EPs posit that there are heavy-duty regularizing structures in human brains that ensure that inferences take a certain form, given a stimulus within some domain defined by content (such as ethnobiology, naïve physics, or theory of mind). These are evolved mental structures that presumably all people share. (As I have just argued, CSs suggest that minds contain evolved biases, if not encapsulated modules, as well.) This would seem to provide everyone with a kind of error-correction mechanism that guarantees that, despite the poverty of the stimulus, the "correct" inference is nevertheless routinely drawn from a signal or message. Thus, the representation that winds up being constructed in the mind of the receiver is very much the same as that which produced the signal in the first place in the mind of the sender, because these coding and decoding mechanisms are shared. (I ignore the additional step of inferring sender intent because it may be irrelevant to the message being successfully replicated.) If inferencing is regularized by evolved predispositions to treat certain kinds of input in a similar manner, then the conclusions reached – even based upon the relatively poor information of a signal – may be stably reproduced on multiple occasions, in which the same stimulus results in the same conclusion by different brains housing the same inferencing machinery. A set of similar mental representations can then be produced by a chain of events in which the same signal is reproduced over and over by a sequence of individuals.

What exactly must hold if replication is to be true of cultural learning? In Aunger (2002a), I argue (based on literature in the philosophy of biology and Sperber 2000) that replication is a special relationship between a source and a copy such that four conditions hold:

- Causation (the source must play an active role in bringing about the conditions that lead to a copy being made)
- Similarity (the source and copy must resemble each other in relevant respects)
- Information transfer (what makes the copy similar to the source must be derived from the source)
- Duplication (the source and copy must coexist for some time)

Based on this model of replication, I argue (in Aunger 2002a) that certain specialized kinds of interneuronal communication could lead to the replication of information within a brain.

As Sperber emphasizes, signals do not contain thoughts; thoughts stay inside our heads; they are private representations of things in the world or things that are purely imaginary. We have to think about the nature of signals and what they can accomplish if we are to understand replication in the context of communication. This "new view" must find a role for signaling that is consistent with significant local reconstruction of information in the recipient's brain. Hints come from Atran (2001, p. 353), who calls signals "elicitors that draw out inferences and information from the mind"; similarly (and independently), I call them "instigators" (Aunger 2002a). The role of signals in this view is not to bring along the information that will be incorporated into the meme copy, but rather to set in motion the kind of local transformation that will result in the copy being produced.

This is a different way of thinking about replication, but one which is consistent with what we know about how human communication works, particularly the "poverty of the stimulus" tenet. The social learning process no longer need to be based on imitation. As Atran (2001) has pointed out, imitation not only is the cause of replication but also represents the information to be replicated – a kind of self-contained form of information transfer. The message contains sufficient instructions for copying itself – a form of self-referentiality. This "complete package" assumption, associated with the traditional approach to memetics, and with its obvious analogue in the form of genes, appears to contradict the poverty of the stimulus assumption. In Aunger (2002a), I argue this poverty could be complemented by a "richness in the response," the ability of mental machinery to reconstruct just what the stimulus "says," regardless of how little information is actually present in the stimulus.

What has not been generally noted is that, at least theoretically, signals and meanings can be informationally independent. That is, the information present in a signal may bear precious little relation in pattern or content to what is present in the mind that generated the signal in the first place. In effect, the copy of the message need not incorporate information from the signal, which only has the job of starting off the message inferencing process. This view of a signal's role as instigator has the virtue of making memetics Darwinian rather than Lamarckian. If we can get the replication of information largely through regularized local reconstruction, then what happens to signals becomes irrelevant. As long as signals can instigate the reconstruction process, that is enough to ensure replication of the message, thanks to the internal guidance and error-correction systems of the mental module itself. Any mutations introduced into signals through their travels do not get incorporated into the "genotypic" line of mental replicators themselves. This is the cultural equivalent of the central dogma of molecular biology that phenotypic information does not get inherited (a proposition which Lamarckianism denies).

This view also suggests that there is no reason to suppose that significant error will accumulate in a cultural lineage. The idea that information replicates successfully, even in the face of significant reconstruction, is thus preserved – and in fact promoted by the notion of universal mental modularity. Those potential elements of culture that are most reliably reproduced by people's evolved, modularized minds are those that recur and persist, just as evolutionary psychologists argue. It just happens that their proximal cause is social signals rather than learning from the environment.

Further, these social signals need not be acquired directly from other individuals – at least in modern societies in which a variety of machines exist for the storage and manipulation of information. Rather than engaging in face-to-face exchange of information, people today spend a lot of time writing e-mails or more permanent kinds of records about their thoughts and beliefs (e.g., novels, diaries) or other kinds of structured information records (e.g., computer game software, media materials) which they hope others will read or more generally experience at some later point in time. Thus a considerable proportion of social interaction is mediated by machines which convert, store, and broadcast information on behalf of the producers and users of that information (Aunger 2002a, b, 2010a, b).

The only question is whether, in the case of "heavy-duty" reconstruction, there is informational inheritance of this information – is the copy similar to the source because information deriving from that source has been incorporated in the copy?

If individuals are largely recreating cultural knowledge for themselves, based on the flimsy evidence of what others signal, this seems to violate the inheritance requirement of an evolutionary system that information be passed from individual to individual in a lineage (as parents "communicate" their genes to their offspring). Sperber (2000) argues that if the reconstruction can be said to be due to genetically inherited modular inferencing mechanisms, then cultural transmission is not the primary cause of cultural similarity between people. Rather, each person individually relearns much of that knowledge thanks to naturally evolved modules for inferring things. The cultural link may appear to be broken by this "on-board" constructivism. But signal-based instigation does satisfy the inheritance condition: the message the signal brings is what causes the desired result in the recipient brain – replication of information similar to that in the source brain. No one has ever argued that replication was achieved without assistance. Even genetic replication requires the participation of many agents besides DNA (like messenger RNA). So the fact that cultural knowledge is inferred, based on the content of signals, does not exclude it from the category of replication events. And the fact that inference is commonly regularizing or normalizing suggests that it is quite often the case that the duplication of cultural knowledge occurs through this transmission process. This argument would seem to invalidate one of the primary criticisms of the EPs, that variation occurs each time information is passed from person to person, leaving memetics little to explain.

The view of memes I have suggested is also consistent with another claim: that those ideas which do disseminate well are those which make good use of evolved domain-specific psychological machinery (Sperber 1996; Atran 2001). The memes that persist are those that "fit" with the evolved psychology; ideas that try to cross or slip between boundaries of evolved inferential categories will not be good replicators. Memetics can thus take on board much of what EPs have to say about the existence of genetic structuring of the brain without tossing out the central notion of replication. And since replication is one possible mechanism producing cultural inheritance, memetics can also be considered a specific hypothesis about how the cultural transmission of information acknowledged by CSs is achieved.

4 Conclusion

Evolutionary psychologists have argued that culture does not evolve through the social communication of information; instead, it is largely recreated anew by each individual, thanks to shared, evolved modules for inferring meaning from messages. In response to this claim, Boyd and colleagues have emphasized that evolutionary processes, including cultural ones, can retain the ability to accumulate useful variation and complexity through even highly inaccurate social transmission. In the CS view, transmission is an important component of inheritance; it just works differently than in the case of genes. In particular, it need not depend on replication as a mechanism. The cultural selectionists have proven their point that there is a real need to understand how individual predilections convert into population trends over time and that we need formal models to assist our poor intuition in this regard. We cannot easily guess what the implications of a pattern of individual interactions will be in our heads. Counterintuitive social phenomena can derive from intuitive propositions about our native psychology. For example, we should not assume that the only process that can give rise to accurate reproduction at the level of the population is accurate replication at the level of individuals. Cumulative cultural trends at the population level can be achieved without replication at the individual level.

At the same time, Sperber's work has had the salutary effect of keeping everyone honest, of recognizing people's need to make the public/private coding switch – a fact too easily forgotten in the abstractions of the cultural selectionists' mathematical modeling, where genotypes and phenotypes can be switched through a purely interpretive move, without a jot being changed in the formulas. Also, the emphasis on mental reconstruction has required some rethinking about how cultural inheritance might work. Any viable theory of cultural evolution now has to be able to jump through the hoops that Sperber has put in place. This restriction of possibilities is just what cultural selectionists long for, to limit the design space they have to explore with their formalisms (Boyd, personal communication).

While we all agree that replication is not a *necessary* feature of cultural evolution, it still may be characteristic of communication in some contexts. Here and elsewhere (Aunger 2002a, 2006), I have argued that, contrary to both the EP and CS positions, you can have replication in the face of significant mental reconstruction. The theoretical work by Boyd and colleagues shows that memetic inheritance can be mimicked by other kinds of processes (such as universally biased transmission). Still, the existence of memes, if proven, would have significant repercussions: cumulative adaptation is much more likely across a broad range of circumstances if there are replicators at work in the inheritance of cultural traits.

The replication question is important because there are limitations to the conclusions reached by CS modeling. First, the CS models depend on everyone having the same psychological biases and over a long period of time. Without a strong bias toward particular values, the population would soon become awash in random variation, and only very strong selection pressure would be able to maintain any directionality or consistency in cultural values over time; it is the shared social bias for certain learning models or trait values that compensates for individuals' proneness to make psychological errors. In the absence of such a bias, we get a very different scenario: near-zero cultural heritability.

Further, such biases are not necessarily going to characterize many real-world instances. Certainly there is no general tendency to imitate prestigious individuals or favor particular cultural values in the case of one extensively studied cultural system: that of food taboos in the Ituri Forest of the Democratic Republic of Congo (Aunger 2002b, 2000). Instead, individuals acquire their ideas about the edibility of particular foods from specific individuals designated for them by other normative rules about culture learning: children should learn food taboos from their father. This norm tends to produce significant variation between the cultural lineages defined by individual-to-individual transmission patterns. No global psychological bias causes the population to adopt consistent beliefs over time; there is, in fact, considerable intra-cultural variation, with each individual exhibiting a unique suite of taboos. If this is an indication of a more general trend for real-world cultural systems to be culturally determined rather than psychologically determined – and the number of things you are supposed to learn from your parents would suggest that food taboos in the Ituri are not the only example of such a system – then the selectionist models are more limited in their implications than CSs would like.

Second, as Henrich and Boyd (2002) admit, it is probably the case that the very fine control over replication in DNA allows a given selection pressure to be more effective over the long term, permitting the accumulation of very precisely adapted traits over time. On the other hand, the constant pressure of drift through errors introduced into what is socially learned washes away some of this precision in cultural evolution. Cumulative adaptation becomes doubly problematic if there is a tendency for psychological biases to shift over time; if biases are not consistent from generation to generation, then no cumulative directional psychological selection of traits will take place. This implies that such biases must not only be universally shared, but slow to change (as might be true of a gene-influenced bias). If biases are themselves culturally acquired, then they can become fad-like, and cumulative cultural adaptation is lost again.

Henrich and Boyd (2002) are also enthusiastic about quantitative models of cultural inheritance; they feel this possibility liberates us from the need to think about replication at all. In their view, we can think of culture as a continuous spectrum of beliefs or values that blends together in our minds, much like height in biology can increase in seemingly infinitesimal increments. This is a perspective which would appeal to some neuroscientists, who think of the brain as existing in a kind of complex global state at any moment in time in which it is futile to tease apart since each part of its big network of neurons can influence every other (e.g., Freeman 1999, McCrone 1999). But at least in the biological world, the quantitative inheritance of traits like height is still underlain by qualitatively different traits: particulate genes. It is just that multiple gene loci are involved in the production of the relevant phenotypic spread. The effects of different genes are blended together to produce an organism's height, but the units of inheritance producing them are not blended together at all: each gene locus simply adds value to the height achieved by an organism. I think the same could be true of mental traits: The global state of the neuronal network will not be the relevant parameter for describing inheritance of a cultural trait; instead, particular segments of the network, working together, will be responsible for the information associated with that trait. Memes will be shown to be partible physical things.

Still, this is a conjecture. Whether social replication actually occurs remains to be discovered through empirical work – primarily in neuroscience. However, it is worth noting that we do not currently have an example of an evolutionary process that is not founded on a replicator – genes, prions, and computer viruses are all replicators, and together account for nearly all the unique evolutionary processes we see around us (Aunger 2002a). (The "epigenetic" inheritance of biological information through cell types does occur, but this tends to account for only a small fraction of organic traits.) Maybe culture is going to be the first case of a major evolutionary process with a different kind of etiological mechanism; we just do not know at present. And even if cultural replication occurs through the kind of mechanism I hypothesize, it may only account for a relatively small proportion of shared knowledge, the rest being produced through independent learning rather than as a result of stimuli coming in from other members of the social group.[1]

Everyone acknowledges at least one contribution from the EP camp: the emphasis on shared learning algorithms or modules. Boyd and Sperber build on this foundation by hypothesizing that one of these mental modules may be evolved to process social signals, enabling the benefits of social learning to be widely shared. Sperber and the memeticists then add onto this foundation specific hypotheses about how social learning works. It therefore seems we have a much larger universe of possibilities for mechanisms of cultural evolution than has been generally recognized.

The question that remains is which view is correct. Possibly, each is a viable explanation for some kinds of cultural traits. Culture might be a heterogeneous body of knowledge acquired through a variety of routes. We just do not know at present. Three routes to cultural recurrence, each with unique features and therefore different evolutionary prospects, continue to be active prospects. The quest to find out which view is most appropriate is on and of great interest because which kind of inheritance mechanism turns out to characterize particular cases will tell us a lot about just what kind of evolution that trait will experience.

Acknowledgments A previous version of this chapter was profitably read by Robert Boyd, Dan Sperber, and Ned Kock.

References

Atran S (2001) The trouble with memes: Inference versus imitation in cultural evolution. Hum Nature 12:351–381
Aunger R (2000) The life history of culture learning in a face-to-face society. Ethos 28(2):1–38
Aunger R (2002a) The electric meme: a new theory of how we think and communicate. The Free Press, New York
Aunger R (2002b) Exposure versus susceptibility in the epidemiology of everyday beliefs. J Cogn Cult 2(2):113–154
Aunger R (2006) What's the matter with memes? In: Grafen A, Ridley M (eds) Richard Dawkins: how a scientist changed the way we think. Oxford University Press, Oxford
Aunger R (2010a) Types of technology. Technol Forecasting Soc Change 77:762–782
Aunger R (2010b) What's special about human technology? Camb J of Econ 34:115–123
Blackmore S (1999) The Meme Machine. Oxford University Press, Oxford

---

[1] In a similar fashion, prions only account for a small proportion of diseases, but the peculiar pathologies they do cause – transmissible spongiform encephalopathies like "mad cow" disease – nevertheless represent an interesting species of disease which requires its own kinds of analysis and treatment. The same would be true of memetic culture: significant interest would attend the discovery of memes, and projects to uncover the replicative abilities of cultural traits and the unique kinds of dynamics they introduce would naturally develop.

Boyd R, Richerson PJ (2000) Memes: universal acid or a better mouse trap? In: Aunger R (ed) Darwinizing culture: the status of memetics as a science. Oxford University Press, Oxford, pp 143–162

Dawkins R (1976) The selfish gene. Oxford University Press, Oxford

Dawkins R (1982) The extended phenotype. Oxford University Press, Oxford

Dawkins R (1999) Introduction to Blackmore (1999)

Dawkins R, Krebs JR (1979) Animal signals: Information or manipulation? In: Krebs JR, Davies NB (eds) Behavioral ecology. Blackwell, London, pp 282–309

Freeman WJ (1999) How brains make up their minds. Weidenfeld and Nicolson, London

Gil-White FJ (2001) L'evolution culturelle a-t-elle des règles? La rechérche Hors Série No. 5(Avril):92–97

Henrich J, Boyd R (2002) On modeling cognition and culture: why cultural evolution does not require replication of representations, J Cogn Cult 2:87–112

Lewontin RC (1970) The units of selection. Annu Rev Ecol System 1:1–18

McCrone J (1999) Going inside: a tour round a single moment of consciousness. Faber and Faber, London

Miller GF (1999) Sexual selection for cultural displays. In: Dunbar R, Knight C, Power C (eds) The evolution of culture. Edinburgh University Press, Edinburgh

Pinker S (1997) How the mind works. Penguin, London

Sperber D (2000) An objection to the memetic approach to culture. In: Aunger R (ed) Darwinizing culture: the status of memetics as a science. Oxford University Press, Oxford, pp 163–74

Sperber D (1996) Explaining culture: a naturalistic approach. Blackwell, Cambridge

Sperber D, Wilson D (1986) Relevance: communication and cognition. Harvard University Press, Cambridge

Tooby J, Cosmides L (1992) The psychological foundations of culture. In: Barkow JH, Cosmides L, Tooby J (eds) The adapted mind. Oxford University Press, Oxford, pp 19–136

Chapter 17
Evolution as Metaphor: A Critical Review of the Use of Evolutionary Concepts in Information Systems and e-Commerce

Bernd Carsten Stahl

Abstract Many aspects of information systems can be described in terms of evolution. Technologies as well as markets and business models evolve by selection of the best and elimination of weaker ones. This chapter argues that the use of such Darwinian concepts can often better be understood as a metaphorical use of language rather than an exact and scientific description of reality. Metaphors, however, are not value-free tools of observation but carry with them assumptions and views of the world. They can, therefore, be used to promote particular interests and limit critical scrutiny and discourses. This chapter will concentrate on the question of ethics to make the case that speaking of information systems in terms of evolution can limit discourses. By describing information systems through the use of biological metaphors such as evolution, alternative discourses focusing on human agency and freedom can be ignored. This negates the possibility of ethical intervention and thereby strengthens the interests of the established players and power holders.

Keywords Information systems · Electronic commerce · Evolution · Critical theory · Metaphor

1 Introduction

The use of technology in general and information systems (IS) in particular, like all other human action, relies on properties of humankind that are a result of evolution. If humans had not evolved visual sight, then the use of screens on computers would not be useful. If humans could not reason abstractly, then they would not be

B.C. Stahl (✉)
Department of Informatics, Faculty of Technology, Centre for Computing and Social Responsibility, De Montfort University, The Gateway, Leicester, LE1 9BH, UK
e-mail: bstahl@dmu.ac.uk

N. Kock (ed.), *Evolutionary Psychology and Information Systems Research*,
Integrated Series in Information Systems 24, DOI 10.1007/978-1-4419-6139-6_17,
© Springer Science+Business Media, LLC 2010

able to link an electronic activity with an expected outcome. Some of the evolution that the use of technology relies on is of a cultural nature. Cultures evolve and only successful cultures survive. One of the important cultural evolutions that IS use relies on is a widespread ability to read and write and do basic calculations. There is thus no denying the importance of our shared evolutionary background in IS. Furthermore, IS in their current form can themselves be seen as the result of evolutionary processes that favoured certain technologies, organisational structures and business models or processes. The concept of evolution thus appears to be useful for comprehending different aspects of information systems. Recently there has been increased interest in the evolutionary perspective on IS which provides evidence to demonstrate the importance of evolutionary mechanisms with regard to the use of IS (Kock et al. 2008; Kock 2008) as well as theoretical and conceptual underpinnings of the application of evolutionary thinking to IS (Kock 2009).

While this idea of using ideas from the theory of evolution and applying them to IS offers benefits of increased insights into relevant IS phenomena, I do not follow this line of research here but instead use a different angle. In this chapter I argue that the evolution of e-commerce can also be understood as a metaphor. The use of this metaphor is not value-neutral. It is not a purely descriptive category. Metaphors are carriers of accepted meaning. The use of metaphors implies certain contexts and understandings. Following the tradition of critical research, I argue that the metaphor of e-commerce can be used as a device that favours particular interests.

Given the positive aspects of the use of evolutionary terminology in a range of disciplines and the already mentioned links between evolution and different aspects of IS, it is important to stress that the current argument does not reject all uses of such terminology. Instead, it points specifically to the problems of using a biological perspective on evolution and applying it uncritically to social and socio-technical systems. This chapter, therefore, does not rule out that broader conceptions of evolution that incorporate aspects of selection but are not necessarily based on the idea of genes and alleles may even be helpful in addressing some of the ethical issues that the chapter raises.

This chapter begins with a discussion of the concepts and develops the relationship between IS and evolution. The subsequent section concentrates on the use of metaphors in IS. I argue that the application of the concept of evolution can be understood as a metaphor and I briefly explore the use and effects of other metaphors in the area information systems. By concentrating on ethical issues raised by e-commerce, I will then develop a critique of the use of the metaphor of evolution in IS. The main argument is that evolution is a biological concept and as such can raise problems with regard to normative ethics. By choosing to depict IS in Darwinian terms, a speaker can imply that it is a natural process that is not in need of intervention and regulation. Acceptance of this view can favour some market participants to the detriment of others.

2 Evolution and Information Systems

This section lays the conceptual foundations of the chapter. I discuss the concepts of evolution as well as IS and explore in which way it may be justifiable to speak of IS as a phenomenon that is the product of evolution. It is important to note that I am not aiming to make strong claims on the truth of evolution of IS. I am not saying that one cannot speak of evolution of IS or that Darwinian concepts lead to false conclusions in this context. This would require a discussion of truth (Stahl 2006a) and acceptability of theories that goes far beyond this chapter. The main interest of this chapter is to explore how the concept of evolution can be used and is used. The use of concepts can have consequences beyond their immediate context. Such consequences can be intended or unintended but they are worthy of our attention. I argue in particular that the use of the concept of evolution in IS can often be interpreted more usefully as a metaphor rather than a literal description. This metaphorical use has implications for normative ethics that need to be taken into account.

2.1 Evolution

Etymologically, the term "evolution" is derived from Latin *e* (out of) and *volatus* (rolled). Its original meaning referred to the unrolling of parchment books. It was only in the seventeenth century when its meaning changed to change, passing through discernible stages (cf. Giddens 1984, p. 229). Until the middle of the nineteenth century, evolution referred primarily to embryological development. In its current meaning, the term describes the "theory of the change of organic species over time" (Sloan 2005). The current use of the term has been influenced by a number of authors but it is most closely associated with Charles Darwin's Origin of Species (1859). Darwin's unique contribution was to link the concept of evolution with that of natural selection. Drawing on the observation that variations within species occur, this could explain the development of species over time as a reaction to the environment. This idea was revolutionary because it replaced a natural teleology needed to explain the development of different species with a relatively simple mechanism. Darwin later borrowed the term "survival of the fittest" from Herbert Spencer, which emphasised the mechanical nature of natural selection and evolution further.

Darwin's concept of evolution was deeply contentious at the time because of its religious connotations. Most importantly, it no longer required the assumption of a supreme divine being to explain the way the world is. This has been interpreted as an attack on Christianity and other religious narratives that posit a Creator. One hundred fifty years after the introduction these debates are still not resolved and now covered in disputes about creationism and intelligent design. Darwinian evolution has to contend with other critique as well (cf. Bringsjord 2001). However, I will not follow these streams of criticism and instead take Darwinian evolution as the generally accepted theoretical basis for the explanation of the development of biological species.

Despite this general acceptance of evolution, I want to point out that there are limits to its use. Evolution is meant to describe the natural world and explain why there are different species. Since humans are an evolved species, this also applies to humanity. However, evolutionary theory is just that, namely a theory. Like all theories, it is a partial description of reality. As such it is constitutive of our perception of reality and arguably of reality itself. One needs to note, however, that no theory can claim to be comprehensive. This means that there are aspects of reality that a theory does not cover. Exclusive concentration on a theory blends out aspects of reality. In most cases this is desired. Theories help scholars describe phenomena and they do this by providing a limited view of reality. Theories concentrate our attention. If, for example, a physicist is interested in the interaction between stellar bodies, she will use theories of gravitation and maybe relativity to describe these and possibly predict them. She will accept that most aspects of the phenomena are made invisible in this approach (e.g., the colour of the bodies, the question whether alien intelligence exists on them, the romantic view of them when seen from earth). This is widely accepted and usually completely legitimate. It is nevertheless important to realise because in some cases it may become problematic.

2.2 Information Systems and e-Commerce

A typical definition of the term "information systems" refers to their socio-technical nature, to the fact that they are composed of machines and technical artefacts but require human and organisational input to be rendered useful (Laudon and Laudon 1999 p. 13). Despite this intuitively convincing nature of the definition of IS, it raises a number of problems, particularly of the delineation of the field of IS. As a relatively new field of research and academic activity, it is built on a number of so-called reference disciplines such as computer sciences, sociology and business studies whose roots are often still visible. This makes it difficult to draw a clear line around the academic field of IS. Some scholars have, therefore, suggested a pragmatic approach to the definition of IS as a discipline (Willcocks 2004). The question of the definition of the discipline has consequences for the definition of the phenomena under investigation. What is an information system that is worthy of our attention? Or, in the context of the current book, which phenomena are appropriate subjects of study if we want to investigate the evolutionary components of IS?

For this chapter, I will concentrate on information systems as socio-technical systems that are used to fulfil certain organisational needs. They are often (but not exclusively) located in commercial organisations, so that typical functions of IS include the organisation and control of processes within and outside of the organisation that are relevant to its goals. Prominent examples of tasks of information systems are those that aim to increase revenue and profit. An example of applications and uses of IS is the field of e-commerce, which I will use as an example to discuss some of the evolutionary aspects of IS. Given that markets and evolution share certain aspects and that e-commerce is a market-oriented activity, I will use e-commerce as an example of IS in order to develop the critical argument about evolution and IS.

e-Commerce or electronic commerce stands for the transaction of economic goods via the use of information and communication technology (ICT). Much has been written about e-commerce which has seen a phenomenal growth during the last decade. That does not mean that the principles of e-commerce are particularly novel (Currie 2000). Authors often cite huge figures to describe revenue and projected growth in order to underline the importance of e-commerce. A considerable percentage of research in ICT and information systems (IS) has been focused on e-commerce. There are many different definitions and classifications. Among the most widely spread ones are the classification of user groups as consumers (C), businesses (B) and governments (G) (or administration (A)), which allows descriptions of different types of e-commerce, such as B2C, B2B, C2C.

In order to understand the relevance of e-commerce, we need to briefly consider its advantages. The use of ICT in commercial transaction is usually held to decrease cost (Shin 2003). This, in turn, is based on the perception that ICT moves markets closer to the models of neo-classical economics (cf. Zerdick et al. 2001). ICT, and particularly the Internet, allows suppliers and customers to find each other as well as information about products, prices and markets. In other words, the use of technology lowers transaction costs, including search costs, information costs, bargaining costs, decision costs, policing costs and enforcement costs. (cf. Welty and Becerra-Fernandez 2001; Castells 2000). Transaction costs decrease while the quality of markets increases (Spinello 2000). Due to the use of technology, new economies of scale can be leveraged (Copeland and McKenney 1988). Because of the acquisition of new customers, costs can be decreased, for example, through disintermediation. Furthermore, the technology allows for network effects that increase the value of certain goods and services (Hanseth 2000).

Despite these many advantages, e-commerce can also have downsides. These can be of a technical, financial, social or other nature. The one set of problems that I would like to emphasise here concerns ethics. Some of the ethical problems raised by e-commerce pertain to all capitalist exchange. There is a long history of debate of the relationship between ethics and commerce, which this chapter cannot recount. Suffice it to say, that commerce as an example of human interaction is of ethical relevance. That is not to say that ethics must rule every single action within a market. But one needs to recognise that the very idea of markets is based on (utilitarian) ethical ideas and that the purpose of markets is to contribute to the greater good of society. At the same time, ethics plays an important role in stabilising behaviour expectations and thereby facilitating successful interaction in the first place. I do not wish to be drawn into the details of the many debates that are being held in business ethics. The purpose of this paragraph is simply to underline that commerce in general and hence e-commerce is not an amoral activity. There are good reasons for considering ethical implications of commercial relationships and to review and possibly regulate them for ethical reasons.

Salient examples of ethical issues in e-commerce include security, privacy, trust and control. In the e-commerce literature these are often described as possible obstacles to e-commerce adoption, but it is important to note that they also have an important ethical component. Security, for example, not only refers to network or database impregnability, but, more importantly, it is a fundamental (and evolved) human need (Brown 2000), which can have implications for technical artefacts. This ethical need for security is linked to a human requirement for privacy (Gavison 1995). A related notion of central importance in e-commerce research is that of trust. Again, the mainstream literature concentrates on the creation of trust with the purpose of facilitating commercial exchange. One should nevertheless see that trust is also a moral notion that refers to our individual and collective views of a good life and a good society (Donaldson and Dunfee 1999; Grabner- Kraeuter 2002; Salam et al. 2005).

Apart from these generally accepted concerns, there is also literature that points out more deep-seated ethical problems of e-commerce. Such problems have to do with the structure of commercial exchange and how technology can change or confirm these structures in a covert manner. Lessig (1999, 2001), for example, points out how technology and its architecture can lead to constellations of social control that are removed from democratic scrutiny. This refers in particular to definitions of property and ownership. One interesting aspect of this refers to the changing nature and commodification of information. While information used to be seen as a public good, it increasingly turns into an exchangeable and tradable good (Stichler 1998). e-Commerce can furthermore be used to stimulate the development of perceived needs, which are not conducive to the good of the consumer (Janson and Cecez-Kecmanovic 2005). On a grander scale, e-commerce can even be interpreted as an important contribution to western cultural imperialism, which extends the dominance of the market system to the detriment of alternative ways of social organisation (Weckert 2000). e-Commerce, furthermore, has ethical implications with regard to digital divides. In principle e-commerce could reduce costs and thereby address issues of poverty. However, the technology and the knowledge required to use it tend to be accessible only to those who are better off. The effect is that the rich can use e-commerce to save money whereas the poor are rarely able to use it. Instead of overcoming social divides, e-commerce therefore has the potential to deepen them.

2.3 e-Commerce as an Evolved Phenomenon

The review of the concepts of e-commerce and evolution shows that it is justifiable to speak of e-commerce as something that has evolved. In the field of IS, one also finds many references on evolution within information systems (Ward and Peppard 1996). Beyond this, one can argue that human characteristics that can be understood as the result of evolution strongly influence our use of technology and thus the development of e-commerce (Kock 2005). Information is a central concept of evolution (Wiener 1954) and it is therefore reasonable to assume that technology used to exchange information is of evolutionary relevance. Furthermore, markets can be likened to nature and the process of biological evolution thus seems to play out in markets as well. One could thus say that liberal markets and societies mimic natural evolution (Rauch 1993). Indeed, the relationship between markets and evolution goes even further. Darwin himself admitted that liberal economic theories of his time inspired his view of evolution (cf. Hawkes 2003 p. 134).

At the same time it should be clear that the concept and theory of evolution do not create a comprehensive description of e-commerce. Evolution is a macro-level descriptive theory that does not take into account the micro-level or individual view. From an evolutionary viewpoint the individual is of relatively little concern. Unless the individual carries a particular evolutionary advantage, she is not likely to make a difference to overall evolution of the species. If she is maladapted, she will simply not pass on her genes. For the theorist of evolution this is of little importance, but that clearly changes if we look at it from the point of view of the individual. Being able to successfully interact or pass on one's genes can be of highest personal importance, independent of whether evolutionary theory supports this. This is not an argument against evolution but an example that shows that evolution does not cover all aspects of social reality. Another such example, which is central to this chapter, is that focusing on evolution renders it impossible to develop a prescriptive ethics that would regulate contentious ethical issues arising from e-commerce, such as those indicated earlier. While ethics can be described as a consequence of evolution, a theory of evolution is not capable of telling us what we should do, whether or how we should address ethical issues of e-commerce such as digital divides. The point I am making is that the evolutionary viewpoint is not the only one that can legitimately be applied to e-commerce. There are aspects of e-commerce that it cannot capture.

The conclusion to be drawn from this is that the use of the term evolution with regard to e-commerce cannot be a comprehensive and objective description of reality. In many cases, it can better be understood as a metaphor. The use of metaphors with regard to technology, particularly ICT, is well researched and I will draw upon this research to further the argument that speaking of the evolution of e-commerce can have ideological roots and consequences.

3 Evolution of e-Commerce as a Metaphor

The Encarta World English Dictionary (1999, p. 1188) defines a metaphor as an "implicit comparison; the application of a word or phrase to somebody or something that is not meant literally but to make a comparison [...]." This definition sounds inconspicuous but metaphors can lead to problematic social consequences. Researchers active in the fields of e-commerce or IS are often not aware of these. There is, however, a research approach that is highly sensitive to the use of language, namely critical research. Critical research, or research based on critical theory, was originally based on a Marx-inspired scepticism of capitalism. It not only is linked to scholars from the Frankfurt School (Horkheimer, Adorno, Marcuse, Habermas, Honneth, etc.) but also includes other streams of research such as postmodern or postcolonial work. It is difficult to define critical research in one sentence, but it is probably fair to say that its main difference to other research is its aim to change social realities rather than just to describe them. Critical researchers typically try to promote emancipation of research subjects (Stahl 2008).

This tradition of critical research has found application in the field of IS, where there is a growing field of scholars interested in critical research in IS (CRIS). Here, critical research is often seen as a third "paradigm", next to positivism and interpretivism (Chua 1986; Orlikowski and Baroudi 1991). In CRIS, as in critical research in general, there are many open debates. Which theories should count as valid? Is there an appropriate methodology (McGrath 2005)? What are appropriate topics? What does it mean to emancipate (McAulay et al. 2002; Stahl 2006b)? Despite these and other open questions, there is general agreement in CRIS that the use of language is of high importance. This coincides with a widespread social constructivist approach which sees social reality as a product of interaction. Since humans interact mostly through language, the use of language is constitutive of reality. This is true for technologies and their use as well (Brooke 2002). Since metaphors are an important use of language that facilitates understanding and interaction, metaphors play an important role in understanding technology. If research aims to promote emancipation, then it needs to be aware of the linguistic constructs that set the scene for the use of technology. This section will therefore look at why we use metaphors and then discuss examples of metaphors used with regard to technology.

3.1 Advantages of Metaphors

We should be aware that everyday language is full of metaphors. The same is true, maybe to a lesser degree, for much academic and scientific writing. It is therefore important to understand why this is so. The most fundamental reason for the use of metaphors seems to be the attempt to promote understanding by using a well-established point of reference. As Alvesson and Deetz (2002) put it, the "advantage of a metaphor is that it captures the imagination and provides a coherent image that one may stick to" (2000, p. 174). For researchers this allows focusing empirical research but, more generally, it allows the enrolment of an audience into a particular view of the world. Another important task of metaphors is the reduction of complexity. By using a well-established concept as a metaphor, the audience can easily understand what aspects of a phenomenon are to be emphasised and which ones can be ignored. Like theories, metaphors are representations, but unlike theories, they are easily understood (Weick 1989). As an interesting twist on the current argument, it has been observed that our use of metaphors seems to be a consequence of evolution. Evolution has equipped our brains with the ability to quickly grasp certain concepts (concrete physical and spacial ones) that hunter–gatherers needed for survival. At the same time we find it much more difficult to deal with abstract descriptions. Metaphors can help us bridge the gap and visualise complex situations (cf. Casacuberta 2005).

Overall, it is important to understand the fundamental value of the use of metaphors. They allow us to communicate and achieve agreement where a purely abstract language would likely fail. There is thus good reason to support the use of metaphors despite the knowledge that they are always misleading to some degree. Consequentially, Carnap (1980) argues for tolerance with regard to metaphors. Metaphors have been described as important ways of creating insight into organisational processes (Tsoukas 1991). And it is therefore not surprising that metaphors are frequently used to explain the constituent phenomena of e-commerce, namely business and ICT.

3.2 Metaphors in e-Commerce

The preceding section has argued that metaphors have positive consequences and are an integral part of all communication. At the same time it is important to note that metaphors are not value-neutral. By focussing attention on known properties, they influence the way we perceive and deal with phenomena. Some scholars have paid close attention to the use of metaphors. Critical management studies researchers, for example, have investigated how metaphors influence the view of business. A good example of this is the use of military metaphors in management, which leads to preferences for aggressive behaviour (Levy et al. 2003). Similar studies have been conducted in the area of ICT, IS and e-commerce as well. I will now discuss some examples of metaphors before I return to general disadvantages of their use.

Metaphors can be sources of information regarding the use of particular technologies, such as the Internet (Wyatt et al. 2002). Their function as sense-making tools can help bridge differences between technology and its social and organisational context in the field of information systems (McBride 2005). Furthermore, they facilitate the "translation" of organisational culture (Doorewaard and van Bijsterveld 2001).

There are groups of metaphors that concentrate on a particular theme. Discussing these will make it easier to understand their function. One of them is the traditional machine/technology metaphor. This draws on our understanding of machinery from the industrial revolution onward to make sense of ICT. In a machine culture, work has to be organised around the physical principles of the machines. Applying such understanding to ICT-based society and work will lead to structures and processes that may not be suited to new technology (Dahlbom 2000). Another example is the metaphor of the "information highway" or "information superhighway" to describe the technical infrastructure of the Internet. The metaphor of the highway implies individual travel and the commercialisation of interaction on the Internet (Yoon 2001). Particularly from a US perspective, the metaphor of a highway simultaneously raises romantic visions of freedom and individuality (Jones 2001).

Another group of metaphors draw on biology to explain the use of ICT in society. Technology is described as an open system, comparable to living systems in biological systems theory. A telling example of this is the use of the word "life" to describe information systems. A widely spread application of this is the "information systems life cycle development" methodology. The metaphor suggests that the technology is independent of humans and has a natural beginning and end (van der Blonk 2003). While this metaphor has positive connotations, biological metaphors can equally be negative. The use of the term "virus" for self-replicating programs immediately signals that they are not desirable. Like biological viruses, computer viruses are viewed bad per se and any action to eradicate them is automatically justified (Klang 2003). One could argue that, from an evolutionary point of view, viruses are not always bad. Viruses can lead to fatal infections but they can also be used in medical therapy and have therapeutic value. But that is beside the point. In ordinary language viruses are associated with disease and thus perceived as bad. The use of the word "virus" as a metaphor has connotations that have political implications, be they intended or not. There are plenty of further examples of the use of metaphors in e-commerce but the above instances will suffice for the current argument.

3.3 Problems of Metaphors

The problems of metaphors should have become clear from the above description. Metaphors can by definition not be true or false. They may be more or less appropriate. Their main problem is that they structure perceptions and consequently spaces of action in particular ways that may not be desirable. The metaphor of the information highway suggests certain ways of defining property rights and securing resources that may not be optimal for the Internet. Speaking of viruses rules out a positive appreciation and thereby a range of possible uses. Such metaphors can translate in strong social norms or laws. Speaking of "piracy", for example, has certainly lent support to stronger legal protection of intellectual property.

The downsides of metaphors need to be weighed against their advantages. In many cases this is no issue because metaphors are easily recognisable as such. It becomes difficult to do a cost–benefit analysis, however, if it is not clear that a given term represents a metaphor rather than a factual description. In such cases, metaphors can take on a life of their own and lead to the closure of discourses and thus to the diminishing of spaces of action and solution. It is this problem that I will explore with regard to the metaphor of evolution when applied to e-commerce.

Before doing this, I will need to discuss the question how we can distinguish between a metaphorical and a theoretical use of the term "evolution" in e-commerce. I have said earlier that one can legitimately speak of evolution of e-commerce but my case rests on the assumption that the term is often used as a metaphor. So, how can we tell the difference? There is no easy answer to this. There is probably overlap between the different uses and the speaker will in many cases not be aware of it. As a rule of thumb, one might say that a metaphorical use of the term is given when the same content could be expressed without the use of the term. Again, this may be difficult in practice and raises the question of who is to determine the difference. Despite this difficulty in drawing a clear dividing line, it is still plausible to assume that it is possible to use the term in a purely or predominantly metaphorical way. Some authors on evolution and e-commerce explicitly point out that the terms are best understood as metaphors (Singh 2001).

4 e-Commerce Evolution as Ideology

I now discuss the problem of evolution as a metaphor under the heading of ideology because this provides a well-established framework. In order to do this, I briefly introduce the concept of ideology and then I show how the metaphor can serve as an ideological tool. My main argument, which I develop in the last subsection, is that, as a biological metaphor, the concept of evolution deflects attention from normative ethical issues raised by e-commerce. By doing so it promotes particular interests and closes down possible solution spaces.

4.1 Ideology

The term "ideology" has negative connotations. When it was developed in the wake of the French revolution, it originally had a much more positive meaning. Ideology was meant to be the science of ideas, which would critically question and empirically test ideas. The decline of the term began with Napoleon, who belittled it, arguably because he saw it as a threat to his dictatorial aspirations. The next assault on ideology came from Marx, who, in his *German Ideology*, depicted the term as an example of the weakness of the prevalent philosophy of German idealism. Most of the critical use of term has its roots in Marx's interpretation. The history of the term ideology is closely linked with critical research. Critical scholars have seen ideology as the embodiment of false consciousness that facilitates alienation and disempowerment. Ideology has often been seen as something that can and should be overcome in order to create a free and just society (for a more detailed discussion of the term, cf. Hawkes 2003; Freeden 2003).

However, critical theorists in the twentieth century have tended to admit that ideology cannot simply be discarded. Ideologies are still viewed critically as "representations of aspects of the world which can be shown to contribute to establishing, maintaining and changing social relations of power, domination and exploitation" (Fairclough 2003, p. 9). However, it is typically recognised that replacing a particular ideology means erecting another one. The purpose of critical scholarship can therefore not be the attempt to overcome ideologies but to point to their existence and to render them open to debate.

With regard to this paper this means that the question of interest is whether a particular use of language, namely the metaphor of evolution in e-commerce, has the characteristics of ideology, which are the exertion of power, the privileging of individual views and the promotion of particular interests. The aim of such an investigation is not to overcome all power relationships, which we know to be impossible but to expose them to critical scrutiny and to thereby render them fairer and more equitable.

4.2 The Evolutionary Metaphor as Ideology

From the above, it is easy to deduce that metaphors have at least the potential to promote ideologies or become ideological tools. There are many ways in which this can happen. The possibly most important one has to do with naturalisation or reification. Social phenomena can become reified (literally: they become things) when their nature as social constructs becomes invisible and their current interpretation becomes part of what is accepted as the natural world. A typical example is the "nature" of women as home-bound child carers. If it is in their nature to spend their lives caring for the family, then there is no need to educate them or give them access to power and resources in society. Such reification of the nature of women is ideological because it promotes the interest of a certain group in society (members of the patriarchate) to the detriment of others (women). Examples of this type of reification-based ideology are legion. It is upheld by the privileging of the voices which are typically predominant in the first place (Mansell et al. 1999).

One of the reasons why such reifications are supremely successful ideological tools is that they remove their topic from discourse; they lead to discursive closure. If women's nature is to stay at home, then it is no longer a political question whether they should be liberated. There is no need for debate, as it is an obvious waste of time to debate whether nature has political intentions. Apart from discursive closures, metaphors as (misleading) representations of social reality can also have manifest political and legal consequences. The metaphor of "piracy" to support strong protection of intellectual property was already mentioned. Another example would be the metaphor of e-"mail" as a letter, which suggests certain ways of dealing with the content of electronic communication.

These arguments are easily applied to the metaphor of evolution of e-commerce. If evolution is applied to the development of technology, then it becomes a matter of mechanistic progress. Only the most "appropriate" ("fittest") technologies survive and these will be most advantageous and desirable. Human interference or even steering becomes impossible and useless, leaving us with a strong technological determinism (cf. Grint and Woolgar 1997). A similar effect can be observed when Darwinian ideas are applied to social environments. Social Darwinism applies ideas of natural selection and evolution to humans in society with the consequence that inequality and injustices become results of natural developments. Such a state of affairs is not only beyond repute, but, moreover, it can be seen as socially benign in improving the overall structure of society (Galbraith 1958/1998). Applied to e-commerce this means that whatever the current state of affairs is, the technology as well as the related distribution of access, knowledge and ability to use it is removed from scrutiny. Only the best technology will survive and those who profit from e-commerce are those who are most suited to survival. The implicit (albeit arguably fallacious) conclusion is that the current state of e-commerce is justified and not in need of any intervention.

One could counter that these views are fallacious because they do not represent the state of the art in the theory of evolution. Evolutionary theorists will be careful in making statements that could be perceived as supporting the above views. One principal reason for this is that the theory of evolution is descriptive and explains why the current state of affairs came about. It can say little about future states because the environment may change and with it the outcome of selection. Furthermore, the theory of evolution cannot create normative statements for reasons explored in the next section. Such considerations are not of relevance, however, if one uses evolution as a metaphor. The metaphorical use does not claim to be exact or represent theory correctly but it is meant to create understanding and agreement. Where evolution is used for such purposes, e.g., in Nazi Germany where social Darwinism was used to legitimate the killing of disabled persons, this was not so much a misunderstanding of the theory but its metaphorical use for political purposes.

4.3 Evolution and Ethics in e-Commerce

The preceding section has shown that evolution as a metaphor can display characteristics of ideology. My main concern about this has to do with the ethical implications it entails. A Darwinist might argue that ethics is the result of social and cultural evolution. Only those societies with a suitable set of moral rules will survive. Furthermore, ethics relies on properties of humans that are evolved, such as the ability to communicate and think abstractly (Bedau 1998). It has also been argued that evolution can serve as a model for systems designer to incorporate ethics (Mumford 1996). All of these are statements that are correct within the theory of evolution but they overlook that there is more to ethics than the theory of evolution can tell us.

Ethics works on different levels. There is the set of moral rules that we follow. These are social facts, subject to positive research, and arguably results of social and cultural evolution. Beyond and above those rules, however, there is the level of ethical reflection and justification, sometimes called meta-ethics. Meta-ethics goes beyond the pure description of moral rules and can have the charge of developing new ones. We can thus distinguish between descriptive and normative ethics. The theory of evolution can be quite useful in descriptive ethics when it explains why certain rules seem to be almost universals whereas others are very specific. What it cannot do is create new moral rules or justify them. In terms of e-commerce, evolution can inform us why certain behaviours are accepted and lead to successful interactions and organisations. It cannot tell us, however, which rules future developments of e-commerce should follow. There are two reasons for this: (1) Since Hume (1948), philosophers have widely accepted that norms cannot be deduced from description. To do so would be what has been termed a naturalist fallacy. Evolution as a scientific theory of the natural world can tell us how present states of affairs came about but cannot tell us which future developments will be desirable. (2) The theory of evolution has little predictive value. It cannot tell which characteristics of organisms (or cultures or societies) will prove beneficial and promote their propagation because future environments are uncertain. That means that, even if we knew which state of society will be desirable in the future, evolution can tell us little about how to get there.

In addition to these problems, there are inconsistencies between the evolutionary natural science view of the world and most ethical views of the world. Most ethical theories require the existence of autonomous individuals who are capable of making decisions and reflecting on these in a rational manner. While there are obvious empirical limits to this, the underlying idea of freedom and autonomy is central to the constitution of modern industrialised democratic societies. Evolution as a biological concept has no room for such freedom and reflection. The subjects of evolution are endowed with desirable characteristics by the lottery of mutation and find themselves winners of the game of evolution without any way of contributing to this.

This does not mean that one conceptual framework is right or the other one wrong. It just means that they describe different phenomena and that these descriptions are not always compatible. In most cases this is not a problem. Neglecting ethical questions in the natural world is unproblematic, because it simply plays no role. Similarly, neglecting evolution in social environments where ethics are relevant is usually unproblematic. An issue only arises if a certain use of language leads to rendering ethical questions invisible in cases where they are relevant, as, for example, when the use of metaphors of evolution leads speakers and listeners to overlook ethical issues.

Speaking of e-commerce in terms of evolution can render ethical issues invisible. There is neither need nor possibility to address questions of justice and digital divides. Changing power structures and their ethical implications no longer are open to scrutiny. Technology is given and determined. Attempts to regulate it turn into misguided (and ideologically motivated) political activism that cannot be justified and stand no chance of success. Overall, the ethical dimension of e-commerce becomes invisible and can no longer be discussed and criticised.

5 Conclusion: Overcoming the Ideology of Evolution?

It is clear from the tone of this essay that I believe this state of affairs to be problematic. e-Commerce is a technology-enabled social practice based on social constructs and as such should be open to ethical debate. If the use of the metaphor of evolution precludes such debate, then it is an example of ideology. As in all cases of ideology, we can ask who benefits and who suffers. The beneficiaries of the exclusion of ethics from debate are the main technical and business stakeholders of e-commerce. This includes hardware and software vendors as well as the big established players in the market. Where ethical interventions are successful they could lead to stronger regulation and the reduction of profits. The holders of market power thus have an important interest in avoiding attention to ethics. The use of biological metaphors, therefore, promotes their interest. On the other hand, those who would benefit from the inclusion of ethical issues are typically the less powerful stakeholders such as employees, consumers, the environment. They would profit from ethical debates because these would allow them to give their viewpoints more legitimacy and thus more chances of success.

One could counter this critique by suggesting that all I am doing is replacing one ideology with another one. Critical theorists typically claim to be reflective, which means they apply their reasoning to their own arguments (Gouldner 1976; Alvesson and Willmott 1992). Doing so shows that, indeed, my argument has produced without justification some concepts that are at least as contentious as the ones I am attacking. Questions of freedom of will and action and human autonomy have a long history of being debated. If it is just a question of exchanging one set of ideological terms and reifications against another, then where is the added value of the argument? The answer to this question will be in a heightened awareness of one's constructs and their implications and a willingness to question these. My main argument is that the use of the term and the ideas of evolution can preclude ethical debates in e-commerce despite a necessity of having them. This does not mean that I have a perfect solution or that my argument has no weaknesses. The emancipatory aim of critical research can only be furthered if limits to debates, in particular invisible limits such as ideology and reification, are exposed.

What are we to do then concerning e-commerce and evolution? One possibility would be to stop using the metaphor of evolution with regard to all social processes, including e-commerce. This is problematic for several reasons. First, one cannot change the use of language by decree. Second, and more important, metaphors have advantages and these can be substantial. Speaking of the evolution of social constructs can promote understanding and communication and thus be valuable. The solution should therefore be in a more reflected use of the metaphor. When we hear people speak of evolution then we should immediately ask who is speaking, are they using the term as a metaphor, who benefits from the metaphor, which implications of the metaphor has been neglected? The ideological implications of the metaphor need to be understood. Once this is the case, they can easily be debated. It is imperative that metaphors become visible as such and lose their reifying property. If this is given, then the advantages and disadvantages of the use of the metaphor can be weighed and justified.

The solution to the problem of ideology is thus to render it visible. Where speaking of evolution of e-commerce leads to discursive closure, the way out is to open new discourses. This is where critical research can help further debates and it is where this chapter finds its use. I do not claim to be able to overcome ideology, and indeed some readers will point out that the chapter is based on ideological assumptions itself. Nevertheless, by opening the debate on ideology, the chapter can help overcoming its effects and, more specifically, to allow the issues of ethics in e-commerce to re-enter the debate. This is important not only for reasons of intellectual honesty but also for reasons of ethical authenticity. Understanding ways in which communication is shaped is furthermore of high relevance to ICT professionals. In exposing the metaphorical use of evolution as a possible cause of the distortion of discourses, the chapter contributes to the emancipation of the reader who is now free to explore new spaces of action and solution that the use of the metaphor of evolution would have closed down.

A final and important conclusion to be drawn concerns the difference between metaphorical and non-metaphorical use of the term evolution in IS. Much research on evolution and IS is not of a metaphorical character but tries to apply the biological concept of evolution to IS in order to understand certain aspects of it, such as media naturalness theory (Kock 2009). In many cases it may not be clear, however, whether a particular use of the concept to evolution is metaphorical or not. How are we to distinguish between the two and determine whether it constitutes an ideological use of the term or not. Given everything that was said so far, I suggest a simple rule of thumb that is based on the fundamental properties of the concept of evolution. As a descriptive concept, evolution cannot provide normative guidance without the support of normative premises. Wherever normative conclusions are explicitly or implicitly drawn from insights drawn from the concept of evolution, the naturalistic fallacy is committed. This may be based on either a metaphorical use of the concept or a misunderstanding of the reach of the literal use of evolution. Such normative conclusions need to be supported by explicit normative statements. If they are not, then they constitute a potential ideology and need to be questioned. In this sense, this chapter should have made a contribution to evolutionary research on IS by pointing out some of the problems it has to avoid in order to be considered a valuable contribution to the IS discipline.

Acknowledgements This chapter is a revised version of "Trust as Fetish: A Critical Theory Perspective on Research on Trust in E-Commerce", originally published in Stahl (2008). Information systems: critical perspectives. Routledge: London, pp 150–161.

References

Alvesson M, Deetz S (2000) Doing critical management research. SAGE, London

Alvesson M, Willmott H (1992) On the idea of emancipation in management and organization studies. Acad Manag Rev 17(3):432–464

Bedau MA (1998) Philosophical content and method of artificial life. In: Bynum T, Moor JH (eds) The digital phoenix: how computers are changing philosophy. Blackwell, Oxford, pp 135–152

Bringsjord S (2001) Are we evolved computers? A critical review of Steven Pinker's how the mind works. Philos Psychol 14(2):227–243

Brooke C (2002) Critical perspectives on information systems: an impression of the research landscape. J Inf Technol 17(4):271–283

Brown WS (2000) Ontological security, existential anxiety and workplace privacy. J Bus Ethics 23(1):61–65

Carnap R (1980) Empiricism, semantics, and ontology. In: Morick H (ed) Challenges to Empiricism. Methuen, London, pp 28–46

Casacuberta D (2005) Loaded metaphors: legal explanations on monitoring the workplace in Spain. In: Weckert J (ed) Electronic monitoring in the workplace: controversies and solutions. Idea Group Publishing, Hershey, pp 158–170

Castells M (2000) The information age: economy, society, and culture. volume I: the rise of the network society, 2nd edn. Blackwell, Oxford

Chua WF (1986) Radical developments in accounting thought. Account Rev 61(4):601–632

Copeland DG, McKenney JL (1988) Airline reservation systems: lessons from history. MIS Q 12(3):353–370

Currie W (2000) The global information society. Wiley, New York

Dahlbom B (2000) Postface: from infrastructure to networking. In: Ciborra C et al (eds) From control to drift: the dynamics of corporate information infrastructures. Oxford University Press, Oxford, pp 212–226

Donaldson T, Dunfee TW (1999) Ties that bind: a social contracts approach to business ethics. Harvard Business School Press, Boston

Doorewaard H, van Bijsterveld M (2001) The osmosis of ideas: an analysis of the integrated approach to IT management from a translation theory perspective. Organization 8(1):55–76

Fairclough N (2003) Analysing discourse – textual analysis for social research. Routledge, London

Freeden M (2003) Ideology – a very short introduction. Oxford University Press, Oxford

Galbraith JK (1958/1998) The affluent society, 40th Anniversary edn. Mariner Books, Boston

Gavison R (1995) Privacy and limits of law. In: Johnson DG, Nissenbaum H (eds) Computers, ethics & social values. Prentice Hall, Upper Saddle River, pp 332–351

Giddens A (1984) The constitution of society – outline of the theory of structuration. Polity Press, Cambridge

Gouldner AW (1976) The dialectic of ideology and technology: the origins, grammar and future of ideology. Macmillan, London

Grabner-Kraeuter S (2002) The role of consumers' trust in online-shopping. J Bus Ethics 39(1): 43–50

Grint K, Woolgar S (1997) The machine at work: technology, work, and organization. Blackwell, Cambridge

Hanseth O (2000) The economics of standards. In: Ciborra C et al (eds) from control to drift: the dynamics of corporate information infrastructures. Oxford University Press, Oxford, pp 56–70

Hawkes D (2003) Ideology, 2nd edn. Routledge, London

Hume D (1948) Hume's moral and political philosophy (1711–1776), edited with an introduction by Henry D. New York, Aiken

Janson M, Cecez-Kecmanovic D (2005) Making sense of e-commerce as social action. Inf Technol People 18(4):311–342

Jones S (2001) Understanding micropolis and community. In: Ess C, Sudweeks F (ed) Culture, technology, communication: towards and intercultural global village. SUNY Press, Albany, pp 53–66

Klang M (2003) A critical look at the regulation of computer viruses. Int J Law Inf Technol 11(2):162–183

Kock N, Chatelain-Jardón R, Carmona J (2008) Incorporating simulated animal attacks in human-technology interaction interfaces: the predictive power of biosemiotics and evolutionary psychology. Int J Technol Human Interact 4(4):68–87

Kock N (ed) (2008) Darwinian perspectives on electronic communication: special issue of the journal IEEE Transactions on Professional Communication. IEEE Computer Society Press, Washington

Kock N (2005) Media richness or media naturalness? the evolution of our biological communication apparatus and its influence on our behavior toward e-communication tools. IEEE Trans Prof Commun 48(2):117–130

Kock N (2009) Information systems theorizing based on evolutionary psychology: an interdisciplinary review and theory integration framework. MIS Quart 33(2):395–418

Laudon KC, Laudon JP (1999) Essentials of management information systems. 4th edn. Prentice Hall, London

Lessig L (1999) Code and other laws of cyberspace. Basic Books, New York

Lessig L (2001) The laws of cyberspace. In: Spinello RA, Tavani H (eds) Readings in cyberethics. Jones and Bartlett, Sudbury, pp 124–134

Levy DL, Alvesson M, Willmitt H (2003) Critical approaches to strategic management. In: Alvesson M, Willmott H (eds) Studying management critically. SAGE, London, pp 92–110

Mansell W, Meteyard B, Thomson A (1999) A critical introduction to law, 2nd edn. Cavendish Publishing, London

McAulay L, Doherty N, Keval N (2002) The stakeholder dimension in information systems evaluation. J Inf Technol 17(4):241–255

McBride NK (2005) Chaos theory as a model for interpreting information systems in organizations. Inf Syst J (15):233–254

McGrath K (2005) Doing critical research in information systems: a case of theory and practice not informing each other. Inf Syst J, 15(2):85–101

Mumford E (1996) Systems design: ethical tools for ethical change. Macmillan, London

Orlikowski WJ, Baroudi JJ (1991) Studying information technology in organizations: research approaches and assumptions. Inf Syst Res 2(1):1–28

Rauch J (1993) Kindly inquisitors: the new attacks on free thought. University of Chicago Press, Chicago

Salam AF, Iyer L, Palvia P, Singh R (2005) Trust in e-commerce. Commun ACM 48(2):73–77

Shin N (2003) Productivity gains from IT's reduction of coordination costs. In: Shin N (ed) Creating business value with information technology: challenges and solutions. Idea Group Publishing, Hershey, pp 125–145

Singh MP (2001) An evolutionary look at e-commerce. IEEE Internet Comput 5(2):6–7

Sloan P (2005) Evolution, the Stanford encyclopedia of philosophy. In: Edward NZ. (ed) Summer Edition. URL http://plato.stanford.edu/archives/sum2005/entries/evolution

Spinello R (2000) Cyberethics: morality and law in cyberspace. Jones and Bartlett, London

Stahl BC (2006a) On the difference or equality of information, misinformation, and disinformation: a critical perspective. Inf Sci J (9):83–96

Stahl BC (2006b) Emancipation in cross-cultural IS research: the fine line between relativism and dictatorship of the intellectual. Ethics Inf Technol 8(3):Special issue on: Bridging cultures: computer ethics, culture, and information and communication technologies, edited by C. Ess, 97–108

Stahl BC (2008) The ethical nature of critical research in information systems. Inf Syst J 18(2), Special issue on: Exploring the critical agenda in IS research, edited by C. Brooke, Dubravka Cecez-Kecmanovic, Heinz K. Klein, pp 137–163

Stichler RN (1998) Ethics in the information market. In: Stichler R, Hauptman R, (eds) Ethics, information and technology: readings MacFarland & Company, Jefferson, pp 169–183

Tsoukas H (1991) The missing link: a transformational view of metaphors in organizational science. Acad Manag Rev 16(3):566–585

van der Blonk H (2003) Writing case studies in information systems research. J Inf Technol 18(1):45–52

Ward J, Peppard J (1996) Reconciling the IT/business relationship: a troubled marriage in need of guidance. J Strategic Inf Syst 5(1):37–65

Weckert J (2000) What is new or unique about internet activities? In: Langford D (ed) Internet ethics. McMillan, London, pp 47–63

Weick KE (1989) Theory construction as disciplined imagination. Acad Manage Rev 14(4):516–531

Welty B, Becerra-Fernandez I (2001) Managing trust and commitment in collaborative supply chain relationships. Commun ACM 44(6):67–73

Wiener N (1954) The human use of human beings – cybernetics and society. garden city, Doubleday Anchor Books, New York

Willcocks L (2004) Foucault, power/knowledge and information systems: reconstructing the present. In: Mingers J, Willcocks L (eds) Social theory and philosophy for information systems. Wiley, Chichester, pp 238–296

Wyatt S, Thomas G, Terranova T (2002) They came, they surfed, they went back to the beach: conceptualizing use and non-use of the internet. In: Woolgar S (ed) Virtual society? Technology, cyberbole, reality. Oxford University Press, Oxford, pp 23–40

Yoon S-H (2001) Internet discourse and the habitus of Korea's new generation. In: Ess C, Sudweeks F (ed) Culture, technology, communication: towards and intercultural global village. SUNY Press, Albany, pp 241–260

Zerdick A et al (2001) European communication councel report: Die Internet-Ökonomie: Strategien für die digitale Wirtschaft, 3rd edn. Springer, Berlin

Index

N. Kock (ed.), *Evolutionary Psychology and Information Systems Research,*
Integrated Series in Information Systems 24, DOI 10.1007/978-1-4419-6139-6,
© Springer Science+Business Media, LLC 2010

9 781441 961389